a special gift

presented to:

from:

date:

The Women's Devotional Series

COLOR MY WORLD
with love

♥

Carolyn Rathbun Sutton

EDITOR

Pacific Press®
Publishing Association
Nampa, Idaho | www.pacificpress.com

Cover design by Erika Miike
Cover design resources from
Mimacz | Dreamstime.com (map);
Dreamstime.com (women)
Inside design by Aaron Troia

The authors assume full responsibility for the accuracy of all facts and quotations as cited in this book.

Purchase additional copies of this book by calling toll-free 1-800-765-6955 or by visiting http://www.adventistbookcenter.com.

ISBN 978-0-8163-6660-6

May 2020

About the Editor

Carolyn Rathbun Sutton
finds great joy in being there for other women, especially those struggling to find renewed purpose after a major life setback. She particularly enjoys helping women share their own personal stories of God's faithfulness.

Dear Reader,

The North American Division (NAD) Women's Ministries team welcomes you to the 2020 edition of the Women's Devotional book. We are pleased and grateful that all proceeds from sales of the book in the NAD will be used exclusively for scholarships in our territory.

We are praying that you will be blessed this year as you read devotionals from women like you—real women with real stories of God's love and providence in their lives. We look forward to hearing from you, and we hope that you will be inspired to submit your own stories to share with others.

We have a two-person department. Carla Baker has been the NAD Women's Ministries director since 2006. Her union women's ministries and teaching background have made her the department's resource specialist. Carla is a Texan who loves living in Maryland with its four distinct seasons. She has a grown son, Brandon, and three grandchildren, who have all been born in Texas while she's been in Maryland. Needless to say, Carla gets back to Texas several times a year.

Erica Jones joined the Women's Ministries Department in 2014. She didn't come far, having grown up and lived all her life just a few miles from our headquarters in Columbia, Maryland. Her background in youth ministry has given her a heart for teens and their struggles. Combined with her media experience, it was easy for her to find her ministry niche in our department—teen girls and social media. Erica lives with her four-legged children, Boots the cat and Maisy the miniature shepherd mix.

♥

"*A new command I give you:*

Love one another.

As I have loved you,
so you must love one another.

By this everyone will know

that you are my disciples,

if you love one another."

—John 13:34, 35, NIV

Women Helping Women

There is an aspect of this book that is unique

None of the contributors have been paid—each has shared freely so that all profits may go to scholarships for women. Approximately 2,559 scholarships have been given to women in 137 countries. Recipients of the Women's Ministries scholarships are talented women who are committed to serving the mission of the Seventh-day Adventist Church.

General Conference Women's Ministries scholarship fund in the North American Division

All profits from sales of the Women's Ministries devotional book in the North American Division support women's higher education in Seventh-day Adventist colleges and universities in the United States and Canada.

Purpose of the women's devotional book

Among Friends, published in 1992, was the first annual women's devotional book. Since then, proceeds from these devotional books have funded scholarships for Adventist women seeking to obtain higher education. But as tuition costs have soared in North America and more women have applied for assistance, funding has not kept pace with the need. Many worthy women who apply must be turned down.

Recognizing the importance of educating women—to build stronger families, stronger communities, and a stronger church—each of us can help. Together we can change lives!

There are many ways to support our sisters

- Pray for women worldwide who are struggling to get an education.
- Tell others about the Women's Ministries scholarship program.
- Write for the women's devotional book (guidelines are available).
- Support women's education with a financial gift or a pledge.

To make a gift or receive materials, send us the following information:

Name _____

Street _____

City _____ State/Province _____

Postal Code_____ Country _____

Email_____

To contact us:

Women's Ministries Department
9705 Patuxent Woods Drive
Columbia, MD 21046

Phone: 443-391-7265
Email: ericajones@nadadventist.org
Website: https://www.nadwm.org/

The scholarship application and devotional book writers' guidelines are available at our website.

I Will Hold Your Right Hand

"For I, the LORD your God, will hold your right hand,
Saying to you, 'Fear not, I will help you.' "
—Isaiah 41:13, NKJV

Last night, New Year's Eve, I experienced a spiritually high evening in Zion. Our church family gathered to reflect on the blessings of the old year and welcome and celebrate the new year with a Communion service. My handbell choir played two songs. It was evident from the response that the music blessed the congregation. To God we give all glory!

The pastor shared a profound message before we separated for the ordinance of humility, where we washed one another's feet and prayed with one another. The retired pastors, along with current pastors and elders, walked down the middle aisle of the beautifully decorated sanctuary holding lit red candles. The atmosphere was heavenly. Surely, the presence of God was in the place. After the Communion service, a visiting choral group, Heaven's Song, presented an inspiring and heart-warming concert. The music and words deeply ministered to us.

One of the singers shared her personal testimony of God's healing. She mentioned that two years ago, she had been diagnosed with multiple myeloma. Such heart-shattering news can have a devastating and debilitating effect on a person, but God was with her in her dark valley experience and upheld and restored her body. She stated that people from around the world prayed for her and how the prayers of the saints encouraged and strengthened her during her painful journey. From this awful experience has come a profound testimony that ministered to and touched the hearts of our church family. She encouraged us to trust God and not be afraid, to trust Him because His promises are sure and true. He will hold your right hand and will never leave you nor forsake you. We can count on Him to be with us through every dark valley.

As we begin this new year, we don't know what the future holds for our families or us. No one is exempt from heartache and pain, sickness or suffering. Yet we pray that whatever comes our way, we will remain unwavering and unmovable as we hold tenaciously to the strong arms of our loving heavenly Father and claim this precious promise: "For I, the LORD your God, will hold your right hand, saying to you, 'Fear not, I will help you' " (Isaiah 41:13, NKJV).

Shirley C. Iheanacho

Maker of Mighty Things

God thundereth marvellously with his voice;
great things doeth he, which we cannot comprehend.
—Job 37:5, KJV

Fear is a normal part of life for all of us, especially for young children. It tends to start when we try something new, something that we've never experienced before, something that is an unknown. During childhood, we develop a fear of certain things like darkness, strangers, monsters, being alone, and separation.

When I was a kid, I was fearful of thunder. One night, Dad was away from our home, and my mom and I were alone. At midnight, I was startled to hear waves of booming, crashing, cracking, and ground-shaking thunder rumbling overhead. It was a very deafening and frightening experience. With every cracking boom, the lightning's crooked smile became a little wider. The lightning seemed to slice the air as if the very heavens might split apart. I held my mother tightly and started to sob bitterly. I can never forget the prayer she uttered that lonely night. She whispered, "Lord, we are cold and frightened, and the night is encroaching, quickly adding to the gloom. Please stop this oppressive, booming thunder. Please help us. Amen." The moment she said, "Amen," the thunder stopped. We slept peacefully for the rest of that night.

That night, I realized that nature is at God's command. Sometimes nature is predictable and structured. Trees shed their leaves in autumn. Birds migrate at certain times of the year. All of creation functions according to a plan set by God. I was happy that night that I worship a God who is able to still the storms.

I am humbled by the thought that if God has a good plan for every plant, bird, and animal, how much more does He have good plans for those who are made in His image? It is enough to know our mighty God has a plan, and He never abandons His children. His eye is on the sparrow, and I am assured of the fact that He watches me.

Dear Father, You are filled with meekness and majesty in perfect harmony, and You are the Lord of eternity. We kneel in humility before You. Help us understand that You are the Alpha and Omega of our lives.

Esther Synthia Murali

Separation

Worthy is the Lamb who was slain
To receive power and riches and wisdom,
And strength and honor and glory and blessing!
—Revelation 5:12, NKJV

I entered the supermarket with my children. "This is going to be quick, guys. We have fifteen minutes." I sent my son and daughter down the aisle to get snacks. Two aisles later, they met up with me. They trailed behind as I quickly moved up one aisle and down the next. The children kept up—or so I thought.

Moving into the next aisle, I thought that my son was right behind me. When I realized that he wasn't, I told my daughter to look for him. She came back empty-handed. I thought, *Keep moving; he'll catch up with us.* I arrived at the checkout line—still, no son. I told my daughter to wait with the shopping cart while I went to look for him. Up and down each aisle I went. As I came back up the aisle, I heard over the store's loudspeaker, "Would Dana please come to the front. Your child is waiting for you." When I reached the front of the store, there my son stood with the floor manager. Guyen held two bags of popcorn. He had been right behind me until he stopped to get the popcorn without telling me. Then he went bravely to the front of the store to tell the manager his mommy's name.

As you can imagine, he was very upset about being separated from his mother. Why wouldn't he be? Of course, what was only a few minutes of confusion to us seemed like a lifetime to my son.

As I thought about this experience, I remembered that God endured separation as well. He was separated from His Son when He sent Him to earth to be born as our Savior. Then God the Father was again separated from His Son when His Only Begotten gave His life for us. The Son experienced the pain of separation as well. Ellen White wrote, "He who had been one with God, felt in His soul the awful separation that sin makes between God and man."*

There is a happy ending. Our physical separation from God will soon end. He is coming back to take us home with Him forever. No more tears of pain. I can't wait!

Dana M. Bassett Bean

---

* Ellen G. White, *Steps to Christ* (Washington, DC: Review and Herald®, 1956), 13.

Pray for Forgiveness

And forgive us our debts, as we forgive our debtors.
—Matthew 6:12, KJV

Unforgiveness is a disease that can be healed only through our Lord and Savior. Sometimes we allow unforgiveness to manifest itself through our entire being. It festers so rapidly we often fail to recognize the symptoms. Symptoms may begin with depression or a headache. And the longer we hold on to unforgiveness, the more serious the symptoms—even to the point of separating us from God.

The Bible clearly states, "And when ye stand praying, forgive, if ye have ought against any: that your Father also which is in heaven may forgive you your trespasses. But if ye do not forgive, neither will your Father which is in heaven forgive your trespasses" (Mark 11:25, 26, KJV). This means that if my probation closes and I haven't forgiven those that have hurt me or if I haven't confessed or repented of my sins, I could be lost eternally.

Yet God also promises that "If we confess our sins, He is faithful and just to forgive us our sins and to cleanse us from all unrighteousness" (1 John 1:9, NKJV). Unforgiveness is a deadly poison that affects our social, physical, emotional, psychological, and spiritual well-being. It is often said that a little of something—taken in moderation—will not hurt you. I strongly disagree. A little poison taken in moderation over a period of time can kill you.

It is impossible to forgive on our own. We need God's help. He is the antidote for unforgiveness. Neither medication nor treatment can heal or alleviate unforgiveness. God is the only one that is able to deliver us. Take your hurt to Him. Confess your sins to your heavenly Father. Repent of them, for He is willing and able to deliver you. He is the greatest Physician in the universe. Nothing is too difficult for Him. He will also ease our pain and make it easier for us to forgive those that have hurt us.

Remember, once we forgive, we can be forgiven. Sin separates us from God. My prayer today is that nothing will come between our souls and our Savior. I pray that we will all spend eternity with Him.

Cora A. Walker

I Want to Know!

How, then, can they call on the one they have not believed in?
And how can they believe in the one of whom they have not heard?
And how can they hear without someone preaching to them?
And how can anyone preach unless they are sent? As it is written:
"How beautiful are the feet of those who bring good news!"
—Romans 10:14, 15, NIV

As my husband and I concluded the process for the sale of our home with our real estate agent, we signed the papers and took a deep breath.

"What do you do?" our real estate agent, Lori, asked me out of the blue.

"I'm what our denomination calls a Bible worker," I said.

"What's a Bible worker, and what do you do?" she asked.

"Though I'm just about to retire, I study the Bible with people who are interested in knowing more about it, and—"

"I want to know more about the Bible!" she interjected unexpectedly. I blinked. Rarely has an interest just dropped into my lap like that. "I became a Christian as a teenager," she went on, "but I've never understood very much. I didn't grow up in a Christian home, and I haven't had anyone to explain things to me. I've been praying that someone would appear who could."

I blinked again. The Lord was present and active in that room at that moment—His presence was obvious.

As I made Bible study arrangements for Lori with my replacement, I thought of the wonderful sequence God put into place. It includes us mere mortals so that others might find Jesus. Someone is positioned to be the conduit; that person acts when the opportunity presents; the provided-for individual hears, believes, and accepts the relationship. And then the riches of the universe are opened to them. Forgiveness, reconciliation, and salvation are all available. The process repeats itself again and again, with each of us privileged to play our part. We can—if we choose (and we must so choose if we wish to remain in a relationship with God ourselves)—play a part in this grand design. It is one of the provisions made for our own salvation.

So let's choose to play our part. There are many people like Lori out there. You never know when the Lord might place one in your life. For sure, you'll want to be ready!

Carolyn K. Karlstrom

Take Courage

But Jesus immediately said to them:
"Take courage! It is I. Don't be afraid."
—Matthew 14:27, NIV

When we traveled in England back in 1965, we saw several signs that read, "Take Courage." *How nice, we thought, that must be a saying leftover from World War II.* Later on, we discovered that Courage was a brand of ale. We were no longer so impressed!

But to take courage itself—not the ale—has always been good advice. Courage is mentioned numerous times in the Bible. One of the first uses appears when Moses speaks to Joshua (Deuteronomy 31:6 and repeated in verse 7). As Joshua thought about the task before him and thought of the trials Moses had endured, I am sure he needed some extra courage. And he received it in verse 8: "The LORD himself goes before you and will be with you; he will never leave you nor forsake you. Do not be afraid; do not be discouraged." God kept telling him to be courageous. We find this in Joshua 1:6, 7, 9, and 18. As a result of Joshua's courageous stand and leadership, when the Amorite kings west of the Jordan and all the Canaanite kings heard how the Lord had been leading, they lost their courage (Joshua 5:1).

Finally, Joshua was also able to tell the people he led to be strong and courageous when they faced their enemies: "Do not be afraid; do not be discouraged. Be strong and courageous. This is what the LORD will do to all the enemies you are going to fight" (Joshua 10:25, NIV). Later, David showed a different type of courage. He wanted to build a temple to the Lord, but God sent word that he was not to do so. David could have become angry and discouraged. But instead, he prayed. And in this prayer, he said, "You, my God, have revealed to your servant that you will build a house for him. So your servant has found courage to pray to you" (1 Chronicles 17:25, NIV). Sometimes it takes courage even to pray.

When the woman who had been bleeding twelve years came to Jesus, He said: "Take heart" (Matthew 9:22, ESV). In other translations of Matthew, this appears as "be of good comfort" (KJV), "be encouraged" (NLT), and "be of good cheer" (NKJV).

When the disciples saw Jesus walking on water and thought He was a ghost, He said, "Take courage! It is I" (Matthew 14:27, NIV). He says that to us whether the danger we face is real or imagined.

Take courage—in Jesus!

Ardis Dick Stenbakken

Homeward Bound

If I take the wings of the morning . . .
Even there shall thy hand lead me, and thy right hand shall hold me.
—Psalm 139:9, 10, KJV

Our grandson, Doug, recently returned home to the United States of America after teaching English in Southeast Asia. The entire family eagerly awaited his return, especially his father, Terry, who gave us periodic reports of our grandson's flight home. These reports were very meaningful and detailed since our son has personal knowledge of aviation.

His reports went something like this: "Doug departed Bangkok for a six-hour flight in a Boeing 787 Dreamliner, one of the most modern airliners flying today. . . . The flight took him over the Pacific, south of China, then up to Japan heading NE over the Pacific at a cruising altitude of 35,000 feet and forward speed of APRX. 600 MPH, flying east of the northern tip of Japan, tracked NE into the North Pacific Ocean. Aircraft passed about 550 miles south of the Kuril Islands (Russia) heading for the Bering Sea. Tracking showed the aircraft flying at 35,000 feet and pushing 596 MPH. . . . Crossing the Bering Sea, it passed 350 miles south of the Aleutian Islands. . . . Made a slow, SE arc toward DFW airport. . . . Speed remains high through 24,000 feet. . . . On final descent for runway 18. . . . His flight has reached the gate!"

With tears sliding down my cheeks, I sensed the heartfelt love and anticipation of Terry as he tracked his homeward-bound son.

Another Father is also tracking the return of His homeward-bound children. Our Father in heaven is watching with anticipation every detail of our lives. Psalm 139 reminds us that He knows of all our comings and goings. Such abundant love! Of this love, my favorite author, Ellen G. White, wrote, "All the springs of tenderness which have opened in the souls of men, are but as a tiny rill to the boundless ocean when compared with the infinite, exhaustless love of God."*

If I had wings and could fly to the ends of the earth, His love would follow me, and when the flight of the saved ends at the gates of heaven, He will gather us in His arms, rejoicing with joy forevermore. His children have come home!

Dottie Barnett

---

* Ellen G. White, *Testimonies for the Church*, vol. 5 (Mountain View, CA: Pacific Press®, 1948), 740.

The Working Commitment

Not slothful in business; fervent in spirit; serving the Lord;
rejoicing in hope; patient in tribulation; continuing instant in prayer.
—Romans 12:11, 12, KJV

Picture Jerusalem in 457 B.C. Our hero, Nehemiah, has a burden to rebuild the walls of the city of David. The burden on his heart is so great that it shows on his countenance when he, a Hebrew captive and the Persian king's cupbearer, goes in to serve King Artaxerxes. The king asks the reason for his sadness, and Nehemiah offers a silent prayer and explains his problem. Because he has found favor with the king, Nehemiah is granted leave and given official letters of support and provision to take with him to begin his God-appointed task.

Nehemiah arrives in Jerusalem to find a daunting task ahead of him. Not only do neighboring enemies threaten to invade, but internal dissension among the Hebrews also surfaces. Nehemiah could throw his hands up in the air and go back to the palace in Persia. Instead, he prays. With God's help, he begins the task.

The Bible says that Nehemiah assigned sections of the broken walls to various families and groups to rebuild. When threats came, the people prayed and armed themselves with swords in one hand and tools in the other. Little by little, because "the people had a mind to work," the wall was rebuilt (Nehemiah 4:6, KJV).

Likewise, we are to occupy ourselves with the building up of God's kingdom until He puts us to sleep or comes for us in clouds of glory. It is hard work because sometimes God calls us to do tasks that are, for one reason or another, downright difficult. Sometimes I want to throw my hands up in the air and say, "Enough! There is more to life than teaching people who have no interest in learning—and under less than ideal conditions."

Yet I have a choice—we each have a choice. We have the choice to (1) run away as Jonah did (Jonah 1:3); (2) make excuses as to why we are not qualified as Jeremiah first did (Jeremiah 1:6); or (3) gird our minds with prayer and the sword of the Spirit (Ephesians 6:17) to face the task with faithfulness and confidence as Nehemiah did. We can believe, as he did, that God is with us and will strengthen us to fulfill our goals. We can believe that for each task and each willing, imperfect hand, God will equip and perfect. Oh, that the world had more Nehemiahs!

Greta Michelle Joachim-Fox-Dyett

Could You Have Gone There?

For we do not wrestle against flesh and blood,
but against principalities, against powers,
against the rulers of the darkness of this age,
against spiritual hosts of wickedness in the heavenly places.
—Ephesians 6:12, NKJV

Before moving to our new pastorate, certain ladies approached me who had previously resided in the pastorate to which we were relocating. "Tell your husband he should object to moving to that pastorate," they said. "It is located in an area where the occult is practiced. Wizardry runs rampant! Under those conditions, you would experience much trouble from people who practice magic." I reflected that those who do not have a personal relationship with the living God have cause to fear witchcraft while those who walk with God need not fear.

Most certainly, I had to inform my husband about the women's concerns for us. When I told him of the women's suggestion that he reconsider making the transfer, he adamantly replied, "The Lord, whom I believe in and serve, has a divine power that far surpasses any kind of occult practice. He will protect us from any magical powers!"

During our second year in the new pastorate, a man (reputed to be chief of the wizards) asked my husband a question: "Pastor, if you underwent severe suffering, wouldn't you look for help from those who practice magic?"

My husband replied, "Should I, or one of my family members, experience great suffering—even to the point of death—I would neither seek help from magic nor abandon my dependence upon the Lord." That man laughed and asked my husband to confirm his words.

A few days later, our firstborn son, nearly four years old, was suddenly taken ill with a strange sickness. We rushed him to our mission's hospital that night. For three days, he was treated for chronic malaria, but without any change. On the evening of the third day, our crying child appeared to be suffering to the point of death. My husband prayed, "Lord, You have the power to heal this child. Please heal him if it is Your will." Immediately our son fell asleep. When our child awoke the next morning, he was completely healed. Today our son is married with a two-year-old son of his own.

Jesus promised that with faith, nothing would be impossible (see Matthew 17:20)!

Naomi N. Otore

Self-Defense

Honour thy father and thy mother: that thy days may be long
upon the land which the LORD thy God giveth thee.
—Exodus 20:12, KJV

My mother lived with my family for twelve years. She moved to Edmonton when my twins started kindergarten. Mom remained with us during the school year and traveled during the school holidays. She was a tremendous help to me. I did not have to juggle working and running a busy household with four children and other relatives.

It was a blessing for my children to know their grandmother. Grandma tended to sick kids, gave them money, fed them, and helped them grow spiritually. As the children got older, she lovingly corrected them when they did not comply with her expectations. My children often talk about how strong their grandma was—for an old lady. Once my daughter, Cassandra, responded to my mom in a way that she did not appreciate. Mom sat and waited until Cassie was within reach and then let her know a thing or two.

Mom experienced discomfort due to congestive heart failure and fluid retention. It broke my heart to see her struggling to breathe, knowing that there was nothing I could do to ease her pain. Jokingly, I once said, "Mom, how about I just strangle you and put an end to all your struggles?" Mom told me that given the way she felt, she would almost welcome the idea. Then I asked her what I could say to the police when they arrived.

She grinned at me and said, "Just tell them you did it in self-defense." She was eighty years old at the time. We had a good belly laugh. What a sense of humor even in her last days!

If you are caring for an elderly parent or relative, enjoy them and seize opportunities to share special moments before it is too late. You may feel overwhelmed and frustrated at times, but don't lose heart. You are doing an honorable thing. I cherish the fond memories and experiences that my mother and I enjoyed for forty-five years. I was born on her thirty-fifth birthday, and we shared many birthdays together. Eight years ago, Mom died at the age of eighty.

I long for the day when Christ will return, and Mom and I will meet again. What a great reunion that will be! I plan to be there by God's grace. How about you?

Sharon Long

Learning to Ride My Bike

"The LORD himself goes before you and will be with you;
he will never leave you nor forsake you.
Do not be afraid; do not be discouraged."
—Deuteronomy 31:8, NIV

I was six when I learned to ride my sister's big bike. I had to ride it standing up because it was too big for me. I believe it was my father who first helped me until I was able to maintain balance on my own. We lived on the top of a hill. One day I rode down the road too fast and slid in the sand and gravel on the tarmac at the bottom of the hill. The bike tipped onto its right side, and I slid several yards. I was dressed in a skirt and socks, and the whole right side of my body was grazed. My leg and arm were bleeding profusely. Ouch, that hurt! I picked up the bike and pushed it up the hill to my home. Then I went to my mother and showed her my injuries. I had tears on my cheeks, but I refused to cry out loud.

Mum tried to clean up my wounds and get the dirt out. I almost felt like an Egyptian mummy with my body parts bandaged up. The next day we were to leave for a seaside holiday. My parents were sorry for me as they thought I wouldn't be able to get into the water with my injuries. But it turned out to be a wonderful vacation. I was constantly in the water and only got out to let the scabs dry up a bit. The salty water helped heal the wounds, and I only have a tiny scar left in the hollow of my knee. After the vacation, my parents gave me a bicycle of my own. It was a blue bike in my size. It was much easier to ride this bike than my sister's big bike.

All of life is a constant learning process. A few months after our birth, we learn to crawl and then walk, then speak, read, and write. And this list could go on and on. How happy I was when our children learned to take their first steps! Then there were other steps I tried to help them learn: riding a bike, swimming, getting a driver's license, and graduating from school and university. Like my father, who helped me keep my balance while I learned to ride a bike, we have tried to help our children reach maturity. Now they don't need us as much as they once did, but as their parents, we will be there for them as long as we live.

God is our loving Father, who wants us to learn things one step at a time. He will never leave us. He will always support and encourage us. He will teach us the things we need to know because He will never forsake us but will always be with us, whatever may happen.

Hannele Ottschofski

The Little Toe

And if one member suffers, all the members suffer with it;
or if one member is honored, all the members rejoice with it.
—1 Corinthians 12:26, NKJV

Recently, I broke my little toe.* I can't tell you how my little toe happened to slam into the leg of the nightstand so hard that it broke, but I can tell you this collision was unmistakable—and painful! I dropped to the floor in instant agony. Before my eyes, my toe swelled up and turned various shades of blue and purple. I'm sure many of you who have had similar experiences are feeling my pain right now, and those of you who haven't experienced it personally are wincing at the thought of it. For weeks, I could not wear shoes or even walk normally because certain movements made my toe hurt intensely. I didn't always know what type of movement would bring on the drop-to-my-knees pain, but I figured it out as the days passed. Who knew that a tiny, seemingly insignificant part of the body could make the entire body fully aware of its needs like that? Ah, the things we take for granted at times!

Amid the pain, the Holy Spirit nudged me and brought an image to my mind. When one part of our physical body hurts, the whole body suffers in some way. That is true in the church body as well. This body of believers is made up of many individual parts—little toes if you will—and when one of them is hurt, sick, or injured, the entire body is affected.

"For as the body is one, and has many members, but all the members of that one body, being many, are one body: so also is Christ. . . . And if one member suffers, all the members suffer with it; or if one member is honored, all the members rejoice with it" (1 Corinthians 12:12, 26, NKJV).

It is our responsibility as Christians—"parts" that make up the body—to make sure that the sick, hurt, or injured members of the church body are receiving the care, nurture, and healing they need. After all, how can the body as a whole be well and all that Christ intended if there is pain and sickness among its members? We have a responsibility to "bind up the brokenhearted" (Isaiah 61:1, KJV), reach out a helping hand to those in need, and speak words of comfort and hope "in season" (Isaiah 50:4, KJV) to the weary and discouraged. Will you join me in making sure the body is as healthy and happy as possible before our Lord returns to take us home?

Samantha Nelson

---

* Samantha Nelson, 2018, "The Little Toe," Facebook, January 3, 2020, https://www.facebook.com /UnlockingTruth/photos/fpp.306521167525/10158361071552526/?type=3&theater

January 13

The Crunch Heard Around Heaven

So when the woman saw that the tree was good for food,
that it was pleasant to the eyes, and a tree desirable
to make one wise, she took of its fruit and ate.
—Genesis 3:6, NKJV

Remember the story about Eve taking the forbidden fruit in the Garden of Eden? In my mind's eye, I imagine the crafty serpent relaxing along a leafy limb of the tree that God had instructed Adam and Eve not to eat from. Slyly, he plucks a piece of fruit from a nearby branch, examining it before taking a bite and smiling. He then looks down at the woman he knows is there. His smile broadens as he surprises her with a declaration: "Mm-mm! This fruit is delicious!" With amazement, the woman looks up into the tree at a talking serpent enjoying some forbidden fruit—apparently with no ill effects. "Would you like a taste?"

Eve knows what God has instructed about this tree, but the serpent assures her no harm will befall her. He appeals to her pride and informs her that she will be like God if she eats the fruit. So because the serpent has so quickly and convincingly turned Eve's attention from God to herself, she looks at the exquisite fruit more closely. Then she reaches out her hand and plucks a piece of fruit for herself. In my mind, I watch in slow motion as the beautiful young woman next raises the fruit to her lips, which she slowly parts, momentarily resting the fruit against her teeth.

Crunch! The sound of this first sin might as well have been a round of thunder that echoed around heaven like a cannon shot. Again, in my mind's eye, I see all the angels, God, and Jesus hang their heads, put their arms around one another, and weep.

This scene also comes to mind whenever I do something that I know hurts God—whether it's speaking harshly to my family, or venting my anger to a friend about someone else, or being dissatisfied with what God has asked of me. My "crunch" is heard in heaven too.

On the other hand, I know that my obedient choices (even when they don't make sense to me) cause cheers of joy to ring through the archways of heaven. Oh, how I want to be the cause of those delighted shouts instead of my sin "crunches," which bring additional tears of sorrow!

May our prayer be for God to give us the strength to obey Him—even when the enemy tries to twist something apparently "good" into a temptation that could entice us to disobey. God desires us to love and trust Him and make choices that honor Him and His Word.

Cyndi Woods

Delayed!

"Watch therefore, for you do not know what hour your Lord is coming."
—Matthew 24:42, NKJV

I was anticipating this trip to celebrate Dad's one hundred and third birthday with great joy. Many family members and friends were coming from far and near to this birthday-thanksgiving party. Aside from the party atmosphere, we anticipated the worship and praise time we would spend together singing the old songs of Zion in four-part harmony. At the airport, my anticipation was mixed with disappointment when we were told that our flight would be delayed for two hours. Then the delay extended to five hours. We just had to listen for the announcement and follow the lead of the airline employees at the departure desk; they were uncertain.

No one ever said why the delay happened, but I finally decided to put away my disappointment and occupy my time with reading. I also continued to work on an article I had started to write.

I shared a few words of greetings and encouragement with some of the other waiting passengers, but many preferred to play their video games, listen to their music through their headphones, or pace back and forth. Suddenly there was a great commotion at the counter—a passenger lost her patience and her faith in the airline. This frustration she expressed to the attendant in a very loud voice with crude language. Many others began to speak in undertones of displeasure, their faces looking haggard and tired.

But there was another scene. Some children were laughing loudly as they tossed a stuffed toy back and forth. They retrieved it and tossed it again, over and over, as if they had no care in the world. They must have been tired, too, but they were happy while waiting.

I reflected on another scene: "The bridegroom was delayed" (Matthew 25:5, NKJV). We are waiting for a very important wedding. We are uncertain of the day or the hour, yet are we ready for His sudden appearing? Are we happy and joyful as we share with others His love, or are we griping about the cares of this life while we slumber spiritually?

Please, Father, help us not to lose our focus. We want to be ready when You arrive. Amen.

Sonia Kennedy-Brown

Voices of Failure

I waited patiently for the LORD; and he inclined unto me....
He brought me up also out of an horrible pit . . .
and set my feet upon a rock, and established my goings.
And he hath put a new song in my mouth, even praise unto our
God: many shall see it, and fear, and shall trust in the LORD.
—Psalm 40:1–3, KJV

Have you ever heard voices of failure? At one point or another in our lives, failure finds us all.

At my hotel, after my first sermon opening an evangelistic campaign in Managua, Nicaragua, I kept telling myself, "Raquel, you failed badly." I went to bed, miserable. Books that address how to succeed in life are everywhere, but you'll look a long time before you find a book titled *How to Succeed While Failing.* Either this is a difficult topic to discuss, or nobody has anything to say on the subject. But God does.

A careful look at the Bible reveals that most great characters from Scripture experienced failure. David had a moral failure, yet God used him. Elijah had an emotional breakdown after Mount Carmel, but God refreshed him. Peter, in his self-confidence and great pride, denied Jesus, but Jesus restored him. Perfect people? No. Yet God used them.

Sometimes God allows us to fail before He enables us to succeed. If we learn from them, our failures are often the beginning of growth.

So, after a long night talking to the Lord in my hotel room, I received strength for the next day. The church was packed that night, and I preached again, confident that God was in control. As soon as I finished, an old man came toward me and said, "Raquel, thank you for your beautiful message yesterday. My son is here with me today and decided to give his heart to Jesus." I looked at both of them, speechless and grateful. I hugged the young man and told him, "The message was just for you."

If you are starting your day thinking about yesterday's failures, I have good news: God can use failures, and He can use you. Today is the day to sing a new song and to leave the voices of failure behind as we embrace a new day full of new mercies. Why? Because "in all these things we are more than conquerors through him who loved us" (Romans 8:37, NIV).

Raquel Queiroz da Costa Arrais

Living With (and Without) Henry

The LORD is my shepherd. . . . He restoreth my soul.
—Psalm 23:1, 3, KJV

Henry is my black medium UltraSling. We became attached at the hip (literally) when I awoke from a surgical procedure that repaired a badly torn rotator cuff on my right shoulder. Henry's job was to bolster my right arm so that my shoulder could heal without being torn again from the weight of that arm. When I got over the initial pain, I discovered what life would be without my right arm. Try washing your hair with only a left hand. Imagine taking a shower, getting dressed, or driving a car without that arm. It's hard to imagine. Just think of living that way for eight weeks! My life changed instantly. I became a baby again—needing help to bathe, dress, and drive from place to place. The novelty soon wore off. I longed to drive again, to comb my hair again, to fix breakfast. But with the inconveniences came lessons from this journey into helplessness.

First, I learned empathy. In my second week with Henry, I visited a friend who could not use his right hand or arm following a stroke. As I sat beside him, I immediately understood how he felt. I had visited him many times before, but only when we sat with both our right arms in slings could I share his feeling of helplessness. My sling, however, was temporary; his condition was permanent.

I also learned, after many decades of independence, to depend on others. I am thankful for the friends and relatives who brought dinner daily, and I am beyond grateful for my husband of forty-seven years who became my nurse—bathing and dressing me, fixing breakfast, and becoming my "right hand."

Finally, I learned the joys of restoration. After weeks of therapy, I regained my mobility. I could peel potatoes again, open tight bottle caps, wash dishes. I could drive again. God restored my mobility. And now it is easy to forget that I ever had to live with Henry. But this restoration is just the beginning. God has promised to make all things new (Revelation 21:4, 5). Hallelujah! Minds ravaged by dementia will be healed. The blind will see; the deaf will hear. Wheelchairs and walkers will be discarded. No one will need a Henry sling again. Shoulders, wrists, legs, and knees will all be restored. Forever! I want to be part of that joyful restoration, don't you?

Annette Walwyn Michael

Three Times Mine

Cast your bread upon the waters,
For you will find it after many days.
—Ecclesiastes 11:1, NKJV

Once I won a very nice acoustic/electric guitar at a fundraiser raffle for fire victims and then gave the guitar to my guitar teacher, whose need exceeded my want. That guitar was mine—*once*. Now, the rest of the story.

About a year later, after my guitar lesson one day, my teacher gave the guitar back to me as she needed something more professional! To say that I was happy would be an understatement. Not only did I get the guitar back, but now it was mine—*twice*.

In the fall of 2018, at church one Sabbath, a woman in that week's praise team told how she had given her guitar to her son when she dropped him off at a boarding high school so he could bless others with his playing. She gave him her most prized possession—her guitar. I knew how much that guitar meant to her.

As I sat there listening, God spoke to my heart. I knew what I needed to do. But I didn't want to do it. I wanted to keep my guitar, yet I couldn't rest until I decided to give my guitar to this lonely mother. As soon as church was over, I went home to get *my* prized possession: my "twice mine" guitar. Since I was using it mostly for my own enjoyment at the time, I felt at peace with my decision. But God had another plan.

I waited outside the church until I saw the woman come out. I called her over to my car, pulled out my prized guitar, handed it to her, and said, "Here, this is yours now. Take it."

"No," she said with a grateful smile. "I can't take it. Someone else here in the church offered me her guitar last night!" I was stunned. I was so sure I would be losing my guitar for good this time. In the end, however, I suspect my being brought to this decision point was a test, to see if I would be willing to give a prized possession to someone who needed it more than I did—again. Mine: *three* times!

What about you? What do you have to which you're clinging tightly? Are you willing to give it up, if God asks you to, so you can be a blessing to someone else?

Sonia Brock

I Met a Virtuous Woman

A good woman is hard to find,
and worth far more than diamonds.
—Proverbs 31:10, *The Message*

I began ministry as a young pastor's wife in Greenwood, Mississippi. This was a culture shock for me, having never lived in the South. I was northern born and bred. But here, the obvious differences were more than I could fathom. I was privileged to meet a woman who taught me so many things about how to become the change you want to see in the world. Her name was Fannie Lou Hamer. She lived in Ruleville, Mississippi, and was a part of the change in her world. Fannie Lou was a child of rural Mississippi; her parents were sharecroppers. She was the only family member who was able to read and write. Mrs. Hamer bore the marks of the struggle on her body. She had been beaten and maimed for seeking to vote. Mrs. Hamer was involuntarily sterilized, so she and her husband adopted two daughters!

I met Mrs. Hamer when Mississippi was on the cusp of change. My husband and I were a part of the Greenwood Movement, and a mutual friend took us to Ruleville to meet Mrs. Hamer. She invited us into her home and made us feel as if we were family. She spoke about her home state and where she envisioned it going. She was upbeat and encouraging. Never once did she complain about the physical and emotional sacrifices she had made. She just encouraged me to keep doing what I could to make a difference. She embodied Proverbs 31:26, as her words were always "worthwhile" (*The Message*), and she always spoke kindly. I thought Mrs. Hamer's words were profound, but when she broke into song, I was mesmerized! Mrs. Hamer said that Negro spirituals were a powerful force in her life. When things got heavy, she could always find encouragement in their words. "Through each night I sing his songs, praying to God who gives me life" (Psalm 42:8, NLT).

I did not realize back then that the Lord had shown me a living example of a woman more valuable than diamonds. Still, when times get dark, I remember the Lord offers a song in my night. I hear the melody, and I sing on. Praise God for the impact of Mrs. Fannie Lou Hamer!

Wilma Kirk Lee

New Focus

For I am the LORD, I change not.
—Malachi 3:6, KJV

Recently, during my devotions, I focused on the verses in Malachi 3:6–12. They are often quoted when the tithes and offerings are being collected during worship services. But for many, because they have repeatedly heard these words, these verses may be mundane. However, I discovered a new and deeper meaning as I meditated on this passage. I realized it could be summarized in the following four points.

1. *Affirmation.* God declares He does not change. In fact, "The tithing system reaches back beyond the days of Moses. Men were required to offer to God gifts for religious purposes before the definite system was given to Moses, even as far back as the days of Adam."* We have the example of Cain and Abel, bringing their offerings to the Lord (Genesis 4:3, 4). Therefore, we are to understand that God expects the same from us today.

2. *Accusation.* In addition to the pronouncement in Malachi 3:6, God says that we are the ones who have changed. "Ever since the time of your ancestors you have turned away from my decrees and have not kept them" (Malachi 3:7, NIV). We are further accused of robbing God (verses 8, 9). This sounds like a threefold charge: turning away from Him, not keeping His commands, and robbing Him.

3. *Admonition.* However, we are not left without hope. There is recourse for us as we deal with the accusation. The Lord instructs us that first, we must return. " 'Return to me, and I will return to you,' says the LORD Almighty " (Malachi 3:7, NIV). Next, we must bring something: "Bring the whole tithe into the storehouse" (Malachi 3:10, NIV). In other words, stop the robbery!

4. *Accumulation.* Finally, Malachi 3:10 throws out a challenge to "prove me" (KJV). When we prove the Lord, the promise is that there will be an outpouring of blessings to the point where we will not have enough room to accommodate them. In addition, God will prevent pests from destroying the crops, and also the fruit will not drop in the fields before it is ripe. When we obey His commands, there will always be "meat" in His house, and we can be the channels He uses to bless others!

Claudine Houston

---

* Ellen G. White, *Counsels on Stewardship* (Nampa, ID: Pacific Press®, 2009), 69.

Miracles—I Didn't See Them Coming!

Before they call, I will answer; and while
they are yet speaking, I will hear.
—Isaiah 65:24, KJV

As my husband faced health challenges, he brought up the topic of downsizing into a smaller home. My heart sank as I had thought this discussion would never come up again. Selling our home and finding another place seemed so overwhelming to me. Twelve years earlier, when we moved from Miami, Florida, to Huntsville, Alabama, to build a home, I hoped our next move would be to heaven. I began to pray earnestly that God would get me on board with this decision.

Then the first miracle happened! Out of the clear blue sky, my son and daughter-in-law came to our home and said, "Mom and Dad, we are building a home and would like you to live with us." My husband and I had no idea they were even thinking about building. It took my husband three days to wrap his head around this answer to prayer, a prayer that God answered before we prayed it. In a whirlwind, decisions had to be made—selling our home, selling most of our possessions, and finding storage space.

The second miracle was that most of our items and furniture sold on the first day of our massive garage sale. Praise God!

The third miracle occurred when a lady from California, who was visiting her son, came to the garage sale. She was interested in our dining room table set. After purchasing the set, she said, "I really like this house." To our surprise, she contacted our Realtor and put a bid on the house—the house sold in four short weeks. Praise God!

The fourth miracle is that although our house sold quickly, our son and daughter-in-law's house was not yet finished. So my husband and I needed to rent an apartment. God was not finished with His miracles. The lady who bought our home had gone back to California to take care of business. We were impressed to ask if we could rent her home. She readily said, "Yes!" Praise God! A few months later, we moved into a brand-new home with our family. The experience we are having is a joyous one.

I encourage you to submit yourself to God in all your decisions and watch Him bestow miracles in your life.

Vivian Brown

Stepping Out in Faith

But Jesus looked at them and said to them, "With men this is impossible, but with God all things are possible."
—Matthew 19:26, NKJV

I don't know about you, but I tend to be a little stubborn. There are also times where I don't like to listen to others because I think I know what is best for my life. Back in my high school days, Dad and I were having a conversation about my university degree and future career path. I have always liked helping people, can stomach "gross" things, and am fascinated by the unusual. So it was obvious—nursing was going to be my career. However, Dad counseled me back then to "do teaching" because he thought I would be good at it. Dad was a teacher in Chile and then became a pastor in Australia, so his bias was evident. However, I always shied away from teaching opportunities because it didn't fit into my plans. Have you ever done that?

Fast-forward fourteen years. I am a registered nurse with a specialty in wound care management and stomal therapy, where *teaching* has been part of my daily job for the past seven years. In 2014, I decided to undertake a master's of clinical leadership degree with adult education to improve my skill and knowledge. I completed the degree in 2016, and it's amazing how the doors for *teaching* keep opening! Some opportunities were "forced" upon me, and other times I decided to say yes despite my lack of confidence. Now let me explain: Every time I had to teach, my stomach would be in knots. I was so nervous, but I would silently pray, *God, You are opening the door for me to teach, so You need to help me. Please give me peace, and let it be to Your glory.* As soon as I opened my mouth, my fear would disappear, my hands would stop shaking, and somehow I would talk and talk and talk—and not have to look at my notes. When I walked out of the class, I would be overwhelmed at how much I was beginning to like teaching. Over the last couple of years, the doors keep opening for teaching where I have even taught medical doctors (daunting), but I also regularly teach medical students.

What I have learned from this newfound God-given love of teaching is the importance of listening to my father's wise counsel (see Proverbs 5:7); but more importantly, I've learned to listen to God when He starts calling me to do the impossible (or so I thought). God can make the impossible happen if we are prepared to step out in faith. He will sustain you and never let you fall!

Jenny Rivera

Children Are a Reward

Children are a gift from the LORD;
they are a reward from him.
—Psalm 127:3, NLT

When I was a little girl, I always hoped—when I grew up—that I would be the mom of a boy and a girl. So when I had my son, followed by my daughter, everything was perfect, and I was done. Much to my surprise, God didn't agree with my decision. Just two years after my daughter was born, we discovered we were pregnant again! Although I love babies, it was a very difficult time for me. During that pregnancy, I struggled with terrible anxiety and several panic attacks, most of which were caused by my perfectionism and control issues. How would I get things done with another baby? My daughter was finally getting old enough for me to be able to relax a little bit and not worry about her getting into things. Besides, I already had the two children I had always wanted.

Thankfully, about six months into my third pregnancy, I warmed to the idea of another baby. We had a different birth experience this time, a home birth, for which I will always be so grateful as it healed in me the discontent I carried from my first two births! I praise God for how my third child, a son, was such a beautiful blessing from the moment of his birth. One thing I noticed shortly after he was born was that my desire to have everything done perfectly all the time greatly decreased. Once I noticed this, I realized that was a part of God's plan for me—to help me let go of all the pressure I put on myself, like the pressure to keep a perfect house and focus on unnecessary details, not to mention the guilt of perfectionism. Despite feeling unsure at times about my parenting, God's trusting me with yet another child truly did feel like a reward!

Currently, we are expecting our fourth child this coming Christmas (2018). We didn't necessarily plan this one either, but we had not shut any doors since our third child has blessed our lives so much. God has given me so much grace, growth, and faith in Him through my children. I can't imagine receiving a greater reward than these precious little lives. I can only keep praying that we parent these kids in a way that continually shows Him how much we appreciate His trusting us with such precious rewards!

Lord, help us never to forget Your children are precious gifts.

Ericka J. Iverson

Wild Kittens to Home Cats

"They shall be My people, and I will be their God."
—Jeremiah 32:38, NKJV

In January, a feral calico cat came to live in our backyard. My husband fed her and tried to tame her, but she chose to remain feral instead of sharing our home. Dave continued to feed her, and she became our "outdoor kitty," preferring to live under our backyard shed.

In July, she blessed us with five feral kittens. We got the necessary shots for all five kittens and the mama, and they all had the surgery that would turn them into responsible cats. We had decided to keep one of the two tuxedo kittens, a female we named Sox. We found good homes for the other the four kittens, including the other tuxedo kitten that we called Boots.

The night the family came for Boots, he would not let himself be caught, so they left with a determination to find a different kitty. You would have said, as we did, "He will never be tame!" I kept thinking of our beautiful but wild kitty, and I worried that no one would ever want him. So we decided to let him be feral in our backyard with his mom if that was what he chose.

But first, Dave would try harder to tame him. His sister, Sox, settled in and became a sweet, gentle kitten. But Dave never gave up on Boots. He worked patiently with him in the house. It took a long time for Boots to learn to trust. Now he, too, is gentle and sweet.

What changed him from wild to mild?

Of course, he knows he will always have food to eat, and our hands will always be gentle, but mostly he knows he is loved. Now he sleeps by my side much of the night, often with his face just a few inches from mine, confident he will never be hurt. Often he puts his paws on my cheeks for a while before falling asleep. His purr says it all—he is home, we are his people, he trusts us, and he feels loved.

Life has not been easy for some, and it can be hard to trust or to love. Yet Jesus works with us patiently and gently, always showing us how much He loves us. He never gives up. But the choice to trust Him is ours. His Word promises, "They shall be My people, and I will be their God" (Jeremiah 32:38, NKJV).

We can be confident in God's love.

Let Him change you by His love!

Ginny Allen

I Will Trust Him

Yea, though I walk through the valley of the shadow of death,
I will fear no evil: for thou art with me.
—Psalm 23:4, KJV

I lay awake, wondering how my good intentions had been interpreted so wrong, wondering how my conviction to show God's love to everyone—regardless of their story—could be interpreted as complacency. I was sad, deeply hurt, conflicted. I called my dad for reassurance and advice. He said, "Working for the Lord in whatever capacity is never easy. The trials are many, but the blessings overflow. Be patient. God will see you through."

Patience has not been my strongest trait, but I have learned to trust in God, His plan, and His timing. I prayed for God's grace, wisdom, and guidance. The days dragged, the sleepless nights were long. However, in the midst of this, I felt God's grace and reassuring presence.

On Sabbath, my teenage daughter randomly decided to go forward and pray during the altar call. A special friend took her hand, walking with her to the altar and praying with her. A special message on my daily devotional reminded me of God's love and presence, especially during difficult times. Regardless of our personal tribulations, life must go on. I had papers to write, articles to read, laundry to do, and a house to clean. My younger daughter and my husband were heading off on a mission trip. There was packing to do, hair to braid, and extra hugs to give. The next morning, as we headed to the airport, my husband looked over and reassuringly said, "Don't worry. It is darkest before dawn. God has a plan; He has never failed us, and He will reveal Himself in an amazing way."

I returned from the airport to a very quiet house. I chatted on the phone with a dear friend. We talked about the challenges women face as mothers, Christians, and professionals. Later, as I settled to do my work, I listened to Wintley Phipps on Pandora sing, "Let There Be Peace on Earth." And I was reminded of my favorite Bible verse, Psalm 23:4: "Yea, though I walk through the valley of the shadow of death, I will fear no evil: for thou art with me" (KJV).

I felt lighter, as if a weight had been lifted off my shoulders. I know that whatever trials I face now or in the future, my heavenly Father is always by my side. "If God is for us, who can be against us?" (Romans 8:31, NIV).

Ngozi Obiocha-Taffe

Perfect Weather

Farmers who wait for perfect weather never plant.
If they watch every cloud, they never harvest.
Just as you cannot understand the path of the wind
or the mystery of a tiny baby growing in its mother's womb,
so you cannot understand the activity of God, who does all things.
—Ecclesiastes 11:4, 5, NLT

Have you ever found yourself planning that special event or trip that required perfect weather? It may have been a wedding, picnic, beach trip, or church event. You may have needed sunshine instead of rain, a cool breeze instead of scorching rays, or birds chirping instead of mosquitoes biting. So you may have checked your local weather channel for the forecast for that day, hoping all would be well. But the weather forecasts we receive are not always perfect predictions. Sometimes the forecast is correct while, at other times, we get worse weather than was predicted. Or, to our delight, we experience better weather than was expected.

So it is with our journey here on earth. We need good weather to plant and harvest our crops, but sometimes we delay planting and harvesting because we are waiting for perfect weather. Have you been waiting for great weather to plant the "crop" of writing that book, starting that craft project, joining the choir, marrying that special someone you have been dating, or starting that charity to help the less fortunate? Maybe you have been waiting for all the things you need to fall into place before you take a step in a particular direction. But in our key text today, Solomon reminds us that if we wait for the perfect weather, we may never plant, and, as a result, we won't have a harvest to reap. Consequently, we cannot be deterred by every cloud that appears to threaten our planting.

So plant your crops despite the cloud of discouragement, lack of funding, or absence of moral support. I challenge you today to ask God to direct you to the things He would have you do so that you can plant those special crops He has given you and reap a bountiful harvest for His glory. It just may happen that the harvest is so bountiful it goes far beyond what you imagined and you do not have enough room to receive it.

May God bless you as you decide what crop to plant and harvest for His kingdom.

Taniesha K. Robertson-Brown

The Unexpected Letter

"Your heavenly Father already knows all your needs."
—Matthew 6:32, NLT

We were out of food and out of money to buy more food. Not that we usually had a surplus of either money or food. We were newlyweds from two poor families who felt called into the ministry. Yet as hard as we tried, our income did not cover our expenses.

My husband was in his fourth year of ministerial training at a midwestern college. His work at a college-run industry paid for his tuition and books. I found secretarial work with a large accounting firm in the heart of the city. My salary barely covered our living expenses. Unexpected medical bills had left us broke.

As I handed the city bus driver my final token, I walked slowly to the back of the bus, wondering how long it would take me to walk into work the next morning. I figured I would have to be up by at least 5:00 A.M. to get there in time. I wished I had summoned the courage to ask the older secretary at the office for a few dimes until our next paycheck, but I felt intimidated by her. I didn't want any of my coworkers to know how desperate our situation was.

I began to count the blocks I would have to walk to and from work, starting the next day! Twenty-two, twenty-three, twenty-four—I couldn't bring myself to count any further. As the bus pulled up to a stop in front of a small grocery store across from the college, I stepped out and, with sadness, watched it depart. Then I started up the steep stairs to our apartment above the store.

I did not expect to be greeted with a big smile by my husband, but he opened the door with a joyful flourish. "I got a letter from my mother today," he said. "And guess what?"

"What?" I responded, with a twinge of hope.

"She sold my sheepskin coat, the one I wore working during the winter on the railroad section crew, and she sent us the ten dollars she got for it!" He triumphantly held up a bill.

I was overwhelmed that God had impressed my mother-in-law to sell the jacket and send us the money so it would arrive just in time to save a young bride a long walk. I felt ashamed at my despair and lack of faith. I had hoped the Lord would help us find ten cents for the next day's bus fare, but He had sent one hundred times that much!

Teresa A. Sales

Train Up a Child

So Jesus told those Jews who had believed in him,
"If you continue in my word, you are really my disciples.
And you will know the truth, and the truth will set you free."
—John 8:31, 32, ISV

As early as I can remember, my parents put two very important gifts into my heart—honesty and the art of apologizing. When my older brother and I would get into trouble, my mother would ask us who was to blame. Our instinct was always to blame each other by saying, "It wasn't me" or, "I didn't do it." But Mom would always throw a mind-bending twist into the mix by saying (before we could avoid temporary punishment by lying or blaming each other), "Whoever tells the truth won't get into trouble, even if it was you."

This twist was a real challenge for a young child who had to weigh the options. It took a great deal of trust to rely on Mom's word and a great deal of restraint on her part. Her emphasis on honesty was our teacher, and I quickly learned that telling the truth about bad behavior and mistakes would always be my best option. My father would often discuss the actions we confessed and determine if an apology was needed. He always said, "Apologizing will make you feel better." He was right! It always did.

In my adult life, there are—and have been—constant opportunities to err, make mistakes, or exercise poor judgment, which have landed me in situations of accountability. My instinct has remained true to what I was taught as a child: if I'm honest, the results will always be better in the end. And the response to a person's honesty is usually the same. It's rare for someone to become enraged when the other party says in complete honesty, "It was me. I made a mistake, and I apologize. How can we move onward and upward from this situation?" The nature of most people is to forgive and understand, because who hasn't made a mistake? This first act of humility brings out the second act of grace.

No matter what the wrong, we can always confess and ask for forgiveness. It takes trust and a willing heart to remove pride and fear, which tend to cripple us. My mom had the right idea about following God's teaching on honesty and forgiveness. As Christians, we've been forgiven too much to constantly revisit the Garden where Adam and Eve fell—and then lied about it. Honesty truly does set us free and then allows love back into the equation.

Naomi Striemer

His Lens on My Life—and Yours

*"Not one sparrow (What do they cost? Two for a penny?)
can fall to the ground without your Father knowing it."*
—Matthew 10:29, TLB

It had been one of the busiest years for me professionally and personally. Our school had lost two teachers just within two months in the same class, and I had to add teaching a third-grade class to an already crowded workload as an administrator. I was finishing my doctoral dissertation, and, in the middle of the school year, I suffered a fall that left me racked with pain.

Now the last school day was here, but rest would come only after my nephew's high school graduation. I was physically and emotionally drained, and, most important of all, I was struggling spiritually as I needed to see the hand of God in my sister's life. She was going through a terrible time, and it appeared that the enemy was winning.

My sister, Nathalie, was hurting, and her troubles kept my heart company as my husband and I drove to graduation. I shared my worries with my husband, Walden, and he listened sorrowfully as I spoke through my sobs until we arrived at the university. Upon our arrival, we joined the rest of the family and took our seats. My brother-in-law, Winston, sat next to me. He shed the camera from across his shoulders, wiggled in his seat for comfort, and adjusted his camera lens on his son, Jared, who sat among more than eight hundred graduates.

For the next four hours, Winston focused his lens on his son, and he did not move. He captured his son's every stir and smile. As Jared scuttled for his diploma, his father caught his happiness and high fives. When the whole ceremony was done, Winston quietly placed his camera down and sighed with relief. Right there, the Holy Spirit spoke a lesson into my heart.

"Do you see this?" He seemed to say. "Do you see how this man's lens was focused solely on his boy? Cannot God see your sister and set things right for her?" The Spirit of God uses the simplest moments to teach the deepest spiritual lessons. Why was I fretting? The One who keeps my sister does not slumber or sleep (see Psalm 121:4), nor does He tire. My faith and joy renewed, I related God's message of hope to my husband and later to my sister. We all prayed and anticipated God's promises to materialize—and they did in time. If God can see the tiny sparrow fall, surely, in times of distress, His lens is centered on me, my sister—and you!

Rose Joseph Thomas

It Seemed Right

Lead me in the way everlasting.
—Psalm 139:24, NIV

I was showing my friend, Melissa, a favorite, special, and secluded spot my father had loved in Stanley Park, British Columbia. After a little while, we settled down on a redwood bench to V and V ("Veg and view," as Melissa liked to say). That's when we saw it. At least a couple of inches in length, the segmented ant body exuded confidence. Its initial trajectory was toward a bank of ferns and delicate forest flowers bordering the opposite side of the sand-packed walkway. "I'll call it ABC," said Melissa, watching intently. "Ant British Columbia." ABC was motoring along well enough, initially. Almost five inches into its journey, the ant turned a right angle and wandered erratically. Next, it made a U-turn, traveling in a series of half circles. Melissa grabbed a twig and, drawing a straight line to the bank, nudged ABC toward it. ABC tumbled over the edge of the straight path, righted itself, and walked a few inches toward the opposite bank. "Look!" cried Melissa. "I made a path, and ABC is following it."

Dream on, I thought. ABC climbed back over the edge of the path and began a set of zigzag machinations. Melissa placed twigs on each side of the path, built higher sand edges, and gave verbal directions. (Obviously, there was a language barrier.) "Two of ABC's cousins are following the path," said Melissa. Not ABC, as it made an about-face and arrived back at Point A.

"I thought ants were wise. This is pathetic! ABC has wasted a great deal of time and energy to go nowhere. It could have already been eating lunch by now if it had followed my path."

"How like humans," I suggested. "Scripture lays out for us a clear path, but so often we deviate from it, wandering here and there and sometimes arriving back where we started—no closer to our original goal." Thirty minutes later, we rose to leave, but ABC was still immobile at the corner of the redwood bench, no closer to the bank of ferns and delicate flowers—and lunch.

"Too bad," Melissa said, shaking her head. "I tried to direct ABC toward the right way, but, silly, it had a mind of its own!"

Lord, I breathed, *renew my mind. Help me follow the path and avoid unnecessary detours. Lead me in the way everlasting.*

Arlene R. Taylor

When God Speaks

Suddenly, a fierce storm struck the lake,
with waves breaking into the boat. But Jesus was sleeping.
The disciples went and woke him up, shouting,
"Lord, save us! We're going to drown!"
Jesus responded, "Why are you afraid? You have so little faith!"
Then he got up and rebuked the wind and waves,
and suddenly there was a great calm.
—Matthew 8:24–26, NLT

It had been an eventful year at work thus far; several changes were proposed for the organization, and there was much talk about the company being sold. Employees watched the proceedings and listened for updates on the new developments and how we would be affected. The events had become personal because the circumstances of our lives were about to change, and everything was now uncertain.

Even though I was concerned, I was not deeply worried. I had strong faith and trust in God that He would see me through whatever storm was about to come my way. This confidence in God came about when, at the start of the year during the New Year holidays, I had felt a strong urge to fast, pray, and consecrate my life to God. I obeyed the Holy Spirit's leading to act because something was about to happen, and I would need extra strength from the Lord to see me through.

I had many financial commitments and was completing the last module in the final year at the university to finish my undergraduate degree. Then, as if this were not enough, one Sunday, I was busy at home with domestic chores when I discovered some changes taking place with my body. I had never seen anything like what was happening to me before and became fearful. A visit to the doctor resulted in hospitalization. I felt as if I would not live through that night. Then I remembered the time of fasting, prayer, and consecration and felt God's peace embracing me.

God speaks! He speaks to His people in different ways. When we have a connection with the Lord, we know when He speaks. There was no questioning God in my mind when urged to fast, pray, and consecrate my life to Him. I obeyed and received peace, hope, and strength to go through a raging life storm, but God was in the midst of it. He spoke, and my path became clear through the storm. God will do the same for you. Will you listen when He speaks today?

Elizabeth Ida Cain

Words to Ponder

Let the words of my mouth, and the meditation of my heart,
be acceptable in thy sight, O LORD, my strength, and my redeemer.
—Psalm 19:14, KJV

With verbal communication, we use thousands of words that, when put together, create messages for conversation. When we think of this function God has created, we can see that His plan was for verbal interaction along with the other incredible functions of the human body. Some words bring comfort and cheer; others hurt. We have choices of words for every occasion. Some have a profound feeling about them. I have chosen to highlight four out of many.

Love reminds me of God's love for me. Jesus said, "For God so loved the world, that he gave his only begotten Son, that whosoever believeth in him should not perish, but have everlasting life" (John 3:16, KJV). We are counseled to love others: "Beloved, if God so loved us, we ought also to love one another" (1 John 4:11, KJV). In 1 Corinthians 13:13, we read, "And now abide faith, hope, love, these three; but the greatest of these is love" (NKJV).

Peace is a beautiful thought. Isaiah 26:3 tells us, "Thou wilt keep him in perfect peace, whose mind is stayed on thee: because he trusteth in thee" (KJV). When I go out in the country amid things of nature, my mind becomes peaceful. God gives us quiet places to renew our minds; He knows we need peace. "And the peace of God, which passeth all understanding, shall keep your hearts and minds through Christ Jesus" (Philippians 4:7, KJV).

Hope encourages me every day when so much in this world can cause despair: "Be strong and take heart, all you who hope in the LORD" (Psalm 31:24, NIV).

Happiness is my fourth word: "A merry heart makes a cheerful countenance" (Proverbs 15:13, NKJV). Jesus desires that we should be happy, for this is a witness before others of His love and care. The first three fruits of the Spirit are "love, joy, peace" (Galatians 5:22, KJV). And Proverbs 16:20 shares that "whoso trusteth in the LORD, happy is he" (KJV).

In this world of sadness and strife, Satan would rob us of love, peace, hope, and happiness. However, there will soon be a day of rejoicing, for when Jesus comes, only words of praise will pass our lips.

Lyn Welk-Sandy

Ski Accident

A cheerful heart is a good medicine,
but a downcast spirit dries up the bones.
—Proverbs 17:22, RSV

During the winter, my husband, Larry, and I skied almost every day. We strapped on our cross-country skis and puffed up the slopes that border the lake behind our house. We raced down through the trees and sped across the frozen lake. Occasionally, on weekends, we'd head to the mountains for more beautiful scenery and more challenging topography. One Sunday morning, we decided to explore a new trail. Friends would drop us off at a trailhead, and we'd ski, ever downward, to the town of Banff where we'd find our car.

We skied in a blaze of sunshine and then traversed areas of shadow beneath evergreen trees, ever watchful for patches of ice on this late-winter day. Suddenly, I slipped, my poles flailing, my skis skidding out of the track. I landed on my face with my sunglasses pushing into my forehead. Winded, I lay for a few moments in the trail. A headache, but no broken bones. I wasn't in bad shape. The next few miles would be uncomfortable, but certainly possible.

"Your forehead's bleeding," announced Larry. He pulled off his reflective sunglasses and handed them to me to serve as a mirror. My forehead was cut in two places right above my eyebrows. "Where's the first aid kit? We need to get you bandaged up and into the emergency room. I think you'll need stitches." He put two Band-Aids on my forehead, and we headed along the trail, skiing more slowly and carefully. I waited several hours at the Mineral Springs Hospital, feeling rather grouchy. Not only had our beautiful morning been marred, but lunch was delayed, and my head hurt. I felt gloomier and gloomier as the afternoon progressed. I started analyzing the injuries of those around me: With three downhill ski resorts nearby, I was the only person who wasn't in pain because of a broken wrist, arm, or leg. Still, the observation did nothing to lift my spirits. I sat morosely and felt sorry for myself.

When I was called in, the doctor removed the Band-Aids. Suddenly, life was much better. I felt almost happy. Yes, the doctor decided that stitches were unnecessary, but my mood shifted primarily because my eyebrows weren't held down. My face wasn't fixed in a perpetual gloomy expression. I could smile. I realized that a cheerful heart—and face—are both good medicine!

Denise Dick Herr

39

Any Spare Salt?

*"You are the salt of the earth. But if the salt loses its saltiness,
how can it be made salty again? It is no longer good for anything,
except to be thrown out and trampled underfoot."*
—Matthew 5:13, NIV

The plot was thickening and the words flowing smoothly. I was having a good time with the keyboard and smirking at the thought that I had, at this point, outrun that dreaded writer's block. The characters were becoming real until the loudest of knocks on my door threw me off guard. "This better be good," I said to myself. Grudgingly, I moved away from the computer to check who this "bad timer" was. I hoped it wasn't my neighbor's boys, who had already disturbed me twice that morning, kicking their ball over my fence and coming around to knock on my door to ask that I throw it back to them. A discreet peep revealed it was the boys' little sister. I pondered if I should hear her out or continue writing—I assumed her brothers had sent her over this time, having sensed they had already gotten on my last nerve. Before I made up my mind whether to hear her out, she knocked again. I opened the door and forced a smile.

"Mummy wants to cook something, and she has run out of salt. Do you have any spare salt, please?" For a moment, I stared at the child, puzzled. She looked me straight in the eye as she said those words.

"Yes, I do have spare salt," I responded. She came in and waited by the hallway as I made it into the kitchen. When I was a young girl, my mum taught me to be sure I always had extra salt in my kitchen cupboards. True to that teaching, I always have one or two extra unopened bottles of salt. I handed the young girl a salt bottle, and she left.

Three days later, Matthew 5:13 came to mind. God requires me to be the salt of the world. He requires us to be well seasoned and to mingle, carrying out the purpose to which He has called us. What good are we if we lose our saltiness or if we allow our saltiness to be overpowering? Had I ignored the little girl's knock, I would have missed an opportunity to reach out even in the most insignificant way. Very unlikely people could need our saltiness, yet there should be no excuse. So, my sisters, the question is, Are you too salty, or are you well seasoned? Do you always have "spare salt" to share: kind words you say to someone or that little act of kindness you extend to others? *Lord, help me be well seasoned and minister to others.*

Regina Jele-Ncube

A Cup of Water, Please?

"Whoever drinks the water I give them will never thirst."
—John 4:14, NIV

With her head bowed, her eyes partially shielded, barely looking up to check her path, too afraid she might be noticed, she timidly walked on to her destination. Her mission was to get where she intended to go and leave as quickly as possible. She was in deep thought, concentrating all her energy on her mission, when suddenly she was startled by a male voice.

Moving her veil ever so slightly, she raised her head, wondering to herself, *Who could this man possibly be?* With her thoughts racing, she thought of the time of day. Had she miscalculated the time? Was it not high noon, the sixth hour of the day? Would not all the women and girls already have attended to filling their water jars? *And yes,* she thought, *men do not usually come to the well to draw water. It's usually the women and girls. So why is this man here?*

When she shook herself back to reality and out of her deep thoughts, the woman was astonished to see a man sitting on the edge of the well, asking, "May I have a cup of water, please?" She looked around. Only the two of them were present at the well. *He must be addressing me,* she thought. Their eyes met, and she noticed His features and His dress. He was not from her tribe.

"Your dress and your features betray you. You must be a Jew! Can you not tell from my clothing that I am a Samaritan? Yet here you are, asking me to give you a drink of water from our father's well—Jacob's well. The Jews hate us Samaritans so much they usually spit on the ground when they accidentally come near us. Yet you ask me, a Samaritan woman, for a cup of water?" Christ met her where she was, a flawed woman with a deep spiritual longing.

I invite you to join the club of *ordinary, flawed, hungry, thirsty* people who are drawn by the incredible grace and love of Jesus. Like John, the beloved disciple, we also can claim to be the beloved of Jesus. I invite you to drink from the well that never will run dry, the well from which just a cup of water will quench your spiritual thirst and make you whole and fit to spend eternity with the Living God.

Avis May Rodney

A Long Wait Home

"Be still, and know that I am God."
—Psalm 46:10, NIV

Many of us struggle with being patient. For instance, we are impatient when we have to wait in line at the grocery store or wait for someone to take us somewhere. One day, my husband, who is legally blind, had an appointment for an outpatient procedure at the hospital. His insurance company supplies transportation for doctor visits, so I called to schedule a ride. The van came, and the driver was very nice. When we arrived at our destination, he gave me a card with the toll-free number to call when we were ready to be picked up.

My husband's medical procedure took longer than expected, but I had informed the nurse that we were riding in the insurance van, so I needed to know when I could call for our return trip. She said she would come and let me know when my husband was in recovery. While in the waiting room, I was surprised to see Kay, a fellow church member, working at the desk. She saw me and came over and hugged me. I had no idea she worked there. After a couple of hours, the nurse came and gave me the OK to call for our ride. I went to the desk and called the number on the card but got only a recording. I waited "patiently," but after about seven minutes, I hung up the phone and redialed. I began getting impatient and frustrated as I was still on hold. The secretary saw my frustration and tried to call the number on her phone but to no avail. Now I was really becoming upset. I asked the secretary if she knew Kay, who worked downstairs. She said, "Yes, you go to the same church?"

"Yes," I responded.

She continued, "Then I'll call Kay, and she'll find you a ride home. Don't get upset." When Kay arrived, we told her the situation. She assured me that she had her church directory and would be able to call someone to pick up my husband and me. I praised God and relaxed.

The Lord places people in our path, and sometimes we don't always know why. I had no idea that Kay worked at the hospital, but the Lord knew. He knew the need I would have, crossed our paths, and—through her—provided us a way home with another church member. Here I was, impatient and worrying, while the Lord was already working things out!

"Rest in the LORD and wait patiently for Him" (Psalm 37:7, NKJV).

Elaine J. Johnson

Our Hope

*Then they cried unto the LORD in their trouble,
and he delivered them out of their distresses.*
—Psalm 107:6, KJV

Which of us has no wounds or scars on the soul? Certainly, the world spares no one. We are marked by pain and afflictions that seem to have no end. Every day we fight against discouragement, and sometimes we fall in this fight. Wounds burn, reminding us that we have limited abilities and need help. Each person, at the soul level, carries the scars from a sinful, ruined world headed for destruction.

Conditions on this planet have worsened to the point where we really cannot expect much quality of life. We are affected by illness, violence, and discouragement, as well as material and emotional needs. The peace and tranquility once found in the Garden of Eden no longer exist.

Yet we give glory to the Lord because in the midst of all this chaos, there is a living hope: Jesus will be with us until the end—and beyond!

His promise is sure. While it assures us that we have help in overcoming our daily struggles with sin, it also reminds us of a new home of unending peace and happiness being prepared for us. We will live without sorrow, death, pain, or suffering. Despite this world's pain, we have a certainty in our hearts—that God created us to be happy and at His side.

What we see, hear, and do in this world of suffering does have a function, however: to keep alive the flame of hope in the promises of Jesus. The afflictions that are part of our lives now are only intruders in what God originally created on, and for, this world. We know that in the better world God is preparing for His children, no evil will ever enter.

Too often, it is easy to become discouraged when facing life's challenges. Yet on this final journey, we must believe and trust in the words of our Savior. He will help us walk on the right path and not lose our way. Jesus said, "I am the way, the truth, and the life" (John 14:6, NKJV). Only He can help us through our tribulations and steady our steps.

Therefore, dear friend, when troubles come upon you, look up. God loves you with an everlasting love. Only in Him will you find hope and lasting security!

Sueli da Silva Pereira

Soap

And it shall come to pass, that before they call, I will answer;
and while they are yet speaking, I will hear.
—Isaiah 65:24, KJV

There is an international program called Days for Girls, which provides feminine hygiene supplies to young girls. I have been involved with the project for a couple of years now.

Most every girl and woman, everywhere, have something in common—a monthly menstrual cycle. Many countries are blessed with adequate means to deal with this area of female life. However, there are places where normal activities almost come to a standstill during the few days of menstruation. When hygiene supplies are made available, it is life-changing for young girls who can continue to go to school all month long instead of missing several days.

Days for Girls volunteers supply needed items along with a washcloth and a small bar of soap. Many times, I have asked motel proprietors if they would consider either donating or selling me a few bars of soap for this special project.

A friend of mine and her husband recently took a trip to a distant city. Jeannie, being interested in my project, asked the motel clerk where they stayed if she could buy ten to twelve small bars of soap. The clerk responded, "How would you like a whole case?"

Jeannie exclaimed, "A whole case!" Then the clerk explained that the motel had recently changed brands, and they didn't need the case of soap they had been using. Jeannie took the case of soap to her motel room and tried to figure out how to get it home. She removed clothes from her suitcase, placed them in a carry-on bag, and crammed both suitcases full of soap.

When they arrived at the airport, the airline check-in clerk asked why Jeannie's suitcase was so heavy. With a grin, her husband responded, "Soap." The clerk exclaimed, "Soap!" And they all laughed. Then Jeannie briefly explained that the soap was for a missionary project. The lady said that she, too, had done some missionary work in the past and gladly waived the forty-dollar excess baggage fee. Back home, I was very surprised when Jeannie presented me with over a thousand small bars of soap, all of which will bless many girls in distant lands. God helped with my project, answering before I even asked. What a mighty God we serve!

Marybeth Gessele

Hear My Prayer

When my heart is overwhelmed:
lead me to the rock that is higher than I.
—Psalm 61:2, KJV

The Lord never leaves nor forsakes us. He hears our prayers. Have you felt hopeless, lonely, and as if you were alone in the dark? I have had these feelings and more, but God has always shown me, one way or another, that He is working things out for me and that it will be OK.

In 1984, I was a teenager in Jamaica trying to find my sister. She lived in a rural area in St. James, and I was visiting her from Westmoreland. I got on a bus whose route led down a lonely, dark road.

Suddenly we passengers saw some activity on the road ahead. A major accident had occurred! Our bus had to stop.

"Everyone will have to walk from here," the driver announced.

I did not know anyone on the bus or how to get back home or to my sister's house. I murmured to myself, "How will I ever find where she lives?"

"Where who lives?" asked the young man seated beside me. When I told him my sister's name, he responded, "Oh, I know her. She just moved to a house in my area." I could not believe what I was hearing. On a bus full of strangers, the person sitting next to me knew my sister!

The young man held my hand in the crook of his big, warm arm and began walking with me for over three hours—the time it took to arrive finally at my sister's house. Though the man was twice my size and height, I was not scared. I felt safe holding his arm, although I did not know his name.

He led me safely to my sister's house.

Today, if you feel as if you are lost in the darkness, please remember that God hears your prayer. He has angels on each corner along your journey. When your heart is overwhelmed, He will lead you to the Rock that is higher than you. So please pray with me now.

Dear God, open our eyes to see Your blessings. Focus our attention on Your love. Hide the fears and doubts that haunt us, and lead us to the Rock that is higher than we are. Amen.

Now accept God's answer and flourish in His loving embrace.

Pauline E. Robinson

Count Your Blessings

In every thing give thanks: for this is
the will of God in Christ Jesus concerning you.
—1 Thessalonians 5:18, KJV

I was completing my master's degree in the United Kingdom. I was homesick, mostly because I missed my only child. In an effort to relieve my distress, I spoke of him whenever possible.

While speaking to one of my colleagues during a diabetic clinic, I emphasized how much I enjoyed raising my son and proceeded to lament the fact that I had only one child. My colleague was quiet for a moment then told me of how long he and his wife had tried to have a child, and how difficult it had been to accept that it was medically impossible. I apologized.

The next day I was asked by another colleague about my children at home and how I was coping. I responded that I missed my son dearly. She then asked if I only had "just the one." I was quick to answer that although I had tried to have a pair of children, I had only managed to have one living child. I told her of my medical condition, which had affected my childbearing ability and how sad this had made me. I was startled by her calm response. She said, "You're lucky; I couldn't have any." I almost bowed my head in shame. Again, I apologized for being insensitive.

I left the hospital that day feeling very cruel and ungrateful. In two days, I had met two people with no children—two people, however, who were still cheerful. I thought of how I must have hurt God by constantly lamenting the fact that I had only one child. I had been so selfish and ungrateful. I thought of how much better it would be to constantly thank Him for a normal, healthy child, indeed a gift from God.

Although I was away from home, God had taught me a valuable lesson in gratefulness.

How often do we complain about what God does or doesn't give to us? Yet there are others around us who have so much less. They continue to be blessings to others anyway and do not cease to smile.

Today let us take the time to thank God for our many blessings. Indeed, He has done great things!

Shana Cyr-Philbert

Don't Stop What You're Doing

*So let's not get tired of doing what is good. At just the right time
we will reap a harvest of blessing if we don't give up.*
—Galatians 6:9, NLT

Once a week at work, we have a meeting with our whole team.* During this meeting, our team is briefed, and we also have a peer share, exchanging pertinent work-related information. I'm a creature of habit, so I frequently mention an interesting article that I've read in the *New York Times*, generally dealing with finances that applies to our business or team members. One morning as I prepared to find an article, I had a discouraging thought: *All your shares are from the* Times. *Why don't you do something different?* So I gave up searching for my would-be article and went to the meeting with nothing to share.

As the meeting progressed, the partner said, "I won't share everything because I'm sure some of you will have the same share." I'm usually first to share, but I responded that I had nothing for the team. He was surprised that I had not brought the article that he had read for what would have been my usual share. You see, he had even dubbed me "queen of the *New York Times*." He had come expecting me, because of my usual routine, to be the one to share about this interesting article—which he proceeded to discuss. I sat there and half smiled to myself. Though thinking that my contributions were going unnoticed, I had created a reputation for finding and sharing articles of interest related to our profession.

Is there something you keep doing but think your efforts aren't being noticed? Keep doing it anyway. Twice yesterday, I came across this verse: "Whatever your hand finds to do, do it with your might" (Ecclesiastes 9:10, NKJV).

Friends, while it may feel discouraging at times because you think your efforts are not being noticed, don't give up! You have a very important role to play, no matter how unimportant you may feel it is. God has a way of multiplying things when we place them in His hands.

Lord, please forgive us for believing that what You have asked us to do is inadequate. Please strengthen us to do whatever it is You have given us to do. Please encourage us along our journey so that we may know we are doing the work to which You have called us.

Kaysian C. Gordon

---

* This entry first appeared as blog post, "Don't Stop What You're Doing," *Kaysi Gordon LLC: Walking by Faith and Not by Sight* (blog), May 24, 2017, https://kaysigordon.com/dont-stop-what-youre-doing/.

Heaven's 911

*When he calls on me, I will answer; I will be with him in trouble
and rescue him and honor him. I will satisfy him
with a full life and give him my salvation.*
—Psalm 91:15, 16, TLB

A contemporary Christian singer, Eddie DeGarmo, sings a song titled "Heaven's 9-1-1." It tells of a person heading down life's highway in the wrong direction. Then the person realizes he can call on Jesus any time of day by offering a quick prayer. We, too, can have a direct line to Jesus anytime, anywhere. Jesus knows our needs and wants even before we ask. He is waiting for us to come to Him and tell Him the desires of our hearts.

My friend Joyce, a diabetic who lives alone, wears an emergency safety button. If Joyce should fall or have a medical emergency, she can push the button. Someone will immediately contact her to see if she's OK, needs an ambulance dispatched to come to her aid, or needs her son to be contacted to come and help. This emergency button option is reassuring not only for Joyce but also for her loved ones, knowing that she can easily summon help.

Have you ever wanted to talk to someone important? Perhaps the president of a school, of a bank, or even of the United States? You may have had something important on your mind, and you wanted to get advice or offer a suggestion, but you knew it would be nearly impossible to reach that person. Maybe you just wanted to meet a celebrity. There was a young actor from a children's movie whom my oldest son resembled. Once I asked my son, about ten years of age at the time, to stand by the television. I stopped the movie on a close-up of the young actor that my son resembled. I took a picture of both of them and submitted it to the movie company. A few weeks later I received a reply from the company, a form letter inviting us to join this young actor's fan club, but it made no mention of my son's resemblance to the young actor.

On this earth, we may not be able to have a direct connection with everyone we wish. However, we can have a direct connection with God and His Son, Jesus Christ, our Creator and the King of the universe. I know it's hard to fathom or imagine that when we get to heaven, we will communicate with Him face-to-face, having no more need for "911 calls." I like to make lists. Perhaps I will make a list of topics that I want to discuss with Him when I meet Him on the sea of glass. How great will that be!

Gyl Moon Bateman

Paying Our Debts

It is better not to make a vow than to make one and not fulfill it.
—Ecclesiastes 5:5, NIV

We live in a world where some people's "word" has been losing its value. Think about your life. How many times have you promised to do things for people? Then try to recall how many of these promises you have actually fulfilled.

And how many times have people who made promises to you kept their word?

Toward the end of his life, during a time of reflection, King Solomon wrote, "It is better not to make a vow than to make one and not fulfill it" (Ecclesiastes 5:5, NIV). His father, David, had written earlier in Psalm 15 that among those who "will stand firm forever" (verse 5, NLT) are people who have kept "their promises" (verse 4, NLT). In other words, they made good on their word.

As human beings, we can control whether we stand behind our word. If we don't, though, we lose credibility and the respect of others. People view us as being untrustworthy.

And here's a further thought: If keeping our promises to others is important, how much more careful should we be when making promises to God? When we are requesting God's help during times of anxiety or fear, we sometimes promise to do something in return. Yet how often have we forgotten to follow through on those promises to the Savior?

But God does not forget. He wants us to fulfill what we have promised. As Solomon wrote, "When you make a vow to God, do not delay to fulfill it" (Ecclesiastes 5:4, NIV). In this verse, the admonition to fulfill a promise takes on the meaning of paying a debt that we owe. So when we promise something either to God or another person, we assume a debt in a sense. And as such, since we have committed to assume this debt, we need to pay it.

Jesus once told a parable of two sons that a householder asked to work in his vineyard. The first son said he wouldn't but changed his mind and went to work. The second son promised to work but did not make good on his word. Jesus implied that the son who did not fulfill his promise—did not pay his debt—did not do the will of his father (Matthew 21:28–31).

As we promise—and are careful—to pay our temporal debts, should we not take our promises to God and others with the same seriousness? In God's strength, we can make good on our word.

Cecilia Nanni

The Kindness of a Stranger

Whoever is kind to the poor is lending to the LORD—
the benefit of his gift will return to him in abundance.
—Proverbs 19:17, ISV

Once, in 1979, I was traveling from Manila to Addis Ababa, Ethiopia, where my husband and I served as missionaries. There was a thirty-hour layover in Bombay (currently Mumbai), India, before I could board the Ethiopian Airlines flight for the last leg of my trip.

As I sat in the corner of the airport observing the busy activities around me, I saw a middle-aged lady sitting alone. She had a worried look on her face; something was wrong. Curious, I approached her. In limited English, she related her sad story.

She worked as domestic help for a family in Saudi Arabia. Unfortunately, she became sick, and the family decided to send her back to Sri Lanka via Bombay. However, the ticket did not include the connecting flight to her final destination. She was stranded in Bombay indefinitely! For several days she had begged passengers for money to purchase a ticket to Sri Lanka. I thought of helping her but did not have the courage to approach people and beg. I gave her my last dollar and prayed that I would not need anything before I reached home.

Before I settled on my makeshift "bed" of airport chairs, I knelt to thank God for His protection and the company of a new friend. Suddenly I heard a voice asking, *"Filipina ka ba?* [Are you a Filipina?]" I looked around to see who asked the question. Seated nearby was an Arab gentleman. In the course of our conversation, he mentioned that he was on his way back to Saudi Arabia from a business trip to Manila. I introduced my friend and mentioned her sad predicament.

Upon hearing her story, this kind stranger handed me money and instructed me to purchase her a ticket to Sri Lanka. My new friend could not contain her happiness. Finally, she was going home, thanks to the kindness of a stranger!

I am reminded of Christ's words: "Assuredly, I say to you, inasmuch as you did it to one of the least of these My brethren, you did it to Me" (Matthew 25:40, NKJV).

The next day I bade farewell to my new friends as they boarded the plane to their respective destinations. I was alone again, but not for long. I, too, was going home.

Evelyn Porteza Tabingo

Praying for Strangers

Pray without ceasing.
—1 Thessalonians 5:17, NKJV

Every day I pray for strangers. It sets the stage for new friendships. Let me explain about my prayer. I decided long ago to ask God to be the One to lead me to friends. This is my prayer: "Thank You, Lord, for the stranger that I'm yet to meet, one who will become my friend." As a result, my friendship coffer overflows.

Life is short. "We can't choose our [birth] family, but we can choose our friends"—a young friend said that to me the day after I prayed with her mother in the hospital, following her father's unexpected death. She and her husband were two strangers for whom I had prayed before we even met, the same as with her parents. It's always wonderful to meet the new people God brings into my life; they are precious gifts.

My husband and I returned to Florida in 2014 after being away for four and a half years. Though we've acquired many fine friends and enjoyed nice experiences while living in other places, I longed for Florida. I'm one of those people affected by seasonal affective disorder, also referred to as SAD. There aren't many gray days in Florida. Even the almost daily summer rain showers are followed by brilliant sunshine. One of the delights upon our return was the frequent flow of visits from our Florida friends, who welcomed us back to the Sunshine State, as well as our many snowbird friends.

Does "pray without ceasing" mean to do nothing except pray twenty-four hours a day? If we tried this, we might be hauled off for a psychiatrist's evaluation. Instead, it means that we maintain an attitude of prayer throughout the day, knowing that God's listening ear is with us. My days are better because of my friends—each one is a tremendous blessing. My husband and I prayed for these friends and continue to pray for them. They are an extension of our family. Thus, let us pray for strangers for, in so doing, they become the ones whom we call, individually, "my friend."

Betty Kossick

Know Us by Our Love

"A new command I give you: Love one another. As I have loved you,
so you must love one another. By this everyone will know
that you are my disciples, if you love one another."
—John 13:34, 35, NIV

"Where are you going?" Cara, the gym class instructor, asked a fellow member of our class.

The question drew my attention. I turned in the direction of her voice. Then I looked at the soft-spoken student. That day she appeared to have spent more time than usual on her appearance and was wearing carefully applied makeup that enhanced her features.

I did not hear the student's quiet answer to the instructor's question. Later that day, however, a spiritual parallel dawned in my mind.

I reflected on how Cara's attention had been drawn to her student's appearance, which suggested that she intended to go somewhere important after class. Likewise, we, as followers of Christ, should "look" as if we are going somewhere important. And we are—heaven.

People should know that we are Christ's disciples and ambassadors before we even speak a word. How can they know that? Because we are "wearing" something every day that's much better than makeup. We are wearing love.

Jesus told His disciples, "By this everyone will know that you are my disciples, if you love one another" (John 13:35, NIV). God calls us to show His love to everyone. People should look at us and notice something different—that we have love for one another. That love should envelop everyone we meet in heartwarming waves, in actions and words of kindness. When others know us by our love, they will want to connect with the Source of our love, God.

When we witness with love, we share hope. We are living testimonies that this world is not our home. We are walking reminders that we are going somewhere important: heaven. Our love will inspire others to love and follow God and be among the faithful followers that He, when the time comes, will take to heaven. The Bible says that we are pilgrims here on this earth and advises us to store up our treasure in heaven, not on this planet. So let us live like we're loved by God, and let us show His love to everyone we meet.

Alexis A. Goring

Coming to My Rescue

"For I am . . . the holy God of Israel, who saves you. . . .
because you are precious to me."
—Isaiah 43:3, 4, GNT

Squealing brakes and the thud of a slammed car door followed by an angry, bellowing male voice abruptly drowned out our quiet conversations. The usual laughter and pleasantries of church potluck vanished. Furious accusations escalated into violent shoving. The recipient of the anger, a tiny teenager, tried unsuccessfully to escape.

From my distant vantage point, I was too far away to protect her. Racing into the community room, I frantically searched for the father of the teen.

"A young man is yelling and pushing your daughter in the breezeway!" I exclaimed. That was all he needed to hear.

The father asked no questions. With coattails flying and brown shoes beating the ceramic tiles, this usually reserved giant of a man was out the door in a flash. There was no time to waste. His precious daughter was in danger.

And that's when I caught a new picture of God.

As a child, I often gazed at a picture of Jesus, the Good Shepherd, inching His way over the ground on His stomach. With outstretched arms, He's reaching for His lost lamb, quivering on a narrow ledge of a steep precipice. I always imagined a slowly moving Shepherd, quietly taking His time so as not to frighten the lamb.

But at that moment, I saw God's fierce reaction to the sound of *my* cries for help. Gone are the slow, cautious movements. He drops everything. He snatches up the hem of His robe as His sandals fly across the ground. God races to my rescue! When I cry to Him, He responds instantly and without hesitation. It doesn't matter whether my choices are the cause of my problems or not. That can be sorted out later. What does matter is His rescuing me from imminent danger just as that father rescued his daughter that day in the church breezeway.

It is this new picture of my heavenly Father, running immediately to my aid, that I will remember. When problems envelop me, when danger overwhelms me, when the enemy seems to outdistance me, I can be sure that God is my Rescuer.

Judy-Ann Neal

Restored

*"Then you will call to me. You will come and pray to me,
and I will answer you. You will seek me, and you will find me
because you will seek me with all your heart. Yes, I say,
you will find me, and I will restore you to your land. I will gather you
from every country and from every place to which I have
scattered you, and I will bring you back to the land from which
I had sent you away into exile. I, the LORD, have spoken."*
—Jeremiah 29:12–14, GNT

Have you ever felt out of sorts? You wanted to cry but didn't know exactly why? Despondent? Depressed? In despair? I know—we Christians aren't supposed to talk or think like this. But it's true; at times, we suffer from emotional lows. At least, I have.

My sister, let me share what has helped me through these exasperating times. The passage of Jeremiah 29:12–14. (I also like to read it from *The Message* as well as in the paraphrase above.)

Look closely. What do you see? God makes four conditional promises. Here are the first three: call, come, and pray. And, if you will *call, come,* and *pray,* God will answer you!

Do you know what will happen when God answers you? He will restore you. He is a *good* Father, and He understands and knows what we need. He only waits for us to call, come, and pray. We suffer needlessly at times because we try to fix the problems ourselves. Then as a last resort, we bring our failed attempts to God.

Sister, make God your first choice, and you won't need any other options.

Then we read that "if you seek Me—I will allow you to find Me" (that's the Cheryl Simmons paraphrase).

When we find God, He restores us, and our emotional needs dissipate. When we sit fully in His presence, the Holy Spirit begins to energize our minds into higher thoughts, and our brain is restructured.

Lord, help me get rid of my stinking thinking! Amen.

Today as you call upon the Lord and come before His throne in prayer, I ask you to seek His face earnestly. Then watch as He begins a restoration in you.

But that's not all—as God restores you, He will also make you a blessing to others.

Cheryl P. Simmons

Lunch With Jesus

He remembered us in our weakness.
His faithful love endures forever.
—Psalm 136:23, NLT

When my lovely granddaughters invited me to lunch, I was thrilled. I arrived at the restaurant quite early and was seated at a table where I could see the front door. I didn't want to miss one second of our time together—I felt so honored! While I waited, the waitress seated an older couple in the booth across from me. They sat down and took out their cell phones. By the time the waitress returned to take their drink order, they had not spoken one word to each other. After ordering drinks and salads, the couple returned to their cell phones. The waitress came back to take their entrée order and remove their empty salad plates. Then their attention once again turned to their respective cell phones. I was fascinated. Their entrée finally came—and so did my granddaughters.

While enjoying the animated luncheon conversation with my granddaughters, I kept glancing at the noncommunicating couple. Not one word had passed between them. When they finished their meal, the man helped the woman put on her jacket, and off they went with the cell phones in their hands. Can you believe they were not interested in talking to each other? Amazing! They didn't seem upset, nor did they act mad. They were simply indifferent.

I guess I am the proverbial magpie. I like to talk, and I enjoy other people talking to me. I feel safe in saying that Jesus is the same way. He is so very accessible to each of us. The Bible reveals that people loved talking to Him. They came alone or in groups. They came during the day and even at night. And Jesus enjoyed talking to people because they were—and still are—the love of His life! The condition they were in, their financial status—none of that mattered to Jesus. He interacted with all who came to Him. Some left His presence healed of their diseases. All left His presence with a deep sense that He loved them and wanted them to follow the path to eternal life. After all, "His faithful love endures forever" (Psalm 136:23, NLT).

So why not make a date to have lunch with Jesus today? Take the time to talk to Him; He wants to hear from you. He is the best Listener ever! He keeps your secrets, and He knows how to solve your problems. He really, really cares about you.

Grace A. Keene

Protection

The angel of the LORD encamps
around those who fear him,
and he delivers them.
—Psalm 34:7, NIV

When Sabbath ended one week, we had a baby shower for one of our church members. It was very well attended, and I helped clean up afterward. The family life leader said a closing prayer, and we all went our separate ways.

I caught a bus to the main bus station and waited for another one to take home. To my surprise, I had missed the last bus! With no other options left, I decided to walk home. I had no choice in the matter, and I had a long walk ahead of me.

The first part of my trek took me down a main highway that was very busy. I decided to get off this busy highway and walk through the neighborhood instead. So I redirected my route from the highway and down a road that would take me to the neighborhood road.

That's when I first noticed a long driveway to my right. It wasn't just the driveway that attracted my attention; I also saw three large dogs walking down that driveway toward me. I just glanced at them and kept walking. *I wonder where they are going* went through my mind as I glanced back. They were right behind me!

Arriving at the main street of the neighborhood, I turned left. To my surprise, I encountered more big dogs there too. In fact, so many dogs that I started to panic.

"They will not harm you," I heard a voice say.

That voice comforted me. I began noticing something different about this "pack" of dogs. They were not barking or growling. It was as if they all knew one another. They surrounded me as I continued walking down the street. When I had walked for about thirty minutes and gotten close to a hospital, I knew I was only ten minutes from my home. When I arrived at the hospital, I looked around and behind me. All the dogs were gone! Soon after, I arrived safely at home.

Tears still come to my eyes every time I recall this experience. The Lord showed me on that dark night when I missed the last city bus that He keeps track of His children and provides protection—perhaps even sending angels in the form of dogs.

Sharon Denise Smith

From Kansas to Oz

Therefore if any man be in Christ, he is a new creature:
old things are passed away; behold, all things are become new.
—2 Corinthians 5:17, KJV

In *The Wizard of Oz*, an American children's book, a cyclone comes through Kansas and whisks off Dorothy and her little dog, Toto—still in their house—to the Land of Oz. After a safe landing, Dorothy exits the house only to become acutely aware that things are different. The colors are different, the people are different, the customs and laws are different, and everything is new. At that moment, Dorothy knows that her whole life is about to change.

Now I know that Dorothy and her experience are entirely fictional. However, one nation in Bible times had a similar experience. God's deliverance of the Hebrews from Egyptian bondage, to me, was a figurative Kansas-to-Oz experience.

The Hebrews had been enslaved for about four hundred years. At the time of their deliverance, most or all did not know what it was like to be free. All they knew was to do what the master told them to do, how he told them to do it, and for however long he told them to do it. This was ingrained into their very being. So when God brought the Hebrews out of Egypt, He made it a point to tell them, "I am the LORD your God, who brought you out of the land of Egypt, out of the house of bondage" (Exodus 20:2, NKJV).

In other words, "What happened in Egypt doesn't have to happen here. You are no longer slaves; you don't have to do what slaves do."

God sends that same message to us today.

His Word tells us, "For God so loved the world that He gave His only begotten Son, that whoever believes in Him should not perish but have everlasting life" (John 3:16, NKJV).

Yes, we were born into the bondage of sin. Yet because of the shed blood of Christ on the cross in our place, God tells each of us, "My child, you don't have to be a slave to sin anymore." We no longer have to do *what* sin tells us to do *when* sin tells us to do it. God has redeemed us from its bondage. When we are in Christ, we are new creatures. We have a new lifestyle. It's sort of like going from Kansas to Oz.

Carmalita Green

The Great Physician

Praise the LORD, my soul,
and forget not all his benefits—
who forgives all your sins
and heals all your diseases.
—Psalm 103:2, 3, NIV

When I was eighteen years old, I suffered the onset of a sickness I can't explain even today. It started as a sharp sensation running from my fingers throughout my right arm. Then my arm began to jerk, and I fell unconscious. The same alarming attack repeated itself later that evening. Immediately following the first incident, my aunt began screaming, "Please, someone! We need help over here!" Some of our neighbors responded to her cries. They sprinkled water on me to bring me back to consciousness. However, after the second attack, I woke up in a hospital bed.

These two events, along with the resulting sickness, left me feeling very weak. For several months I lost weight, and the pain in my arms was intense. In fact, my arms became so weak that I could hardly wring water out of a towel. I had lost all my strength. In addition, the back of my head felt as if water were running through it and down to the base of my neck.

My right side was weaker than my left. When walking, I had an abnormal feeling at the back of my knee as if I were limping a little bit. My life dreams faded as I expected either death or paralysis. All this time, though, God's people were praying for me.

The following year I was able to study at a college. Though still feeling weak, I determined that with the Lord on my side, my life would go on. I am convinced that the prayers of God's people, together with the vegetarian diet served at the college, eventually led to my healing. The Lord truly did renew my strength day by day.

Praise be to God because now I am forty-four years old. Those severe and troubling incidents that brought about my sickness have never returned. The strange feeling inside my head is gone, and I can work hard, whether in the house or the garden. Indeed, God is the Great Physician. He heals our diseases.

Trust Him to renew your strength day by day as He did for me.

Zandile Mankumba

Our God Is a Faithful God

And my God shall supply all your need
according to His riches in glory by Christ Jesus.
—Philippians 4:19, NKJV

It happened so quickly that I couldn't believe it. Two friends, Jennifer and Barbara, and I were getting together to prepare some food and desserts for an upcoming family bridal shower for my grandson, Christopher, and his bride-to-be, Flory.

We needed a couple of items from the grocery store, and after I picked them up, I had just backed out of my parking space and straightened my car to pull forward when I heard a crunching sound. The car across the lane had just backed into my car's rear fender on the passenger side. The young man who hit my car was driving a borrowed car. "I was in a hurry," he said, "and didn't look in my rearview mirror to see that you were directly behind me."

Since this accident happened on private property, the police informed me we would have to drive to the police station to fill out the necessary accident form. My insurance company and the other insurance company were notified of the accident.

My insurance company gave me the name of a collision shop where I was able to have my car repaired. When the work was completed, my car looked like new. But there was just one rather large problem: the other insurance company was slow in paying. So the collision shop said I would have to pay the one-thousand-dollar deductible myself. Then my insurance company would be responsible for collecting that sum from the other car owner's insurance company. However, my insurance company also informed me that not only would it take a while for them to collect the sum but also that I might never receive the money. The other insurance company informed me that I could take the insurance client to small claims court. This would be complicated since I live in Tennessee, and the accident happened out-of-state.

All along, I had been praying for the Lord to come to my aid. My son, Jack, made a couple of phone calls, and so did I. But in the end, Jack and I gave all the credit to God for what ultimately happened. After three and a half months, I received a thousand-dollar check.

I had promised the Lord to give a thank offering when I received the check, so I mailed two checks to two wonderful ministries. Remember, our God hears and answers our prayers.

Patricia Mulraney Kovalski

Who's Coming Tonight?

Faithful is he that calleth you, who also will do it.
—1 Thessalonians 5:24, KJV

By nature, I am an introverted person. So when I got the chance to host a weekly care group in my home, I was a little anxious. The idea came as my friend, Jasmine, and I were discussing how we could share God with our nonbelieving friends. Many of these friends worked or went to school six or seven days a week and had no time for church. Those who did have time were wary about Christianity. But they loved spending time with us, so inviting them to my home seemed like a good plan. But for me to be the hostess? I wasn't the charismatic one; Jasmine was. She was the fun one, the one always making new friends. Unfortunately, her apartment was on the edge of the city while mine was conveniently located in the city center. We prayed about it and decided to host this care group together at my home.

And we did! For several months Jasmine and I hosted, and our friends came. We would have dinner, share our experience of God's blessings, discuss a passage from the Bible, and pray together. Our friends were shy at first but eventually shared their problems and asked for prayer. They began to show interest in God and also began to bring their friends to the care group, filling my little apartment and my life.

Then one day, Jasmine couldn't come to our weekly event. I panicked. How could I do this by myself? I thought about canceling the meeting. Instead, I prayed. "God, this is Your event. You asked us to do this, so You bring the people." Then I prepared the apartment and waited. Twenty minutes passed. Then thirty. Then my phone rang.

"I'm at the gate; can you let me in?" Someone had come! Before long, our meeting was full.

I learned a lot from that experience. Sometimes when God asks us to do something, we depend on other people in the ministry to help us do it. Sometimes we might depend on them so much that we forget God is the one in charge. The people we reach out to don't come because of us. It is the Holy Spirit that moves their hearts toward God. And the Holy Spirit will use anyone who is willing to be used, even a shy girl like me. Even you. God is the one who calls us. He will never leave us to do it alone.

R. Bowen

Acid Can Be Awesome

Because you know that the testing
of your faith produces perseverance.
—James 1:3, NIV

As I proceeded to handle the rice water mixture, its pungent, acidic odor slapped me. I could not believe how much that fermented rice water stank! It had been soaking for a few days, and I now doubted the advice of the hair care video. *How could something so acidic be any good for my hair?* A Google search confirmed that though rice water was acidic, it was very beneficial to hair. It was reputed to restore pH balance and repair, rejuvenate, and promote hair growth.

A colleague in science explained to me that some acids are actually helpful. Hydrochloric acid is found in our stomachs. It helps with digestion through the breakdown of food. Vitamin C, ascorbic acid, is good for skin, gums, and our immune system. Even vinegar is helpful with preservation. My colleague's explanation led me to think that even unpleasant circumstances, like some acids, have their place and function in our lives.

Quite like my rice water experience, we may encounter situations that stink. We question their usefulness to our Christian experience. *Lord, what good could come out of this?*

The widow of 2 Kings 4 was about to lose her home and two sons, but it was this "acidic" calamity that built her faith and trust in God as He provided for her and her sons. The effects of sin, rebellion, and loss can help us become more spiritually disciplined. Debt can elicit creativity and faith that we did not know we had. Betrayal can sharpen our focus on God and His faithfulness. Personal mistakes help us be humble and gracious when dealing with others.

The rice water did work. My hair looked awesome. Eventually, though not immediately, I saw evidence of growth and sheen. Similarly, there is much that we might learn from trials if we pay attention. They are sent to transform and not destroy. David, in Psalm 119, noted that his afflictions caused him to learn God's laws. The Father knows just the right amount of "acid" to apply. First Corinthians 10:13 also assures us that God will not allow tests we cannot bear.

If you are going through what seems like an acidic trial, keep trusting God. Be encouraged that God can use something unpleasant to restore, repair, rejuvenate, grow, and preserve. His plans for us are awesome.

Judelia Medard-Santiesteban

My Dream

"Do not fear, for I am with you. Do not be afraid, for I am your God.
I will give you strength, and for sure I will help you."
—Isaiah 41:10, NLV

I dream a lot, but usually, I do not remember the dream's content. A few times, I have had a dream that moves me, and I have even had one that redirected my life.

Recently I awoke from a dream of which I remember only the following: I was holding a small child's hand. Another adult held his other hand. I could not see their faces or who they were, and they didn't talk. We were leaving a house, and as we opened the door, I saw what appeared to be a dark angel with a gold head looking down on us with a foreboding expression. I told those with me not to look up but to move forward and hold tightly to each other's hands. As we moved on, I felt the child's hand start to slip from mine. After reminding him to hold on, I prayed and asked God to keep us strong. As I continued praying, the child's hand tightened its grip, and we moved on. I awoke from my dream at this point.

I reflected on what I had dreamed and thought of how our leaving the house (in my dream) could represent our going out into the world every day with all the enemy's temptations and distractions to keep our minds from Christ. I believe that holding the child's hand represented our loved ones, those we want to see in the kingdom one day. The advice not to look up at the evil angel could mean keeping our eyes on God and "pushing through" by not allowing distractions to keep us from Him. My prayer in my dream was for God to give us the strength to hold on to Him because we cannot do this on our own.

I believe in the power of prayer and have, for several years, been part of a weekly prayer group. This group of seven started because of our mutual concern for loved ones and the belief that Jesus will return soon. We want our loved ones to experience His protection, His guidance, His drawing their hearts to Himself, His help in difficulty, and, yes, the strength to follow Him.

My dream touched me deeply. I hope my sharing it will touch you, the reader, too. Prayer is the key to experiencing peace, for we know that God cares more about our loved ones than we do and that He has answers for everything that burdens us. He loves us and will give us the strength we need as we go through life, no matter what comes our way.

Sue Anderson

Keep the Devil Out!

And do not give the devil a foothold.
—Ephesians 4:27, NIV

I saw changes in my life as I began to read the book *Adventist Home* by Ellen White. One Friday was a particularly rough day. Instead of turning to YouTube or Facebook for amusement like I used to do, I picked up this book and began to read. I read the chapter about how what we read has such a powerful influence on us. The following quote impressed me: "Works of romance, frivolous, exciting tales, are, in hardly less degree, a curse to the reader. The author may profess to teach a moral lesson; throughout his work he may interweave religious sentiments, but often these serve only to veil the folly and worthlessness beneath."*

I thought of my mom and how she loves to watch television movies that play out love stories in various settings.

The next Sabbath afternoon, I felt impressed to read my mom this quote. I started upstairs to my room to pick up the book, praying that it would go over well with her. I fell hard and landed on my left arm as I climbed up the stairs. I immediately recognized this as spiritual warfare. I thought, *The devil doesn't want me to make it up the stairs to get this book to read this quote to Mother.* I carefully walked down the stairs, sat down, and read the passages to her. I explained that since the author did not have a television in her day, we could easily apply the same principle of reading to viewing television today. Mother quietly listened and took it all to heart. She said that I had already won the victory over television and that she had done so in the past. Now she needed to claim the victory again. I told her, "Claim it!"

Throughout the week, I noticed that Mother was very productive and a lot more even-tempered. She didn't complain of her back hurting her so much. She got up and cleaned the house, painted the kitchen, and scrubbed the floors. I didn't hear her comment on a great movie she had recently watched. Nor did she rush back to her bedroom with her dinner plate to finish watching the movie she had already started. Praise God! I could clearly see why the devil didn't want any of this to happen. It just all goes to show you what God can do in your life when you don't let the devil have an opportunity to be invited into your home.

Mary C. D. Johnson

---

* Ellen G. White, *The Adventist Home* (Nashville: Southern Publishing, 1952), 413.

Miracles Still Happen

Behold, I am the LORD, the God of all flesh.
Is there anything too hard for Me?
—Jeremiah 32:27, NKJV

Nothing is too hard for God, and God is ready to help us in our weakest moments.

One Friday evening, I started having excruciating pain in my wrist. I knew that it was my rheumatoid arthritis acting up again, so I went to bed.

Sabbath morning, I woke up with my wrist swollen and very painful. My fingers were also very stiff, and I wondered if I would be able to go to church. My husband, who is a pastor, was going to preach at another pastor's church, and I wanted to go. I prayed and asked God to give me some relief. Although I was hurting, I got dressed.

The trip took more than an hour. When we arrived at the church, my wrist was still swollen and painful and needed some medical attention. However, I insisted that I was going to attend church no matter what the situation. Shortly after we entered the sanctuary, the Sabbath School song leader invited me to play the piano for the Sabbath School service. I turned and looked at my husband, for there was no way I would be able to play the piano.

Nevertheless, I walked up to the piano and sat down. "Our first song this morning will be 'Great Is Thy Faithfulness,' " announced the song leader, giving the page number of the hymn.

Lord, I am asking You to take over, I prayed silently. I started playing the piano and was able to play three more songs. Then I played for the divine service. At the end of the service, people thanked me for playing that day as their regular musician was absent.

I was still in shock that I had been able to play the piano despite the pain in my fingers. In the fellowship hall, a church elder noticed my fingers and my wrist and commented that he never heard the piano being played so well. I told him I was just a vessel used by God, and that I was not the one who had played. He called some of the other members to look at my hand. They were surprised at what they saw and wondered how I had been able to play so well.

This experience taught me that even though we might feel helpless and suffer from severe pain, attempting to do something for God can be rewarding, for God can enable us to do the task undertaken.

Cynthia Mighty

I Am Claiming the Song of Moses

"The LORD is my strength and song,
And He has become my salvation;
He is my God, and I will praise Him;
My father's God, and I will exalt Him."
—Exodus 15:2, NKJV

When I read this verse, written by Moses, it spoke to my heart, reminding me of who God is to me and how I am to relate to Him.

First, this verse states that God is my strength. All my life, I have been told, "Oh, you are so strong." At times, I have believed that. At other times, I have not believed it. Sometimes I have felt like an impostor, faking my way through difficulties. But this verse tells me that I am strong when I rely on the Lord, my God, who gives me strength in whatever situation. In fact, Paul wrote, "That's why I take pleasure in my weaknesses, and in the insults, hardships, persecutions, and troubles that I suffer for Christ. For when I am weak, then I am strong" (2 Corinthians 12:10, NLT).

Second, this verse tells me that the Lord is my song. I don't think I am alone when I say that I have a few songs, secular and sacred, whose lyrics I repeat or that I listen to, for they motivate me. Some of them bring me peace. I listen to different ones depending on what mood I'm in. But according to this Bible verse, Moses declares that God is his song. I am claiming that for myself too. God is the song that picks me up. He is the song that comforts me and reminds me I am loved and blessed. I can dance to and sing along with songs that speak of God's love, grace, and mercies every day.

Third, this declaration of Moses goes on to say that God has become his salvation. We can't have salvation any other way or from anyone else. That's why I want to cooperate with the Lord, to be a habitation for Him to indwell. After all, Paul tells us that each of our bodies is "the temple of the Holy Spirit" (1 Corinthians 6:19, NKJV).

I am so blessed that my mother, Jill, and my Aunt Robin cultivated a love for God in my sister and me. I pray that our children and their children's children will be just as blessed because they know for themselves the God of their mothers and fathers—and of Moses.

Erika Loudermill-Webb

God Will Make a Way

"Trust in the LORD forever.
The LORD himself is the Rock.
The LORD will keep us safe forever."
—Isaiah 26:4, NIrV

My friend and I were sitting at the airport of Port Moresby in Papua New Guinea.

We had worked in a hospital in the Highlands of Papua New Guinea for a few weeks and were filled with many memories and impressions. Now it was almost time to go home again. We wanted to spend the last weekend on the campus of the local church school. With our domestic flight behind us, we waited now for our luggage as well as an acquaintance who had promised to pick us up. Soon we were reunited with our luggage—all except my friend's backpack, which was missing. We tried to find out where it could be. However, we received only contradictory information. The fact of the matter was that the whereabouts of the backpack were not even traceable.

Our other predicament was that the friend who had wanted to pick us up had not shown up either. How could we get to the school campus then? We had no idea where the school was located (these were the days before GPS). All our attempts to phone were in vain. Unfortunately, Port Moresby is known for a high crime rate and is not a safe place for two foreign women to be stranded. So there we sat, trying to think up all kinds of solutions—then we finally turned to God. My friend and I prayed, pouring out our hearts, reminding Him of His promises.

His answer came through a worship song that suddenly came into our thoughts. Softly, we began singing some of the words of "God will make a way." That's just what we needed. We became calm and confident. Our problem was not solved right then, but we had the assurance that God would take care of us. We finally found a taxi driver who took us safely to the campus. We were so thankful for God's protection and His care.

Some weeks after we had returned home, we experienced another surprise. My friend's backpack with all of its contents was found and sent home. God takes care of even the little things in our lives. Shouldn't we trust Him with everything?

Dagmar Dorn

From Deserter to Daughter

"Yet the Israelites will be like the sand on the seashore,
which cannot be measured or counted. In the place
where it was said to them, 'You are not my people,'
they will be called 'children of the living God.' "
—Hosea 1:10, NIV

My sophomore year of college was a time of intense spiritual battles. Ever since I was twelve, I had given in repeatedly to a specific sin. Eight years of back and forth with God had exhausted my soul, and I had reached my breaking point. When I looked at my life, I saw only battlefields of defeat. The future looked completely hopeless, and my past was no different. At my lowest point, I considered ending a life that was not going to turn into anything worthwhile.

Yet the story of Hosea spoke to me during that time. God leads Hosea to marry a harlot named Gomer to illustrate His willingness to forgive His unfaithful "bride" (Israel) and reconcile. Gomer's second and third children were named Lo-Ruhamah (in Hebrew, meaning "she has not obtained compassion") and Lo-Ammi ("not my people").

I grew up in the church. During a portion of my life, I even toyed around with the idea of becoming a pastor. The contemplation of suicide just a few years later, therefore, was not something that I would have thought possible. Even with all of my history, I knew that I was not one of God's people; I was living in sin.

However, the Lord refused to leave me the way I was. He refused to leave Gomer's children that way as well. Like ancient Israel, the situation in my life was utterly hopeless, but God made a profound promise. He said to me, "I know your future looks empty right now. I know what you have done and what sins you have committed, but you do not have to let them take over your life. Let Me turn your defeats into My victories." As God had changed Abram's name to Abraham and Jacob's to Israel, He changed my Lo-Ammi into Ammi. It was a painful process; accepting His forgiveness is harder than anyone had ever told me. Yet as I looked at my life, my perspective began to change. All the places that used to showcase my defeats now showed me God's victories. My weakness changed to His strength. My darkness turned to His light. In all the places I thought I was all alone He introduced me to His people.

I was no longer a deserter when it came to my battles; I was His daughter.

Jaclyn Myers

I'm Smart Enough, Aren't I?

Be not wise in thine own eyes: fear the LORD, and depart from evil.
—Proverbs 3:7, KJV

Why are some people cocky? They provide the illusion that they are always right, that they've had plenty of experience and have the best solution ever! Sure, experience does provide many solutions and answers, but could pride possibly be involved sometimes? The sorrow of Sarai and impatience of Abram caused them to go forward with a plan that brought only pain and trouble to their household. Disbelieving God's promise that they would birth a son of their own, Sarai suggested that her husband marry her Egyptian handmaiden and raise her son as their own. Abram agreed, and the results have been family squabbles and war ever since.

Many years ago, my husband wanted to leave one employment for another, but the fear associated with that caused me to disagree. My husband even asked for a sign from God. And though "it came to pass," my fear was very great. One day I listened to a religious radio program and was convicted to surrender everything to God. My heart melted. Kneeling, I prayed the prayer of surrender. Getting up from my knees, the devil again brought fear and turmoil into my heart. Fear took over rational thinking. I convinced my husband not to press forward in the direction he felt God was leading. The results of my know-it-all opinion and decision wreaked havoc on our lives. So much of the pain and results of this unwise fear did not bring peace.

Praise God, though, He is the Restorer and Repairer of the breach. He can turn pain and poor decisions into something wonderful—He beautifully did so in my life. *The Message* says:

> Trust GOD from the bottom of your heart;
> don't try to figure out everything on your own.
> Listen for GOD's voice in everything you do, everywhere you go;
> he's the one who will keep you on track.
> Don't assume that you know it all.
> Run to GOD! Run from evil! (Proverbs 3:5, 6)

We can always trust God to provide the answers needed for each situation. If you lack trust and faith, flood your mind with His beautiful promises. Let His power and peace fill your heart to overflowing, so much so that you can allow Him to work things out as He sees best.

Valerie Hamel Morikone

Cake, Careers, and Celebrations

For I know the thoughts that I think toward you, says the LORD,
thoughts of peace and not of evil, to give you a future and a hope.
—Jeremiah 29:11, NKJV

My sister and I sat in a booth enjoying our Chinese food in celebration of a not-so-local cultural holiday. We weren't really invested in the holiday itself—other than that it included a delicacy called moon cake—and cake of any kind was reason enough for us to celebrate. I had just completed planning and successfully hosting a workshop for the children's ministries leaders in my area. My sister and I laid aside our daily challenges to celebrate the hopes, dreams, and careers before us. As we were laughing about our fortune cookie predictions, a woman from an adjacent booth cautiously approached us. She was shaking nervously and apologetically addressed us. "I never do this, but ever since you two ladies walked in, I have the strong impression that I am to pray for you. I don't mean to offend you," she said, turning to me, "but I feel it the most with you. I get the feeling something big is weighing you down, and you're not sure about the path before you. Are you ladies Christians?"

We confirmed that we were and cautiously inquired of her background. It became clear to my sister and me that this woman's impression was of the Lord. We prayed together and thanked her for listening to the promptings of our heavenly Father. She seemed slightly less embarrassed now. We shared a piece of cake with her and her husband.

I have often thought about the incident since then, always dismissing it with a shrug and a passing comment of, "Well, that was strange." Yet today, the things that have been on my mind are before me with the same intensity the woman seemed to have felt for me that day. Career decisions I've had to make over the past couple of days will place me on an uncertain path, and if there's one thing I'm certain of, it's this: I don't like uncertainty. The strangeness of the restaurant encounter has given way to the message I believe God was sending me. God is still in control. He sees and knows all. He can speak anytime, anywhere, and through anyone.

Always be kind to one another. We don't know what others are carrying behind those jokes and smiles. Most important, celebrate what God has done and is about to do in your life!

Wendy Williams

The Christian Challenge

Discipline yourself for the purpose of godliness.
—1 Timothy 4:7, NASB

A few years ago, I joined a twenty-one-day fitness challenge. I agreed to follow a strict diet and engage in at least one hour of exercise six or seven days per week. What was I thinking?

The first week was challenging, to say the least. On day two, I said to my husband in frustration, "If this is what it takes to lose weight, well, I am just going to be fat all by myself!" But praise God, I did stick with the program, and I lost twenty pounds.

Soon, however, I realized that losing twenty pounds was just the first step in the journey—the real work was continuing to discipline myself to maintain the healthy habits I had learned. That takes continued and intentional effort. Some days, apple pie and french fries are calling my name. Some days, my bed is so nice and warm that I do not want to get up to exercise. Yet I recognize that if I want to keep the weight off, I have to discipline myself to do the things that will lead to success.

This experience made me appreciate even more the analogy Paul uses when he describes the Christian journey as a challenging race. In this race, he advises Timothy to "discipline yourself for the purpose of godliness" (1 Timothy 4:7, NASB). Paul was saying to Timothy: "Do you see how athletes train their bodies for an outcome that is temporary? You must train yourself so that you can reflect the character of God."

But what does that training look like? We need to look no further than the example set by Jesus Himself. How did Jesus spend His time on earth? Was there any doubt that He was radically and fanatically devoted to God? No! That inner reality was evident in His actions. For one thing, we read that Jesus would wake early in the morning and go off to pray and spend time with His Father.

When we, like Jesus, discipline ourselves to spend time with the Father, we open up spaces in our lives for Him to indwell and then to change us. Then our lives "will be molded more and more after the life of Christ."*

Will you discipline yourself to make space for Him in your life every day?

Kathy-Ann C. Hernandez

---

* Ellen G. White, *Steps to Christ* (Washington, DC: Review and Herald®, 1956), 70.

Parenting Chronicles

*Love is patient, love is kind. It does not envy, it does not boast,
it is not proud. It does not dishonor others, it is not self-seeking,
it is not easily angered, it keeps no record of wrongs. Love does not
delight in evil but rejoices with the truth. It always protects,
always trusts, always hopes, always perseveres.*
—1 Corinthians 13:4–7, NIV

After a fun time with my son, he turned and said to me, "Mum, I love you, but you only seem to love me when I obey you. It doesn't make me feel good, and Jesus doesn't like it."

Wait, what just happened? I wondered. I was totally blindsided. I was immediately tempted to defend myself; however, the Lord bridled my tongue. After staring at him in disbelief, all I muttered was, "I'm sorry." The Lord reassured me that was all that was needed to be said.

God, in His wisdom, knew the lessons we could learn in dealing with children. My first lesson was one of listening. Often we listen to respond and not to understand. We believe we must defend ourselves, rationalize, and explain our actions. However, God desires us to listen more and talk less. James 1:19 tells us that "everyone should be quick to listen, slow to speak and slow to become angry" (NIV). Consider Jesus when Mary expressed disappointment over His tardy arrival after her brother's death. Our Savior listened to the emotions that hung on her words: grief, loss, even confusion. He was moved to empathetic tears.

Then came a powerful revelation: Jesus loves me unconditionally, but am I doing the same? My son was convinced that I loved him only when he did what I wanted. This truly was not my intent. I had ascribed to so many schools of thought when it came to discipline: "Spare not the rod," so the child won't be spoiled. "Nip it in the bud" to minimize reoccurrence. And the one that trumps all: "His behavior is a reflection of my parenting."

God allowed me to see that my methods lacked love. God's love is the preface for His discipline (Hebrews 12:6). In the beginning, God established a loving relationship with Adam and Eve. When Adam and Eve sinned, He disciplined them—yet He also stayed to help them navigate the consequences of their actions. The best thing that we can do as parents is lovingly guide our children on the righteous path. May our discipline be administered in love, for love is what converts hearts, changes behaviors, and saves souls. This is truly Christ's method.

Shevonne Dyer-Phillips

An Angel in the Office

And thine ears shall hear a word behind thee, saying,
This is the way, walk ye in it, when ye turn to the right hand,
and when ye turn to the left.
—Isaiah 30:21, KJV

J oy, I need to go home right away. I don't feel well; I think the air-conditioning in the office is affecting my sinuses." This, coming from my husband, meant that he really needed to get out of the office. I sensed the urgency in his voice. So although it was about 1:30 in the afternoon, I responded immediately. I left my office, drove to his office, and took him home.

As soon as he entered the house, he headed for the bedroom and went under the covers. After spending a few minutes with him to be sure that he was all right, I returned to work. That night he had a fever and did not seem to rest very well.

The next morning before I left for work, I administered some home remedies and left my husband to rest, as it was obvious that he needed more. At work early in the afternoon, I casually remarked to the secretary that my husband had a fever and a cough and was unable to go to work. "Go home and take him to the doctor!" she told me in a commanding tone. I tried to explain that I would see how he was by the next morning. But she insisted, "Go home and take him now!" I obeyed. The doctor said my husband had a viral infection, which turned out to be dengue. The extent of his illness was such that he was ordered to rest for three weeks—something unheard of for my husband.

I have since thought, *What if I had not obeyed the secretary? Would my husband have needed to be hospitalized? Would he have died?* After all, the doctor explained that without adequate rest and fluid intake, my husband certainly could have died.

One of the ways in which God speaks to us is through ordinary people—a friend, a sibling, a child, a colleague, or a secretary. Am I willing to listen and obey? God also speaks to me through His Word. My devotional text the morning I left my sick husband at home to rest was Isaiah 30:21: "And thine ears shall hear a word behind thee, saying, This is the way, walk ye in it, when ye turn to the right hand, and when ye turn to the left" (KJV).

Lord, help me be willing to listen to Your voice by whatever means You choose. May I, like Samuel, say, "Speak, your servant is listening" (1 Samuel 3:10, NLT).

Carol Joy Fider

God's Love Is Made Complete in Us

If we love one another, God lives in us
and his love is made complete in us.
—1 John 4:12, NIV

I learned early in life that bad stuff happens. It just shows up anytime, making us innocent victims. Sometimes it drastically changes our lives. As a quiet and timid child, I usually kept to myself. That's who I was, but it was exacerbated when I was a preteen. I was sexually assaulted numerous times by an extended family member that my mom and dad trusted. I never told them. Instead, I hid my feelings and withdrew. Back in the fifties, no one talked about inappropriate touching or child sexual predators. I was clueless and didn't know what to say, and my parents were having their own crises. I became fearful and sad, completely nonchalant about life. Life went on, but fun times with my three younger brothers helped.

Attending Sabbath School and church with my grandma gave me some respite. I sang songs about Jesus and learned about God and His special love. Creepy feelings would sneak back into my mind occasionally. Why did God let these terrible things happen? He didn't stop them, so did He really love me? And how could a man in our family hurt me and still be buddies with my parents? I was emotionally conflicted—ashamed, angry, confused, fearful, and feeling worthless. It was impossible to discover who I was or dream about who I could be because trying to be normal was all I could handle. Bits of hope sometimes brought short-lived encouragement.

Sadly, child sexual assault happens more times than we admit—in communities, churches, and families. This trauma is rarely talked about, and when uncovered or divulged, it's often quickly buried. Victims suffer—often all their lives. It's taken almost sixty years to slowly overcome my pain and begin seeing the gifts God planted within me. Probably you know a woman like me with her own agonizing story of what she went through or is going through. People won't understand when she retreats, stuck in a dreadful past she can't forget, unable to live happily. We can make a difference through our empathy, compassion, kindness, and love. The love of God within each of us can help her become who God destined her to be. May we recognize the weight she bears. Let's diligently and willingly share God's love—a love that completed us and will complete her when she is finally ready to receive it.

Iris L. Kitching

An Angel Indeed

For thereby some have entertained angels unawares.
—Hebrews 13:2, KJV

It was just a few weeks after we had gone through a horrific time with the loss of my baby brother in a car accident two days before his sixteenth birthday. We were struggling, heartbroken, of course, and trying desperately to encourage one another to accept things and heal, but we really didn't know where to begin.

Then someone in the community mentioned that they knew where some new puppies were, and Mama and I perked up a little bit. The next day we went to see if we could buy a puppy. The man was anxious to find homes for the puppies, but he gave us plenty of time to look them over carefully. We asked all the right questions and made all the right promises, even though he wasn't listening. Then we decided on a little dark-brown, bearlike puppy.

As we started to walk away, the man's wife came out of the house, holding the cutest light-brown pup the color of sand. She had beautiful, shiny amber eyes to match. Mama and I just stood there with our mouths open. I never figured out exactly what drew both of us to that little girl pup at the same time, but I do know that she turned out to be an angel.

The woman noticed our tears and graciously asked if it would help if she gave us the runt of the litter. When we finally understood that she meant the puppy she was holding, our hearts melted. She placed the wiggly pup in my arms, and Mama carefully returned "Bear" to his box and reached for what would become a best friend to both of us.

We never saw those people again, but I have been forever grateful for their kindness and the beautiful gift they gave us. Before we even reached home, we had named our little friend Cinnamon.

I can't say that our hearts never again missed my little brother, but, oh, the joy that came from taking care of that pup and watching her grow! She never knew she was the runt. God has myriad ways of showing us His love, and in a way, we can return that love by caring for His creatures, and most times, they turn out to be very special.

Carol Wiggins Gigante

Twenty-Four-Hour Week

The LORD will perfect that which concerns me;
Your mercy, O LORD, endures forever;
Do not forsake the works of Your hands.
—Psalm 138:8, NKJV

After officially retiring from a nursing career, which spanned fifty years, I was asked to be the director of a small home care agency.

The job was not physically strenuous. Furthermore, free transportation was arranged to and from the job as one of the coordinators lived right around the corner from me. I worked four or five days a week, as needed. My patience, I learned, became a source of encouragement and cohesiveness at the agency.

One day the owner of the agency walked in. Without much ceremony and looking directly me, he abruptly announced, "I am cutting your work hours down to twenty-four hours a week."

I opened my mouth to ask for an explanation. However, I could sense the Holy Spirit restraining me. I wasn't the only one surprised by the announcement. Yet when the other staff members tried to bring up the topic for discussion, I quickly discouraged the conversation. Again, I felt the Holy Spirit was advising me to do so.

Traveling to new countries is my delight, and I had several trips planned for that year. Now I wondered, *How will this weekly work-hour change affect my travel plans?* Well, 2014 ended up being the year I traveled the very most. In fact, I traveled to eight countries and three continents and the Caribbean that year. In addition, I was a financial blessing to more people than I had ever been before.

God wanted to confirm that He is the Source of my blessings. My job was just another source of blessings. When I discovered the promise in Psalm 138:8, I could describe my feeling as one of exhilaration. It was as if I had found precious jewels and gold. I can hardly comprehend how important I, along with the desires of my heart, am to God. What blessings He brought into my life despite the reduction of my weekly work hours!

God is faithful, and you can trust Him to fight all your battles.

Vashti Hinds-Vanier

I Will Be With You

He shall call upon Me, and I will answer him;
I will be with him in trouble;
I will deliver him and honor him.
—Psalm 91:15, NKJV

I'm afraid that I don't have any other alternative for you. We have to operate and remove these fibroids," the doctor announced. This wasn't my first time to have fibroids. The first time they occurred, the doctor had also suggested surgery. But, you see, I do not like any part of my body being altered unless it is a life-and-death matter. I knew, once I was cut, I would never be the same again. So I wanted to try other alternatives. We prayed, and God opened a way for the fibroids to come out without an operation. So, here in the doctor's office, I thought, *God did it then; surely, He can do it again!* The problem was that this time, these fibroids were different; they sucked the blood out of me. My hemoglobin kept dropping. I tried changing my diet and herbal treatments. I had people praying for me, but the problem persisted.

At last, my doctor told me, "If you do not want an incision, why don't you consider laparoscopy?" I talked to God and asked Him to either "let this cup pass from me" or give me a clear indication to proceed with the operation. *Lord, I need to know what Your will is in this situation,* I prayed. It took almost nine months before I knew what to do. The day came when I needed an operation. This time there was no hesitation in my heart. When I was admitted to the medical facility, I had great peace. I was taken into the operating room, smiling and with no fear. God had promised that He would be with me, and that was all that mattered. I could feel I was being lifted up in the prayers of my loved ones and friends.

A month later, a friend asked me to encourage her colleague, who was in a more serious medical situation than I had been. After I spoke and prayed with the woman, she testified of the peace she felt. Then I wondered, *Could it be that God wanted me to go through this experience so that He could use me to help encourage His other daughter?* I praise God for being with me in trouble, for delivering me, and for honoring me!

Could it be that He also wants to be with you in your troubles today? Of course He does. Take courage, for as long as He is there with you, all will be well.

Lynn Mfuru Lukwaro

Mangosteens or Durian

He who does not love does not know God, for God is love.
—1 John 4:8, NKJV

I remember years ago, on my second trip to Indonesia to hold evangelistic meetings, I fell in love with a wonderful fruit called mangosteen. No, it's not a mango. It's small with purplish skin. Inside are large seeds covered with a white, soft, sweet layer of deliciousness. I knew I had found my heavenly fruit. Yes, this must have been what tempted Eve, for it tempted me.

On the second night of our meetings, I shared with the audience that I had fallen in love with mangosteens. That brought a smile to their faces—and large bags of mangosteens to me. From the third night until I left Indonesia, I always had that wonderful fruit with my dinner.

On that same visit, I was introduced to another fruit called durian. I must confess I never attempted to taste the fruit because of its obnoxious scent. The people of Indonesia, and most of Southeast Asia, love this fruit, saying it tastes like heaven. Really? You can smell this fruit a mile away! It's so bad that hotels will not serve it, and airlines will not let people bring it on board. Yet, it is still a beloved fruit to many people in this part of the world.

People remind me of these two fruits. Some are like mangosteens. Easy to love. Easy to talk to and beautiful personalities. Others are like durian. Bitter. Angry. Critical. When you see them coming, you walk the other way. Yet today's text says that if I don't love others, I don't know God. God's love is not only indwelling, healing, and affirming in my life, but He wants to love others *through* me in the same way—to touch the lives of the "durian" people around me.

How do we love difficult people, whether family, neighbors, coworkers, or strangers? As human beings, our ability to love is limited to the "mangosteen" people we meet. We love them as long as they love us and treat us with love. But to love the "durian" people in our lives . . . that comes only from God, because "love is of God" (1 John 4:7, NKJV). He is the only source of unselfish love, and He offers that love to us—so we can share that love with others.

It's possible. The love we give to others—whether to durian or mangosteen people—begins with God. And we can receive that love each day as we stay connected to Him.

So go out and love a durian person today, but first, take some time to be filled with God's healing and unconditional love.

Heather-Dawn Small

Humble Me, O Lord

In all your ways acknowledge Him,
And He shall direct your paths.
—Proverbs 3:6, NKJV

As my husband, Walter, entered the room for the ordinance of footwashing one Sabbath, he saw another man sitting alone. It appeared as if no one was going to offer to wash his feet. Walter couldn't help but notice that the man appeared to have just wandered in off the street and was, perhaps, only a step away from being homeless. Walter wasn't excited about washing the man's feet, but the Holy Spirit kept nudging him. *This is what Communion is all about. If you can't serve him, then you don't need to be here*, said that still, small Voice. So Walter walked over and introduced himself to the man.

I met the newcomer the next Wednesday evening at Bible study, where we became his friends. Several times Walter and I talked about inviting him home for dinner, but we couldn't figure out how to go about doing so. After all, he really wouldn't "fit in" with our other guests. Our church is very large, so we assumed that, on Sabbaths, the newcomer was probably sitting on the other side of the church, in the balcony, or downstairs. Out of sight—out of mind.

Many months passed, and then, out of nowhere, the man entered the church and sat right in front of us. As I listened to the sermon, the Holy Spirit spoke directly to me and must have spoken to Walter as well. "He is on my mind. What do you think?" whispered my husband.

I whispered back, "Invite him, but only if he is willing to take a shower when we get home." The man accepted our proposal. As his clothes washed, he showered, put on some of Walter's clothes, and came out sprinkled in cologne. We all gave him big hugs as he grinned from ear to ear! As we ate, he talked about his former home church many miles away, where he regularly ate in the soup kitchen. That's how he first joined our church back in 1987.

"When I got up this morning," he said, "I had no idea that I would be invited to your home for dinner. I can't believe this! Thank you." Tears surfaced in my eyes as I thought about the lesson we needed to learn and the blessing we almost missed.

Lord, help us humble ourselves so that each day we can be used by you.

Shirley Sain Fordham

Jesus Can Fix Anything

Whatever your hand finds to do, do it with all your might,
for in the realm of the dead, where you are going,
there is neither working nor planning nor knowledge nor wisdom.
—Ecclesiastes 9:10, NIV

My grandpa, Josef Kopitar, moved from Austria to Brazil after World War I when he was a teenager. Everyone who has been an immigrant knows how hard it is to start all over in a country where everything is different from one's homeland. He had many adventures traveling on foot around Brazil. During his life, he worked as a baker, pizza chef, upholsterer, carpenter, builder, and farmer. He also learned about God and gave his heart to Jesus. He taught us by his faithful example how to do things well. He used to walk long distances to study the Bible with others. We could offer him a ride in our car, but he would respond, "Thank you, but I prefer to walk."

Having a father like Josef Kopitar ensured that my father learned how to fix things—starting from his earlier years. Even now, we always have a list of broken things waiting for my father to fix. He fixes them better than they were when they were new. He saws, sands, retouches, and glues until they are perfect! If he feels his work is not perfect, he starts all over again. He measures carefully, aligns the fruit trees in the garden, levels and centers pictures, and repairs toys, so they are like new once more. This is the way my father does things.

My older nephew, Kaíke, was still a little child when a friend broke one of his toys by accident. After inspecting the severity of the damage, my nephew told him, "Don't worry. My grandpa is like Jesus. He can fix everything!"

Kaíke is now an adult, but we were taught a great lesson that day by the words of a faithful little kid. Jesus really can fix everything. He can fix broken hearts, broken health, broken relationships, broken bank accounts, broken businesses, broken dreams, and even broken faith.

Sometimes life is not easy for us because we want to do things our way. But I am learning to surrender all to Jesus. He knows better than we do how to cut, mend, sandpaper, and retouch us so that we can become new in Him.

Would you like to surrender to Jesus your "broken toy" today and watch patiently what the outcome will be? Whatever is broken in your life, keep in mind that Jesus can fix anything!

Kênia Kopitar

A+ Parenting

"I will set out and go back to my father."
—Luke 15:18, NIV

As I parented my two girls (now adults), I frequently asked God to give me a grade at the end of the day. I wanted to know how well—or how poorly— I was doing in the parenting department. *Did I get an A today, Lord? Or was it a D-?* I would have appreciated this information from God, as I was trying so hard to be a good parent. Frequently, however, at the end of the day, I could only recount all the blunders I had made with my girls. I would be discouraged and self-condemning and grade myself with a big fail, F. Parenting children, in itself, can be exhausting—but coupled with self-doubts and self-condemnation, it is self-defeating!

The Lord had me on a journey of discovery as both my husband and I brought up these two bright young daughters. Our deepest desire was that they would grow up loving God and would want a relationship with Him. Knowing that our influence was great as their parents, it propelled us forward to read books on parenting, pray every day for our girls, and endeavor to teach and model Christ for them. We knew we needed to deepen our own relationship with Christ so that those things could even be possible. But what we had to discover was the part that we all fear and yet respect about our God: free will. No matter how "perfectly" we raise our children, God has granted us all free will. Because we have free will, we can reject all that has been generously given by God, even though we see it clearly and consistently. And the fear is that one's children will, in the end, reject Him.

Unfortunately, it is a sober reality for all parents. And yet, it keeps us always praying for our children, never giving up on them, and hoping they will choose what we know is the heart of God for them.

I don't ask God anymore for a grade on my parenting skills. I ask God to be God. I ask God to do what He does best: find lost sheep. I pray this prayer for all my fellow parents who have children that are not walking with God. I pray that the lost sheep will be found. I pray that the lost children will desire something better than what they are currently experiencing. I pray that each will be like the prodigal son in Christ's parable and say, "I will set out and go back to my Father!"

Lee Lee Dart

A Legacy of Faith

*I have no greater joy than to hear
that my children are walking in the truth.*
—3 John 1:4, ESV

I have fond memories of Grandpa Francis, but I don't recall my very first distinct memory of him. Was that first memory the sight of him leading out in a Friday evening vespers program? Or perhaps it was saddling his donkey to go to his farm? He was always busy doing something.

I was raised surrounded by my father's side of the family. Mom and Dad separated when I was very young; yet, somehow, we three girls found ourselves surrounded by the Francis clan. As such, I received my spiritual nurturing from Grandpa Francis. I recall many family worship sessions that were held in his room. Then there were the family choir practice sessions directed by—yes, you guessed it—Grandpa Francis. I smile as I remember those rehearsals. The songs had to be just perfect based on Grandpa's standards.

As a child, I knew my grandfather was blind. Yet, in the midst of his darkness, he brought me to the light of God's love. He modeled industry. Grandpa's lack of vision did not impede his ability to farm his land and provide for his family. He was a man of faith who was dedicated to serving his God. Another great legacy of faith that Grandpa left me was the value of being on time for church. No one, not even his precious wife, Lynn, could make him late for his divine appointment with God. Decades after his death, the values Grandpa Francis passed on still resonate in my heart and mind. I live in the anticipation, as he did, of Christ's return so I can be a part of the great reunion with loved ones.

I am encouraged by the words of the first song I sang with my family choir:

What! Never part again?
No, never part again. . . .
And soon we shall with Jesus reign,
And, never, never part again.*

I challenge you to live according to the legacy of faith in Jesus that you have received and to improve on it as, by God's grace, you endeavor to impart it to succeeding generations.

Andrea K. Francis

---

* Isaac Watts, "Never Part Again," 1707, public domain.

"It's Not All About You"

And we know that in all things
God works for the good of those who love him.
—Romans 8:28, NIV

I was coming to terms with being left out yet again by my family with things not happening the way I wanted them to. But surely God had blessed me, truly blessed me, beyond my wildest dreams. So why was I so disappointed? Yet I was. I was still feeling "hard done by" and "woe is me," but why? Hadn't God been good to me and performed miracles before my very eyes?

Yet God is patient with us and goes on loving and loving, which He did for me that night. In His infinite grace, He gave me the words with which I have entitled this devotional. He shared them in a soft, loving—and not harsh—way: "It's not all about you." And it isn't.

I felt Him reveal this to me, and I began to see that the situation troubling me really wasn't all about me. In those early hours of the morning, I penned these words, which I felt came from Him: "When an artist paints a picture, or someone creates a tapestry, it is not one single brushstroke. It is a combination of many different strokes and many strands of thread. So this situation is also part of something bigger and more beautiful."

God was doing something amazing to bring about an end result, incorporating my loved ones and friends. Things hadn't happened as I felt they should have. Even so, this situation wasn't all about me. It had never been nor ever would be. God wants to have my family in the picture too. How silly I had been. All these feelings of abandonment would pass. I had felt bad about being left out, yet I wasn't being left out at all. Eventually, when I stood back, I realized that I was included and had a vital part to play, as does every thread in a tapestry and every brushstroke in a painting. All things were working together for good.

It is true that God could use anyone, but He chose to use me and He chooses to use you to complete His works of art. So let's not be disheartened or hurt and upset if we are not always where we want to be and doing what we want to do. When we see the whole picture, we will shine, give glory to God, and be so pleased that we were part of something bigger than we had thought. Be blessed knowing you are part of His amazing work no matter what life brings.

Laura A. Canning

To Touch or Not to Touch

And, behold, a woman, which was diseased with an
issue of blood twelve years, came behind him,
and touched the hem of his garment:
For she said within herself,
If I may but touch his garment, I shall be whole.
—Matthew 9:20, 21, KJV

A touch can be a powerful force for good or evil. From an early age, we teach our children to recognize a good or bad touch. If a touch makes them feel uncomfortable, they should report it to a parent or another responsible, protective adult. Though physical contact and kissing were common in biblical days, Levitical law forbade many forms of touching. A Hebrew could not touch an unclean animal (Leviticus 11:8), a woman following childbirth (Leviticus 12:2), or a woman during her menstrual cycle (Leviticus 15:19). In so doing, people could become ceremonially unclean.

When Jesus came on the scene, however, He brought about a dramatic transformation in the way He dealt with people. He touched a great many people for their good. He touched a leper (Mark 1:41), and the healed man was never the same again. Jesus touched a blind man's eyes. After this man's eyes were opened, he had a testimony (John 9:6–41). At the touch of Jesus, the little daughter of Jairus came back to life (Mark 5:41, 42).

Jesus not only brought healing and restoration through His touch but He also allowed Himself to be touched. Remember the woman who perfumed and washed His feet with her tears and kissed them (Luke 7:37–39)? On another occasion, a woman with a flow of blood touched the hem of Christ's robe. She pushed her way through the crowd in order to reach Jesus. I can only imagine her sense of urgency and longing to meet the Healer. Nothing was going to stop her from her mission. She was able to reach out. Just touching the hem of His garment was good enough for her (Matthew 9:19–21). So many times, unlike this determined woman, I have allowed obstacles to stop me from accomplishing a mission when I was supposed to go somewhere or do something.

Is there a part of your life that needs a touch today? Or maybe Jesus is impressing you to do whatever is necessary to touch someone else on His behalf. Sisters, let us allow ourselves to be used by Jesus today, for any touch in His name brings transformation.

Joan M. Leslie

Living Like a Christian

Those who say they live in God should live their lives as Jesus did.
—1 John 2:6, NLT

Speak—don't be still—when somebody's reputation is being spoiled. The most important way to identify true religion is to see if it affects our daily lives. Yet many Christians still tell lies if they feel doing so can benefit them in one way or another.

Once I was working in an office where I faced challenges. Another woman wanted my position. She did her best to taint my good name, hoping to obtain my job. She was someone I knew well as a fellow Christian. Yet, sadly, she still behaved in that way.

As followers of Jesus, we should not take delight in finding fault in others, nor should we look for wrong in the lives of others—especially as a way of avoiding our own problems. The apostle John wrote that those who practice deception or tell lies will not enter the kingdom of God (see Revelation 21:8; 22:14, 15). Neither will their names be "written in the Lamb's Book of Life" (Revelation 21:27, NLT). John also wrote that since Jesus will come as a thief in the night, "blessed is he who watches, and keeps his garments, lest he walk naked and they see his shame" (Revelation 16:15, NKJV). What if Jesus were to come when the situations at work, such as I have described, were still happening? How tragic that would be for some.

Yes, it was a bad experience for me at work, yet I also learned that it pays to be patient. When unpleasant things are happening to us, we might not immediately see what God has in store for us. We need to remember that He allows things to happen for a purpose. Finally, in my office situation, I saw God's hand at work. That has strengthened my faith. I knew, as I saw Him working on my behalf, that God has me in the palm of His hand. Also, God can use us to help others see the truth that they may have been avoiding.

A responsible relationship with others is essential to our spiritual growth. Jude 15–19 lists several unchristian behaviors that will keep people out of heaven when Jesus comes. Jude counsels us to keep ourselves "in the love of God" (Jude 21, NKJV). He also reminds us that it is God who is able to keep us from stumbling (or exhibiting unchristian behaviors) and present us faultless when He comes (Jude 24). Let us be kind and truthful when dealing with others.

Behold, He is coming! My friend, may Jesus find us living as He lived.

Pauline Gesare Okemwa

The Solutions of Jesus

But Jesus said unto them,
They need not depart; give ye them to eat.
—Matthew 14:16, KJV

What do you do when you have a problem that you cannot solve? Do you ask God for help, or do you tell God how He must solve your problem? Many times in our supplications to God, we tell Him how He should solve our problems. This is what happened in the story found in Matthew 14:13–21. There was a problem: it was evening, and people who had come a great distance to see Jesus were hungry. The disciples told Jesus to send the people into the villages to buy food. But that was not Christ's solution. His solution was that the disciples should feed the people. How were they going to feed several thousand people? Christ's "solution" sounded crazy, while theirs seemed to be more reasonable.

Has this ever happened to you? Have you ever asked God to solve a problem, but the solution He gives you seems crazy? That is when we need to exercise faith, accept the will of God, and trust in His Word. When we ask for solutions from God, we must also ask for the necessary faith to accept them and trust that His solutions are better than ours.

The disciples agreed to do what Jesus had told them to do. They brought to Him the only food they could find: five loaves of bread and two fish (Matthew 14:17). Jesus took this small amount of food from the disciples. He prayed over it, asking His Father's blessing. And from that small quantity of food Jesus miraculously fed more than five thousand hungry people!

If we put what we have at God's disposal, even if it is small, He can use our "little" to create amazing solutions to problematic situations. Even if we think our talents are small but give them to God, He will use them to help work out His solutions. In fact, God's solutions may often exceed our expectations.

That is what happened when the disciples gave Jesus five loaves of bread and two fish. This was nothing compared with the problem at hand. Yet all the many people "ate and were filled, and they took up twelve baskets full of the fragments that remained" (Matthew 14:20, NKJV). Not one person left hungry, and there was much food left over to share with others.

Do not tell Jesus what to do with your problem but accept whatever solution He has. Leave your problems in His hands. Give Him what you have, and watch for His solutions.

Pamela Catalán

Wait on the Lord

Wait on the LORD: be of good courage,
and he shall strengthen thine heart: wait, I say, on the LORD.
—Psalm 27:14, KJV

Patience is a virtue that few of us have. We live in a busy world and rush through life, trying to get ahead. Even on our roads and highways, everyone seems to be in a hurry to get to their destinations. This has often resulted in vehicle accidents.

I have a magnet on my refrigerator door that says, "Give me patience, Lord, but hurry." I get impatient waiting for others because I like being on time. I don't like it when I am cruising on the road and other drivers cut me off. I always say that if you are rushing or driving too fast, then you simply didn't wake up on time!

In the Bible, Abraham and his wife are prime examples of impatience. God told Abraham that Sarah was going to bear him a son. Instead of being thrilled at this news, Sarah thought she was too old to bear children. So instead of waiting on the Lord and claiming His promise that Abraham was going to be the father of many nations, they took matters into their own hands. Sarah offered her maidservant as a surrogate mother in order to provide her husband with a son. They didn't have the patience to wait for God's spoken word to come true. The decision that they made so long time ago has brought a lot of discord into our world today.

On the other hand, we read about the story of Hannah, who was childless and desperately wanted a son. She fervently prayed and waited patiently for the Lord to grant her request. Eventually, she conceived and gave birth to a son. She named him Samuel. When the boy was old enough, Hannah took him to the temple as she had promised God she would. She gave little Samuel to the Lord to serve Him. He eventually became a great prophet in Israel. Hannah had learned, through waiting on God, that He answers prayers according to His purposes. Only He could make her life complete.

I pray for patience every day. I have learned that God answers prayers in different ways, and I just have to wait on Him. He is never late; He answers our prayers at the right time and in the right place. I need to put my trust in Him and give Him full control of my life.

Rhona Grace Magpayo

The Fruitarian Family

That was the true Light, which lighteth every man
that cometh into the world.
—John 1:9, KJV

It was Friday afternoon, and we, the pastor's family, were busily preparing for Sabbath, though he was away. Suddenly, we were surprised by an urgent knocking. "Come quickly," said our friend, Dimitris. "There is an English family. They don't eat meat." At that time in Greece, vegetarianism was quite a novelty.

With Dimitris, I saw a young, long-haired hippie wearing sack-like clothes secured by a rope belt. His fingernails were uncut, and he was pale and thin, as was his little boy, who clung to his hand. Our friend had offered to treat the family to a hot meal, but they would eat only fruit. In desperation, he had brought them to us. I agreed to take them in and feed them, so Dimitris and the hippie left for the station to bring the man's wife and baby, leaving the little boy with me.

Soon the rest of the family arrived. The young hippie mother was as pale and thin as her husband, and she held a tiny baby in her arms. After they had accepted my offer of a warm shower, I laid out a variety of fruit (they would eat nothing else), which they ate, sitting on the floor without plates or cutlery. Tired after their journey, mother and children were ready for bed—but not in a bed. They would sleep on the floor! However, the floor was stone and very cold, so I dismantled the Ping-Pong table and put it on the floor under their sleeping bags.

By this time, I was more than ready for bed, but the young father wanted to talk, so we settled down to a long discussion. He had been very impressed with the robust appearance of our four boys, especially as his little son had not grown at all in the last three years. He talked on, explaining his strange religious beliefs and his problems with sinful cravings for fried potatoes. The hours ticked by. I tried to answer his endless questions, and eventually, deep in thought, he joined his family on the Ping-Pong table. The following day they continued their journey.

I decided to send their name and address (they lived in a tent on the moors) to friends in England who could perhaps help them on their return home. Through my friends, I heard that the hippie mother and children were being treated at a hospital for malnutrition, and the father was having Bible studies with the local pastor.

God surely works in mysterious ways His wonders to perform!

Revel Papaioannou

Just One Banana

And my God shall supply all your need
according to His riches in glory by Christ Jesus.
—Philippians 4:19, NKJV

I have always enjoyed reading the true stories of missionaries and learning how, through terrible trials and suffering, they have remained faithful to the Lord. One of these stories is documented in Darlene Deibler Rose's autobiography, *Evidence Not Seen.** She told the Lord that she would go anywhere with Him no matter what the cost. In 1938, at the age of twenty-one, she was the first American woman to enter the rugged interior of Dutch New Guinea with her pastor husband, Russell. The young couple, however, was captured during the Japanese invasion of World War II and sent to separate prison camps, never to see each other again.

Through the crack of her cell window, she witnessed a guard in the courtyard sneak a bunch of bananas to a woman. At this point, Darlene was only skin and bones, and she dropped to her cell floor, exhausted and craving bananas. She looked up and pleaded to the Lord for just one. But how could God possibly get her a banana through these prison walls, especially with the fact that she was not allowed to have any visitors? Through an amazing series of events, her past camp commander had bananas delivered to her cell. Not just one banana but *ninety-two*! She credits these bananas with keeping her alive until her rescue at the end of the war.

For ten years, I was a single parent with four children to raise. I felt like Darlene, isolated in a dark prison cell with no one to help me. I cried out to the Lord daily; many times, I didn't know where our next meal would come from or how He would provide for our basic needs. But provide He did! In one instance, a church friend took my children for the afternoon to play at the park. When she returned in the evening, she had fed them and bought them new school shoes.

God can do miracles even in the most unlikely circumstances. He knows our situation and cares for us with an everlasting love.

If you find yourself in a difficult situation, trust in Him with all your heart. We cannot lean on our own understanding, for His ways are not our ways.

He will not fail us even in the darkest of situations.

Karen M. Phillips

---

* Darlene Deibler Rose, *Evidence Not Seen* (New York: Harper and Row Publishers, 1988).

The Missing Cell Phone

Don't worry about anything; instead, pray about everything.
Tell God what you need, and thank him for all he has done.
Then you will experience God's peace, which exceeds anything we
can understand. His peace will guard your hearts
and minds as you live in Christ Jesus.
—Philippians 4:6, 7, NLT

Excitement filled the air. I was going to Washington, DC, to attend the graduation of my goddaughter, who had completed the doctor of philosophy requirements in clinical psychology. My brother greeted me at the airport and took me to my son. The next morning, Friday, I awoke very early, dressed, and waited for my son to take me with him to his work at the hospital. From there, we would work out the transportation logistics to get to the graduation venue.

All went as planned. The graduation was beautiful, followed by a lovely dinner on the waterfront. All too soon it was Sunday and time for me to return to Huntsville. Since my son was on call, he took me to the airport on his way to work. After checking in for my flight at the kiosk, I went to the bathroom and placed my cell phone on the tissue dispenser. I proceeded downstairs, joined the security line, and waited my turn to be scanned. While in line, the attendant reminded passengers to remove electronics, phones, keys, or other items from their person. Hearing that announcement, I immediately realized my phone was missing.

I continued to place my items on the belt and then collected them on the other end. I quickly headed back up the escalator to the bathroom, praying all the way that I would find my phone. Reaching the stall, I thanked God that it was vacant and rushed in, only to find my phone waiting for me where I had left it! Again, I went through security to have my items scanned. This time one of my bags was selected for extra scrutiny. I was amazed since these were the same bags, and I had not put anything new in them. *Why was this bag not selected the first time I went through?* God knew I needed to go back to find my phone as quickly as possible.

Despite all this, I was able to arrive at my gate in time to board my flight. God is interested in every detail of our lives. Let us continually thank Him for His promise of peace. He kept His eye on my cell phone and protected it in that busy Reagan Airport.

Lydia D. Andrews

Hoax

And the serpent said unto the woman, Ye shall not surely die:
For God doth know that in the day ye eat thereof, then your eyes
shall be opened, and ye shall be as gods, knowing good and evil.
—Genesis 3:4, 5, KJV

In the coming days, DO NOT open any message with an attachment called [subject of email message] regardless of who sent it to you. It is a virus that will destroy the whole hard drive of your computer. This virus usually comes from a known person who you have in your contact list." Anyone with a computer has undoubtedly received a similar email message at some point. Sometimes we believe the message and immediately forward it to all our email contacts. Other times we wonder or go to fact-checking websites to determine if the message is a hoax. But what about the noncomputer parts of our life? How many hoaxes do we face daily? The first hoax ever was whispered by a serpent into Eve's ear because she hadn't followed the warning to stay away from the tree of the knowledge of good and evil. When she bit into the forbidden fruit, she opened, in a sense, the "attachment" that destroyed her future.

Did she share this "wonderful" news with Adam about becoming as gods and knowing good from evil, sincerely believing she had found something new that God had not allowed them to know? Or did she already realize she had triggered a virus?

When God came for evening worship with Adam and Eve, He had to call for them. He knew, of course, that they had opened the attachment, and their hard drives were infected. Many centuries passed, and each generation has passed on the virus of sin to the next. Daily the "inboxes" of our minds can be filled with viruses if we are not careful. Yet we have the opportunity to heed the warnings and invitations of Jesus: "Thou shalt not. . . ." "Come unto me. . . ." "If I abide in you, and you in me . . ." Or, we can click on Become as Gods.

Jesus, our Creator, had a virus-removal plan in place. The process to rescue and protect us has been a lengthy one and personally expensive for Him. There is no way to clean out the virus of sin from our lives except for Him to remove our confessed sins through His own blood. His factory reset renews our minds so we can become virus-free. *Lord, help us daily to beware of hoaxes and delete those dangerous viruses before they destroy us. Amen.*

Elizabeth Versteegh Odiyar

Paid in Full

"You can do all things;
no purpose of yours can be thwarted."
—Job 42:2, NIV

The memory from when I was five is vivid still: the trailer behind our car swayed gently. Facing backward in the back seat, I can remember only one item in the trailer—it was our piano.

My father paused at a strange little one-room building; my mother called it a "guardhouse." A man in a uniform with bright buttons stepped out of the cubicle, saluted, and handed my father a key. The man walked crisply to his vehicle, and both cars parted; the last soldier representing the Army of the United States of America drove away, and we, and our piano, continued deep into the 379 acres to the modest General's House. The war had ended, the property was deserted, and we three were the first civilians to enter Camp McQuaide.

The sparkling sea, purple-blue flowers, and staccato-stepping quail were a constant source of delight to a five-year-old. The mini army office was now a backyard playhouse, a wafting curtain at the window! God's faithful leading, Dad's tenacity and unswerving dedication to Christian education, and Mother's constant encouragement made the vision continue: a boarding school where the good news of a risen Savior would be the message to teenagers now seemed, perhaps, obtainable. The words *answered prayer* come readily to mind when one recalls this academy has stood as a sentinel "to go and teach" Jesus' love for more than seventy years.

God honors unselfish diligence to His Word, His calling, and service to others as well as giving glory to a God who searches until He finds willing servants, forming a partnership and, most importantly a friendship, to fulfill His will. Take a boy or girl from ordinary pursuits, teach them faith and confidence in God, and they can do extraordinary things in God's name.

At the close of the first week of school, as was his custom, my father took an early morning walk on the shore. On this early Sabbath day, Dad returned and recounted the beach scene he had witnessed from a distance: a circle of bobby-socked young ladies forming a prayer band. His words to Mother and me: "It's all been worth it—I've been paid in full."*

Darlene Joy Grunke

* For more information on the history of Camp McQuaide and Monterey Bay Academy, visit http://history.montereybayacademy.org/grunke.html.

God Loves You

I will instruct you and teach you in the way you should go;
I will counsel you with my loving eye on you . . .
but the LORD's unfailing love
surrounds the one who trusts in him.
—Psalm 32:8, 10, NIV

Sometimes we find ourselves in what appears to be an impossible situation. When it seems we are standing alone, we're tempted to forget about all that God has been to us and what He has done in our lives. We wrap ourselves in self-pity and clothe our minds in darkness. We see all the things that have gone wrong while failing to recognize the abundant blessings that we have. We allow ourselves to be crushed by those who reject us and fail to appreciate that there are others who love us.

Even mighty men of God like Elijah experienced moments of discouragement and fear. Elijah had just had a spectacular victory on Mount Carmel over the false prophets of Baal. God had rained down fire from heaven in response to His prophet's bold assertion that Jehovah was the only true and living God. Elijah had been a courageous and effective spokesperson for God's glory. Now Queen Jezebel's wrath reduced this mighty man of valor to a quivering, dejected soul. He feared for his life. In the depths of Elijah's despair, God sent an angel with food to nourish and sustain him. God also has innumerable ways to encourage and nurture us.

Once, in a moment of doubt about my ministry, I said, "I'm not sure if I'm enough."

My friend said, "You're enough." I was concerned about my weight. My friend said, "Stop thinking about what you can't eat and focus on all the things that you can eat." We are not alone; that's just an illusion. God has promised to be with us always. In His generosity, He also sends people to love and care for us.

Have you become so discouraged by the disappointments and dark moments of your life that you want to throw your hands up in despair and, like Elijah, say, "I have had enough, LORD" (1 Kings 19:4, NIV)? Have you thrown in the towel, given up the fight?

Be encouraged, children of God. You are not alone—God has a plan and a place for you. He has extraordinary ways and means to sustain you. He loves you.

Beverly P. Gordon

Does God Care?

Delight yourself also in the LORD,
And He shall give you the desires of your heart.
—Psalm 37:4, NKJV

Moving from one place to another is very demanding for us homemakers. This was the eleventh time we had moved, the last four times being overseas. We had just arrived at our new mission field, Paraguay, in South America, straight from Nepal on the other side of the planet. House hunting was difficult; the new culture, challenging; and the city's scenery boring.

We landed in Asunción; the container of our belongings arrived from Calcutta, India; and we finally rented a beautiful house. However, I was not happy. My heart was heavy. I wanted to return to my beloved Himalayan peaks and walk again through those precious rice and wheat terraces. I needed a job desperately—something to keep me occupied.

"Lord, why did You bring me here? I hate it . . . I need a job. . . . Please, heavenly Father!" I prayed, kneeling beside my bed, in an otherwise empty house. I cried and claimed God's promises.

That was when the owner of a bilingual school called me for a job interview. "I have no positions for a music teacher," she told me. I waited, patiently wait, on the Lord while claiming His promises and furnishing our home.

Just as I had finished, the school owner who had interviewed me two years earlier called again. God is so good! The offer was far above my wildest expectations. I would teach physics in English and would receive a high salary. God had me wait for two years so that I could adjust to a new culture, turn the house into a home, and learn to trust Him more. I loved my job and my students. I testified to them of God the Creator—the God of all the laws of physics and the Creator of colors and beauty. I added Bible verses to every topic we dealt with in class. This made an impact on my students' bright young minds.

My God, who has my name written in the palm of His hands and knows all my needs and my heart's desires, had given me far more than I could ever ask for or even imagine. This job gave me the peace of mind and acceptance I needed so much.

Put Him to the test and wait on Him always. He will do the same for you.

Marli Elizete Ritter-Hein

March 28

The Joy of Honest Living

Pray for us; for we are confident that we have a good conscience,
in all things desiring to live honorably.
—Hebrews 13:18, NKJV

My husband and I spent many years as missionaries in a country where people were kind and generous. While my husband worked as a pastor, my job was teaching English to high school students. During those years, there were only three schools where English was the language of instruction. Our school had always had a long student waiting list, for we could accommodate only five hundred students from first to twelfth grades.

Most of my students came from rich families whose chauffeurs drove them to school in Mercedes-Benzes. One day during the class discussion, we happened to talk about the challenges of driving in that very large city. At some point in the discussion, I shared, "I am in the process of preparing to take a road test. I want to be able to drive here, especially when my husband is away for a week or two."

"Teacher, just relax," said one of my students. Then he continued in a happy tone, "I'll take care of it. I'll pay for your driving test fee. Just wait a few days, and you'll have your license." I thought I had not understood very well what my student had just said. Yet he confirmed, "I will bring you your driver's license in a week."

"Well," I hastened to explain, "I don't operate my life in dishonest ways. However, I do appreciate your kind offer. Yet I cannot accept it."

I thanked him profusely before the discussion ended.

Shortly after that episode in the classroom, my family and I decided to immigrate to Canada. It was in my new country that I was able to take my driving test. God was gracious enough to allow me to pass the test so that I could drive in my new country.

Sometimes we are faced with situations that seem to offer shortcuts out of, or through, our dilemmas. Yet God cannot bless choices that cut corners on honesty. The writer of Hebrews 13:18 affirmed that he had a good conscience because he desired to live his life honorably.

We can have that good conscience, too, when we live lives that honor God.

Ofelia A. Pangan

The Chocolate Incident

But this I call to mind, and therefore I have hope:
*The steadfast love of the L*ORD *never ceases;*
his mercies never come to an end;
they are new every morning; great is your faithfulness.
—Lamentations 3:21–23, ESV

That morning, it looked like a crime scene after some sort of chocolate and rice puff battle! The bowl was facedown. Its entire contents were splashed 360 degrees across the floor, up the walls, between kitchen cupboards and appliances, pebble-dashing everything with soft brown rice puffs! *Even with my best cleanup efforts, this would be an easy job for forensics!* I thought.

I stared in horror at the rice puff particles and streaks of sweet sticky brown milk. *What was he trying to do?* I was about to express my disappointment when I stopped myself. Looking into the widening eyes of my son, I saw concern that he would indeed be on the receiving end of a verbal lashing, and for what? For trying to make his own breakfast? The verbal lashing suppressed, I expressed my pleasure at his effort to prepare his own breakfast and assured him that the mess looked worse than it actually was. Together we strategically absorbed the mess with reams of paper towels that were easy to condense and dispose of.

We all mess up at times, don't we? We feel deflated and discouraged when only our failures, not our efforts or achievements, are acknowledged. This can discourage us from trying again, from growing and developing. I was reminded of how God treats us when we wander offtrack to do our own thing when we make mistakes and leave behind far worse than a mess of chocolate rice puffs. It is often not a pretty sight. But God—loving, patient, and sympathetic—shows infinite mercy. He helps us clean up and in a way that would leave forensics totally baffled! Then He sticks with us, reminds that we can trust Him, gives direction, encourages us to try again, and lets us know that He is always there to see us through any future difficulty. He gives us second chances over and over; every morning, there are new opportunities. His faithfulness is great, indeed. Let us be grateful. Let us stay faithful to Him!

Denise Roberts

With Glowing Hearts—Part 1

"I tell you the truth, everyone who acknowledges me
publicly here on earth, the Son of Man will also
acknowledge in the presence of God's angels."
—Luke 12:8, NLT

My heart skipped several beats. My grasp on the steering wheel tightened as I started down the Smoky River hill. Through the Holy Spirit, Jesus impressed me that my son would have a "significant role" as time in this world approached its end. Sonny is my autistic son, born on June 19, 1986, in Grande Prairie, Alberta, Canada. I was driving home that particular evening after an intense discussion with Pastor Dan. I had shared something with him that I'd shared with only a select few. In school, I had had to study and work very hard to get good grades. Having my name on the honor roll meant the world to me. I needed this recognition to help gain victory over very low self-esteem, the result of molestation at the age of six.

I have noticed that sometimes, when we need it most, God sends us reminders that He is with us in life's challenges. He did this for me during those difficult years of struggling for self-esteem, and my mother affirmed that reality to me years later.

When Sonny was three years old, he survived a medical emergency. I knew guardian angels were surrounding my family and me, but I had an uneasy feeling that the enemy of our souls wanted to kill my little boy. We dedicated Sonny to Jesus on Sabbath, November 25, 1989. Almost three months later, on February 9, 1990, Sonny fell down the basement stairs and fractured his skull. Hurtful things were said, including words from a neighbor who insinuated that I had hurt my son. I felt as if I were being pushed to my emotional limits. I wrote my first article three months later and then dozens more. Then, when it seemed as if the enemy were targeting my son—especially at night—I would rock him back to sleep, singing him songs such as "This Little Light of Mine." That memory and song brought a glow to my heart.

By mid-July, I willingly obeyed when I sensed the Lord's instructing me to go to the hospital for a much needed "time-out." While there, I shared copies of my writings and boldly witnessed for Jesus. The two-week stay in the psychiatric ward was an experience that I never want to repeat. Yet, even during that time, God assured me of His presence with me.

Truly, no situation is ever beyond His attention, His help, or His love.

Deborah Sanders with Lila Bailey Romp

With Glowing Hearts—Part 2

So, my dear brothers and sisters, be strong and immovable.
Always work enthusiastically for the Lord,
for you know that nothing you do for the Lord is ever useless.
—1 Corinthians 15:58, NLT

Despite life's difficult times—early childhood molestation, my three-year-old Sonny with a brain injury, and my hospitalization for a much-needed emotional "time-out"—I have always sensed God's presence with me. He has always kept His glow in my heart. He also assured me that He had a work for my child, Sonny, to do for Him, and this gave me additional peace.

Sonny began to talk at age twelve. In a sense, he has become our local community's ambassador of love and singing "evangelist," though he will always require a 24-7 caregiver. His vocabulary is severely limited, so most often, he speaks in "Sonny language." It's open to interpretation! Yet his heart also glows with love for Jesus and a desire to witness for Him in his own unique ways.

Furthermore, out of life's setbacks and challenges has emerged a writing ministry through the years, which has allowed me to witness to people from many walks of life. I like to say that every story I have written represents the "grade" of life that I was in at the time of the writing. Some "grades" are more difficult than others.

In January 2018, for example, I was diagnosed with severe osteoarthritis. Those who deal with unbearable pain can feel as if life is draining out of them. Five months after my osteoarthritis diagnosis, I was anointed by Pastor Dan and was so grateful, despite an MRI the following month that revealed my need for back and hip replacement surgeries.

In Romans 8, Paul asked, "Does it mean [God] no longer loves us if we have trouble or calamity?" (verse 35, NLT). He answers His own question with words that always bring a glow to my heart: "I am convinced that nothing can ever separate us from God's love. Neither death nor life, neither angels nor demons, neither our fears for today nor our worries about tomorrow—not even the powers of hell can separate us from God's love" (verse 38).

Therefore, as I used to sing "This Little Light of Mine" to Sonny as a baby, I have not lost my resolve to have a heart that glows for Jesus. He is coming soon to take His family to their new home in Paradise. "Please come quickly, Lord Jesus" is my daily prayer. Forever amen!

Deborah Sanders with Lila Bailey Romp

The Walk

So the disciples went and did as Jesus commanded them.
They brought the donkey and the colt,
laid their clothes on them, and set Him on them.
—Matthew 21:6, 7, NKJV

Today I completed the Palm Sunday Walk, an annual event held on the Sunday before Easter. My mom and I went together. Every year people from the Bermuda National Trust pick an area of Bermuda to explore. This year's Palm Sunday Walk explored Paget and Warwick parishes. We walked along the shoreline, up hills overlooking the ocean, through the Alfred Blackburn Nature Reserve, across a school field, and through hotel properties. When I say we, I am talking about hundreds of people. During the walk, I was able to take some beautiful pictures of flora and fauna. We passed two water stations. In an hour and forty-five minutes, I traveled just under five miles.

It wasn't until after the walk, though, that I reflected on its significance. As Christians, we know that many people who had come to see Jesus walked with Him during what is known as the triumphal entry into Jerusalem. The story is recorded in Matthew 21. I began to wonder about the people who had walked to see Jesus that day. Was their walk long or short? Did they feel thirsty, and were they able to get water along the way? Were their minds on Jesus, or were they just excited to be on their way to keep the Passover? Were they hoping to see Jesus as a king? We know that the people asked, "Who is this?"

Their question did not mean that the people of Jerusalem had not heard of Jesus. Rather they were asking, "Who is this person who enters Jerusalem as if He were the Messiah?"

To describe this amazing event, Ellen G. White wrote, "All nature seemed to rejoice. The trees were clothed with verdure, and their blossoms shed a delicate fragrance on the air. A new life and joy animated the people. The hope of the new kingdom was again springing up."[*]

Jesus will soon set up a new kingdom. Someday soon, there will be another triumphal entry, another "walk," but this time into the New Jerusalem. And the faithful of all the ages will be with Him. Before that day, though, will you recognize the Savior as the Messiah?

Will you be ready?

Dana M. Bassett Bean

---

[*] Ellen G. White, *The Desire of Ages* (Mountain View, CA: Pacific Press®, 1940), 569.

Without Spot or Blemish

He paid for you with the precious lifeblood of Christ,
the sinless, spotless Lamb of God. God chose him for this purpose
long before the world began, but only recently was he brought into
public view, in these last days, as a blessing to you.
—1 Peter 1:19, 20, TLB

Spinach seems to grow better than anything else in my little garden patch. Bugs bite the pumpkin leaves and attack the tomatoes, but my spinach eludes the little critters, producing healthy new leaves every day. Yet I do see a few defective leaves among the healthy ones. Those imperfect ones I cut off immediately, letting them fall to the ground.

Then my reaping begins.

In a brown bag, I collect the freshly cut spinach leaves. I select carefully, knowing that since these leaves will feed my family, only the best will do. If there is a slight imperfection, even a calling card from a visiting bug, down that leaf goes. Soon, my bag fills with the spotless selections.

As I select and reject, I think of the children of Israel choosing lambs to be offered to God as sacrifices. I can imagine them looking at a defective lamb, the one born with three legs or the bleeding one bitten by a lion. They look at it, knowing it cannot be offered because it is not spotless; it is not one without a blemish. I want to believe that without regret, they will move on to another lamb, one that is perfect, all woolly and cute, baaing softly.

I hope that without regret, they would take a knife and sacrifice that perfect lamb for the sins they had committed, knowing that it was their lies, their infidelity, their theft that had caused the death of that perfect animal. They would have given their best lamb as a sacrifice for their sins.

Then I think of the irony of Jesus selecting us to be part of His kingdom, selecting us, undeserving, in our sins, our imperfections. He, the spotless Lamb of God, takes what anyone else would have rejected, seeing our flaws, our sins, our glaring transgressions. Nothing we can do can ever make us acceptable to Him. What love, what matchless love!

Humbled, I will eat my spinach dish tonight, made from perfect, healthy leaves, and remember that I do not deserve to be so richly blessed.

Annette Walwyn Michael

Blind Bartimaeus

Jesus stopped and said, "Call him."
—Mark 10:49, NIV

This morning my Bible study blessed me through the story of blind Bartimaeus (Mark 10:46–52). Jesus is headed to Jerusalem, His final trip. He knows betrayal and death are ahead; He has just told His disciples about it (verses 32–34). He is focused on His difficult mission when He hears a cry for mercy. The cry grows louder, and Jesus stops and says, "Call him." Bartimaeus immediately throws off his cloak, jumps to his feet, and comes to Jesus. When Jesus asks what he wants, Bartimaeus responds, "I want to see." Jesus says, "Go," and assures him that his faith has healed him. Immediately, Bartimaeus receives his sight, but he does not go away. He goes with Jesus. Luke 18:43 tells us he not only follows but he also praises God as he follows.

No matter what Jesus is doing, He always hears our cries for mercy, and He stops to respond. He calls, "Come to me, all you who are weary and burdened, and I will give you rest. . . . My yoke is easy and My burden is light" (Matthew 11:28–30, NIV).

This story speaks to me today. Like Bartimaeus, we must throw off what hinders us from coming to Jesus. It might be our "cloak" of sin tripping up our feet. It might be our "cloak" of self-righteousness and its impression of protection and comfort. The writer of Hebrews puts it this way: "Let us throw off everything that hinders and the sin that so easily entangles. And let us run with perseverance the race marked out for us" (Hebrews 12:1, NIV).

When Bartimaeus tells Jesus his need, Jesus proclaims his faith has healed him. I don't know about you, but sometimes I feel I don't have enough faith. Yet we know from Romans 12:3 that God gives each of us a measure of faith.

And, we are called to "[fix] our eyes on Jesus, the pioneer and perfecter of faith. For the joy set before him he endured the cross, scorning its shame, and sat down at the right hand of the throne of God. Consider him who endured such opposition from sinners, so that you will not grow weary and lose heart" (Hebrews 12:2, 3, NIV).

Let us follow Him joyfully and with praise!

Myrna L. Hanna

The Road to Emmaus

"For I know the plans I have for you," says the LORD. "They are plans for good and not for disaster, to give you a future and a hope."
—Jeremiah 29:11, NLT

H ave you found yourself on the wrong road going in the wrong direction? Do you ever feel that all hope is gone? Take courage from disciples who traveled to Emmaus with heavy hearts.

The disciples struggled to believe the testimony from the women who had found an empty tomb and heard from angels that Jesus was alive. They left Jerusalem—the last place where they had been with Jesus—and walked back to their former life in Emmaus. Since the disciples arrived home together and prepared a meal, we can assume that the unnamed disciple was the wife of Cleopas. She joins a long list of unnamed women mentioned in the Bible. Read Luke 24:13–25 to discover how the Savior gives the woman "a future and a hope" (Jeremiah 29:11, NLT) on that sorrowful morning when she could not see Him.

As the couple walk toward Emmaus, Jesus joins them and overhears their distress. Filled with compassion, He engages them without an introduction. He walks for miles, giving them His full attention. Even if you feel like a nobody, you are the most important person in the world to Jesus. He never ignores you and always accepts your invitation. He is available for the sinful woman to anoint His feet. He does not judge the woman caught in adultery. He eats with the unnamed publicans and prostitutes.

Jesus walks with you, no matter where you are. You may be walking to "nowhere," to a place that isn't on the map, but Jesus shows up for you. You may not recognize Him, but He is your Companion the entire journey, no matter how far you go before detecting His presence.

Jesus walks with you to remind you of who you are. The two disciples think they have reached their destination, but then they recognize Jesus and notice their burning hearts. Suddenly aware that they are not fulfilling their purpose as His disciples, they rush back to Jerusalem, overjoyed to share their story of hope.

If you are walking down the wrong road, invite Jesus to walk with you. He knows where you are. He will remind you who you are, where you are going, why you need to get there.

As told by Joanne Cortes to Rebecca Turner

April 5

"Never . . . Never"

Never will I leave you; never will I forsake you.
—Hebrews 13:5, NIV

You never know what to expect when you get onto a plane in bad weather. I always check the weather forecast before going to the airport as part of my routine. But one thing I have found over the years is that what you see in the app is not always what occurs. This is what happened during my flight from Zagreb, Croatia, to Sarajevo, the capital of Bosnia and Herzegovina.

Clear skies, beautiful sunny day, no winds. Perfect! I was not worried until I found out the plane was delayed due to heavy winds. My heart started to pound. The plane, the very small plane, finally arrived. Immediately, my thoughts pictured this small aircraft bouncing in the middle of dark clouds between Croatia and Bosnia. It is funny how the mind can picture something terrible before it even happens.

So, I prayed, "Lord, help me replace these thoughts of dread with Your promises." We always have a choice to find good or bad in any situation. As a remedy for seeing reality, the Bible counsels, "Set your minds on things above, not on earthly things" (Colossians 3:2, NIV). Firmly grasping this verse, I boarded the airplane.

Sure enough, thirty minutes later, the aircraft began shaking and losing altitude as the strong winds made that small plane dance in the dark, rainy skies. I was afraid. You, like me, have had moments of fear, especially when we feel alone and not in control. In whatever part of the world you are today, in rough circumstances that have brought you to tears, let God cradle you, comfort you, reassure you—you are the beloved of the Lord.

In that little plane, when I was frightened about crashing and dying in the middle of rain and wind, these two words, "Never . . . Never" moved me toward peace and trust that God was indeed with me and in control of the situation. Listen as He speaks to your heart right now. He declares that He will *never* leave you; He will *never* forsake you. Never. Never.

The bad weather that day was scary, but God cradled me, and the plane landed safely. You are always in a safe mode with Jesus despite what happens. Trust. Pray and let God guide you into positive, hopeful thoughts for the day. In Him, there is always a safe landing.

Raquel Queiroz da Costa Arrais

Weakness Is Strength

And He said to me, "My grace is sufficient for you, for My strength is made perfect in weakness." Therefore most gladly I will rather boast in my infirmities, that the power of Christ may rest upon me.
—2 Corinthians 12:9, NKJV

I had been having a pretty rough few days. Everyone and everything was annoying me. It was hard to pinpoint exactly why I was annoyed and getting irritated with my husband and my kids. Then I realized it was my same old problem creeping back. The "voices" that I thought were behind me again taunted: *You're stupid and weak; you can't do anything right. God can't use you because you aren't good enough. Your family doesn't need you.* I'm sure many of you reading this can relate to those voices. They can be very strong and overpowering at times and discourage us easily. Have you ever thought you are too messed up to be of any good to anyone?

What helps me get through these times, besides the support of a loving family, are God's promises. If we listen to *His* voice, He will tell us the truth. One Sabbath, during this time when I was feeling down, we sang—fittingly—a hymn whose words started going through my head, "I need Thee every hour, most gracious Lord."*

How true that is! I do need Him every hour, minute, and second of every day. The negative words in my head are not God's, but rather those of the great deceiver. He wants his words to make us give up. But God has different words. He tells us that He is strong when we are weak, and when we realize our weakness for the opportunity it is—to let God perfect us and His grace to cover our imperfections—then we can have victory. We are strongest when we are weak and rest in God's strength. Paul said that the power of Christ is perfected in our weakness.

I know that you and I will still have rough days sometimes, but we have the promise that, despite our infirmities, we can rest in Christ's strength and know His grace is enough. So the next time you feel less than enough—weak, powerless, and defeated—remember that you have a Father who has given everything to make you strong. He will always be enough for you if you will believe in Him instead of in the enemy's lies.

Debra Snyder

---

* Annie Sherwood Hawks, "I Need Thee Every Hour," 1872, public domain.

What's in Your Heart?

Create in me a clean heart, O God;
and renew a right spirit within me.
—Psalm 51:10, KJV

As I sat in church on a recent Sabbath, the pastor was preaching about prayer. He was making a point that God wants to know what's in our hearts. He doesn't see us as others see us; God looks at our hearts.

"If you cut open your heart, what will God see?" asked the pastor.

Hmm. This got me thinking. I couldn't focus on the sermon anymore. I began to think about my heart and what was really in there. What *does* God see? My life hasn't been a Disney movie. There has never been a happily-ever-after for me. I thought about my day at church and what was in my heart just that day. I knew that in my heart, I had pain, hurt, grief, loneliness, sadness, and remorse. And that was just from that day.

So, thanks to my smartphone, I began a search for the word *heart* in the Bible. Many texts came up. I needed to find out what I could do to have a heart that is acceptable to God. As I searched the Scriptures, I found several promises that gave me peace, assuring me that I could be acceptable to God, regardless of my heart condition.

First, 1 John 3:20 reads, "For if our heart condemn us, God is greater than our heart, and knoweth all things" (KJV). OK, so God knows my pain—hallelujah! He knows my life experiences that have caused my heart to hurt. Then in Ezekiel 36:26, I found this promise: "A new heart also will I give you, and a new spirit will I put within you: and I will take away the stony [painful, hurting, lonely, grieving, remorseful, sinful] heart . . . and I will give you an heart of flesh" (KJV).

In Proverbs 3:5, I read, "Trust in the Lord with all thine heart; and lean not unto thine own understanding" (KJV). So instead of trusting myself and my feelings, I must trust God to work out my life for me.

And last, I discovered that I must "delight [myself] also in the Lord: and he shall give [me] the desires of [my] heart" (Psalm 37:4, KJV). My heart desires peace. My heart desires to be free from loneliness and pain. My stony heart wants to be replaced with a heart of flesh, so I can be available for God to go where He leads me.

Eva M. Starner

Fire! Fire!

Only be careful, and watch yourselves closely
so that you do not forget the things your eyes have seen
or let them fade from your heart as long as you live.
—Deuteronomy 4:9, NIV

S-c-r-e-e-c-h! Piercing, screaming sounds of, "Fire! Fire!" knifed through the darkness of the night. I jerked straight up and glanced at the clock: 3:27. I walked into the living room. No smoke, no flickering flames. But the alarm sounded again, the robotic voice repeating, "Fire! Fire!" Dick got up too, checking each area and room. No fire. No need for an alarm. It was a relief when the alarm quit screaming, and the night became quiet once again.

This false alarm was not the first occurrence. Further, it seemed like it always occurred in the middle of the night. We were almost used to it. So we returned to bed, but before I slept again, I thought about what had just happened; I remembered the old story of the little shepherd boy who yelled, "Wolf! Wolf!" too many times. In fact, he did it so many times that when a wolf did come, and he yelled, "Wolf! Wolf!" once again, no one came to rescue him or his sheep. So now: *What if this had been a real fire?* We had rather casually gotten up and walked through the house instead of grabbing what we could and running safely out of the house.

Which led to the next scary thought: *What if so many bad, awful, terrible things keep happening in our world (and they do) that we get used to them?* What if we turn over and go back to sleep and don't even realize that these warnings are for real—that our world is in great danger, and the "Fire! Fire!" alarm is real, and it is time to get out?

Just as we installed fire alarms throughout our home, God's Word gives warnings as to what is to come: In Job 33:15–17, Elihu tells Job that in dreams or visions of the night, even in a deep sleep, God may speak to people and terrify them with warnings to keep people from wrongdoing. His Word certainly warns us away from wrongdoing—and danger.

What if we get so hardened to terrible things around us that we don't recognize and react when the real thing happens? That will be more than tragic, because it won't just be the loss of a house or even a life, but a loss of eternal life. Jesus warned, "Be on guard so that your hearts are not weighed down with dissipation and drunkenness and the worries of this life, and that day does not catch you unexpectedly" (Luke 21:34, NRSV).

Ardis Dick Stenbakken

She'll Never Walk Again

Jesus saith unto him, Rise, take up thy bed, and walk.
—John 5:8, KJV

When I was thirteen years old, I contracted polio. The paralysis was in my left hip, which caused my left leg to be two inches shorter than my right leg. After a week in isolation, I was transferred to a ward where one of my roommates was in an iron lung. I used to brush her hair since she couldn't. Later on, I watched her take her first step! It was exciting to be a witness to her recovery. I loved saying goodbye to her when she was able, with assistance, to return home to her husband and children. I was treated with deep heat treatments and given salt pills and ice water all day long. Remaining behind, I endured hours of physical therapy, which necessitated the stretching of my body. My parents were told that I would never walk again. But I did.

When I was almost sixty-two, I suffered two strokes, which robbed me of all motor skills. After a month of therapy, I learned to walk again. It took me a year to completely recover, but I did. I developed a program I called Walking with Jesus and led early morning walks at women's ministries retreats in Michigan. Then I repeated the program at our church's camp meeting where some men joined in for the 6:00 A.M. daily walks. I walked in the Susan G. Komen three-day breast cancer events for four years in Michigan and then in Chicago, Phoenix, and San Diego. In 2017, I walked again in San Diego but only for the final day—in deference to my age—so only twenty miles. I have raised more than fourteen thousand dollars for breast cancer research. The past two years, I have headed up a walking group for Newcomers Club (which includes men) on monthly hikes to spectacular outings along the coast, foothills, mountains, and deserts in north San Diego County and Riverside County.

The amazing journey from a prognosis of never walking again to leading out in major walks and hikes at my age is only because God has richly blessed me. Did I mention that I am eighty years old? I was fortunate to be stricken during the polio epidemic in 1951, since an Australian nurse named Sister Elizabeth Kenny had already developed the deep heat treatments that helped me (before polio vaccines were available). I was fortunate that the strokes in 2000 occurred while I was undergoing a diagnostic test in radiology so I could have immediate medical care. I praise God each morning when I awaken that I can walk. Maybe you should too!

Patricia Hook Rhyndress Bodi

God's Resolution

And we know that all things work together
for good to them that love God.
—Romans 8:28, KJV

Have you ever needed grace and mercy? Well, I have. One year, during October and November, my financial resources were quite challenged. Due to unforeseen emergencies, I was unable to make my car payment on the twenty-eighth of the month. I contacted my car loan financier to request a payment extension until the thirtieth. The request was declined. I continued to pray for the extension and for God to intervene on my behalf.

The loan representative was very compassionate toward my request, but she refused to extend the payment beyond the twenty-eighth. Before hanging up the phone, I stated, "I believe God will provide the means to make the payment." This phone transaction took place on a Wednesday, and on the following Wednesday, the payment would be due. Once again, I went to God in prayer regarding the matter and left the situation in His hands. On Monday of the following week, I was impressed to go to my bank for service. For whatever reason, I could not log into my account at the service desk. I decided to log into my account from my mobile phone. To my surprise, I saw that someone had extracted three unauthorized debit transactions out of my account for more than three hundred dollars!

Already at the bank, I was able to report the incident and file an immediate report. The bank representative was very helpful and began the refund process. The representative said the fraud transaction would be restored in three to five days. The return took seven days. After my morning prayer and worship time on the payment date, I decided to check my bank account to see if the fraudulent transactions had been restored. I prayed about the matter and said, "Lord, it's Wednesday. My car payment is due, and I do not have the money." I was impressed to phone the car loan financier and share about the fraud transactions. Once again, I asked for the two-day extension of payment. Praise God, from whom all blessings flow: the extension was granted!

The Bible shares that God "is able to do exceeding abundantly above all that we ask or think, according to the power that worketh in us" (Ephesians 3:20, KJV). Although I was not happy about the fraudulent transactions, I am thankful for my heavenly Father's continuous love, grace, and mercy. Grace and mercy await you, too, especially when they are needed the most.

Barbara Stovall

What a Mess

And I am certain that God, who began the good work within you,
will continue his work until it is finally finished
on the day when Christ Jesus returns.
—Philippians 1:6, NLT

My hair needed some attention. Since my granddaughter is a beautician, I went to the shop where she works so she could provide the necessary services. Looking around, I quickly spotted a beautician engaged in the challenging job of untangling and cutting a thick head of hair that looked as if it had been neglected for weeks. Sometimes two beauticians had to work at it. They had started the process before I arrived and had not yet completed the task when I left. It was hard for me to believe that anyone would ignore her hair for that long. How could the individual stand her appearance, let alone the itching discomfort this neglect must cause?

This incident in the beauty shop reminded me of times when my life has been a mess, caused by my neglecting very important aspects of it, day after day. For our walk with Christ to progress, necessary steps must be taken. First and foremost, beginning the day with Him is important. He is eager for us to talk to Him, and prayer enables us to do so. His ear is always open to anything we want to talk about: our joys, our sorrows, our concerns, and our need for guidance in making good choices. Whatever concerns us concerns Him.

The study of His Word is also imperative. Sometimes we don't know how to pray or what to pray for. Reading His Word and letting it speak to us brings our condition and situation into focus. Reflection during our time with God also allows Him to speak to us through impressions brought to our minds. When we spend this daily time with our Savior, He untangles our lives by empowering us to have the courage to carry out our convictions and the strength to overcome those out-of-control aspects. His scissors, the Holy Spirit, cut away that which is sinful and offensive.

How I wish I could have seen that young lady when her hair transformation was complete. What a testimony it must have been to the work of her beautician. What a difference her cared-for hair must have made in her appearance. When we walk with Jesus and the Holy Spirit is living in us, it will show. There will be smiles on our faces and joy in our hearts. Our words and our works will speak volumes for Him!

Marian M. Hart-Gay

My Gift

My [daughter], give me thine heart.
—Proverbs 23:26, KJV

While taking my morning walk, I noticed that the trees along the sidewalk had a U-shaped cut out from their crowns down to several feet above the top of the trunks. Upon further observation, I realized that the cutting had been done to facilitate power lines passing through them. The houses along the way, as well as the street lights, got their electricity from those lines.

As I pondered the view, I seemed to hear a soft, inner whisper: "That's what I want from you—your heart." The phrase "Give me thine heart," from the book of Proverbs, immediately came to mind. Suddenly, my thoughts seemed to tumble over one another.

The trees had no choice in the "heart" of their crowns being removed for the electric company's purpose. There was no benefit for the tree. On the other hand, God sent His Son, Jesus Christ, to take the punishment for my sins. Then He grafted me into His family. By believing and accepting Jesus—giving Him my heart—I become His child.

Unlike the tree trimmer, though, God gives me a choice when He says, "Give me . . ." I could hear Him continuing, "Love gives. I gave." And I thought, *He gave me His best gift—His only Son. Now it's my turn. He is asking for my gift—my heart, the center of my whole being. But why this inquiry now? I surrendered my life to You a long time ago, Lord. Why this request now?*

My question led me to reflect further on how, as a consequence of recently submitting my retirement letter, I had been plagued with uncertainties. *Will I be able to sustain my daughter in college and continue meeting my living expenses? Will I be able to keep on participating in mission trips and helping international students with their college expenses? Will I . . . ? Will I . . . ?* As a result of these uncertainties, my prayers had become, *Lord, please . . . ! Lord, please . . . !*

Now He was telling me, "Enough already! Get rid of your doubt." Then He directed my attention to my gift to Him—my heart. Through the promise in Ezekiel 36:26–30, He reminded me He could not only exchange my fearful, faithless heart for a new one but also give me a new spirit that would empower me and establish my heart. He could give me rest. Finally, He pointed my thoughts to His promise in Philippians 4:19—He would supply all my need.

What loving promises God has given us! *Forgive me, Father, and help Thou my unbelief.*

Florence E. Callender

He Has Not Forgotten Us

*God is not unjust; he will not forget your work
and the love you have shown him.*
—Hebrews 6:10, NIV

My husband and I had booked a trip to the Dominican Republic to celebrate our twenty-second anniversary. Then, about a month before our dream celebration, my husband made an ill-advised decision and was taken to court to face a lawsuit. Our world started to fall apart. Everything that we cherished was taken from us. We had to hire a lawyer, who requested $12,500 just to begin the case. I cried, asking, "Where are You, God? I'm a woman of God. My husband and I are leaders in the church and have dedicated our lives to Your service. Why have You forgotten us?" We went on our anniversary trip since everything was paid for, but our hearts were filled with sadness and disappointment. We didn't enjoy the trip the way we'd planned.

The year before this unexpected lawsuit, my husband had been diagnosed with cancer. During this very difficult year, he had undergone surgery. Since my health insurance covered everything, I hadn't used my supplemental cancer insurance. Now, a year later, we decided to cancel the cancer insurance since we needed every possible dollar to help pay the lawyer's fees. I called the insurance company and asked for a cancellation. "Why?" asked the representative. I explained our situation. "I can't believe that you didn't file a report about your husband's cancer," she said. "Let me assure you that he can still be compensated for all the stress he went through during the discovery and treatment of his cancer."

I sent her the requested documents and waited to see how much the compensation would be. Three days later, I awoke, troubled and depressed. *Why has God forgotten my family?* After work that day, I stopped by the mailbox. In it was a check from the insurance company—for the amount of $12,500! I phoned my husband. Crying, I said, "God has not forgotten us!" We still had to face a huge storm ahead of us, but now I was at ease, knowing God was with us.

I do not know what hardships you are facing today. Difficult situations sometimes make us wonder if God has forgotten us, but He has not! He will never leave us, forsake us, forget about us, or turn His back on us. In the moments when you feel lost and alone and abandoned by God, remember that the truth is . . . He has not forgotten you!

Andrea Rocha

Lord, Let Him Serve in the Temple

For thou hast possessed my reins:
thou hast covered me in my mother's womb.
I will praise thee; for I am fearfully
and wonderfully made: marvellous are thy works.
—Psalm 139:13, 14, KJV

At the six-month point of my second pregnancy, I was already having problems. I walked around, appearing as though it were past time to deliver my baby. An ultrasound examination was urgently needed. However, during those days in Jamaica, where I live, the ultrasound machine was a novelty. There was only one on the island. After a very long road trip from the western end of the island to the eastern section, my husband and I arrived in Kingston, Jamaica's capital. There we went to the medical facility to which I had been referred and were quickly ushered into the examination room. After being prepared for the ultrasound, I was allowed a little time to rest before the examining doctor joined us.

Sometime later, an energetic man entered and introduced himself as the doctor in charge. He appeared warm and caring. After asking me a few health-related questions, he began moving the ultrasound probe across my overextended abdomen. Upon seeing the unborn child, he excitedly exclaimed, "What a big boy!" As the doctor continued his checks, he conversed with my husband. I closed my eyes and lifted my heart heavenward in prayer. *Dear God, thank You for giving me a son. I thank You that he is well and strong. Could You please bless him and make him be like the biblical child Samuel? Lord, let him serve in Your temple all the days of his life. Now, I give him back to You from his mother's womb. Please receive him. Amen.* In God's time, my son was born.

I was extremely careful with my son's training and development. After all, I had made a promise to God. I wanted to use every opportunity I could find to ensure my boy would serve in "the temple." In my mind, I visualized him helping sweep and clean the church, along with other domestic-related church activities. That was my limited vision of his serving in the temple. Today, God has given me more than I ever expected. That baby is now a humble, grown minister of the gospel. He not only preaches and teaches but is an accomplished musician and singer of the songs of Zion—all to the honor and glory of God. God had mercy on the simple prayer of an anxious mother's heart and gave her far more than she expected. What a mighty God we serve!

Jacqueline Hope HoShing-Clarke

Our Mighty God

Is anyone among you suffering? Let him pray.
Is anyone cheerful? Let him sing psalms.
—James 5:13, NKJV

The gradual development of pain and burning in my right leg left me with deep concerns. Then I noticed a small red, itchy, and moderately swollen area, along with periods of weakness in the leg. After four visits to the dermatologist, urgent care, and the emergency room, no one had a diagnosis. The practitioners were puzzled. The ice pack application, anti-inflammatory pills, and anti-itch medication (self-prescribed) were only temporary solutions. Every time I breathed a sigh of relief, the symptoms returned.

On my fifth visit, due to the increasing discomfort of the symptoms and the swelling, I was given antibiotics. I began to have hope again as the symptoms subsided. Yet, about a week and a half later, I was again in agony and almost felt foolish returning to the emergency room as the doctors had said other interventions were not necessary. One of the doctors even ordered a slew of blood work and stated, as she read me the results, "You look beautiful on the inside." My blood work was normal.

The question remained, What was wrong with my leg? I had a busy schedule, and I needed my leg to get well, but the discomfort was distracting me. A biopsy of the red area on my skin was scheduled for three weeks in the future. I was not fully convinced that I needed a biopsy, but I reluctantly agreed as I had previously had several squamous and basal cell cancers.

On one particular day, the symptoms returned with a vengeance. I never stopped praying for healing, but on this day, I went to my prayer closet. There I opened my Bible to James 5:13, "Is anyone among you suffering? Let him pray" (NKJV), and Jeremiah 17:14: "Heal me, O Lord, and I shall be healed; save me, and I shall be saved" (NKJV).

I anointed my leg with olive oil and earnestly claimed the promises. While praying, I felt the gradual reduction of pain and burning. Then I went to my personal physician. Led by the Spirit, we suspected a tick bite. The treatment for Lyme disease was ordered. Within six weeks, I was better. No biopsy needed. Sisters, I encourage you to trust God's promises and always pray.

Sonia Kennedy-Brown

Stop and Pray

And he went a little farther, and fell on his face, and prayed,
saying, O my Father, if it be possible, let this cup pass from me:
nevertheless not as I will, but as thou wilt.
—Matthew 26:39, KJV

It was 2:00 on Sunday morning. I finished packing our bags, and my husband did a final check of the car. Then, along with our one-year-old son, we drove out of our garage and headed for the shore. At 6:00 A.M., the anchors were lifted, and the ferry set sail. We made ourselves comfortable, for, in another six hours, we would be at our first stopping point. Then we would drive our car the rest of the way to our home village, another seventy-seven miles beyond. We reached our first stop at approximately noon and drove off the ferry. We sent our prayers up to our Lord and started for our home village. It had been eight months since we had seen our relatives, so we were excited to get home!

At 2:00 P.M., we were about forty-three miles away from our home village when I realized my husband was driving way below the speed limit. I did not ask him why he drove so slowly because I was enjoying the calmness on the journey. However, it wasn't too long until my husband brought our car to a stop. After an inspection, he said, "I'm not comfortable with the way this car feels, but I don't know why." Feeling uncertain, we prayed and continued. With no mechanic shop open, my husband drove slowly until we reached our final destination. We were overjoyed to see our relatives! The next morning we awoke to find one tire flat on the car. After an examination by a mechanic, we discovered that the tire was worn and that we needed a new one. The problem was diagnosed and resolved.

There are times in our lives when we are not certain about what to do when life becomes "uncomfortable." We don't know where to go when the journey we are on seems long and threatening. However, there is something we can do: stop and pray. We may not know what the problem is, but God knows. We may not understand the circumstances, but God does.

Our journey that day was long and terrifying, but we prayed. We thanked God for His protection. We gloried in the fact that God watches over us and leads us. He did it for us, and He can do it for you today. Just remember to stop and pray.

Jenel A. N. Campbell-McPherson

The Gift

"For God so [greatly] loved and dearly prized the world,
that He [even] gave His [One and] only begotten Son,
so that whoever believes and trusts in Him
[as Savior] shall not perish, but have eternal life."
—John 3:16, AMP

Now thanks be to God for His indescribable gift
[which is precious beyond words]!
—2 Corinthians 9:15, AMP

My friend was celebrating her birthday, and I decided I would do something different from former years as I wanted her to have a gift that she could treasure for a long time. After spending a substantial part of the day gathering necessary materials, I made what I thought was a gift she would love. I presented it to her and eagerly awaited her response on her special day.

On the day of her birthday, my friend sent me a text message that, at first, shocked and then angered me. She made it clear that she did not appreciate my gift, saying it was in poor taste. I called her a couple of times to clarify our perceptions of the gift, but she did not respond.

Have you ever had someone reject your love or a tangible gift that you sacrificed to give?

As I pondered the incident with my friend, I couldn't help thinking of my spiritual walk. In many ways, I have rejected Jesus, heaven's Gift to me. I wonder how He must feel. I reject Jesus when I refuse to let Him be Lord and Savior of my life. "It is through the gift of Christ that we receive every blessing. Through that gift there comes to us day by day the unfailing flow of Jehovah's goodness. Every flower, with its delicate tints and its fragrance, is given for our enjoyment through that one Gift. The sun and the moon were made by Him. There is not a star which beautifies the heavens that He did not make. Every drop of rain that falls, every ray of light shed upon our unthankful world, testifies to the love of God in Christ. Everything is supplied to us through the one unspeakable Gift, God's only-begotten Son. He was nailed to the cross that all these bounties might flow to God's workmanship."*

Dear friend, do you appreciate Jesus? When was the last time you showed Him your appreciation? Why not spend some time right now to whisper a prayer of gratitude? Then let your gratitude touch the life of someone else today.

Tamar Boswell

---

* Ellen G. White, *The Ministry of Healing* (Mountain View, CA: Pacific Press®, 1942), 424, 425.

Impossible

I love the LORD, for he heard my voice;
he heard my cry for mercy.
Because he turned his ear to me,
I will call on him as long as I live.
—Psalm 116:1, 2, NIV

S ooner than we thought, Adjei, my husband, and I had an empty nest. Our children all left home. We didn't need the extra rooms, so we thought about moving into a smaller, less expensive apartment. We tried to present some application forms to the management of our hoped-for apartment. As the clerk read through my application, she said, "Oh, Wite-Out® is not accepted on forms." Next, she rejected my Internal Revenue Service (IRS) 1040 tax forms because we had self-filed. "You need to contact the IRS for a real transcript," she said. Then she added, "Your yearly income is too low to qualify you for one of our apartments." As I was on my way out the door, she said, "Besides, we don't have a vacant apartment anyway."

I told Adjei about my experience. He just bowed his head for a moment. So I whispered a short prayer too. Then my husband asked that we pray together over this issue. After the prayer, he said, "Do not worry. It will be well." We wondered why our income looked insufficient because we had been paying three hundred dollars more each month than we would have to pay in the new apartment. We called the IRS and were assured that their official transcript would arrive within five to ten days. Adjei and I thanked the Lord and left the situation in His hands.

Dear reader, God assures us that He hears our voice when we pray to Him (Psalm 116:1, 2). And God heard our prayer. The writer of Psalm 63:3 stated, "Because your love is better than life, my lips will glorify you" (NIV). So I did not worry about the apartment. I just kept praising God as I waited. I knew that the Lord would never put me to shame. Two days before the arrival of the IRS transcript, I received a letter from the housing management that my application had been approved! Really? How? Even if they had ignored the Wite-Out®, how about the annual income? Oh, and I was still waiting for the IRS letter. Did they check my application thoroughly? One thing I do know: "I love the LORD, for he heard my voice" (Psalm 116:1, NIV). So, as my girls used to say, "Clap for Jesus, everyone!" With Him, all things are possible.

Mabel Kwei

A Still, Small Voice

Trust in the LORD with all your heart
and lean not on your own understanding;
in all your ways submit to him,
and he will make your paths straight.
—Proverbs 3:5, 6, NIV

It was a very busy morning at work; I needed to hang an intravenous antibiotic for one of my patients, the one in "contact isolation." This meant I would have to wear a special protective gown and mask. As I was about to hang the medication on its hook, a still, small Voice asked, *Are you sure this is the correct patient?*

I continued with what I was doing. Again I heard: *Are you sure this is the right patient?*

I muttered to myself, "Yes, I'm sure. I'm not taking this hot gown off to put it back on." I didn't realize I'd spoken aloud until the patient asked me if I was OK. I assured her I was.

Then, for the third time, I heard the question: *Are you sure this is the right patient?*

This time I said, "OK, Holy Spirit, You win." I took off the gown and exited the patient's room. Once outside, I obtained the patient's chart and checked the medication. I thought my heart would stop beating as my knees began to shake. I checked with a colleague. You see, I had two patients with the same last name. I had been trying to hang the antibiotic for the wrong one!

Humbled, I worshiped my God right there in the middle of the nurses' station, thanking Him for the Holy Spirit's guidance and blessing after I was obedient to His voice.

I recently read this reminder in the book *Steps to Christ*: "Consecrate yourself to God in the morning; make this your very first work. Let your prayer be, 'Take me, O Lord, as wholly Thine. I lay all my plans at Thy feet. Use me today in Thy service. Abide with me, and let all my work be wrought in Thee.' "*

I believe that had I not given all my plans to God during my daily morning devotional time—and been willing for the Holy Spirit to use me—I would not have recognized the Holy Spirit's prompting. As we submit ourselves to Jesus, He promises to direct our paths. May we always lean on His wonderful promises!

Jannett Maurine Myrie

---

* Ellen G. White, *Steps to Christ* (Washington, DC: Review and Herald®, 1956), 70.

Learn to Be Content With What You Have

But godliness with contentment is great gain. . . .
And having food and raiment let us be therewith content.
—1 Timothy 6:6, 8, KJV

Birdfeeders greatly enrich my life. Although feeding birds is an expensive hobby, I am rewarded with a variety of appreciative voices from sunup to sundown. I have the opportunity to observe patterns of behaviors that are all too often similar to those of people I know. Some seem to have a sense of entitlement, while others are content with living simply.

The chickadees and goldfinches cohabit happily, no corner or cranny is beneath them, and every seed counts. "Waste not, want not" appears to be the motto of these happy little creatures. They take one seed at a time, perch on a branch, and peck away.

Then there are the beautiful jays and woodpeckers, vying for the positions in the food line. They greedily send seeds flying in every direction, or worse, attempt to gulp down a full day's supply. Then, screaming, they fly away with beaks full of seeds to bury somewhere else. I wonder if they think that personal appearance qualifies them to bluster and bully other birds.

The chickadees remind me of the apostle Paul's statement about having learned to be content in whatever situation he found himself (Philippians 4:11). That is a true portrait of these little birds. They bubble over with joy when even one seed awaits them.

A third group of birds enjoys my feeder every day—doves. They waddle around under the trees and check out the leftovers on the ground. Their cooing is a peaceful end to my hectic day. I try to get outside to sprinkle a few choice offerings before the doves arrive. I want them to know that I appreciate their peaceful ways.

I have friends like those doves. They are the kind of people that calm down the restless rush of my life. For just a bit, I am able to forget deadlines and duties.

Jesus, mighty Creator that He is, knew the value of quiet times. When I read about the times He spent in solitary places away from the demanding life He led, I picture Him reclining under a tree, listening and observing the sights and sounds of the natural world around Him.

It seems to me that it is better to be small and grateful than to be gorgeous and graceless.

I pray for the wisdom to be more like the contented chickadee and less like the blue jay.

Patricia Cove

Turning Our Darkest Day
Into a Blessing

Blessed are they that mourn: for they shall be comforted.
—Matthew 5:4, KJV

The call from my sister came on a Monday night. Mother had been in an accident. The car in which she was a passenger had hit a pole, and now she was in intensive care. This news seemed surreal since we had just celebrated her ninetieth birthday a few weeks before. My sister assured me that Mom was fine. She had even opened her eyes. However, as the week progressed, Mother's condition did not improve. We all decided to go home and see our mom.

When I arrived at the hospital on Thursday, I could see that she was not doing well. She was not responding to the medical personnel, and she did not respond to me. The doctor requested a meeting with all six of her children as soon as possible. In the meeting, the doctor informed us that Mom was being kept alive artificially. The doctor confirmed our deepest fears. Therefore, she requested a decision from us regarding the removal of Mom's life support.

How do you even make such a decision? We sat together and talked about what to do next. Just a few weeks earlier, we had planned her birthday party; now we were gathered at the hospital. In that room, there were different points of view. Some wanted to remove life support immediately, while others wanted to wait a week or two. Which decision would be best? What would Mother want us to do? We talked, but we were at an impasse. Then my brother suggested that we pray. We prayed and implored God's direction and asked for unity in the decision-making process. We wanted to be in one accord. God answered our prayer.

We all decided it was best to remove the life support that day. This is what our mother would have wanted—though it was not an easy or pleasant decision. However, it was a God-led decision. After the life-support devices were removed, we surrounded Mom's bed with hearts full of love. We prayed, sang, hugged her, and kissed her as she took her last breath. God led us all the way, step-by-step. Even in our darkest hour, He was there all the time. From this experience, we began a weekly prayer time in honor of our mom. God made something good come from this tragedy. "Weeping may endure for a night, but joy comes in the morning" (Psalm 30:5, NKJV).

Edith C. Fraser

A Modern-Day Lydia

*For this reason we also thank God without ceasing, because
when you received the word of God which you heard from us, you
welcomed it not as the word of men, but as it is in truth, the word of
God, which also effectively works in you who believe.*
—1 Thessalonians 2:13, NKJV

After the first September meeting of my husband's Bible prophecy seminar, an exuberant lady, Lydia, approached me and asked if I would pray for Rhonda, her daughter-in-law, to accept Jesus. I said that I would and contacted several others to pray for Rhonda as well.

A few weeks passed and, night by night, Lydia, her husband, and her son continued to attend the meetings. On October 2, I peeked ahead into the next few pages of my women's devotional book, *Notes of Joy.* The October 5 devotional caught my attention. The title was "Lydia"! I read with interest the beautiful story of Lydia (found in Acts 16), originally from Thyatira. She responded to Paul's message and wanted her family to accept Jesus as their Savior.

This sounds like our Lydia, I thought. That evening I took the devotional book to Lydia and asked if she would like to read that devotional. She read it and was appreciative when I told her that she was a "modern-day Lydia." She had even more in common with the biblical Lydia than I knew, for the next evening, she brought me a pretty bag. Inside was a beautiful blue and pink apron with butterflies. Attached was a paper reading, "Sewcrafty by Lydia." I learned that Lydia makes quilts, pillows, purses, and aprons, among other things. Wow! This modern-day Lydia sews and sells fabrics. I'm sure she shared purple fabrics, too, as well as the love of Jesus.

But the story doesn't end there. On Friday evening, as Rhonda's husband came in the door, he said, "Rhonda would like to be baptized when I am." I told him that I would speak to the pastor so they could arrange a meeting. The next morning, as this man approached the door, I noticed a beautiful lady on his arm. I approached them and said, "Welcome, Rhonda! I'm so happy to meet you." A short time later, we witnessed Lydia and her husband and Rhonda and her husband get baptized. It was such a special occasion to see two couples commit their lives to Jesus. I think everyone there could feel the joy of these four individuals. Lydia was so happy and later said, "I'm praying the rest of my family will be baptized." She truly is a modern-day Lydia.

Lord, help us each to be a modern-day Lydia!

Rita Kay Stevens

Before They Call

And it shall come to pass, that before they call, I will answer;
and while they are yet speaking, I will hear.
—Isaiah 65:24, KJV

We rented a house for five months in 2017 while we waited for construction to be completed on our new house. Our girls, Alyssa and Natalia, enjoyed playing outside on the trampoline and deck during those summer days.

I bought two pinwheels one Friday afternoon, and the girls were very excited about playing with them outside. That Sabbath, we went to a church close to our house. Alan, my husband, decided that since we were close to home, he and the girls would return home on the walking trails. As I drove home, though, I noticed that dark storm clouds were gathering, and a strong wind began to blow. *The perfect time for those pinwheels*, I thought.

Alan and the girls got home soon after I did. I stopped to talk with Alan for a bit. Then I noticed the house was extremely quiet. A thought came to my mind: *Where are the girls?* I searched the house, then went to the back door and saw their shoes. I heard a voice say, *Check on the girls.* I opened the back door, and there they were. Both girls were on the deck, spinning and twirling with their pinwheels in hand, having a wonderful time. Alyssa was nearest to me by the door while her sister, Natalia, was at the farthest right side of the deck. Suddenly I noticed a black cloud of *something* rising from the far side of the deck. A whole *swarm* of something!

"Come inside right now! Natalia!" I shouted. "Run! Quickly!" Both girls raced toward me as Natalia started screaming. The seconds it took for them to get to me felt like an eternity. Alyssa got to me first. As soon as Natalia got inside, I slammed the door with all my might. The girls had just made it to safety. The swarm of wasps that had come up from under the deck were very angry, having been stirred up by the vibrations of two little girls spinning around. Sadly, Natalia got stung on her foot, but as far as we could tell, she had only one sting. I can only imagine how much worse it could have been if I hadn't gone looking for the girls when I did. Later, Alan found a huge wasps' nest under the deck that was about twelve inches long!

We thank the ever-watchful Lord for protecting our girls as only He was able to do.

Noella (Jumpp) Baird

VBF

The LORD has appeared of old to me, saying:
"Yes, I have loved you with an everlasting love;
Therefore with lovingkindness I have drawn you."
—Jeremiah 31:3, NKJV

I was pondering the other evening where some of my old "very best friends" (VBFs) are today. With social media, I have stayed in contact with many friends and coworkers. Yet I lost contact long ago with others. I haven't heard from childhood friends, Vonnie, Diane, and Barb, since our high school days. Another high school chum and I stayed in contact for a long time. In her last letter to me, she asked for money but didn't say why. I wrote back that I couldn't help right then because of my divorce and having barely enough money for my daughter and me.

I had a couple of other VBFs: another Barb and Shelia. We hung out together as young mothers. In fact, Barb and I took Shelia for a ride on her wedding day, trying to talk her out of marrying her fiancé because we felt she could do better. The funny thing is that her marriage has lasted, but neither Barb's nor mine did. Shelia and I are still in contact . . . but where is Barb?

Friendships in this sinful world are fragile and can be destroyed for the simplest of reasons. But we need not despair, for there is a Friend who will stick with us through thick and thin. He will never desert or leave us. He will never get so angry with us that he severs the relationship. Proverbs 18:24 states the following: "A man who has friends must himself be friendly, but there is a friend who sticks closer than a brother" (NKJV).

That friend is Jesus. As recorded in John 15:13, Jesus said, "Greater love has no one than this, than to lay down one's life for his friends" (NKJV). A beautiful contemporary Christian song states that Jesus didn't want to be in heaven eternally without us, so He brought the blessings of heaven down to us. More and more, I am learning that He is the true Friend we all long for deep within our souls. He knows me and loves me just as I am. I am so thankful for that! In the lonely times when I feel like I am deserted by the world, I have only to think about Him, my faithful Friend, Jesus, and I don't feel lonely anymore.

The beautiful thing about Jesus is that, since His heart is so big, He can be your VBF too.

Mona Fellers

God Always Sees Us Through

Casting all your care upon him; for he careth for you.
—1 Peter 5:7, KJV

It was time to go. We had spent fourteen wonderful years as snowbirds in southern California. We had enjoyed golfing, swimming, and "hot-tubbing" in the natural hot mineral pools. We had played games with friends and had fun with our family, who were also snowbirds from various places. But now we were getting old. Our bodies were not doing what we wanted them to anymore, so one day, my husband and I sat down and decided it was time to sell our little desert home.

We set a price, which was pretty much the same as what we had paid for it. Of course, we had spent a lot of money on remodeling, but we knew that mobile homes—even sitting on the land that we owned—were not selling for much. Yet we asked the Lord that if it was His will for us to sell our place, He would send us a buyer. We placed a "For Sale by Owner" sign in the front yard, showed the place to a couple of prospective buyers, and then went to the beach for a week with two of my cousins and their husbands.

We kept praying for God's will to be done. While we were away, our neighbor called to say that he had sold our house to a single lady who had come by. After he showed her our house, she said she was going directly to the escrow company to put down her earnest money. Our neighbor encouraged my husband to call the woman. When we returned home the following Sunday, she came by again. We discussed more details with her, and she was even more determined that she wanted to buy our place. Since it would be a year-round home for her, she felt it was just the place for her. We did have some doubts, however. The woman went by four different names and had a foreign bank account. We wondered if everything was on the level with her. However, I remembered how we had prayed for a buyer to come if it was God's will that we sell. It appeared things were working out just the way He had planned.

Every morning, as we prepared to move, I asked God to remind me of everything I needed to do and give me the strength to do it. He definitely answered my prayers, and the day before we were to leave, escrow closed. The following day the funds were wired to our bank.

We can safely cast our cares upon Jesus. He will always see us through.

Anna May Radke Waters

The Dog on the Golf Cart

The angel of the LORD encampeth round about them
that fear him, and delivereth them.
—Psalm 34:7, KJV

The vast expanse of lush green spread its carpet—dotted with holes. I was visiting a Caribbean island, and a former student invited me to the golf course.

Unhesitatingly, I agreed, and we soon arrived. At the office, we spotted a canine lying at its entrance.

Cautiously, we proceeded to ask for Uncle, an employee who would give us a tour of the grounds on the golf cart. He asked one of the workers to do it since he was busy at the time. After I had taken my place opposite the driver, the dog, Whitie, instantly appeared.

The driver started the motor of the golf cart, and we began to move. The dog accompanied us at a slow trot.

Whenever the driver accelerated the speed of the golf cart, the dog accelerated his speed as well, keeping pace with the moving cart.

The tour finished, I disembarked.

Whitie resumed his position at the entrance of the golf course grounds.

"Why don't you let me get a picture of you sitting on the golf cart?" my friend suggested.

"OK, that would be fine," I responded. Having said that, I climbed up into the driver's seat to pose for the picture. Before I had settled into the seat, however, Whitie was already situated in the adjacent seat. He wanted to be part of every activity associated with his master.

What devotion! I thought. *This faithful dog runs alongside his master's golf cart. He sits beside anyone who takes his master's seat in the cart. Being a devoted guardian of his master is this dog's life!*

Then another thought struck me: we each have a heaven-sent guardian. The angel of the Lord *encamps* about us who fear Him. From our birth to death, angels keep untiring vigil to protect us from dangers of which we are unaware. They travel with us wherever we go and fight off evil influences on our behalf. In short, they are "ministering spirits" (Hebrews 1:14, KJV). What a marvelous gift we have from God in the form of guardian angels! Thank You, Lord.

Hyacinth V. Caleb

April 27

Prayer Meeting

After this I looked, and there before me was a great multitude
that no one could count, from every nation, tribe,
people and language, standing before the throne and
before the Lamb. They were wearing white robes and
were holding palm branches in their hands.
—Revelation 7:9, NIV

I was asked to lead out in the praise and worship portion of the Wednesday evening church prayer meeting—for the entire month. I gladly accepted because music is my passion.

As I was looking through different songs in order to choose which ones the congregation could sing, I was impressed to select "How Sweet Are the Tidings" for the opening song of the prayer meeting. The third verse especially touches me:

There we'll meet ne'er to part in our happy Eden home. . . .
From the north, from the south, all the ransomed shall come,
And worship our heavenly King.*

My mind went back to July 1990, when I was able to attend just one day of my church's global convocation held every five years. That year it was held in Indiana. The day I attended, I caught a glimpse of what I think heaven will be like. I saw beautiful, happy faces as people greeted one another with hugs and kisses as if they were longtime friends. I saw people from all over the world greeting one another with phrases such as "I love you" and "God loves you." What a beautiful picture that was! That was one of the happiest days of my life.

The chorus to the hymn I chose as our prayer meeting's opening song states, "He's coming, coming, coming soon, I know."

So the question I must ask myself is, "Am I ready for Jesus to come?" The cares of this world can cause us to be sad and self-absorbed. Not much good news is shown on television. So let us keep God's promises deep within our hearts as He prepares us for heaven's prayer meeting: "So do not fear, for I am with you; do not be dismayed, for I am your God. I will strengthen you and help you" (Isaiah 41:10, NIV).

Patricia Hines

* "How Sweet Are the Tidings," in *The Seventh-day Adventist Hymnal*, no. 442.

Protective Power

The angel of the LORD encamps around those who fear him.
—Psalm 34:7, NIV

So shall they fear the name of the LORD from the west, and his glory
from the rising of the sun. When the enemy shall come in like a
flood, the Spirit of the LORD shall lift up a standard against him.
—Isaiah 59:19, KJV

One scary night taught me to count my blessings. It was late on a Friday night. Just before midnight, I went to the kitchen to get a hot beverage. Had I gone half an hour later, I could have been injured by a prowler seen in my yard. I count this as blessing number one.

Providentially, that same night I had put a thick green blanket over the window to keep the lights out so I could sleep better—an action that was highly unusual for me since it was much thicker than the cloth I usually place there. Therefore, when I heard the prowler late in the night at the back of the house close to my bedroom window, I knew that though the window was approximately 75 percent closed, the blanket offered added protection. Right then and there, I was comforted that God had already made a way of escape to ensure my safety from the enemy. I count this as blessing number two.

I discovered blessing number three when I awoke the next morning only to realize that the mesh from one of my living room windows had been completely removed. So the prowler had had access to all the spaces between the metal bars on the window. I would not dare say that it was the bars that prevented him from coming inside the house because a metal cutter could have done the job. Rather, what I do sincerely believe is that the hand of God protected me and lifted up His standard against the enemy.

From a human perspective, it was challenging, initially, to cope with this intrusion, not knowing whether the prowler would return at a later date since he had already scanned the property. I thought of relocating, but, in the end, I stayed. It is only God that can provide the refuge that we desperately need.

My dear sisters, whatever situations you find yourselves in on life's journey, know that you are never alone. God already has a master plan and, yes, He has you covered.

Althea Y. Boxx

Weeds

And thou, son of man, be not afraid of them, neither be afraid
of their words, though briers and thorns be with thee, and thou
dost dwell among scorpions: be not afraid of their words, nor be
dismayed at their looks, though they be a rebellious house.
—Ezekiel 2:6, KJV

I am the true vine, and my Father is the husbandman.
—John 15:1, KJV

Nothing can send a gardener into a state of urgency quicker than finding weeds overtaking the garden. I have watched my husband spend hours pulling weeds from his garden. His training is in agriculture, so tending the garden is his domain. I don't mind setting the seeds, but my tending the garden would lead to dead plants. Weeds can be a pain in the garden, but they have provided some valuable spiritual lessons that I will share.

Weeds are classified as plants that are growing in the wrong place, undesirable plants that can interfere with the welfare of people. Weeds, which are stronger by nature than desirable plants, can choke the desired plant and limit its growth, leading to a loss of crop. For the Christian, the bad habits we allow to grow can be likened to weeds: unforgiveness, self-righteousness, and wasting time, just to name a few. These harm our spiritual growth, along with the weeds of frequenting the wrong places or cultivating relationships that lead us away from God.

Second, I have discovered that weeds are prolific. They can grow anywhere, lying dormant for years, just waiting for the right moment to spring up. Wind, soles of shoes, tools, the tractor tray—all can transport seeds that then germinate. I must guard against weeds that appeal to human nature. Every day through prayer and quality time with God, I must submit my will to Him. Like weeds, my habits do not like to be controlled.

Finally, a weed can be a plant whose virtue has not yet been discovered. When we look at ourselves in our sinful state, we tend not to see virtue or value. Yet God, the true Husbandman, sees our possibilities. He can add value; He knows where our true purpose can be revealed and where we can bloom. Only the One who knows true value can distinguish between that which is a weed and that which is a true plant. Allow God to tend you today and replace the unwanted seeds and weeds in your life with good seeds and fruit.

Greta Michelle Joachim-Fox-Dyett

Women of Courage

If you can find a truly good wife, she is worth more than precious gems! Her husband can trust her, and she will richly satisfy his needs. She will not hinder him but help him all her life.
—Proverbs 31:10–12, TLB

I take courage from the many missionary wives who have come to the islands of the Pacific with their husbands, sailing away from loved ones across wild and stormy seas—some never to return home. Others courageously faced cannibalistic warriors, lost all their possessions before reaching their destination, or lost babies for lack of medical help.

Edith Carr was the very first missionary woman of my denomination to come with her husband to Papua New Guinea in 1908. She and her husband, Septimus, were offered a small shack beside the beach until they found something more permanent. Weeks passed before they walked and rode horses on rugged paths to the plateau, twenty miles inland, to set up their mission station. Edith worked hard alongside her husband to establish a rubber plantation, teach school, and conduct morning and evening worships. They had to wait five years before they baptized their first convert. Now there are three hundred thousand church members there.

Emily Campbell started mission work with her husband, Alex, in 1926 in the Solomon Islands. She cooked hundreds of meals, sewed, delivered babies, and treated spear wounds. During World War II, enemy soldiers shot at her house. When Alex was doing mission work on another island, Emily had to fly in an old-fashioned plane with her two babies to a distant hospital where one died. Emily became known as "Namba Wan Missus" (Number One Missus).

Mavis Barnard was a quietly courageous woman who lived in Papua New Guinea for most of her life, along with her intrepid nurse-missionary-pilot husband, Len. Their first house was constructed of bamboo poles and grass on the mountainside at Togoba. Here they lived for the first four years with their little girl. One night the house caught fire from the dying embers. Although the family escaped unharmed, Mavis lost everything. Len traversed on foot for thousands of miles before becoming the first missionary pilot in the Pacific Islands. All during those many years, Mavis supported and provided a safe place and home for him.

Let us remember—and be inspired by—these women of courage.

Joy Marie Butler

Unconditional Love

I have loved thee with an everlasting love: therefore with
lovingkindness have I drawn thee.
—Jeremiah 31:3, KJV

As a child, I loved to go to church. My mother and grandmother helped me know the goodness of God and His everlasting love. Eagerly wanting to follow God, I decided to be baptized in 2015, and what a joy I experienced in my Christian walk!

However, after a year passed, I faltered. I even left the church, forgetting all the good God had done in my life. I felt empty and unhappy. It seemed as if life had no meaning anymore, and I felt lost.

Then I began to blame God and question Him as to why He had allowed me to wander so far from Him. I also began to doubt His promise never to leave nor forsake me. In May 2017, I was angry about everything and with everybody. Yet God sent a dear friend to encourage me to pray and read my Bible. In frustration and anger, I replied, "God does not love me. He has forgotten about me."

Two days later, I was spared from the hands of gunmen who shot my child's father in the head while I was holding our six-week-old child closely to my chest. Then I realized that God had kept His promise! My baby and I were unhurt and safe from harm. God indeed said to me through that dreadful experience, "I will never leave you nor forsake you" (Joshua 1:5, NIV).

As I reflect on my Christian journey, I can say that despite my being upset and angry at God, He has never left me alone. When I let go of God's hand and go my own way, He reaches out to me, and His arms are always open to receive me when I return home.

Thank God, I have recommitted my life to Him, and I am rejoicing again in His love.

Friend, are you burdened under a load of discouragement and depression? Do you feel as if God is far away or has forgotten you? Do you doubt His tender care for you? Just remember that He has promised to be with you even when you walk through dark and dangerous paths. His grace and mercy will see you through.

Dear Lord, please always give me the courage to return to You if I ever falter or lose my way. Amen.

Kareal Getfield

God's Promises Are Sure

Fear thou not; for I am with thee: be not dismayed;
for I am thy God: I will strengthen thee; yea, I will help thee; yea,
I will uphold thee with the right hand of my righteousness.
—Isaiah 41:10, KJV

God has blessed me with a sweet and wonderful grandson, Max. When he was about one and a half years old, I babysat him one Sunday. I had a lot of fun playing with him, and then it was time for his usual afternoon nap. So I put him in his crib that was against the foot of my bed. Once he was asleep, I went to the kitchen to do some chores. I did not realize how quickly the time was passing by since I was so busy washing dishes and cleaning the kitchen.

When I finished my work, I heard Max cry, so I quickly ran to see him. To my shock, I did not see him in the crib! When I looked around, I saw him sitting on the floor next to my bed with teary eyes. Immediately, I picked him up.

Apparently, he had climbed up the side of the crib, which was rather high. Then he had crawled onto my bed before rolling down to the floor. When I saw him, I was so worried that he had hurt himself in some way by falling from the top of my bed. I carried and hugged him. He seemed to be fine. However, I still wanted to make sure everything was all right. I gave him toys to play with and carefully observed. He appeared to play normally and looked unharmed.

I thanked God numerous times that afternoon and praised Him for taking care of Max. I would have been devastated if he had been hurt in any way, especially when his parents had depended on me to take good care of him.

I did not inform them of anything until they came to pick up Max in the evening. It is a blessing my daughter is a pediatrician. When I shared with her what had happened, she was able to check him thoroughly and verify that he was doing fine. That was a great relief to me, and again I thanked my loving Jesus for protecting my dear grandson.

The assurance God gives us in Isaiah 41:10 is so soothing. We can know that God is with us no matter what we may face in life. We can always trust Him and depend on His wonderful promises!

Stella Thomas

When the Dogs Came

*The angel of the LORD encamps
around those who fear him,
and he delivers them.*
—Psalm 34:7, NIV

I shot upright in bed and listened to the rattling from the carport below my bedroom. Someone was trying to pry open the padlock on the carport grill. My heart thumped, its pounding intense around my temples. Someone was trying to break into the house where my special-needs son and I lived. What was I going to do? Other faculty members of the Christian college where I served as academic dean lived nearby, but none were close enough to hear any shouts for help.

I sprang out of bed and switched on the floodlights. Immediately, the yard was awash in white light. Half-hidden by the drapes, I stood by the window. The rattling stopped, but I saw no one. As I shook with fear, my mind dredged up the incidents of murder and break-ins that were prevalent in the area. *Dear Lord, please help me!* My prayer pierced the night sky into the heavenly courts. I don't know how long I stood by the window watching to see if anyone would run toward the driveway. Then I saw something amazing happen. A pack of dogs came trotting up the driveway and stopped. They began barking in the direction of the trees and shrubbery on the far side of the yard. They stood together and set up quite a racket. *Maybe the culprit is hiding in the bushes,* I thought. As the dogs continued their loud barking, my attention was drawn to one of them that seemed to be the leader of the pack. He was huge, twice as big as the others. He looked like a small pony and had a gleaming, light-colored coat. He appeared powerful as he led the yowling chorus. I had never seen any of those dogs in the neighborhood before. Yes, there was one dog in the neighborhood that always rushed out of its driveway, chased my car as I drove by, and then returned to its yard as soon as I passed, but no dogs had ever come into my yard to set off such a cacophony of late-night barking. I watched, hoped, and prayed. The dogs kept up their barking for quite some time. Then, as mysteriously as they had come, they turned and trotted off down the driveway. They never came again.

I remained by the window for a while before going back to bed. Then I lay in the quiet of the moment, unable to sleep but no longer afraid because something precious and memorable had happened to me when those dogs showed up.

Judith Nembhard

Calmed by Silent Songs in the Night

*And we know that God causes everything to work
together for the good of those who love God
and are called according to his purpose for them.*
—Romans 8:28, NLT

One night, I constantly prayed for the safety of my husband and his colleagues while looking at the clock, which seemed to move very slowly. To my relief, he came back after about thirty minutes and related to me his side of a most frightening story.

He and our school's accountant had been surrounded by four bandits armed with knives, a revolver, and a spear. They ordered the cashier to come with them to the office where he gave the bandits all the money he had there, amounting to about six million Malagasy francs (about six hundred dollars). How fortunate that earlier that day, my husband had deposited the excess funds in the bank! Most of the teachers and staff had already collected their pay from the office. So what had remained—and what the bandits had obtained—were the uncollected salaries.

The brigands hurriedly left, leaving behind the laptop and other things they had intended to take with them, they had warned my husband, "If you tell anyone about this, we will return and burn down the school buildings!"

My husband and I offered a prayer of thanksgiving for protection and presence of mind. Then the principal was notified.

Suddenly we heard running footsteps and loud wailing. We ran outside and saw our students, both men and ladies, screaming out their terrifying stories. The outlaws had next gone to the girls' dormitory, where they had molested five of our students.

That was indeed a very sad night for all of us! Our questions as to why God had allowed these things to happen at one of His institutions are still unanswered. The only thing we could do, though, was trust Him even if we didn't understand why these traumatic events had occurred on our campus. I found reassurance not only in God's Word but also in a song whose words call us to trust in God even when we cannot see His hand in the midst of our adversity.

Can anything good come from this tragic experience?

Yes. I assure you that God can turn even traumatic experiences into something good for those who love and trust Him.

Forsythia Catane Galgao

The Royal Wedding

*Behold, he cometh with clouds; and every eye shall see him,
and they also which pierced him: and all kindreds of the earth
shall wail because of him. Even so, Amen.*
—Revelation 1:7, KJV

On May 19, 2018, all eyes were focused on England for the wedding of Prince Harry and his American bride, Meghan Markle. In the weeks leading up to the royal wedding, all you could hear was people discussing the upcoming wedding and wondering, in anticipation, about the details: the outfits, reception venue, guest list, and participants. History was made, and England was reminded about Christianity because of the way the services and festivities were conducted.

We have another royal wedding that is soon to take place. The Groom is coming for His "jewels" that comprise His bride, the church. Too often, however, we seem to forget that we should be focused on this wedding: the second coming of Christ. For this wedding, however, Jesus will descend through the clouds with His angels, and every eye will see Him.

We do not know when the Second Coming will take place, but we do know Jesus is coming, and we need to be ready. "So then, just as you received Christ Jesus as Lord, continue to live your lives in him" (Colossians 2:6, NIV).

We should not be too focused and troubled about worldwide troubles, news headlines, and all the different ideas about how the last events will take place. We need to be thinking about Jesus. Are we allowing Him to prepare us, His jewels, so that we will be ready when He returns?

Let us not focus on the trivial things of this world but rather on Jesus and His plans for us regarding His soon-coming royal wedding. May we be ready as were the five wise virgins in Christ's parable (Matthew 25:1–10). Let's not waste our energy on that which does not have eternal value but rather on helping others be prepared to be jewels in His crown as well.

When He cometh, when He cometh To make up His jewels. . . .
Like the stars of the morning, His bright crown adorning,
They shall shine in their beauty, Bright gems for His crown.*

Camilla E. Cassell

---

* William O. Cushing, "When He Cometh," 1866 in *The Seventh-day Adventist Hymnal*, no. 218.

Holy Angels Are Real

The angel of the LORD encampeth round about them
that fear him, and delivereth them.
—Psalm 34:7, KJV

My husband and I were flying from Brazil to Paraguay. Soon we heard unusual sounds, and the plane made sudden lunges as one of the wings began to break. I prayed intensely and then envisioned God's angels holding it together, yet how I wished to see them for real! After the plane's safe landing, the airline director offered us a lift in a private taxi. After the director reached his destination, the chauffeur transported us further.

That evening we stopped at a restaurant. Entering, we passed by some cowboys with guns and guitars who sat on the floor singing. We were directed to a table. I checked out the whole of the restaurant. In one corner was a bar where a cowboy stood, boldly staring at me.

Oh, I thought, feeling immediately uncomfortable. A second glance confirmed his continued, nearly frozen stare. "Why is he looking at me like that?" I asked my husband.

"Just don't look back," my husband advised. "Or he'll think that you like him. Then he may shoot me and take you away." I shivered and lowered my head, starting to count the red squares on the red-and-white checkered tablecloth. A waitress brought us our meal, which included roast chicken, rice, and beans. The chauffeur was starving. No conversations! He was too busy devouring his food. In fact, he sucked his chicken bones clean and threw them on the tablecloth (to my disgust and shock). "Are these normal manners?" I quietly asked my husband.

"I don't know his culture!" was his reply. By now, still surrounded by cowboys and guns, my imagination was going wild, thinking of the worst-case scenario. *Please, God, protect us! Help me calm down.* When the meal was over, we made our way to the car.

"Oh no! That's not possible!" I gasped. "Who removed the wheels from our car?"

I held tightly to my husband's hand; my long fingernails were almost embedding themselves into his palm. "They are going to kill us!" But soon, some men appeared—carrying the same wheels they had just stolen—and sold them back to the driver. We were glad to leave! *Thank you, God, that holy angels are* real.

Monique Lombart De Oliveira

The Copper Pitchers

"He will sit like a refiner of silver, burning away the dross.
He will purify the Levites, refining them like gold and silver,
so that they may once again offer acceptable sacrifices to the LORD."
—Malachi 3:3, NLT

Once I was given a set of three tiny copper pitchers. Years before, I had played with them when I was a child, not knowing where they came from, only that they were part of my mom's collection of things.

After my precious auntie and uncle were killed in a car accident in 2017, my mom gave me the pitchers and told me they came from Peru, where my aunt and uncle had served as missionaries. She told me to give them to my cousin, whom I was going to visit.

When my cousin found out I used to play with them, she insisted I keep them, so I brought them home with me to Alaska.

The little pitchers were very old, badly tarnished, and dull. One day I decided to see if I could clean them up. I got out the copper cleanser powder and an old toothbrush and went to work; it didn't take long before the brilliant copper color showed through all the tarnish. The little pitchers had only needed polishing to make them look clean and beautiful again. Not only did they shine, but I could almost see my own reflection with each subsequent polishing. Eventually, I contacted my cousin and sent her a picture of the now shiny copper pitchers.

It struck me how like our lives those pitchers are. We become tainted and tarnished by life's events and the poor choices we make. We need polishing. No, our characters don't always emerge as "perfect" after just one polishing. They need polishing again . . . and again, just like those little copper pitchers. The polishing process isn't usually fun. In fact, it's often quite painful, but the finished product is spectacular!

So, where are you in the polishing process? How has God been polishing your character lately so that, more and more, He is able to see His reflection in your life?

Most importantly, are we allowing the polishing process, through trials and losses, to purify our characters so that His beauty not only shines through us but also brightens the world and lives of those around us?

Sonia Brock

Keep Pressing On

"The Son of Man came to look for and to save people who are lost."
—Luke 19:10, CEV

Grandma is a white cat with a black patch on her head and a black tail. She got the name Grandma after giving birth to four sets of kittens, which she nursed and ably cared for. When we first moved into the area, she was just a young kitten roaming across neighborhood properties. Grandma was a very independent cat that we saw only occasionally. Yet, with her fourth set of kittens, she became less independent and more dependent on us for her meals.

In March 2018, Grandma had kittens. One evening about three weeks later, I heard, "Meow! Meow!" Looking up the hill, I saw a cute black-headed kitten with a body as white as snow and a black tail. She was going around in circles on the cliff above our house.

The next day, after thunderous evening showers, I went outside again. This time I heard, "Meow! Meow!" much closer to the house. After searching, I found the rain-soaked kitten, shivering and hungry, in some bushes. I dried it. Then Grandma picked up her baby, climbed a tree, and disappeared. The following day the crying kitten was on a cliff over the neighbor's property. I stood at the fence for an hour, saying, "Meow! Meow!" and hoping the kitten would slip my direction and come to me. Stepping away, I prayed, "Lord, let the kitten fall so that I might rescue it." In my peripheral vision, I saw something white fly through the air. Yes, it was the kitten! We rescued it again, cleaned it, and Grandma took him home.

Friend, have you strayed from the safety of home and gotten lost in the hills of despair, doubt, and depression? Are you wandering on a cliff of loneliness? Like Grandma, God the Father is waiting to welcome you home into His family. You may have been like the lost sheep in Luke 15 that wandered from the fold. Jesus, the Good Shepherd, has come to get you and carry you home on His shoulders. Or, you might be like the lost, dust-covered coin. Press on, for the light of the gospel is still shining on your path. Or perhaps you have been a prodigal son or daughter for years, squandering your life, time, and money in the pigpen of drugs, immorality, crime, or violence. Repent, get up, and go home. Your Father is waiting for you.

Today I implore you to keep pressing on. The feast is being prepared, and there will be joy and celebration in heaven over one repentant sinner that comes home to the Father.

Bula Rose Haughton Thompson

Doing It All While Single

I can do all things through Christ which strengtheneth me.
—Philippians 4:13, KJV

To be a parent is one of the hardest jobs in the world. Yet parenting while single is on a completely different level. When I think of single parenting, my mind goes to Hagar. She was already a slave when given to Abram by Sarai. Because she was a slave, her pregnancy by Abram was not optional for her. To make matters worse, by traditional law, she was considered to be Abram's wife (because they had had relations) yet she had none of the privileges. So here she was, a single parent raising her son in a difficult environment with seemingly no support.

I don't know if you can relate to any part of her story, but know that if you're a single parent, you're not alone. Some of us understand having no one else to help in the middle of the night, having to clean every diaper, runny nose, and sticky hand. Then we help with every homework assignment and buy all the shoes and clothes.

You may want to run away like Hagar, but understand that only God gives life. Whether by adoption or from artificial or traditional insemination, anytime God allows you to parent one of His precious little ones, you're blessed and highly favored. Even if you didn't plan the little one, God's plan provided for and equipped you to handle all that may be involved.

I treasure this wonderful and empowering quote about motherhood: "The king upon his throne has no higher work than has the mother. The mother is queen of her household. She has in her power the molding of her children's characters, that they may be fitted for the higher, immortal life. An angel could not ask for a higher mission; for in doing this work she is doing service for God. Let her only realize the high character of her task, and it will inspire her with courage. Let her realize the worth of her work and put on the whole armor of God, that she may resist the temptation to conform to the world's standard. Her work is for time and for eternity."*

So, my single-parenting sister, daily repeat to yourself, "I can do *all* things through Christ that strengthens me" and, "God will never leave me nor forsake me."

Now breathe deeply, pray, smile, and clean up any mess that has taken place while you were reading this devotional.

D. Reneé Mobley

---

* Ellen G. White, *The Adventist Home,* (Nashville: Southern Publishing, 1952), 231, 232.

God Is Always With You

*"When you pass through the waters, I will be with you;
and through the rivers, they shall not overwhelm you;
when you walk through fire you shall not be burned,
and the flame shall not consume you."*
—Isaiah 43:2, ESV

My father passed away when I was thirteen years old. At the time, I turned my emotions off, without knowing how to turn them on again. I didn't shed a single tear. I didn't know it at the time, but, of course, I was depressed. I slept through an entire year, hardly eating or speaking. My grades suffered tremendously, but, by the grace of God, I made it into and out of high school. Looking back now, I figure it was simply the only way I could cope. I was in so much pain that I closed myself off in order to avoid being hurt again. I shut everyone out.

In the years that followed, there were times when all I wanted to do was cry, but the tears wouldn't come. I felt so much guilt for not feeling the sadness that my mother and sister felt.

The summer before my first year of university, I got back down on my knees for the first time in years. It felt wrong. It didn't feel like anyone was listening, but I burst into uncontrollable sobs that went on for hours. That night I realized I wasn't sad. I was angry. I was angry at God. He was the only one who could have answered my prayers and kept my family intact.

That same night I prayed for forgiveness. I asked for help with all the anger and bitterness I had bottled up for years. I asked that God would continue to be there for me throughout my years in university. Only He could open every door that I believed was closed and allow me to attend a university where I could not only receive an education but also strengthen my relationship with Christ. He is the only one who fully understood my father's suffering through his illness, his inner thoughts, and his spiritual life. He knew when the time was right for my father to close his eyes and go to sleep.

God is the one who will reunite my family once again in heaven. He was by my side every step of the way, waiting patiently for me to open up and allow the healing process to begin. He stayed by my side as I wandered away during my first year of university, and He will stay by my side as I continue my schooling and spiritual journey.

Aiyana Duran

Jim's Journey

Search me, God, and know my heart. . . .
and lead me in the way everlasting.
—Psalm 139:23, 24, NIV

Jim Johnson had just started a new job working for a heating company. One of his first assignments was to service the furnace of a farming family, Dan and Clara Oster, southeast of Greeley, Colorado. They wanted their furnace checked for the winter season. An older man, Phil, was training Jim. Phil soon found a furnace part that needed replacing, so he left Jim and went back into town to purchase the part.

Jim soon completed his assigned task, sat down in the semidark musty cellar, and began smoking cigarettes. It seemed to Jim as if Phil was taking a very long time. Being quite bored, he noticed—and began to read—some old Christian magazines. Having a good bit of time, he sat there smoking and reading. As he continued reading, the Holy Spirit began to work on Jim's heart. Things from his past began to stir in his mind. His grandmother had been a Christian, and Jim had been baptized years before in 1958. But his family had left the church as quickly as they had joined it.

Phil eventually returned to the farm with the furnace part. He and Jim installed it, cleaned up their mess, and were ready to leave when Mrs. Oster began talking with Jim. "I read some of your church magazines in the cellar. My family were once members of your denomination," Jim shared. Mrs. Oster shared her faith with Jim. Jim's encounter with the Oster family stayed with him. A couple of years later, during a hospital stay, a church elder came to visit him. Jim shared his story, the Holy Spirit continued working, and Jim and his wife were baptized. Jim says the kindness of the lady who had saved her old religious magazines had changed his heart.

The Oster family for whom Jim did his work are my in-laws, so he shared this story with me. No doubt, if someone had seen Jim sitting in that cellar smoking cigarettes, they would not have held out much hope for a conversion story. But God saw Jim's heart. "People look at the outward appearance, but the LORD looks at the heart" (1 Samuel 16:7, NIV).

We must never stop praying for family members and friends who have not yet given their hearts to Jesus.

Sharon Oster

Without Purse

Then Jesus asked them, "When I sent you without purse,
bag or sandals, did you lack anything?"
"Nothing," they answered.
—Luke 22:35, NIV

I love bags and purses—most of us ladies do. I love them in all colors, including red and yellow. I have crocheted and faux leather bags. I just love them! One morning I decided that what I had on didn't match the bag I'd been using, so I transferred its contents into the one that I now needed. I stepped out of my house. As I began walking, a car pulled alongside me. "Would you like a ride?" offered a neighbor. At school that day, a colleague shared her lunch with me. Then, lo and behold, I got another ride home. These same blessings followed me the next day.

Sometime during the next day, I sat at my desk and grew hungry. I decided to purchase something to eat and rummaged through my bag for my wallet. It wasn't there! I frantically searched my desk drawers—still, no wallet. My handbag had been near me all morning, so I knew that my wallet had not been stolen. The only place it could be was at home, and that's where I found it.

It dawned on me that I had taken this wallet out of my handbag during the transfer of contents from one purse to the other. For almost two days, I had not even realized that it was missing. I was amazed by how God had taken such meticulous care of me. He had covered me while I was unknowingly vulnerable. For two days, I had flown around like a sparrow, unaware of how God had been lovingly taking care of my transportation and food needs through the small, loving favors of others.

As the enormity of what could have happened enveloped me, I asked myself, *What if I had taken a bus and realized that I had no money when I was about to pay?* A still, small Voice replied, *I would have taken care of that too. Trust Me.*

It was true. I had been out in the world "without purse," yet I had lacked nothing. If God could take such meticulous care of me, our heavenly Father can surely take care of you. Matthew 10:29–31 assures us that we are worth much more to Him than many sparrows. Today, let's trust God for our modern-day-manna miracles and pillar-by-night provisions. He will provide day by day, moment by moment, and from one need to another.

Judelia Medard-Santiesteban

From Payday to Payday

*But my God shall supply all your need
according to his riches in glory by Christ Jesus.*
—Philippians 4:19, KJV

Many people live from payday to payday, and I admit that I am one of them. But when I look at what the Lord has done for me and continues to do for me, my outlook about payday changes. We received a notice from the landlord that our lease would not be renewed and that we had sixty days in which to move. Twenty-three days later, we found a much better apartment that was closer to work. We signed the lease and moved into our new home. What a blessing!

The move, however, came with challenges. We hired a guy to help with the move, but we had to fire him the first day. That left my husband and me with everything to do. The U-Haul rental company kept phoning about the return of their truck. When we finally returned the truck, it cost much more than the credit we had on our card. The rental company told us we could make payments. Blessed! The new apartment manager required a security deposit of eleven hundred dollars, which was eight hundred dollars more than required for our previous apartment. This was an unexpected expense. We were almost completely moved in, but our funds were very low, and payday was still about fifteen days away! We prayed that the Lord would bless us with the funds we needed.

A few days later, I went to the mailbox and retrieved the one lonely envelope inside. The return address was designated as "Class Action Settlement." I thought I was being notified of another class-action suit—that seems to be what's "in" these days. However, when I opened the envelope, I found a check for $129. Praise the Lord! That would certainly last us until payday. Another blessing.

But where did this come from? I wondered. Believe it or not, the sentence above the actual check read, "Please do not call and ask any questions!" *Well, OK, Lord. I will not question what You are doing. I now know I must live from blessing to blessing.*

How true that God, unlike us, never changes His mind. He never goes back on His word. "God always keeps his promises" (Numbers 23:19, CEV).

I just thank Him and now go from blessing to blessing, giving Him the glory!

Sylvia A. Franklin

"May I Hold Your Hand?"

"Do not fear, for I am with you;
Do not anxiously look about you, for I am your God.
I will strengthen you, surely I will help you,
Surely I will uphold you with My righteous right hand."
—Isaiah 41:10, NASB

My cell phone rang as I was leaving the grocery store. Hastily looking at the caller ID, I saw my doctor's name. After sharing about my recent breast biopsy results, she said the dreaded words: "You have cancer." She continued. "I've already made a referral to one of the best surgeons I know."

I remembered my recent physical exam. "I want you to have a mammogram every year," my doctor had stated. My new insurance company recommended one every two years. Thankfully, the small lump had been found early. I sat in total silence. *God, why me?* Tears were lurking. During the next few weeks, my emotions often drifted in anxiety's direction.

My surgery date arrived. Before my 12:30 P.M. surgery, diagnostic and nuclear medicine procedures had to be completed, including the biopsy of dye-injected lymph nodes. Apprehensively, I lay down on a cold gurney. Suddenly someone grabbed my right hand. Looking up, I saw a very kind face. "Harryette," she greeted, "may I hold your hand?" The stranger continued, "Most of our patients find this procedure very painful. I want you to squeeze my hand just as hard as you need to. I can assure you my hand will not break!"

The pain was incredible—worse than I had imagined. As I winced, tightly squeezing her hand, I felt the technician grab my left hand. I heard, "You may squeeze my hand too!"

That day, along with my prayers, I felt the strength from many other prayers ascending heavenward. Yet in the gesture of one caring person, I felt a loving heavenly Father holding my hand, being there for me exactly when I needed Him. Suddenly fear subsided. Even as I was wheeled into the operating room, I no longer felt anxiety but a heaven-sent peace.

At the moment we need Him most, God is there! All we have to do is ask. I had shared with Him my thoughts and frustrations all along this journey. And at the moment I needed to feel His presence, He was there—holding my hand just as He promised.

Harryette Aitken

Power Source

Abide in me, and I in you. As the branch cannot bear fruit of itself,
except it abide in the vine; no more can ye, except ye abide in me.
—John 15:4, KJV

I always anticipated the Sunday-morning Olive Press Prayer Ministry meetings. I would wake up early to join others in connecting with the Godhead through the study of the Word and standing in the gap for others who need prayer, as well as ourselves. What refreshing and rewarding experiences! One Saturday night, before tucking myself into bed, I connected the charger to my mobile phone so it would be fully charged for the nearly two hours of prayer, praise, thanksgiving, inspirational readings, and praying over the prayer requests.

The next morning I offered the opening prayer, thanking God for the blessings He showered over us during the unconscious hours of the night. Then praise reports were given. A prayer of thanksgiving was offered, followed by a reading from the inspirational book *The Desire of Ages*. I read along in my copy of the book while the eloquent reader occasionally paused to explain certain portions as we progressed.

My phone speaker was on, but, all of a sudden, it went silent. *The phone is acting up*, I thought, as I repeatedly pressed a button, but to no avail. I got up and plugged the phone into the charger again. No power. I went to unplug the phone from the charger and try another outlet. Then, I discovered that although the charger cord was in the phone, the charger was not connected to the electrical outlet. But then, with all connections intact, the phone lit up, and the battery sign came on. Immediately I learned a lesson. We read our Bibles and pray, but are we truly connected to the Source of life-giving power? Are we grounded in and rooted in that Source? Are we powered up to witness effectively? I had been disconnected from the group, missing the prayers and the devotional. During that time, I felt powerless and defeated.

When I shared this experience, my friend Mandy encouraged me, saying, "Write, Rubes, write! Write about this powerful thought." The Holy Spirit was at work, for I had already thought about sharing this experience in writing the very moment I realized what had happened.

Ladies, I admonish us all to get—and stay—connected to the Source of our strength, God. He is able to keep us powered up as we study up and pray up every day.

Ruby H. Enniss-Alleyne

Unsubscribe!

I decided to deal with only one subject—
Jesus Christ, who was crucified.
—1 Corinthians 2:2, GW

A wise friend recently reminded me about the importance of setting boundaries in even the small matters of life. So the next time I booted up my computer, instead of simply deleting those unsolicited email advertisements, I scrolled down to the bottom of each one in search of a permanent solution—the Unsubscribe link.

Clicking that link will most certainly put control of the inbox back into my hands, I thought. *I should have done this a long time ago. This will be a piece of cake!*

My click on the minuscule Unsubscribe link at the bottom of the first email advertisement summoned a pop-up screen. It bore the message, "We value our friendship with you, Carolyn, and are so sorry if we've worn out our welcome. May we contact you once weekly instead of daily?" Was that a twinge of guilt I suddenly felt since the reply seemed so personal? Yet with resolve, I clicked the No option.

My click of the next email's Unsubscribe link brought, "Carolyn, may we share just future flash deals with you?" Sigh. But again, no. The third electronic ad queried, "Why do you want to end this pleasant relationship? We feel so bad about losing you!"

Come on, people, I groaned. *I'm not resigning from membership to some elite club. I just want you out of my* inbox! Ignoring the "Click here to be reinstated on our mailing list" and "Continue shopping" links, I finished my laborious task—but only after unsubscribing to fifteen additional email ads. I had no idea I'd been getting so much unsolicited email.

Then I suddenly wondered, *Am I fully aware of distractions, situations, and temptations sneaking into my soul's inbox from which I need—intentionally and perseveringly—to unsubscribe?* The apostle Paul wrote, "Have no fellowship with the *unfruitful* works of darkness" (Ephesians 5:11, KJV, emphasis added). Was that his way of warning us to guard against time-wasting pastimes and influences that would distract from a total focus on Jesus? Reflecting further on his words, I suspect Paul was reminding us that whatever slips into our mental, emotional, or spiritual inboxes—which does not keep us focused on Jesus—we must make every effort to unsubscribe from, getting it out of our lives. From what might you need to unsubscribe today?

Carolyn Rathbun Sutton

What's Your Sign?

"For God so loved the world that He gave His only begotten Son, that whoever believes in Him should not perish but have everlasting life."
—John 3:16, NKJV

As I drive to the church where I worship during the summer months, I travel on the Second New Hampshire Turnpike, a scenic route that winds its way through several small mountains. This winding rural road passes through the center of several small communities. This road provides me with a lot to see on my way to church: wildlife such as turkey, deer, and moose; American flags hanging from utility poles; a wind farm with impressive windmills atop a mountain ridge; and the vivid fall foliage of New England.

This year, however, I noticed that as I travel through the town of Unity, two houses have quaint little signposts that hold changeable signs. I have seen, among others, the following messages: "Repent or perish!" "God is not mocked!" "Prepare to meet thy God!"

These signs took me by surprise the first time I noticed them. While I do admit the truth of these messages, they are not what I would choose to hang from a signpost in front of my own home.

So I started to ponder: *What message would I hang if the signpost were in my front yard?* Certainly, I would want people to know that my God is a God of love and that believing in Jesus is a wonderful experience. I would want to communicate the hope available to all who believe in Him and the life-changing power and joy that comes from a love relationship with Him.

As I traveled along the bumpy road, my thoughts returned to my reality. It would be futile to put up a signpost in my front yard. My house is on a narrow back road on which very few vehicles travel. No one would notice a sign in front of my house.

Then it hit me—I don't need a sign in front of my house to communicate the many truths about Jesus. I already *am* the sign!

When people interact with me, I hope they are learning about God's love at the same time. Today, we have the opportunity to reflect the infinite love of Jesus to all who are around us. We get to decide what the sign of our lives will communicate to others about Him.

What's your sign?

Marsha Hammond-Brummel

The Unforgettable Event

When my father and my mother forsake me,
Then the LORD will take care of me.
—Psalm 27:10, NKJV

It was a thrilling experience when my husband received his admission letter from a university in Zimbabwe to pursue his studies after fifteen years of pastoring, twelve of them with me by his side. We were told that during my husband's studies, we would be given a half salary and that the church would give us additional financial support. We had also been saving money to further his education. Finally, completing our arrangements, we flew from Kenya to Zimbabwe for his studies.

Very soon, we made several new friends on campus. Everything went very well during the first two years. However, at the beginning of our third year, the situation changed drastically. Not only had we used up all the money we had saved back in Kenya for education but also—for one reason or another—we had not received the promised financial support from the church. These factors led to an acute financial crisis. You see, besides my husband's working hard to earn good grades, he had also been working day and night to provide for our family's needs as well as to contribute to his school fees. I did my best to support him in all his endeavors, especially in praying hard for him. I formed a prayer group with my fellow believers: Mrs. Mugadza, Mama Hope, and Night. I would share my prayer requests with them. They also knew how hard I was working to raise money to help provide for our family needs.

The most unforgettable experience during this time was when our barrel of food became exhausted! I asked my husband, "Are you aware that in the next three days, we shall have no more food in the house? How shall we survive?" He told me that God would provide. At the end of that third day, I scheduled to meet with someone. When I arrived, I was told that a good Samaritan had offered to feed us for the next whole year, and he did so!

Sisters, "when my father and my mother forsake me, Then the LORD will take care of me" (Psalm 27:10, NKJV). How true that "God is our refuge and strength, a very present help in trouble" (Psalm 46:1, KJV)!

May we always trust in Him regardless of the hardships we suffer.

Naomi N. Otore

Who Am I?

I am my beloved's and my beloved is mine.
—Song of Songs 6:3, NIV

I had worked as a board-certified chaplain for ten years. For eight of those years, I was the department director of a chaplaincy department; then, my family felt a call to move.

I searched high and low for work in my field. I did on-call work a couple of weekends a month and found other miscellaneous short-term jobs for two years. Yet my heart was set on a chaplaincy position. My identity was wrapped up in it. I loved the ministry, I loved the people I met, and I loved feeling like my work mattered. But opportunities just were not to be found.

I prayed, begging God to open the door for me. I did my best to trust Him. I had great support from my husband and friends. But most days, I was home, caring for grandchildren or cleaning the house—and feeling sorry for myself. I didn't understand what God was doing. He had opened the original doors into chaplaincy in an amazing way.

One day I visited my former chaplaincy training supervisor. I told him what was or wasn't going on and explained my frustrations and feelings of loss.

Instead of being sympathetic, which I had expected, he asked me a crucial question: "Who are you, and is your identity only in being a chaplain?"

It seemed he was sending me down a rabbit trail. After all, I was a chaplain, wasn't I? Didn't God call me to this work for Him? To say I prayed a lot about these questions to gain insight would be an understatement. Somehow, I couldn't seem to get water from a stone.

One morning in the shower, a children's song came to me that went something like this: "Who am I? Someone special to Jesus."

That was it! That was my identity! Of course, I am Jesus' child and totally special to Him. Right after this realization, I recalled answers from my childhood Bible study questions. I remembered that I am a child of God, one of heaven's heirs, and a temple of the Holy Spirit. My heavenly Father loves me. Who could ever find a more precious and perfect identity than that? Amazingly, a week after God gave me these precious insights, I received a call to full-time chaplaincy work. God had just needed me to be clear, first, about who I was!

Carolyn J. H. Strzyzykowski

When Angel Hands Intervened—Part 1

The angel of the LORD encampeth round about them that fear him, and delivereth them.
—Psalm 34:7, KJV

It was our first trip to large area-wide meetings in Montego Bay, Jamaica. We were a very new pastoral couple and had decided to carpool as that was the most economical practice in the seventies. Three other young church workers were traveling with us.

"This is going to be an exciting day!" exclaimed one of the passengers. We all agreed with the statement because the speaker for the youth rally was well known for his stirring presentations and was a favorite among young people.

We arrived safely at the meeting site and in good time. The amphitheater was buzzing with excitement, and the largely youthful audience was busy meeting and greeting one another. Although the meeting went on for several hours, no one was ready to leave when it was over. The youth leader had motivated, energized, and challenged the youth to return to their home churches and set their communities "on fire!"

The five of us loaded back into our little compact car and started our journey back to our respective places of work. We were all excited about the great day we'd had. By the middle of our journey, the three passengers in the back seat had fallen asleep.

Then it happened! Our car suddenly went out of control, careening from one side of the usually busy road to the other. "Jesus!" I screamed, a one-word prayer.

In a split second, the car suddenly veered toward a high bank on the side of the road and then came to a complete stop. I believe an angel had intervened and taken the steering wheel, getting us off the usually busy road. Upon examination, we discovered that the right rear wheel had disengaged from the car because of a broken axle. Again, I thought, *Only an angel!*

The first person to arrive on the scene of our accident was a human "angel." We hardly knew him. Yet not only did he get us to his mechanic nearby but he also paid the repair bill on the spot and in full. "Just pay me when you can," he said. "I know you are young workers."

To this day, we call that corner "angel curve." God had put us into the protective and caring hands of two angels in one day. Praise Him!

Claudette Garbutt-Harding

When Angel Hands Intervened—Part 2

For he shall give his angels charge over thee,
to keep thee in all thy ways. They shall bear thee up
in their hands, lest thou dash thy foot against a stone.
—Psalm 91:11, 12, KJV

Some time had passed since our "angel curve" experience when God had miraculously spared us five occupants returning from church meetings in a compact car that suddenly lost a wheel when the axle broke. Now He had granted my pastor-evangelist husband and me a new baby. These were some of the most exciting days of my life! After waiting for more than seven years, I was now happily mothering Keithia, my bundle of joy. She was just over three weeks old, and her dad was beside himself with joy taking her to meet Grandma.

I cradled the baby in my arms and took my seat behind the excited driver. We set out early, wanting to spend most of the day with Grandma and return to an important Sunday-night meeting at a village church where my husband was conducting a six-week evangelistic series.

We were traveling on the same road that connected this western town to Montego Bay and on which we'd experienced the broken axle accident. Yet that day, even the little one seemed excited, as this was her first long road trip. There was so much joy in the car. I still cherish the memory. The joy, however, came to a sudden halt when our car came around a well-known and sharp corner. A flatbed trailer truck, loaded with equipment, was precariously parked on the corner. Another trailer truck was coming head-on. There was no place to go—death seemed inevitable. The workmen covered their faces and turned their backs, waiting for the impact. Our adrenaline kicked in as we anticipated the worst.

In seconds, we found our vehicle in a safe spot beside the parked trailer. A clear miracle! Our angels had intervened again. This time, they must have lifted the car with us in it, for we had not crashed into a "stone" of any kind (see the Bible text above). Immediately the truck crew was on the scene, this time with a measuring tape to prove there was no way our car could have passed between those two trailer trucks. We agreed. God had done it again!

Today we have not one but two "angel curves" on that road, not even four miles apart. We even got to spend some "alleluia moments" with Grandma. I have written "PP" in my Bible beside Psalm 91:11, 12. That is a "proven promise" for me in God's Word. I still praise Him!

Claudette Garbutt-Harding

The Forked Tongue

The remnant of Israel shall not do iniquity, nor speak lies.
—Zephaniah 3:13, KJV

One day one of my husband's younger employees informed him, "My grandmother died, and I need to leave work early today to attend her funeral."* My husband readily gave this young man permission to be off work for the afternoon. Several days later, however, my husband was surprised when he met the young man's grandmother in a local store where he shared with her the news of her "funeral," which was to have taken place a few days earlier! It does not take long to know if someone is honest or not, for time has a way of revealing the truth.

Dishonesty has many faces. I was once in a conversation with a man who was trying to convince me of something that I knew was false. When finally aware that his tactic was not working, he admitted that he was trying to manipulate me. I suppose he thought I would at least be impressed with his verbal skills. I quietly told him I was well aware of what he was trying to do. No matter what wrapping we place around a lie, it is still unacceptable and remains a lie. Sophistication or cunning cannot whitewash a lie.

Then there is the visitor who finds you down in the garden dirt, digging and weeding. Standing before you in their finest, they ask, "May I help you with what you are doing?" Time reveals this individual does not get his or her hands in the dirt, if possible. The pretense is to give the impression of what one is not! Or what about the teenager who reports to his parents that he "went to church"? In reality, he did intentionally step into the foyer but promptly left the church, taking a joyride with a friend. This is just another example of "telling the truth" with the intent to deceive—the most dangerous of all lies!

Pure, absolute truth cannot be stretched, embellished, sensationalized, or colored. God's true followers must be transparent, straightforward, and honest in all things. The apostle Paul counsels, "Put on your new nature, and be renewed as you learn to know your Creator and become like him" (Colossians 3:10, NLT).

Dottie Barnett

---

* This entry first appeared as "The Forced Tounge" *Whispers of His Wisdom* (blog), October 26, 2015, https://www.whispersofhiswisdom.com/2015/10/.

Give Me This Mountain

I will lift up my eyes to the hills—
From whence comes my help?
My help comes from the LORD,
Who made heaven and earth.
—Psalm 121:1, 2, NKJV

Reading the story of Caleb reminded me of the mountains of the Maracas Valley, where I lived during my childhood. It was the most awe-inspiring experience to view their magnificent splendor each morning. It was as if I stood in the very presence of the divine Creator. The mist rising among them like torrents of smoke brought to mind the greatness, beauty, and power of God.

Perhaps eighty-five-year-old Caleb envisioned such a scene when he asked Joshua for the three-thousand-foot, giant-populated mountain of Hebron. Through faith-inspired eyes, he saw the grandeur and beauty that could evolve after the nine- to thirteen-foot tall giants were vanquished. But could the Anakim be driven out? Caleb was not a fainthearted man! Although his own tribe of Judah lived among the Jebusites (which they could not drive out because of fear and unbelief), Caleb faced his own challenge with courage, faith, and wholehearted trust in the mighty power of the living God. Despite Caleb's forty-year journey in the wilderness and then having to wait five more years until all tribal allotments had been assigned, Caleb remained undaunted. He would claim his inheritance. And like Jesus, the Lion of the tribe of Judah, he was determined to be victorious. Maybe Caleb intended to prove that nothing is too hard for God, that His promises and supply of strength never fail. And they didn't. "Caleb drove out the three sons of Anak from there: Sheshai, Ahiman, and Talmai, the children of Anak. Then he went up from there to the inhabitants of Debir" (Joshua 15:14, 15, NKJV).

It matters not how rough the terrain, there is a mountain to climb. So my question is this: Are you a Caleb, willing to undertake the challenge of conquering the giants in your life? Not just the disturbances of daily living but also the spiritual forces of evil in "heavenly places" (Ephesians 6:12, NKJV)? Today, be a woman of faith. Ask God to give you the mountain that may so severely intimidate you. Then, like Caleb, rely on God to make you a conqueror.

Maureen Thomas

Slow and Steady

So then, my beloved brethren, let every man be swift to hear,
slow to speak, slow to wrath; for the wrath of man
does not produce the righteousness of God.
—James 1:19, 20, NKJV

The text message stopped me, took my breath away for a second, and felt like a knife that had been plunged into my heart. It was my oldest son's birthday, and I was planning on making him a special dinner. I had texted him to tell him to try to be hungry this evening as I was going to make him something special. I was not prepared for the answer I got back. "Try to be hungry? If I am hungry, I am hungry, and if I'm not, I'm not. Also, a 'birthday supper' is completely unnecessary." There it was, like a slap in the face. *How could he say that? See if I do anything like that for him again. So ungrateful. Doesn't he care about how I feel? I'm done.*

Normally, my son is very logical and straightforward. He doesn't have a vindictive or mean-spirited bone in his body. He is just very matter-of-fact and tells it as he sees it. So I should have known, from his perspective, a special fuss made just for him wasn't necessary. But I reacted emotionally instead of slowing down and thinking through what he said.

Luckily, I didn't respond quickly or out of my anger and hurt. Instead, I waited and took counsel from my husband. Then the first chance my son had to come in the house and see me, he apologized, saying, "I didn't mean for it to come out the way it did. I was only trying to tell you that you needn't go to a lot of trouble for me. That's why I hate texting."

How many times in our lives do we not take the time to slow down and let words and situations sink in before we react? I can tell you, friends, that I have done it more times than I care to admit—causing more harm than if I had just waited and prayed before saying or doing anything. Thankfully, I didn't react out of my misunderstanding of my son's text, which could have caused more pain than just my hurt feelings.

God wants us to be mindful, careful in how we act and react when dealing with one another. He urges us to be slow to anger and slow to speak, two areas that can cause great damage in relationships. In the busy, fast-paced lives we live, let's all make sure we take the time to listen carefully, to be slow to speak, and to be even slower to become angry.

My prayer for you, dear friend, is that you will live a slow and steady life in Christ.

Debra Snyder

My Sister

In the multitude of my anxieties within me,
Your comforts delight my soul.
—Psalm 94:19, NKJV

At the time of writing, my sister died this week. I'm very sad; I was not present. However, she was surrounded by children who loved her. The pastor called to express his sympathy, and I appreciated his call. He quoted some Bible texts about the blessing of the resurrection. That should have given me peace; it didn't. I felt surrounded by a heavy cloud, as I explained that I was afraid those texts did not apply in this situation.

We grew up in a Christian home and were raised by godly parents who daily prayed for both daughters, committing them to God at a very young age. I'm sure they claimed Bible promises about "saving children" before they died. I also prayed regularly for my sister and tried to reach out with spiritual books and suggestions, but each time I felt that she shut me out. My sadness increased. How can I have a happy thought about the future in heaven without my sister?

An opportune story came up in my Bible reading this week—the story of Samuel, who followed God's instructions in choosing the right person to take King Saul's place. As Samuel was led to Jesse's sons, he was impressed with the oldest one. However, the Lord told him, "God sees not as man sees, for man looks at the outward appearance, but the LORD looks at the heart" (1 Samuel 16:7, NASB). I had to acknowledge, gratefully, that all I saw was the outward appearance. I'm so glad God knew my sister's heart! I'm too quick to judge by externals. How thankful I am that God knows us inside and outside, from the beginning of life to the end, and His judgments are always fair and loving. My time of influence is over with my sister. At this point, I must choose to trust God's judgment, and I do.

I know that God is "not willing that any should perish but that all should come to repentance" (2 Peter 3:9, NKJV). My dad used to say that God would save all who are safe to save. He knows those who love Him and would be happy in heaven. That's who He wants there.

I'm confident God knows best! He gave me this promise: "Fear thou not; for I am with thee: be not dismayed; for I am thy God: I will strengthen thee; yea, I will help thee; yea, I will uphold thee with the right hand of my righteousness" (Isaiah 41:10, KJV). And what's better than that?

Roxy Hoehn

Don't Doubt, Just Believe

Your wife will be like a fruitful vine
within your house;
your children will be like olive shoots
around your table.
—Psalm 128:3, NIV

How could the promise in today's verse be true for us? My husband and I had been married for twenty-five years! The older we got, the fewer chances we had of having children. Then one January day in 2017, while driving, I poured out my heart to the Lord in tears (as did Hannah when pouring out her heart for a son) and reminded Him of the promises He made in His Word.

"Ask and it will be given to you; seek and you will find; knock and the door will be opened to you. For everyone who asks receives; the one who seeks finds; and to the one who knocks, the door will be opened" (Matthew 7:7, 8, NIV). Driving and praying, I mentioned that perhaps we could adopt a child.

Around 4:00 (European time) on an April morning, I received a phone call from the Christian layman we support in the Philippines. He said, "I have two kids here, a four-year-old boy and a two-year-old girl. Do you want to accept them?" I was speechless. I said I could not decide by myself and that I would call him back. To make a long story short, the kids—a brother and sister—are now in my hometown in the Philippines. We send them to school and provide for their needs. When their young mother died, their father didn't know how to support them with only his low-paying job. No one in his family wanted to accept the children, so we decided to help them. The promise of Psalm 128 is now a reality in my life. The Lord has provided seven children for us—not only financially but also spiritually. God is so good (all the time)!

He has granted me the desires of my heart (see Psalm 20:4). May He grant your heart's desires as well. And may He fulfill in your life the purposes for which He created you.

He knows what is best, and He remarkably answered our prayers. He is always on time. So when doubts are clouding your mind about God's promises, brush away those doubts. Tell yourself, *My God is so big, and He knows my needs.*

Even if it's difficult, trust, believe, and wait. God will do the rest.

Loida Gulaja Lehmann

"Don't Be Afraid"

Overhearing what they said, Jesus told him,
"Don't be afraid; just believe."
—Mark 5:36, NIV

Life is hard sometimes. God never promised us that we would not suffer or that we would not have problems. But He did promise that He was going to accompany us each step of the way. However, there are situations in which—even though we have asked for help and blessing—we do not feel He has answered. Perhaps Jairus, the synagogue leader, felt that way after he pleaded with Jesus to come and heal his dying daughter. Though Jesus accompanied Jairus, He stopped to heal someone else on the way. How much faith Jairus must have had to believe that if Jesus just touched his daughter, she was going to be healed!

When we are facing our own problems and difficulties, do we have the same faith as Jairus? Do we pray with the same assurance?

After Jesus had finished healing another woman on the way to Jairus's house, some people came from the leader's house with a discouraging message. " 'Your daughter is dead,' they said. 'Why bother the teacher anymore?' " (Mark 5:35, NIV). Jairus had seen Jesus heal others, but his daughter died. His world must have fallen apart, but what about faith? Jesus, with His characteristic empathy, could understand what was going on in the emotions and mind of Jairus. Jesus told him, "Don't be afraid; just believe" (Mark 5:36, NIV).

Jesus knows that our faith falters when we do not receive what we ask for. He knows that fear floods in if what we expect is not fulfilled. Yet today, He tells us the same thing as well: Don't be afraid; only believe. Jesus went into Jairus's house, where He said, "Why all this commotion and wailing? The child is not dead but asleep" (Mark 5:39, NIV). Jesus redefined the situation, giving it new meaning and hope. In other words: "It is not what you think; go beyond."

Jesus took the child by the hand and said to her, "Little girl, I say to you, get up" (Mark 5:41, NIV). And the girl got up. Jesus did not answer the leader's request, as Jairus had asked it. First, the father had to experience the desperation of his daughter's death. Yet, in the end, Jesus responded to the father's request in a way that glorified God the most. Therefore, if today you are living through a difficult situation about which you have asked God for help (yet you have not received the anticipated answers), hear Jesus say to you, "Do not fear; only believe."

Cecilia Nanni

My Amazing Church Family

Beloved, let us love one another: for love is from God;
and every one that loveth is born of God, and knoweth God.
—1 John 4:7, KJV

April 8, 2018, was the most devastating day of my life. My beloved husband of forty-three years, Ezra, passed away peacefully in his sleep. Earlier that day, Elaine, one of the women's ministries leaders, and I decided to go shopping for gifts for our annual women's tea party scheduled for April 15. Back at home, I chatted with my husband about our new waterless cooking pot set, which we had just purchased. We decided we would cook lasagna in it for dinner. It was our first time making lasagna in a pot. When dinner was ready, I informed Ezra, but he said he was not quite ready to eat and would let me know when he was. He was working on information for our tax form and wanted to complete it first. I waited for his call to tell me he was ready to eat, but it never came. So I went to where he was working. At that moment, I realized that my husband had quietly slipped away.

The next few hours were a blur as my daughters, siblings, and church family were all around, praying and consoling me. Everyone was offering to help in any way possible. I felt overwhelmed with all types of emotions, but most importantly, I also felt loved. Assuredly, it was at that time when I knew I would not be bearing this burden alone.

My brother, Stanley, and sister, Norma, sprang into action and took charge. Thus began the love and support that played such an integral role in helping us navigate through this difficult time. I can only say it is heavenly to be a part of the family of God. My brothers and sisters of my home church were with me every step of the way on this sorrowful journey. They phoned and prayed, brought flowers, provided food, gave monetary gifts, and visited me. This care and love continued through the day that Ezra was laid to rest on April 22. Today, their encouragement continues unabated. A day never passes without someone calling, sending a text, or praying with me through WhatsApp.

On April 8, 2018, my life radically changed, but with the love and support of my immediate family and my church family, I can say that my God is good, and He loves me.

My sisters, God loves you and will never forsake you. Be a part of His amazing family.

Maureen Ferdinand

Cheerfulness Amid Chaos

*Although the fig tree shall not blossom, neither shall fruit
be in the vines; the labour of the olive shall fail,
and the fields shall yield no meat; the flock shall be cut
off from the fold, and there shall be no herd in the stalls:
Yet I will rejoice in the LORD, I will joy in the God of my salvation.*
—Habakkuk 3:17, 18, KJV

We all have opportunities every day to get upset and to go around frustrated. I used to get stressed and think, *I would be happy if my spouse was never rude and always treated me better. I would be happy if I got a promotion. I would be happy if my child behaved well.* Every day I came across circumstances that were stealing my joy. And this stress caused me to be irritable, short-tempered, and sleepless. I forgot how to smile, until one day I read Philippians 4:6. It states, "Do not be anxious about anything, but in every situation, by prayer and petition, with thanksgiving, present your requests to God" (NIV). It was then that I realized that I shouldn't let others influence my happiness. I must have a childlike trust in the Father for my everyday needs. He will lead me through every difficult circumstance. I need to keep my spirit filled with heavenly joy. "Happy is that people . . . whose God is the LORD" (Psalm 144:15, KJV). So that is the secret to ultimate happiness.

Joy is something that comes out from the inside and affects the countenance of a person. The writer of Proverbs 15 says, "A merry heart maketh a cheerful countenance" and, "He that is of a merry heart hath a continual feast" (verses 13, 15, KJV). "Those who in everything make God first and last and best, are the happiest people in the world."* I continue to be happy no matter what the situation is because I trust God's Word (see Proverbs 16:20).

When I saw things in my life from the perspective of God's truth, it brought happiness to my heart and a continual feast into my life, even in the midst of troubles. I started to develop a cheerful countenance. It's our privilege as Christians to be the happiest people on earth, demonstrating that joy and happiness to all around us.

Dear Father, please make these truths sink into our hearts so that we can trust in Your goodness. Help us know that doing so will bring us happiness.

Esther Synthia Murali

---

* Ellen G. White, *Messages to Young People* (Nashville: Southern Publishing, 1930), 38.

Perfection

I praise you because I am fearfully and wonderfully made;
your works are wonderful,
I know that full well.
—Psalm 139:14, NIV

London, the owner of one of my favorite day spas, is from Vietnam. She has clear porcelain skin, dark hair, and kind eyes. I've always thought that she is beautiful, not just because of her looks but also because of her heart for people. She goes above and beyond for her clients, delivering five-star quality service and treating each client as if she were the only person in the spa.

But one day, I overheard her say something that made me sad. I was sitting in the comfortable leather chair, getting a pedicure, and London was giving a pedicure to the woman in the chair next to me. The woman was very stylish in her white capris, boatneck navy top, and gold jewelry. Her blond hair was cut short, perfectly framing her heart-shaped face. She had a flawless tan that many women would envy.

Sadness washed over me when I witnessed London gaze at the woman with awe and say, "I want to be a carbon copy of you."

It bothered me that London wanted to look different than the way that God had intended she look. The woman that London was serving was beautiful, but London was equally as beautiful in the way that God made her to be.

It was also a lesson for me. How many times have I looked at someone else and wished I looked more like that person rather than how God created me to be? Too many times! As an adult who's more seasoned by life now, I'm "growing out of" my pursuit of perfection in how I look because I realize that in God's eyes, I am already perfect. He said in His Word that I am "fearfully and wonderfully made" (Psalm 139:14, NIV).

We all have our own ideas of what it means to embody physical perfection. However, we need to see that God already thinks we're perfect just as He made us, and He doesn't want us to be the carbon copy of anyone else.

Alexis A. Goring

Blessed Are the Peacemakers

"Blessed are the peacemakers,
for they shall be called [daughters] of God."
—Matthew 5:9, NKJV

For many years I was a "stringer" for a city newspaper, writing historical pieces and human-interest stories. My editor asked one day, "How would you like to take a crack at writing up what goes on at the county supervisory board meeting? Since you live near the courthouse, it would save me some running." I agreed and quietly took notes at the meeting. Then a much-debated topic came to the floor. The county had earmarked ten thousand dollars for firefighting improvements. Each of the three firefighter departments hoped they would be the lucky department. One of the supervisors announced the board had strongly considered dividing the money into two equal parts.

The question, "Who gets left out?" was answered with, "We haven't decided yet."

Each group clamored to explain why it needed the money more than the others. Everyone's reasons were valid. The arguments became loud and angry. At open-forum meetings, anyone can offer ideas. Praying silently that God would help me with my words, I stood.

When the chairman recognized me, I began, "Apparently, the only thing we agree on is that nobody wants to be left out. Why don't we split the money three ways? That would eliminate hurt feelings. Think of it as seed money—enough to start your projects. You can raise the extra money you need by selling the products that you already make for tourists to buy."

People looked at one another and nodded. The chairman smiled. "Would you like to make that a motion?" My motion was affirmed unanimously, and everyone excitedly discussed their fundraising plans. I thanked God that they were willing to solve their problem peacefully.

My editor liked my report but decided not to miss future meetings and covered them himself. I accepted that God meant for me to be at the courthouse that one time and prepared to be a "stringer" again. But God had another plan for me. My editor assigned me to a project that lasted several months. It gave me great satisfaction to contribute to the July 4, 1976, collector's edition of the city newspaper commemorating the bicentennial of the United States of America.

May you, as a daughter of God, be blessed as one of His peacemakers as well.

Bonnie Moyers

No Delay

"This vision is for a future time.... It will not be delayed."
—Habakkuk 2:3, NLT

I love the book of Habakkuk. It gives me permission to bring my questions to God. Even if God does not answer, it's wonderful knowing that He is there listening to not only my praise, thanks, and requests—but also to my questions. I think we've all questioned God about His long delay in returning for His children. Life gets harder and harder, and sometimes we are overwhelmed by the disasters we see on TV, lives lost from senseless violence, political turmoil, and much more.

I confess to feeling that time needs to move faster. Since my children were toddlers, I've told them Jesus is coming soon. Now they are adults, and I'm still saying the same words.

Sometimes I look at the world in which we live and ask myself if Bible prophecies are being fulfilled—*anything* to make His coming seem sooner rather than later. Then I read this verse from Habakkuk. Here, God is making His second reply to Habakkuk's questions. He reassures the prophet that his vision refers to the end of time. If it seems slow in getting here, though, we are to wait patiently, for the end will definitely come (see Habakkuk 2:3).

As I read God's words of comfort to Habakkuk, I realized God was also comforting me. His words comforted and strengthened my heart as I thought of the Second Coming. There *is* an "appointed time" for Christ's return. God *never* lies. He said He would return in John 14:1–3, and He *will*!

Finally, God says that "though it tarry, wait for it; because it will surely come, it will not tarry" (Habakkuk 2:3, KJV). To us, the fulfillment of this promise may seem late in coming, but God wants us to wait in faith and trust, knowing that not only will He return but also the fulfillment will *surely* come. God's time is not ours. Though we may be late at times, God is never late.

I don't know what "when" question you are struggling with today. "When will I get married, Lord?" "When will we be able to buy a home?" "When will I get a job, Lord?" The gentle reply comes back—there is an appointed time . . . so surrender.

Take heart, my sister. God does not lie, and He is ever faithful.

Heather-Dawn Small

Leaving a Legacy

This is the day the Lord has made;
We will rejoice and be glad in it.
—Psalm 118:24, NKJV

[We] shall see His face, and His name shall be on [our] foreheads.
—Revelation 22:4, NKJV

As I write this devotional, it is 2018. In three years, I'll be ninety, unless Jesus comes beforehand and time is no more. I hope that is the case. Or I may be in my grave awaiting Jesus' return. However, if you're reading this as a devotional in published book form, it is 2021.

Most of us have the good sense to prepare both an advance directive, regarding our care when our health issues seem terminal, and a will for distribution of our worldly assets with money set aside to pay for our burial or internment. But are you also leaving a legacy? With intention, I want to leave a legacy of both inspiration and encouragement.

Earlier this year, I wrote an article that appeared in our denomination's flagship publication. It was entitled, "At the Corner of . . . the Voice of an Anti-Retirement Advocate." As a result, I received via my email address—which appeared with my information at the end of the article—letters from readers across the United States of America and even one from the mayor of Chetwynd, British Columbia. Each email mentioned that the article had inspired the reader. These letters affirmed my desire to write to inspire others, to bring praise, honor, and glory to Jesus in some way. As correspondence ensued between the readers and me, I also learned my writing had helped them feel encouraged. And guess what? Each of them also inspired and encouraged me. They helped to send me on my way with the joy of service to my fellow wayfarers, as we travel the path to heaven together—most of whom I'll probably never meet until the kingdom of God is our home. Readers have always done this for me as I hope that I've always done for you.

So, this day, I ask you to reread the two memory verses at the top of this devotional. First, rejoice in this day, and rejoice further in the thought that soon we will see our Lord Jesus Christ and His very name will be on our foreheads. (I assume that means on the frontal lobes of our brains.) What a glorious day that will be! I look forward to our friendship throughout eternity.

Betty Kossick

You Are Loved

I have loved thee with an everlasting love:
therefore with lovingkindness have I drawn thee.
—Jeremiah 31:3, KJV

I had come back to work from a three-week vacation. More than six hundred emails waited for me, and I had pending work that needed my attention. While I tried to focus on my work, students kept coming to inquire about whatever they needed since it was the end of the semester. As I was speaking to one student, he asked me about something that he should already have known. Had he read the email that I usually send to all graduating students before they graduate? Just before I asked him why he had not read the email, I remembered. *Oops!* I had not sent the email to this group of students—I had been on vacation!

After attending to this student's needs, I hurried to send the email right away. This was their last day on campus, and they needed to receive it before they left. As I started to prepare the email, I remembered another email that I also needed to send to students. It was more important than the one I was working on. In order to prepare the second email, I needed to consult with my colleagues to be sure that they were done with their part of our work. As I was speaking to one of them, she asked me, "How did you remember this email now, having just returned from vacation?"

I just answered, "God loves me."

She replied immediately, "I'm sure He does. Just in case *you* doubt it, *I* know that He really loves you. I have known this about you for a long time now." I was taken aback; I had not expected such a response, especially because my colleague is not a Christian.

I kept on asking myself, *What is it that she has seen in our daily interactions that gives her such an impression that God really loves me?* I long for her to have such assurance for herself; nevertheless, it was so good to be reassured of God's love for me.

Have you ever questioned whether God loves, hears, knows, or accepts you? Do you ever feel like you are not worthy of anyone's love? As my colleague told me, let me say to you: "God loves you. Just in case *you* doubt it, *I* know He really loves you. He has always loved you, and He will always love you." How do I know? The Bible tells me so.

Lynn Mfuru Lukwaro

Super Strength or Angel Power?

*"Keep on asking, and you will receive what you ask for.
Keep on seeking, and you will find. Keep on knocking,
and the door will be opened to you."*
—Matthew 7:7, NLT

One day, a short time ago, I was faced with the monumental task of orchestrating a move from one house to another. Organizing this was the easy part, but the challenge came when it was time to move the really heavy items.

It so happened that my husband was traveling at the time, so I was left without any masculine strength to complete the heavy tasks.

To make the situation more challenging, I was cramped in a small space with many boxes, and I still had a lot more to pack. So I came up with the idea that I could create more packing space by moving the bed from its location in the center of the room to a spot in a corner.

The bed, however, was no ordinary bed. It was huge and heavy. So I muscled up and made several attempts at pushing the bed out of the way. Every attempt failed.

Unfortunately, I did not do what I should have done at the outset—pray. Many times when we face challenges, we try our own solutions instead of starting by seeking help from God. After a few failed attempts, reality hits and we realize there is not much that we can do.

So I came to my senses and prayed. I asked God to give me the strength to move the bed or send an angel to help. At the end of my prayer, I launched out in faith and tried to move the bed. Guess what? The bed moved!

I pushed and pushed until the bed was moved into its new location. I was stunned but elated. So whether God gave me super strength or provided angel power, the bed was relocated, and I glorified God.

This experience reminded me that God hears the prayers of His people and is more than able to answer them, no matter how small or great the problem may appear to us or others. God cares about us so much that He takes the time to tend to our troubles. Our text for today says we should ask God because He will answer while we are still speaking.

Today, is there a prayer you are waiting to have answered? Persevere in prayer—God is listening.

Taniesha K. Robertson-Brown

Our Biggest Cheerleader

"If you, then, though you are evil, know how to give
good gifts to your children, how much more will your Father
in heaven give good gifts to those who ask him!"
—Matthew 7:11, NIV

My daughter's new school has a policy of matching students with advisers. They sent me an email asking for some information in order to match her with an adviser that best suited her.

It was important to me that I get my daughter's input in the process, as she would most likely work with, collaborate, and trust this adviser for the next four years.

I asked my daughter, "Honey, if you could imagine the best adviser for you, what kind of person would that be?"

She replied, "Mom, I was talking to my friend Madison.* She told me that when she was new to her school, she was not popular, but she wanted to run for class president. She knew her chances of winning were very slim, but she ran for office anyway. On the day of the election, she had to give a speech to the entire student body. As she gave her speech, there was only one person in the audience clapping and cheering for her. That person was her adviser. Mom, I want an adviser like that, someone who will support and cheer for me even if my dreams seem far-fetched."

Our heavenly Father is our biggest Supporter and Cheerleader. He believes in us and loves us so much He sent His only Son to die for us. He also tells us to reach out to Him and express our needs to Him. Jesus said, "Ask and it will be given to you; seek and you will find; knock and the door will be opened to you. For everyone who asks receives; the one who seeks finds; and to the one who knocks, the door will be opened. Which of you, if your son asks for bread, will give him a stone? Or if he asks for a fish, will give him a snake? If you, then, though you are evil, know how to give good gifts to your children, how much more will your Father in heaven give good gifts to those who ask him" (Matthew 7:7–11, NIV).

If our earthly parents, teachers, and advisers can be our biggest earthly cheerleaders, how much more will our heavenly Father cheer for us, provide for us, and comfort us?

Let us trust Him, ask for what we need, and boldly claim His promise!

Ngozi Obiocha-Taffe

---

* Not her real name.

What? No Water?

"Give us water to drink."
—Exodus 17:2, NIV

Water is a precious commodity. No one can make water; it's only God that can send us rain. In 2016, when we had no rain, water restrictions came into force in the Western Cape, starting November 1. Dams were drying up. Water restrictions kept tightening until we were at Level 4. People's gardens were the first to suffer as less and less water was allowed. If people did not adhere to the laws, they risked having their water supply cut or even paying a heavy fine.

On July 17, 2017, I needed water. I opened the tap, but not a drop of water came out. Since it was around 11:45 P.M., it was too late to phone anyone. Why did I have no water? I had tried to be so careful using it. I went to bed with my mind churning over the problem and couldn't fall asleep till 3:00 A.M. The next morning, July 18, I was up around 6:30. I phoned the water department to ask why I had no water. A young man answered the phone.

"In what kind of shape is your water meter?" he asked. I went outside to have a look. A dirty packet of some sort was lying on the spot where the meter is. As I lifted the packet, a thick, strong spray of water squirted all over, drenching me. That's when I noticed that my water pipe had been cut, leaving the uncontrolled stream of water to run along the garden path.

I ran back to the phone in a wet and emotional state to report what had happened. The complaint was logged. Now I needed to get my water stopped! I phoned my neighborhood watchmen to come and stop the water. The next hour an inspector came to check the problem. "Your water meter was stolen," he informed me. "Probably for the copper."

An hour later, the water department sent two men to install a plastic water meter outside my front wall, for the thugs had jumped over the high, alligator-spiked wall into my property to steal the copper pipe and the meter itself. I am so thankful to God that the meter replacement job was completed by 2:10 P.M. that same day. Having no water was a problem!

I thought of the children of Israel in the desert, complaining to Moses about having no water (Exodus 17). I remembered the thirsty Hagar and Ishmael (Genesis 16). We can now buy water at the supermarket in gallon jars. In addition, we discovered fresh spring water a half hour's ride from home. Isn't God wonderfully good to supply for the needs of His children?

Priscilla E. Adonis

Have You Made Your Reservation?

And if I go and prepare a place for you, I will come again, and receive you unto myself; that where I am, there ye may be also.
—John 14:3, KJV

Every year all of our family members who anticipate attending our family reunion must make hotel reservations within a certain period of time. Reservations are usually made months in advance, and a certain number of rooms are reserved for an estimated number of guests. A special room is reserved for the meetings as well. As time draws near to the date of this grand occasion, my adrenaline level increases, and I become overwhelmed with excitement. The big question is, Guess who's coming to the reunion?

Among the attendees are relatives that I've kept in touch with during the year. On the other hand, there are those with whom I've not communicated for almost a decade. And, of course, there are always some that I'm meeting for the first time. We meet and greet one another on the evening of our arrival. This is very interesting because you don't know who you're going to see.

Once we've become acquainted with one another, we look forward to attending a well-planned picnic the following day. There is generally at least one activity that everyone can take part in. We go on tours, play games, take short cruises, take pictures, and reminisce about old times while enjoying the food provided for us.

After the picnic, we return to the hotel to wind down. I proceed to take a nap before I shower and prepare for the banquet. There is usually a fashion show and a talent show during the banquet. The entertainment is phenomenal. We don't know who is going to do what until the night of the occasion. You would be amazed at the hidden talent your family members possess. The banquet is the highlight of the reunion. Everyone generally participates in the program, including the children. We end our stay with family worship.

There is much to thank God for. Yes, we may lose a family member during the year, but we have the hope of being reunited with our loved ones upon Jesus' return. God has scheduled a greater reunion for us, and everyone is invited. Lodging is available and was paid for at Calvary. Have you made your reservation? Call today. I hope to see you there.

Cora A. Walker

We Belong

The LORD is my shepherd;
I shall not want.
He makes me to lie down in green pastures;
He leads me beside the still waters.
He restores my soul;
He leads me in the paths of righteousness. . . .
Surely goodness and mercy shall follow me
All the days of my life;
And I will dwell in the house of the LORD
Forever.
—Psalm 23:1–3, 6, NKJV

We are His people and the sheep of His pasture.
—Psalm 100:3, NKJV

The house was vacuumed, the kitchen mopped, the toys picked up, and the clean clothes folded and put away. The smell of freshly baked bread wafted through the house.

At last, it was sundown, and our little family had gathered together to welcome the Sabbath. After reading about Jabel the shepherd from *My Bible Friends* and a chapter from the Bible, we knelt for prayer.

As was our custom, we ended our prayer time by reciting the Lord's Prayer. I smiled as I heard our two-and-a-half-year-old daughter pray, "For Thine is the kingdom and the power and the Laurie and the baby and the mommy and the daddy forever. Amen."

I thought, *How true!* Whether we remember it or recognize it, we belong to Him. He created this world and everything in it; we are His—no two ways about it. The Sabbath is a special reminder that we belong to Him.

The story of the shepherd tells us that we are His people and the sheep of His pasture. Too often, we worry ourselves out of His arms and try to make it on our own. I daily need to remind myself that I am one of the sheep of His pasture. I am loved and cared for, and I am here to follow my Shepherd and rest in His provision for me.

Kay Dorchuk

It's Fourteen o'Clock

And do this, knowing the time, that now it is high time to awake out of sleep; for now our salvation is nearer than when we first believed.
—Romans 13:11, NKJV

It was one of those rare occasions when I had the privilege of spending some quality time with my grandchildren, my nieces, and my nephew. The memory of that day is as fresh and alive in my mind as though it happened yesterday. We had fun, played games, read stories, ate delicious food, and enjoyed one another's company.

After a while, my two-and-a-half-year-old granddaughter, Kyrah, became visibly fretful.

She was not happy about something. I watched her keenly. Then at about five o'clock, she came to me and asked, "GG, where are at my parents?"

I explained to her that her parents were at work but that they would be on their way anytime now. A few minutes later, Kyrah came back. "GG, it is fourteen o'clock, and where are my parents? *Now* it's time to go home!" (I smiled when she said, "fourteen o'clock." That must be a very long time to a two-year-old who cannot yet read a clock.)

The essence of "fourteen o'clock," however, left an indelible impression on my mind. Kyrah knew that she had spent a long enough time with us and that it was time for her parents to come and take her home. *Now.* Today I ponder *now.* What are the things that we have been putting off? What do we need to do *now* since the time is right or the time has long passed?

This morning I pray that whatever it is you need to do *now,* you'll find the courage, the tenacity, the strength, and the resolve to do it. Time is passing quickly. It is past time for us to do whatever should already have been done.

Precious Lord and Savior, today I want to surrender myself to You, along with my sisters and others reading this message. Thank You for the reminder that

> *there is a time for everything,*
> *and a season for every activity under the heavens* [Ecclesiastes 3:1, NIV].

Thank You, Lord, for removing anything that is slowing us down or preventing us from doing what needs to be done before it is too late. Thank You for hearing and answering. Amen.

Gloria Barnes-Gregory

June 10

Falling in Love With Jesus

Evening and morning and at noon
I will pray, and cry aloud,
And He shall hear my voice.
—Psalm 55:17, NKJV

When I look back over the last year or so of my journey, I am amazed and humbled.* God kept reaching out for me, wanting one thing: my obedience. Though hard to give, doing so has been rewarding. And somewhere along the line, I realize that I have fallen in love with Jesus. I read somewhere that you can't come into God's presence and be the same as you were before. Since I began taking time to sit at God's feet, speak with Him, and listen to His instructions, I realize how much He has changed me and my perspective.

I recently shared a post on social media that stated, "You need a regular appointment with your Creator. God is ready to talk to you, and you should prepare yourself each morning to talk to Him." A social media friend responded with a suggestion based on David's practice of praying three times a day. I subsequently found today's text in the Bible and couldn't agree more.

Some years ago, my morning worship was sufficient. Over the years, I've gone through some things that have made me realize that I need to meditate on God's words both day and night. As a result of constant searching, I've fallen in love with Jesus. Yes, it's been a slow and gradual process until the day when I woke up and realized this was the case.

Just as with an earthly relationship, this is where the "work" happens. I can fall in love, but I need to be intentional about my relationship to stay in love. I have to continue digging deeper into God's words and seek Him day and night. We need to have regular conversations to maintain our relationship. He fell in love with me before I was born and chose me. He tells me, "Before I formed you in the womb I knew you" (Jeremiah 1:5, NIV). He chose me!

Dear heavenly Father, thank You for a loving relationship into which You have called me as Your own. Thank You for coming after me, time and again, even when I haven't felt worthy enough to be called Your friend. Yet You saw fit to pursue me, wanting nothing more than my obedience and trust. Thank You for loving me so much that You died for me.

Kaysian C. Gordon

* This entry first appeared as "Falling in Love With Jesus," *Kayci Gordon, LLC, Walking by Faith Not by Sight* (blog), January 24, 2017, https://kaysigordon.com/falling-in-love-with-jesus/.

Treasures of the Heart

*"Wherever your treasure is, there the desires
of your heart will also be."*
—Matthew 6:21, NLT

M any people collect things. To some, they are treasures to be displayed and kept. These treasures can be cars, record albums, toys, magazines, or books with monetary or sentimental value. Collecting things can be a special pursuit, but it can also be detrimental.

Collecting things can become detrimental when it turns into hoarding. Hoarding is when a person holds on to things—or people—to try to relieve uneasy thoughts or emotions, such as loneliness. Sometimes we hold on to things when we do not want to let go of relationships that have ended.

I have been guilty of "hoarding" relationships. Sometimes I have put a value on things connected to a family member or put an unrealistic value on someone who has moved out of my life for whatever reason. Then, because of my hoarding whatever was emotionally connected to the relationship, I have become stuck.

Then I had an aha moment. It happened when I was quietly reading Matthew 6:19–21. I related it to what was going on in my life and why I was feeling like Lot's wife—a pillar of salt (see Genesis 19:15, 16, 26). I had been placing value on the wrong things and people. Keeping things to remember is not bad, and remembering loved ones or keeping memories of them close to your heart is not evil. However, if we value the things or relationships above God, we will stay stuck in a destructive pattern.

Our heart is where our treasure is. People leave, relationships end, items burn up and get lost, but God is everlasting, true, and honest. He will never leave or forsake us. My treasure is in my relationship with my heavenly Father, not here on this earth where dust and moth can destroy, or where I am rejected for who I am or who I am not. Just as I am loved by God, you, too, are loved and blessed.

Today, be mindful of what you are treasuring. Ask yourself, "Does this thing or person bring true, eternal value into my life, or does it weigh me down, keeping me frozen like a pillar of salt?" My prayer is that the desires of our hearts will focus on what—and who—bring eternal value. And what we should value above all else is our relationship with our heavenly Father.

Erika Loudermill-Webb

Can I Really Do All Things Through Christ?

I can do all things through Christ who strengthens me.
—Philippians 4:13, NKJV

Sometimes we read Philippians 4:13 that tells us we can "do all things through Christ" who provides our strength. And we may feel a bit distant from that verse. We may keep that verse "far away," for its "umbrella promise" covers things like moving mountains. Yet perhaps we should bring that verse a little closer to home.

I was recently invited to speak at my church following a season of prayer. Sometime earlier, I had told the Lord that if He ever wanted me to speak for Him, it would have to come by way of invitation. Then I would be assured that He, in fact, was the one doing the asking. So when I received the invitation to speak, I accepted with a willing, "Yes, I'd be honored!"

Then the panic set in. Why? Because I had considered my earlier talk with God to be one of those "far away" prayers. I hadn't honestly thought God would ask me to speak in public, but He had! Now I began questioning why I would strike a deal like that with Him. After all, I couldn't use any notes, cue cards, slides—none of those. You see, those types of "cheat sheets" don't work for a blind person. So I began thinking myself a bit foolish for having prayed that prayer—with no idea how I would be able to make good on my promise.

Nevertheless, I *had* prayed. God *had* answered, and now I was to preach a message. The scripture God laid on my heart was John 9:3—and how God works through infirmities to bring Him honor. All I could do was make a few mental notes, keep my cool on the platform, and pray like crazy. Well, two out of three isn't bad, as they say. For when I took my place at the microphone, I forgot *every* word I had planned on saying! I babbled on for thirty-three minutes about who knows what. Assuming my presentation had been awful, I held back the tears and waited outside the sanctuary doors after the message. I was prepared for words of pity: "Not bad for the first time." Instead, I heard, "What a great message! Just what I needed to hear today," and, "That really touched my heart. Now I'll always remember that scripture, for sure."

Were these people in the same church service I'd been in? That day, I experienced Philippians 4:13 coming to life for me. God took a bunch of jumbled words and turned them into a message for each person there. You, too, can trust Him with your "all things."

Cyndi Woods

Let God Lead the Way

Thy word is a lamp unto my feet, and a light unto my path.
—Psalm 119:105, KJV

My family lived in a two-bedroom apartment, and only one parking spot was allotted to it. When my son gained admission to a university, it became necessary for us to rent a bigger apartment with more parking spaces to accommodate his car. The landlord we approached offered us a three-bedroom apartment with ample parking spaces. Sometime during the time we were filling out the rental forms, I had a dream about driving on a long road and making a left turn into a certain house. Waking up, I remembered the dream. The house in my dream, however, did not match the place we were renting. We moved into the rental and lived there for three years.

One evening a fellow tenant attempted to steal our car, but the alarm scared him away. Another time, he drove his truck into the passenger side of the same car. Again, the alarm went off, and he drove away in the middle of the night. At daybreak, the police were contacted, and the tenant returned while the police were examining the damaged car. The tenant tried to deny what he had done, but the police were able to get a confession from him. The law enforcement officers told me to call them if the tenant failed to pay up. He did make a few payments and then stopped. Finally, my husband decided it was time for us to move elsewhere.

A real estate agent took us to see a house. She made a left-hand turn onto the property. I remembered my dream of three years prior and connected the dots. I recalled how God had revealed the future to Joseph through dreams; little did he know their fulfillment would take him from his father's house to a pit, from the pit to slavery, from slavery to jail, and from the jail to Pharaoh's palace for those dreams to come true (see Genesis 37, 39–45).

"For I know the thoughts that I think toward you, saith the Lord, thoughts of peace, and not of evil, to give you an expected end" (Jeremiah 29:11, KJV).

Soon, we read in our local newspaper that our previous adversary had been caught by the police and jailed for whatever illegal trade he had been engaged in. Is God mindful of His children, and does He avenge His own that cry up to Him night and day? He certainly does!

Margaret Obiocha

Squeaky Clean

Create in me a clean heart, O God,
And renew a steadfast spirit within me.
—Psalm 51:10, NKJV

Have mercy on me, O God,
because of your unfailing love.
Because of your great compassion,
blot out the stain of my sins.
Wash me clean from my guilt.
Purify me from my sin.
—Psalm 51:1, 2, NLT

Have you ever noticed when it's time to do household chores that you always find more that needs to be cleaned? Often when we clean house, our home can never get clean enough.

King David prayed that God would create in him a "clean heart." When we ask God to clean us up on the inside, then the outside will show that the inside is clean.

Many times when we first start the housecleaning process, we find it hard. *How long will it take for me to get this whole area finished?* But if we stay faithfully at our task, before we know it, the whole house is clean.

As with housecleaning, it also takes God time to clean our hearts. Renewing a right spirit within us also takes time. In my heart, I pray that the Lord will do this for me regularly. I want to be clean, inside and out, just as you do. I believe that if we pray, asking God for His help, He will answer our prayers.

Cleaning the house also takes a great deal of effort to get things just right. We go from room to room, sweeping and dusting and mopping. We wipe down mirrors, do laundry, make up the beds, and clean the bathrooms. When all is finally done, we can sit back and congratulate ourselves on the excellent job we have accomplished.

Jesus promises to do the same thing for us. He will refine our characters like gold tried in the fire. When Jesus is finally finished cleaning us up, He will have prepared us to be received into His kingdom. It is my prayer that Jesus will prepare us all to be ready when He returns to this earth so that we can finally go home with Him.

Kristen Hudson

Sheer Delight

Delight yourself also in the LORD,
And He shall give you the desires of your heart.
—Psalm 37:4, NKJV

My friends were always talking about their experiences and the encounters they had giving Bible studies and knocking on doors. To me, people shutting the door in your face and looking at you through their window blinds but ignoring the knock on the door, not to mention the dogs barking on the other side of the door, seemed anything but exciting. But there was no denying that these women and men enjoyed what they did. "That's not my gift," I said under my breath as they told many stories of how God had captured the hearts of people who later took that leap of faith and gave their lives to Him in baptism. That's the part that captured my heart—winning souls for Christ.

How many times had I quoted the Great Commission scripture and encouraged women to share Jesus and to win souls? The Bible says that he who wins souls is wise. So it was time for me to move from my role as the leader and get down to the grassroots level where people lived if I wanted to be a more effective leader. I prayed to God about my heart's desire to win souls for Him, and He opened a door! For three weeks, I served as a volunteer Bible worker in an evangelistic series. The first week was taxing for me because it took me out of my comfort zone. There were so many who knew about God but needed the assurance that He loved them. They needed to see Jesus, up close and personal. My teammate was a master at engaging people. I was in awe at how she met people where they were, took time to engage them in small talk, and handled objections like a pro.

Each morning as we traveled to our training, I prayed for those we had befriended and asked that they would receive Christ as their personal Savior. I realized that they were just like us—in need of a Savior. They needed to know the God we know and to experience His unconditional love for them. As my focus changed, I found myself enjoying knocking on doors, our visits to the park, and to a special family who lived in a housing project. Our visits took on a new meaning. I witnessed the Holy Spirit bless our feeble efforts, and souls gave their hearts to Christ in baptism. This is what my friends were talking about. It was a sheer delight!

Shirley P. Scott

Uprooting Weeds

He adds, "Their sins and their lawless deeds
I will remember no more."
—Hebrews 10:17, NKJV

I finally decided to take on an exercise regimen after putting on almost fifty pounds within three years. The first morning, I was so excited that I decided to take on another project in our yard. Our new home had been under renovation for almost two years, with my husband doing the majority of the work, but the outside needed some renovation as well. And I felt that I was ready for the task. So, I took on the job of pulling out weeds. I thought it was good for me because it gave me more time outdoors in nature with sunshine and fresh air. My weeding would also add aesthetic value to our home. For more than half an hour, I pulled out weeds. On days two, three, and four, I did the same thing.

I noted a few things that quickly became obvious. Some of the weeds were terribly hard to pull up. Even though I had used all the force I could exert, I was unable to pull out all of them by their roots. With others, I was able to pull them out very easily. Still others had small prickles that made them uncomfortable to pull. But I believe one of the most valuable lessons I learned is that pulling weeds has to be accompanied by other practices, such as ensuring that a Weed Eater is handy for use. You see, after four days of my hard work and a portion of the yard looking so beautiful, it rained! Because of the damp and dark weather, I took a break from pulling weeds. To my amazement, the very area that I had cleared had weeds again.

Oh, how disappointed I was to see that my work of uprooting weeds did not prevent them from growing right back! That made me think of sin in my life. I thought, *Sins can be so much like these weeds. We can, in our own effort, try to uproot them. But without God's help, our efforts are short-lived because those weeds—rooted so deeply inside of us and "watered" by our own lives of sin—can grow right back.*

I now understand on a deeper and more personal level that I cannot uproot sin on my own. Instead, I need to be fully dependent on God to do that work through me. I am now more able to conceptualize that the deep-rooted sinful ways, inherited tendencies, generational curses, and besetting sins are nothing new for God to uproot. If I, if we, continue to submit to God, He will forgive our sins and lawless deeds—which are like weeds that He will help us uproot.

Nadine A. Joseph-Collins

Reaching Beyond Our Own Pain

"So do not fear, for I am with you;
do not be dismayed, for I am your God."
—Isaiah 41:10, NIV

I couldn't make sense of the negative circumstances that kept happening in my life. I called out to God—actually, I screamed out to Him. *Please, God, can I just heal from the last negative situation that transpired? I'm really stretched.* There seemed to be no response, just silence. Yet I never doubted that God was listening. However, from my human perspective, questions remained. While I was in my state of bewilderment, God impressed a scripture upon my heart. "Lean not unto thine own understanding. In all thy ways acknowledge him, and he shall direct thy paths" (Proverbs 3:5, 6, KJV). I felt a sense of relief.

However, I was still facing a challenging situation. It was three days after my seventieth birthday. I had spent the day out, reflecting on the seven decades of my life and how God had directed me through my failures and accomplishments. As I was returning home that evening—in my haste to catch the bus—I fell and sustained a radial head fracture to my forearm. It was extremely painful, and I had very limited mobility of my arm. I had to learn how to use my less-dominant arm for all of my day-to-day tasks. And the doctor informed me that the healing would take from six to eight weeks.

Before I left the hospital, I stopped by the bathroom. As I was washing my hands, a young woman walked in. She appeared to be seven months pregnant. As she walked closer, I greeted her and inquired when her baby would be due. She paused and sadly stated, "This is not a baby. I have an illness that requires a tube to be placed in my stomach, which makes me appear to be pregnant." She began to sob. I asked her name and asked if I could pray with her. She said yes. I prayed with her, and our heavenly Father uplifted us both. She smiled and thanked me, and I thanked her.

It became clear that God answered my dismay through this young woman. Sometimes healing comes through reaching out to others and helping them through their pain. God was not silent and never is. He hears us and is working for us at all times, sometimes in unexpected ways. He tells us, "I am with you; do not be dismayed, for I am your God" (Isaiah 41:10, NIV).

Brenda Alexis

Emergency Medical Services

So He touched her hand, and the fever left her.
And she arose and served them.
—Matthew 8:15, NKJV

I went to work that day not feeling the best. By midmorning, I was hurting all over and felt like I had the flu. I told my boss that I was sick and going home but would be in contact with her. The drive home was excruciatingly difficult, for all I wanted to do was crawl in bed and sleep off whatever this was. I tried resting but to no avail. All I did was toss and turn. The thought of food nauseated me. I then decided that maybe a hot bath would help. However, this did not work either. What was going on? I had never before felt this way. I waited a few more hours but knew that I was in trouble.

At the time, I was a single parent. When a crisis arises for a single parent, there often isn't anyone who can help. Out of desperation, I called a friend and asked him to take me to the emergency room. I knew something wasn't right. He dropped me off at the door and left me there to be checked in by the nursing staff. After IVs and blood work, the results indicated that my appendix was about to burst! I needed emergency surgery.

The next thing I knew, I woke up in a hospital bed somewhat disoriented but grateful that the medical team had been able to save my life.

When Jesus was on this earth, He demonstrated that He deeply cared about relieving human suffering. He healed lepers, enabled the lame to walk, and gave the blind their sight. He extended the invitation: "Come to Me, all you who labor and are heavy laden, and I will give you rest" (Matthew 11:28, NKJV). He restored them to perfect health, and they were then able to go and serve others.

I praise God that He has instructed physicians to be coworkers with Him in the healing work of ministering to our bodies. Just as Jesus healed Peter's mother-in-law from her fever with a simple touch of His hand, He is there to heal us with power from above that only He can give.

Are you in need of healing today? Does there appear to be no one who can help? Reach out to the Great Physician. He can restore and revitalize our bodies, minds, souls, and spirits, for He created us and loves us with an everlasting love.

Karen M. Phillips

Jip and Nana Forgot

Commit your works to the LORD,
And your thoughts will be established.
—Proverbs 16:3, NKJV

Several years ago, when our first grandson started to talk, he chose to call his grandfather Jip. When another three grandsons joined our beautiful family, they all continued to use this term of endearment. At the time, my husband, Reg (Jip), and I (even in retirement) managed to fill our days with a variety of activities within our local church, playing in our church music ensemble, visiting, and caravanning.

Last Father's Day, our daughter helped our four-year-old grandson fill out a questionnaire about his relationship with Jip.

One question got us thinking about the priorities in our lives. Cameron's word picture said it all: "Jip always forgets to come and visit me."

We all know that it is our mission as a church to carry the gospel to the world. So by the time we do our exercise, look after our dietary needs, practice with our music ensemble, and fulfill our responsibilities at church, there is very little time left in our week. But our grandson wanted us to visit more!

How blessed we are to have a Savior who lived on this earth amid trials and temptations such as we encounter. How do we as Christians ensure that our priorities are right? Jesus set us an example in all things. His principal aim was to reach out to the masses, but I am sure that He also spent precious family time just as He visited with His friends, Lazarus and Mary.

Today's scripture reference shares that we should commit all our actions to the Lord. Some of us commit our actions only superficially. We may say that some of our favorite projects are being done for the Lord when, in reality, we are actually doing them for ourselves.

It is indeed difficult to maintain a delicate balance in our lives. I believe the secret to our success as Christians is committing our ways to the Lord. He guarantees He will give us direction in getting all our priorities right.

Since that day when Cameron filled out his questionnaire, we have endeavored to travel the two hours to visit him on a more regular basis. Each one of us needs to be aware of the fact that one day Jesus will say to us, "Where is your beautiful flock?"

Lynn Howell

Father's Day

The LORD is like a father to his children,
tender and compassionate to those who fear him.
—Psalm 103:13, NLT

It is Father's Day as I write this, but I don't feel like celebrating. Just a few weeks ago, my darling dad passed away. Though he was nearly ninety-two years old, he was still independent and active. In fact, he was still working a little, making spare parts for some of the locomotives he and his brothers had built years ago for their family engineering business.

Despite his age, Dad's passing was unexpected, the result of a sudden stroke—a few hours later, he was gone. I know I was fortunate to have had him in my life for so long, yet his passing still felt too soon.

I am blessed, however, with precious memories to cherish. I remember so many things about Dad: his large work-worn hands, capable and strong but gentle. I recall his warm hugs and gentle humor as well as his quiet, reassuring presence and the feeling of security he engendered. I remember his love, care, and respect for my mum all through their sixty-seven years of marriage and his love and support for each of his children. He had a strong sense of loyalty and service to his family, his God, and his church. He persevered through life's challenges.

The tributes at his funeral not only confirmed the professional respect Dad had attained as an engineer but also confirmed the consistency of his life. Many people described him as "a quiet, gentle man" and "a true gentleman." While I am proud of my dad's work achievements and engineering expertise, I am even prouder of his quiet Christian witness. As my sister wrote in an email to a friend whose late father had also been described similarly, "Considering that we do not get to choose our parents, we are blessed indeed to have the ones we were given. It must give you some comfort to know how your dad was viewed by others, as it does me. What a wonderful legacy to know someone about whom no one had a bad word to say."*

Though I am heartsore right now, I realize that I do have something to celebrate: not only the well-lived life of my dad but also the sure promise of my heavenly Father that I will be reunited with my dad one day very soon. What a special Father's Day that will be!

Jennifer M. Baldwin

---

* Used with permission.

The Best Is Yet to Come

The glory of young men is their strength:
and the beauty of old men is the grey head.
—Proverbs 20:29, KJV

I want to share with you today someone very special to me—my father, Norm, who reached his 101st birthday on January 12, 2018. He still lives in his own home alone and is enjoying good health, which allows him to continue the activities of living independently, such as doing his own cooking. He loves being out of doors, attending his plants, or quietly watching the birds while enjoying the sun. Also, he likes driving his scooter around the footpaths and going up to the local shops. Dad's life has been blessed with many interests, and he has achieved much despite lowly beginnings.

To me, it seems Dad was able to fix everything. He gave anything a go, even making playable didgeridoos. We still find him in his work shed, happily planning new projects. When he was younger, he played in a brass band—he has always loved music. One of his biggest achievements was building an observatory and making telescopes. He studied with the Astronomical Society and shared his facilities and knowledge with students studying astronomy. His last employment was in refrigeration engineering, where he worked for thirty years.

Dad has been a wonderful father and provider. I'm blessed to see him every day as we have access to each other's property through the back fence. Each evening we discuss the day's activities or reminisce about when life was so different. We have worship and prayer together, conversing about things that encourage and strengthen our walk with God.

People have asked, "What's your secret, Norm?" I love his answers and try to apply his seven principles to my own life. Live one day at a time (Matthew 6:34). Be content with what you have (Hebrews 13:5). Value time (Psalm 90:12). Practice the golden rule (Matthew 7:12). Keep occupied (Ephesians 5:15, 16). Keep your faith (1 Corinthians 16:13). Focus on God's promises, especially the "blessed hope" (Titus 2:13, KJV).

For my father, the coming of Jesus is the hope that gives him peace and strength each day. When he bids me goodnight, he reminds me: "Another day"—a day nearer to Jesus' return. Consider the relatively short length of 101 years on this earth compared to eternity with Jesus in heaven.

Lyn Welk-Sandy

Special Needs

"Do to others whatever you would like them to do to you."
—Matthew 7:12, NLT

I am back from a wonderful cruise, a family vacation. It was special to have so many of us together for a great time. We saw many interesting things, ate good food, and basked in fairly cooperative weather. I thoroughly enjoyed the cruise and the needed time away.

One of the most meaningful "incidents" I observed on the cruise occurred when several of us were getting ready to ride the carousel. Directly in front of me was a young family: a dad, mom, little sister, and eight-year-old brother. I don't know what set the boy off, but he began to scream and stomp his feet, waving his arms wildly, his little face growing as red as a beet.

I could at least understand the phrase, "I won't do it!" Mom and Dad were calmly getting little sister strapped onto her chosen carousel horse and seemed oblivious to their screaming son. The mother looked over at us and said, "He has special needs." Suddenly the screaming stopped, and the boy scrambled up onto the horse next to his sister. As the carousel began to move, I was impressed by the look of serenity on the mother's face and the sense of calmness with which the whole family had handled the episode.

I thought, *What a lucky little boy he is!* Not lucky to have special needs, of course but lucky to have parents who love him and encourage him, parents, who work to help him have as normal a relationship as possible with those around him.

In a sense, we are all "special-needs children" to Jesus. We live in a world filled with degradation. We are warped by sin, and it is only when we realize how wretched we really are that Jesus is able to change us into His likeness. He is patient, enduring, and willing to help us become candidates for eternal life. Though our righteousness is as filthy rags (Isaiah 64:6), we have hope in Jesus, who can deliver us. In Him, we also have freedom and comfort. He will take away all of our debilitating "special needs" and make us whole.

So we, in turn, need to treat others as He treats us by being tolerant of one another's special needs. No, life here is not fair at all, but we have a better life awaiting us. Jesus has promised that if we accept His saving grace, loving Him in return through our trust and obedience, we will be partakers of eternal life. I, for one, do not want to miss out!

Grace A. Keene

Stuck in a Jam (Jar)

*"Are not two sparrows sold for a penny? Yet not one of them will
fall to the ground outside your Father's care. . . . So don't be afraid;
you are worth more than many sparrows."*
—Matthew 10:29, 31, NIV

The sun felt warm against Pauline's face when she heard her mother's soft, "Oh." Blinking her eyes in the bright Florida sun, Pauline saw Mom, Dad, and Granddaddy all leaning over the wooden railing of the beach boardwalk, staring down into the tangle of sea grapes, palm fronds, and morning glories.

Peering over the rail, Pauline saw the big black eyes of a baby raccoon staring back up at her. Its face was magnified by the glass of the jam jar tight around its head. Its little pink tongue lapped at the sides of the jar, claws scratching fruitlessly.

Pauline could see its ribs against its matted fur. Farther away, in the bushes, the mother raccoon watched them cautiously with a second baby clinging to her tail. That twin was so much bigger and healthier than its trapped sibling.

"It probably tried to eat the jam inside," Dad said. "Must have gotten its head stuck. Poor thing's starving."

Wordlessly, Granddaddy reached down and plucked up the little raccoon. The baby thrashed against him, scratching his large, calloused hands. Cradling the critter, he gently twisted the jar. After a minute of tense silence, the jar popped off.

Granddaddy placed the baby down in the rushes. Confused, it looked around, then sneezed and ran off to its family. Granddaddy rubbed his scraped-up hand and smiled, saying, "I think he'll be OK."

Often, we can unintentionally get ourselves into trouble. Maybe it's not willful ignorance but something that we think is good for us, which can end up leading to problems and heartache. In these times, God comes along and sees us in our distress. The baby raccoon didn't ask for help. It didn't even want it and fought back, but Granddaddy took care of it anyway. He loved that baby raccoon and wanted to see it thrive, just as our heavenly Father will swoop in and care for us in our most dire moments.

Elizabeth Bearden

Dressed From the Sea

"Therefore I say to you, do not worry about your life,
what you will eat or what you will drink; nor about your body,
what you will put on. Is not life more than food
and the body more than clothing? Look at the birds of the air,
for they neither sow nor reap nor gather into barns;
yet your heavenly Father feeds them.
Are you not of more value than they?"
—Matthew 6:25, 26, NKJV

In March 2015, several of my family members traveled from Edmonton and Vancouver for a wedding in Jamaica. All of the guests stayed at the same resort in Runaway Bay, so we hung out together. It was wonderful to visit with my son, Jarett, from Vancouver, who was the best man. His twin sister, Cassandra, was happy to have some bonding time. We also met family and friends of the bride's and quickly became one large family. We ran into someone from our group at every meal, and after breakfast, we headed straight for the beach to relax until it was time for lunch.

One day several of us were lounging by the beach. Miguel, a young family member who loves to swim, headed straight for the water. Amid the chatter and application of sunscreen, we watched as Miguel dove in the water and then got out, enjoying the sun on his skin. Down he went on another dive, but this time something was different when he came up. He emerged, holding up a wire hanger with something dangling on it. We tried to figure out what the "catch of the day" was. As he got closer to the shore, I realized that he was holding up a dress!

Laughter erupted as Miguel approached us with his treasure in hand. I quickly jumped to my feet and grabbed the dress. It was local print fabric with coconut trees and "Jamaica" written all over it and in a one-size-fits-all style. Immediately my kids began shouting for Miguel to go back into the water as someone wanted shorts and another a top. Everyone laughed hysterically.

I decided to take the dress to our room and wash it, which I did. The color was a bit faded from being in the sun and water; however, the dress fit perfectly. I could not wait to wear it the next day. What a concrete, tangible manifestation of God providing clothing—we are not to worry about our basic needs!

Won't you trust Him today to meet yours?

Sharon Long

Blueberries Needed

*Call unto me, and I will answer thee, and show thee great
and mighty things, which thou knowest not.*
—Jeremiah 33:3, KJV

You will need to take this medication for your eyesight," the optometrist told me. I knew that I had a long-term vision problem, so the news wasn't unexpected. However, blueberries also contain an ingredient that helps. When at our annual church camp meeting, I usually bought a supply that would last all year.

"Sorry, we have no blueberries to sell this year," answered the clerk to my request for four boxes of berries. To say that I was disappointed would be an understatement. I was devastated! What could I do? But God knew, and He was in control.

When the camp meeting was over, there were still no blueberries. On our way through the town of Hope, I noticed a grocery store. I am sure the Lord prompted me to ask, "Harmony, would you mind stopping at this store to see if there are any boxed blueberries?"

"Sure," she answered. She swung her car into a parking space and went inside the store. Much later, she came out with several boxes of blueberries, a big smile on her face, and a story to tell. Harmony had spoken to the manager's assistant about blueberries. Yes, they had blueberries—and only five boxes left. It was Sunday of a long holiday weekend, so the assistant wanted to sell all five boxes, not just four.

"If you will take all five boxes," Harmony was told, "you can pay for just four." It was a good deal for both parties. All the store's boxes would be gone, and we would get the berries. The manager's assistant topped four boxes with the remaining berries, and we saved thirty-five Canadian dollars on the deal! I had been so disappointed when I'd not been able to obtain blueberries at camp meeting. Now I had more than a year's supply! Truly God loves us and desires our good. He answers us even before we ask. We need to trust Him more. God wants us to.

His Word tells us, "Trust in the LORD, and do good; so shalt thou dwell in the land, and verily thou shalt be fed. Delight thyself also in the LORD: and he shall give thee the desires of thine heart. Commit thy way unto the LORD; trust also in him; and he shall bring it to pass" (Psalm 37:3–5, KJV).

Muriel Heppel

Pro Bono Case

*Trust in the LORD with all your heart
and lean not on your own understanding;
in all your ways submit to him,
and he will make your paths straight.*
—Proverbs 3:5, 6, NIV

I sat next to my client, O. A., at the plaintiff's table, trying to calm her. The judge was looking at us, and this was not a good time for a blowup. Opposing counsel had just told the judge that her client, C. C., wanted O. A. to pay child support, although the child lived with O. A. Opposing counsel cited O. A.'s higher income as justification.

I took this divorce case, pro bono, as a favor to someone and because attorneys in my state are encouraged to do some free work. The case proved to be an enormous stressor. The two parties fought constantly, and both requested restraining orders against the other. The whole process was scheduled to take one year. Opposing counsel was determined to intimidate us into submission. This was not my specialty, and I tried everything I could to get O. A. another lawyer. O. A. could not raise the large retainer fees other lawyers demanded. I exhausted every avenue I had to get out of the case, but nothing worked. I felt ineffective, so I doubled down on the prayers. I prayed about the case every day, all day long.

One day, during the second deposition of O. A. (we had walked out of the first), things suddenly started to come together. *Thank You, Lord.* We were able to move from deposition to negotiation. We settled the issues except for child support.

We were in court to get a judge's ruling on child support. O. A. was willing to forego it, but she also did not want to pay it. The law says the parent who makes the most money pays unless the other party waives. The other side did not waive, and I began to pray. The judge sent everyone outside to talk. I kept praying.

Unexpectedly, the other side proposed that no one pay anyone. We agreed, then told the judge we had an agreement. She said, "Let's finalize the divorce right now and not wait for the scheduled hearing in six months." O. A. was thrilled—the legal case was finished. I thanked God. I still do not understand why He wanted me to stay in the case, but He got me through it.

Jean Arthur

We Are God's Heart

The LORD hath appeared of old unto me, saying, Yea,
I have loved thee with an everlasting love:
therefore with lovingkindness have I drawn thee.
—Jeremiah 31:3, KJV

One of the many blessings that God has bestowed on my family and me is a beautiful home. There's a window inset above the sink in our kitchen that affords me the opportunity of looking out onto God's masterpiece of creation and being renewed by so many evidences of His love for us. On one particular day, as I was wallowing in mounting despair, a beautiful pink-lilac *something* caught my attention—peering out from behind the shed located in our foliage-and-tree-filled backyard. *Hmm, I mused, could that be the hanging, dying, flowering plant removed from the deck at summer's end and placed there? Can't be, for flowering plants usually cannot survive winter's cold temperatures. So, how is it moving?* Then I saw that the object was a pink valentine-shaped balloon slowly being blown by the wind beyond the shed's shadow into a more open space. Then I was able to clearly discern the large, heart-shaped balloon that was now in my direct view. At that moment, God reassuringly spoke to me, saying, "Cynthia, you are My heart!"

Wow! Think about this. We, God's children, made in His image, are His heart. God gave us His only begotten Son, who died for us, rose again, and is faithfully interceding on our behalf in the heavenly sanctuary. Why? Because we are His heart.

His greatest desire is to save us so that when He—our loving heavenly Father—comes again in the clouds with power and great glory, we will be ready to go home to be with Him throughout the ceaseless ages of eternity. He will be our God, and we will be His people. Where He is, there we—His heart—will be also.

So whatever ongoing obstacles, disappointments, and endless problems are assailing us today, let's be encouraged, for God hears both our audible and inaudible cries for help. The deeper our problems, the more powerful our mighty God. The greater the conflict or storm, the more abundant His blessings. He is always able to make a "way out of no way." Remember, because we are God's heart, we can rest in His faithful promise that He will never leave us or forsake us. He will see us through.

Cynthia Best-Goring

Emily, Dollar Tree, and So Much More

On either side of the river, was there the tree of life.
—Revelation 22:2, KJV

I'd love to meet the owner of this wonderful store!" Five-year-old Emily bubbled over with excitement. She had just been introduced to something new to her: Dollar Tree, where everything is a dollar. Her parents had given her five dollars to spend, and she was having a real shopping spree.

I am also a fan of Dollar Tree, so much so that my friends tease me about its being my favorite store. I don't mind because I can often find brand-name items that would cost a lot more in a regular retail store, and, like most people, I enjoy finding a bargain.

When the dollar store concept was new, our son, Tim, and his family were visiting. We took them to the store. While the others browsed, granddaughter Kelly, a toddler, went around picking up items that had fallen to the floor and carefully putting them on the shelves. Years later, as a young adult, she worked at a well-known department store, refolding garments customers had rummaged through and putting them back in place. Maybe she got that training at Dollar Tree!

We once had another special tree. We were moving from one location to another, and our friends surprised us with a money tree—a small artificial one with real dollars attached. I don't remember how much money was on the tree, but it was very welcome, and we put it to good use.

Some charities have angel trees at Christmas, decorated with tags that bear the ages and needs of individuals. Those wishing to help take a tag, buy an appropriate item, and take it to the tree.

Then there is nature's wonderful variety of trees. When we first bought land on which to build, we had no trees. Years later, thanks to my husband's efforts, there are now magnificent maples and other kinds of trees. We haven't done as well with fruit trees, though one "dwarf" apple tree reaches high into the sky! A little peach tree has never figured out that it is supposed to bear peaches. Others eventually died. Yet there is a tree that will never disappoint or die. You can read about it in Revelation 22:2. It is "the tree of life, bearing twelve crops of fruit, yielding its fruit every month" (NIV). Best of all, we will finally meet the Owner of that wonderful tree and enjoy the delicious fruit forever—no dollars needed!

Mary Jane Graves

Scarred, Bruised, and Bloody—but Safe

The LORD heareth, and delivereth them out of all their troubles.
—Psalm 34:17, KJV

My husband and I have two cats, Gabriel and Meowth. Gabriel will not leave the house for any reason. However, Meowth tends to escape and go exploring as soon as he notices a way out of the house—no matter how we try to contain him. "Baby, have you seen Meowth?" my husband asked one Sabbath as we prepared to leave for church. "When I was putting items in the car, I don't think I completely closed the door into the garage because I noticed it was open. We cannot leave since Meowth might be outside." Then my husband, through a back window, spotted Meowth in the backyard, walking in the wooded area.

Oh, no! I thought. *We are dressed for church, and now we have to search through the woods for our cat.* We headed out to rescue him. Needless to say, I was poorly dressed for the task. As I looked and called for Meowth, I encountered trees, weeds, mud, and thorny shrubs. Finally, after about fifteen minutes, I caught a glimpse of the cat. My husband had remained just beyond the perimeter of the wooded area in case Meowth decided to run out that direction. As soon as Meowth saw me coming toward him, he turned around and began his trip back to the house. I turned around, thinking, *I wish I could get out of the woods just as easily as the cat.* My husband had wisely stayed at the perimeter, but I was attempting to disentangle myself from the trees, weeds, and mud. The thorny shrubs slashed like knives at my skin. I felt blood flowing down my legs. Every way I turned seemed to take me further into the woods. Finally, I called out to my husband with a loud and frantic voice, "Help me! I'm trapped in here!" He did help me, and I was able to make it out of the woods.

What happened that day made me think of how my situation was indicative of how we become ensnared in sin. It is easy to walk into a path of sin because we don't comprehend the danger. However, as time passes, we realize that we are trapped—as if in a maze. In trying to find our way out of the danger, we begin to understand that we are lost. It is only after we emerge, only after we have cried out to our heavenly Dad and Father for help, that we find ourselves scarred, bruised, and bloody (just as Jesus was)—but returned safely into His loving arms. Meowth was rescued as well, but I have some battle scars to remind me of this experience.

Zandra LaMar Griffin-Willingham

Found

"Rejoice with me, for I have found my sheep which was lost!"
—Luke 15:6, NKJV

The persistent clanging of the bell reverberated through the clear summer air, calling all campers to an emergency headcount. I watched them straggle in—-curious and bewildered. My daily job was to check in the campers at their various activity centers and locate any "strays." Each camper was always accounted for. Until today.

Little Christopher hadn't shown up for his canoeing class. We'd checked the other classes, the cabins, and the washrooms. We'd asked everyone we'd seen, but no one knew his whereabouts. I was sick. Christopher wasn't just an ordinary little boy—he had special needs and severe communication problems. How could we know what was going on in his little mind?

Just then, Rolly drove up in the farm truck. They'd heard the clanging over at the stables and wondered what was happening. I jumped into the truck and directed him to head for the hill that led to the water. Someone thought they might have seen Christopher in that area. The truck crested the hill and before us spread a large open field, the swimming hole, and the woods beyond. Counselors and workers were fanning out to search every square inch of the area.

"Please let him be OK!" I begged God. A short prayer, but I knew my Father understood. Suddenly I caught a movement out of the corner of my eye. I swung around to face the woods and was certain I saw a small figure dart behind a tree.

"There he is!" I yelled. Was I just imagining it? Rolly was out of the truck in a flash. "Don't frighten him," I called. I needn't have worried. By the time Rolly had gathered and placed the trembling little fellow into my arms, the others were already being alerted. My fear collapsed into concern and pity. Christopher's faltering answers told us that he had been afraid of the canoe. Who would have known? Just the day before, he had gone for a ride and laughed and had a great time.

My thoughts turned to a Bible parable about a lost sheep. All night the shepherd searched in the cold and storm until the one missing lamb was safely back in the fold. As I held little Christopher that day, I better understood how the Good Shepherd felt as He placed that little lamb safely back by its mother's side.

Dawna Beausoleil

Surfin' on Interstate 10

But let all who take refuge in you be glad.
—Psalm 5:11, NIV

Every medical student needs an escape. For my group of friends, our getaway was the ocean, and sometimes we chose to exchange microscopes and textbooks for sand, sun, and surf. What differed this Friday from our other surfing expeditions was that the surfboards would be strapped to the SUV's roof instead of being placed inside the SUV. I was a little apprehensive as a search for strapping instructions produced online tutorials with ominous warnings: "Flying surfboards can kill people!" After we triple-checked the strap security, we started the journey. The car was filled with the usual chatter when, abruptly, someone said, "Wait! We didn't pray!" Immediately heads bowed, and we asked for God's hand of protection over us. Less than one minute later, we were on the highway. Then we heard rattling sounds from the top of the car.

Suddenly I watched my worst nightmare unfold in my side-view mirror as four surfboards went flying across all lanes of the interstate, careening toward unsuspecting drivers. As I pulled to the shoulder of the road, I envisioned everything that could go wrong—a ten-car pileup, crushed surfboards, and, potentially, much worse. But by the grace of God, two semitrucks behind us stopped on a dime, blocking all traffic. We sprinted down the highway to retrieve our surfboards. Within seconds, traffic resumed as normal; no one even honked their horn. There was not one collision, and the surfboards were just fine despite having flipped across four lanes of traffic. Lying on the side of the road was the culprit responsible for this harrowing experience—the attached metal roof rack had been ripped off of our vehicle, taking the strapped surfboards with it. Huddled together on the side of the highway, we were struck by how differently this situation could have played out. The heavy metal rods hurtling through the air at sixty miles per hour could have easily pierced through a windshield.

Literally seconds beforehand, we had prayed for God to protect us. In a situation we never even dreamed would unfold, He had done just that—shielding every person and us on the busy highway by sending two semitrucks to drive behind us at the perfect moment. Our next words to God were of deep gratitude. Prayer is profoundly powerful. Surfboards, semis, and Interstate 10 reminded me of this in a way that I will never forget.

Briana Greene

The Struggling Pepper Tree

Can the rush grow up without mire?
can the flag grow without water?
—Job 8:11, KJV

I love to use cayenne pepper in my cooking, and one of my neighbors, who has several pepper trees, always supplied me abundantly. One day as I was picking peppers, it suddenly dawned on me that I should plant a pepper tree. I immediately asked the gardener to give me a starter, which I planted right away in my garden. I nurtured it myself by giving it water and natural manure and applying mulch around the root. It grew nicely, and I was so proud of it. Then I needed to travel overseas for ten days. Before I left home, I pleaded with my gardener to give my pepper tree water daily so it could withstand the extremely hot tropical sun, but he did not. When I returned, I was shocked and almost cried when I saw my pepper plant all dried up. So I thought, *Let me try one more time; maybe the root is not dead.* I was right. A few days after watering it, I saw two tiny leaves popping out. I was happy, and it thrived.

Two months later, I went on vacation for a month. I got a new gardener and begged him to keep my pepper plant alive and healthy. After hearing of the struggles of this poor plant, he promised to do just that. When I arrived home from my trip, I hurried to the garden—only to be greeted by several dried-up plants, including the cayenne. I wallowed in disappointment and grief. I learned the gardener had not shown up to work every day; when he did, it was when the water in the tank (which I share with a neighbor) was low. I observed that my pepper tree was very firm in the earth, even though the leaves were all dried up and fallen. I resorted to my nurturing technique, and the second morning I noticed a little green bud popping out. My joy returned. To date, my cayenne plant is maintaining a flourishing, healthy appearance, praise to His name.

As I stooped down by my plant, I could not help but reflect on the daily Christian walk. I asked myself, *Isn't this how it is with us Christians, more specifically with me?* When we do not stay connected to the Source of our spiritual nurturing—the Water of Life, the Vine—our walk takes on the form of a struggle, accompanied by disappointment, loneliness, frustration, and discouragement. But we have the choice to stay connected to the Vine. For us to grow and be productive Christians, we must abide in Christ. This is possible through prayer, spending time in His Word, and daily surrendering to Him as we live and serve by His grace.

Theresa M. McDonald

The Motorbike

I called upon the LORD in distress: the LORD answered me.
—Psalm 118:5, KJV

Not long after our family began mission work at our denomination's hospital in Banepa, Nepal, something terrible happened to me. I still carry the scars and pain of this incident.

On Friday evenings and Sabbath mornings, we gathered at our local chapel to worship with expatriates and the local people of our community. On one of those occasions, we met the surgeon from the United States Embassy, along with his wife. We shared our religious beliefs with them and developed a close friendship. It was through this physician's intervention that God saved my life.

My husband loved to ride motorbikes, but I had never ridden one before. One beautiful spring day, we both climbed on a Kawasaki and rode the eighteen miles to Kathmandu, the nation's capital, a trip that lasted around forty-five minutes. Winding down the hills, we delighted in viewing the eternal, snow-covered mountain peaks until we gradually entered the dusty outskirts of the city. The streets were full of cars winding through crowds of people, bicycles, and cows all over the road. Then on one curve, our motorbike slipped in the thick dust and fell to one side, continuing to skid for several yards. My husband, an experienced biker, drew his knees inward for protection; but I, a beginner, did not. My left knee scraped violently against the pavement. My jeans were torn to shreds, and blood started oozing from the open wound. I thought I would die. Instead, I was rushed to the United States Embassy's clinic. A bone in my knee protruded as a result of the serious injury, causing unbearable pain and the risk of permanent loss of motion in my leg. After the surgeon patched me up, I remained bedridden for weeks while God graciously put His healing hand on my shattered knee. I walked with a limp for many weeks until my injury healed, and my health was completely restored.

To this day, whenever I kneel to pray, I feel the cavity in my left knee. A part of my ligaments stayed in Kathmandu—and a large portion of my heart remained there as well! In heaven, I hope to meet all the lovely Nepalese friends we made, loved, worked with, and worshiped with during those blessed years in that part of the world. Heaven will be wonderful!

Marli Elizete Ritter-Hein

We All Scream for Ice Cream

Whom shall he teach knowledge?
and whom shall he make to understand doctrine?
them that are weaned from the milk, and drawn from the breasts.
For precept must be upon precept, precept upon precept;
line upon line, line upon line; here a little, and there a little.
—Isaiah 28:9, 10, KJV

I t had been a long day. I had a coupon for free ice cream, and I knew the exact flavor I wanted. As I made my way to the frozen food section in the store, I didn't see that flavor upon first glance. Should I get another flavor, another brand that was on sale? I really wanted to use my coupon and get the flavor my taste buds wanted. I looked again; I still didn't see what I wanted. Then I decided to take the time to read the product labels on each shelf to see if that flavor was one they even stocked. Searching each shelf, I saw my flavor listed. But the actual ice cream on the shelf wasn't the one I wanted. Disappointment filled me again. Then, I decided to dig deeper for my flavor and move some of the ice cream cartons around on the shelf. There it was! A few cartons back, hidden behind unappealing flavors, was the flavor I wanted! It was in the right place, only hidden.

Things aren't always as they appear. On the surface, we may or may not see "it" or understand "it." We might even look at "it" several times and still not see "it."

The "it" can be anything from understanding someone else's perspective to understanding God's Word. Just as I had to take the time to read the product labels on the ice cream shelves, we, too, must go beyond what our eyes see. We must go beyond the initial glance—to read, even investigate if necessary. After a surface reading, we probably need to dig deeper. We must move aside any preconceived biases we might already have and push them out of the way. This can take time, and patience will be needed. Yet if I had left the store after my initial glance at each shelf, I wouldn't have gotten my ice cream that day.

Some health-conscious readers might be thinking, *She didn't need the ice cream anyway.* Yes, that may be true. However, I did need to "hear" and "see" the valuable lesson that God revealed to me that day.

Angèle Peterson

That Little Yellow Flower

Pray ye therefore the Lord of the harvest,
that he will send forth labourers into his harvest.
—Matthew 9:38, KJV

The farmer planting grain in one of Jesus' parables (Matthew 13) reminds me that some seed falls by the wayside, some on stony paths, some in thorny areas, and some on good ground. The results are obvious to a careful observer. It is marvelous to see the results of planting on carefully prepared soil. But many treasures are to be found in the wasteland.

Several years ago, I commented on a lacy gold flower growing in the ditch at the far end of Grand Manan, where we spend our summers. My friend stopped, handed me a plastic spoon, and said, "Go get one." I did. Now several years later, the flower is growing in many spots in the front yard of my cottage. I spread it by deadheading the original plant and casting the seed-filled heads around the yard.

I have used this process many times as I turn an old gravel driveway into a wildflower haven. The lupines, honeysuckles, mallows, daisies, yarrow, and black-eyed Susans have all been generated by the casting of seed or seed heads. Some plants take several years to mature before they produce any blooms. There are still a few species that my seed casting has not reproduced. Every seed I cast faces many dangers. There are always greedy little seed-eaters such as sparrows and mice that love to find banquets of seed. I am close by but miss them as they creep along under the already successful plants.

I think God's work in other people I meet (and in me) follows this program as well. A comment gleaned from a visitor's conversation, the scene through my cottage window, or a thought-provoking daily devotional combine to mold and shape my perception of the world. These golden orbs, the coreopsis, remind me that I am also shaping the characters of those I rub shoulders with. They remind me of how my actions and words affect others and that words spoken in season will eventually reap a harvest of yet another soul for the kingdom.

It is not up to me to decide which seeds will germinate. I must keep sowing and watering and watching. God will take care of the rest.

Patricia Cove

In God's Service—Part 1

*I will say of the LORD, "He is my refuge and my fortress,
my God, in whom I trust."*
—Psalm 91:2, NIV

On July 9, 2011, South Sudan became the newest country when it gained its independence from the Republic of Sudan, thus ending Africa's longest-running civil war. The country is officially the Republic of South Sudan with Juba City as its capital. During more than twenty years of civil war, thousands of people died and millions were displaced. Then the civil war of December 2013 brought turmoil and bloodshed, which lasted for a week.

In January 2015, my husband, Harville, and I accepted a call to serve in South Sudan. We were informed that there were still some insurgencies that could cause some disturbances. But our faith was strong that God called us to serve Him, and we trusted that He would keep us from danger. Our church mission compound is a large enclosed, multi-acre area, located in one of the districts of Juba. That area's church headquarters, disaster relief office, medical clinic, church, elementary school, guesthouse, and homes for administrators and department heads are all inside the compound. The months of January through March are the hottest months of the year there. Temperatures can reach as high as 105.8°F. A generator runs electricity in the city. Since our main compound office owned only one generator, electricity was limited to the office hours of 9:00 A.M–1:00 P.M., 2:00–5:30 P.M., and 7:00 P.M.–12:00 A.M. With the guesthouse unfinished, we were housed in a twenty-foot container van owned by the disaster relief ministry. The van had a tiny window and could accommodate only a bed, a table, and a locker. After a month and a half, we moved to the completed guesthouse. It was a challenge without air-conditioning after midnight. Windows had to be opened so air could circulate in the room. Harville and I had bouts of malaria that made us terribly ill. After several months, we were provided a comfortable house to live in.

One night I was awakened by the sound of gunshots. I feared it was the beginning of another civil war. The gunshots I heard turned out to be a nightly "normal" occurrence. We finally got used to it. Despite the dangers around us, I was not afraid for "[God] is my refuge and my fortress." Today He is your Refuge and Fortress as well.

Ellen Porteza Valenciano

In God's Service—Part 2

He will cover you with his feathers,
and under his wings you will find refuge.
—Psalm 91:4, NIV

After a year and a half of our living in South Sudan, civil war again broke out between rival parties. Unlike the war in 2013, this war used heavy ammunition, bombs, and high-powered weapons. Civilians were advised to leave their homes and seek shelter in refugee camps or in our church's mission compound, which was surrounded by high concrete walls. Around seven thousand people came to our compound, staying in the elementary school, church buildings, and the extension room at the clinic. Those who could not find space in buildings sought shelter under the trees. As the fighting continued, the internally displaced persons suffering from malaria, cough, and fever came for medication. Having fled their homes, many had no money for the consultation fee and medical treatments. After I made several trips to the clinic, the president of our area church headquarters asked me to stay home for fear stray bullets might hit me.

The rain was heavy the night that I heard a knock at our back door. When I opened the door, people—dripping wet—rushed inside the laundry room. Aside from the four families already crowded inside our house, every inch of the laundry room was now occupied. Without electricity, the compound was pitch-dark. The next day, while I was working at the clinic, I had to go home for a glass of water. Soon after, gunshots rang out as a jeep load of soldiers entered the compound. The refugees who were crammed in the clinic's extension room fled at the sight of the soldier who barged inside. From our home, Harville and I watched the commotion outside. We were in a crouched position, anticipating the sound of gunfire and earnestly praying that God would protect us. After several days of intense fighting, both rival parties declared a temporary cease-fire. Our world church headquarters ordered us to evacuate immediately because peace and order in the city were uncertain. Two days later, roadblocks were removed, and the airport reopened. We left the compound and drove through what looked like a ghost town.

Yet God was in control. Seeking a glass of water saved me from encountering a soldier. God spared my life from stray bullets as I repeatedly walked to the clinic—in His service.

We serve a great God who will keep us safe under His wings according to His promise.

Ellen Porteza Valenciano

Our Guide

He guides the humble in what is right
and teaches them his way.
—Psalm 25:9, NIV

I recently traveled to Jamaica, my country of birth. Before leaving the United States of America, I made arrangements for a family-and-friends trip to Dunn's River Falls, a famous tourist attraction that boasts a natural waterfall that ends in the sea. This iconic beauty involves a rocky, treacherous climb best navigated by experienced tour guides who guide hand-holding "human chains" of visitors. Though difficult to climb, the experience is exhilarating, and the vista of the dazzling blue Caribbean Sea serves as a backdrop to the ever-present lush vegetation. My friends and I opted out of a paid guided tour, deciding to make the ascent by ourselves. We had seen many others ascending and descending without guides. After all, how hard could it be?

However, we hesitated when we saw the warning signs and overheard comments from visitors, warning others to be careful. As my friends and I pondered our decision, two young men approached us and held out their hands as an invitation to climb the falls. We were a bit hesitant but then threw caution to the wind. The difficult climb over slippery, uneven terrain was not for the fainthearted. There were moments when I wanted to turn back and take the easy way out, especially when I saw other visitors exiting via the various paths designed for those who are unable to complete the ascent. However, our guides were gentle and patient as they reminded us of our goal—reaching the top. Eventually, we saw the sign: "Congratulations! You have just completed the climb of the world-famous Dunn's River Falls." We were jubilant as we thanked our guides and departed. Later in the day, as I recalled this incident, I couldn't help but compare my spiritual walk with the climb up the falls. I didn't know these guides, but I took the journey with them, believing they would keep me safe and get me to my destination, the "prize."

We also have a perfect guide in Jesus. He has promised to keep what we have committed unto Him until that day when our reward is sure (2 Timothy 1:12; 4:7, 8). Look at your life right now. Maybe you have become discouraged by life's twists and turns, and you have slipped away from our Guide. Why not take a moment now to reconnect with Him? I know for sure that when we trust God, our paths will be made perfect.

Tamar Boswell

Progress Over Perfection

*Now faith is confidence in what we hope for
and assurance about what we do not see.*
—Hebrews 11:1, NIV

When times are going well, it can be easy to think we have things figured out. But as soon as something goes wrong and the world crashes down around us, the last thing on our mind is having faith that things will be OK. My life was getting out of control, and all I wanted to do was run away. Yet, no matter where I went, my problems seemed to follow me, and they were getting worse.

The start of the second semester of my senior year of college was the complete opposite of what I had hoped for. As things started going downhill, so did my faith in God and my faith for a great final semester. My schoolwork, my mental health, my job, and my relationship with my friends started to deteriorate, and I began to lose faith in everything.

One particular day I wasn't feeling my best, and a friend was trying to convince me to go to a Bible study with her. "When was the last time you left your room and hung out with people? Ate a meal? Did your homework?" asked Alexa.

"I don't care, and it honestly doesn't matter. Everything in my life fails, so I figured that I would just stop trying," I responded.

"How about we go to the young adult group tonight and see how it goes? We can stay for as little or as long as you would like. I just want to see you back to normal," Alexa said to me with deep desperation in her voice.

I decided to go to the Bible study with her, not because she asked but because she's my best friend. I couldn't stand to see her hurt, especially knowing that I was the cause of her pain.

When we got there, the youth pastor immediately greeted us with a warm and welcoming smile that I didn't know I had missed until I saw it. The message that night was about having faith in God; He will take care of the things that we need if we ask and put our trust in Him. At first, I couldn't see all the wonderful things that God had done for me, but after exercising my faith a little bit, everything started to become normal again.

We can always focus on progress through faith in God.

Caroline Guchu

The Cursed Woman

"Are you the king of Israel or not?"
Jezebel demanded. . . . "I'll get you Naboth's vineyard!"
—1 Kings 21:7, NLT

N o one will get away with sin forever. God delays His judgment to give people time to repent (2 Peter 3:9), but His patience can run out. After neglecting to repent when given numerous opportunities, Jezebel would eventually meet her unhappy end (see 1 Kings 21:23–25). Ahab's desire to own a vineyard drove Jezebel to plot the death of an innocent man, Naboth. An obsession such as greed can severely taint our sense of good and bad. If we allow sinful passions to control us, then we are in danger of committing a multitude of other sins.

If we allow God to help us follow in His footsteps, however, our lives will reflect honesty, genuineness, kindness, and empathy. He will be able to fulfill His plan for our lives. We follow Him when we surrender our lives to Him through faith in Jesus Christ.

What kind of influence are we in our homes, churches, workplaces, and communities? Some people behave righteously on the Sabbath day but not on weekdays. In their everyday lives, some people move fence lines, coveting the property, jobs, or positions of others. They appear to be no different than those who do not profess to be Christians.

Ahab and Jezebel surrounded themselves with people of like mind. They avoided—or punished—people who held them accountable. When we are surrounded by people with bad behavior and evil hearts, we can be influenced by their characters. Ahab and Jezebel were "good examples" of bad role models and bad behaviors. They had opportunities to understand and pursue the ways of God since the righteous prophet Elijah often confronted them in the name of God. However, they chose to work against God.

Jezebel was a self-styled prophetess who encouraged a profligate lifestyle (see Revelation 2:18–23). Her fury knew no bounds when the God of Israel was victorious on Mount Carmel—and her false prophets were killed. Jezebel's story of rebellion and punishment reminds us how dangerous it is to have relationships with people who would lead us astray. We need to choose friends wisely and spend time with people who would point us to God.

Friends, let's be careful to walk in the light of God's Word and be good role models.

Pauline Gesare Okemwa

The Making of Disciples

Do not be concerned about your own interests,
but also be concerned about the interests of others.
—Philippians 2:4, ISV

A few years ago, I went on a mission trip with a group of American undergraduate students. We spent time helping church members in a rural community build an extension to their church building. These students had never used an outhouse and never had to carry water in buckets or mix cement by hand. Yet on this trip, they met people who were content with much less than they had—people who pooled together their limited resources to cook a meal for us over an open fire as a gesture of appreciation. It occurred to me then that service to others is as much about changing us as it is about introducing others to the great Life Changer.

Not only have I experienced the transforming effect of service in my own life but I have also witnessed it in my own children.

One Sabbath day, when my daughters were ages seven and nine, we offered a visitor a ride home after church. As she got into the back seat of the car, she mentioned that it was her birthday. My daughters overheard this exchange and got right to work. They created a makeshift paper barrier between themselves and our passenger and worked furtively to create a birthday card for her. When they handed it to her, she was moved with emotion and gave them a long, hard hug.

Later that day, my daughters convinced my husband to take them over to a construction site next door to give Popsicles to the workers because, they said, "They must be so thirsty on such a hot day." When the girls came back home from this "mission trip," their faces were flushed. With a sense of deep satisfaction, my younger daughter said, "Mommy, I have a really good feeling in my heart!"

I believe that mission encounters transform us even as we serve others. Service teaches us about doing the Word—living the gospel truth among those we encounter. It is as much about sharing God's love with others so He can change their lives as it is about engaging us in work that changes our hearts, making them more like His.

Today, look for an opportunity to *do* the gospel wherever God has placed you.

Kathy-Ann C. Hernandez

Glad Rags and Bird Droppings

*"For whoever exalts himself will be humbled,
and he who humbles himself will be exalted."*
—Luke 14:11, NKJV

My spirit was low, I was experiencing a major, life-changing upset and did not feel inclined to go to the wedding, but I rallied myself. I put on my glad rags (which happened to be my newest, most glamorous dress) and highest heels and checked out my reflection. *Looking good*, I thought. I stepped out to attend the wedding. The event was enjoyable, elevating my spirit despite the heaviness in my heart. The ceremony over, I began walking back to my car, feeling even higher than my heels allowed, having received compliments on my appearance. Then something landed on my head. It was not rain! I was not pleased that a passing bird did what it had to do—on my head. Having no mirror, the only option was to humble myself and ask for assistance from a very kind lady who was a few steps behind me. She graciously cleaned my hair with a tissue. It was either that or strut back to my car with a lump of a bird's waste matter on my head. Not the best of looks! The passing bird did not consider the fact that I, in my sleek satin glad rags, was not an appropriate target.

Life can land a whole heap of undesirable matter on our heads, and sometimes these metaphorical droppings are exactly what we need to bring us down from our lofty heights. They help us turn our sight away from ourselves to reach toward the Source of our being and strength, God. Only He can lift us up and away from our difficulties. Only He can successfully see us through our challenges. And it doesn't matter who we are, how dressed up we may be, or how well things appear to be going; underneath it all, we are sinners in need of the Savior. Rather than spending energy keeping up appearances, we need to make a shift in our focus to acknowledge our helpless state. Then, falling to our knees in humility, we can seek grace, favor, and deliverance from the God who, despite our sometimes overinflated selves, loves us unconditionally.

Let us maintain a spirit of humility as we petition and accept help from God to deal with life's "droppings" rather than having a preoccupation with being clad in superficial glad rags! (By the way, bird droppings are not pleasant, but, when they land in the right place, they enable seeds to germinate, perpetuating life. Now that's another lesson in itself.) Count it all joy!

Denise Roberts

Mourning Hope

" 'He will wipe every tear from their eyes.
There will be no more death' or mourning or crying or pain,
for the old order of things has passed away."
—Revelation 21:4, NIV

As I drove Yary home from her first grief support group, she lit up, telling me, "It was nice being able to talk with others who are also grieving the loss of a loved one."

Before turning twenty-five, Yary lost both her parents due to illness. She felt lost, not knowing how to move on without their guidance. Talking to others who had not experienced the loss of someone they love was difficult.

"How can they ever understand fully what I'm going through?" she'd say.

As her best friend, I wanted to do something to help, but I didn't know what. Then one day in my college fundraising class, the teacher presented us with information about some charities that we could help. I grabbed information on the charity named Mourning Hope, not knowing what it was about.

During the next class period, a representative from each charity met with students to go over their charity's mission and provide more information. While talking to the representative of my chosen charity, I thought of Yary and how this charity might help her.

"Do you have any programs for young adults who've lost their parents?" I asked the representative.

"Yes!" she answered. "I have a handout about a ten-week program for eighteen- to thirty-year-olds. They meet at a coffee shop after hours. Your friend might be interested in this."

Right then, it hit me. God chose this charity for me, knowing it could help Yary in such a difficult time. Even though I wondered if she would attend, I gave her the handout.

Yary scanned the details on the page. "I think I could try going once. I appreciate your telling me about this. Thank you."

Sometimes God hands opportunities to us that might be what someone else needs. I realized I need to keep my eyes open, because we never know when God will hand us opportunities that will benefit others.

Roxi Peterson

Your Choice

"In the world you will have tribulation;
but be of good cheer, I have overcome the world."
—John 16:33, NKJV

There we were at the airport, ready to return home with great anticipation—until the ticket agent said, "You're booked but not ticketed, and unless you pay six thousand dollars now, you can't go on this flight." Then she said, "There is no available ticket for Sunday because your tickets have been canceled, and all flights are full." What had seemed too good to be true was just that—too good to be true. The car had been returned; we'd checked out of the hotel and discarded or given away all unnecessary items, such as food, water, and walking shoes. Now we would be staying two more days in Sydney at a greater expense due to the airlines' mess-up. About two weeks before, the ticket agent had canceled the wrong ticket and created a major problem—unknown to us until that day. Now, after spending an extra hundred dollars for an unneeded taxi, two hours on the cell phone at the overseas charge, and returning to the hotel we'd checked out of almost four hours earlier, we had two options. We chose to make the best of the situation. The following quote is a good one to read every so often to get a better perspective on life's unexpected challenges.

"God in His great love is seeking to develop in us the precious graces of His Spirit. He permits us to encounter obstacles, persecution, and hardships, not as a curse, but as the greatest blessing of our lives. Every temptation resisted, every trial bravely borne, gives us a new experience and advances us in the work of character building. The soul that through divine power resists temptation reveals to the world and to the heavenly universe the efficiency of the grace of Christ."*

Returning to the airport on Sunday, we were thankful to see the same lady that had helped us on Friday and who knew our situation. We were able to fly out that afternoon. During that extra time in Sydney, we enjoyed a youth Sabbath program and time to take pictures and go for walks. We recharged and recuperated, not having realized how tired we'd become.

A few weeks later, we received a travel voucher from the airlines for $250 each. May God help us to make good choices when trials come, and may we remember He (Jesus) has overcome the world!

Rita Kay Stevens

---

* Ellen G. White, *Thoughts From the Mount of Blessing* (Mountain View, CA: Pacific Press®, 1956), 117.

Warriors

"Come to me, all you who are weary and burdened, and I will give you rest. Take my yoke upon you and learn from me, for I am gentle and humble in heart, and you will find rest for your souls."
—Matthew 11:28, 29, NIV

Are you a weary warrior? I've been learning from exhaustion. It's different than falling in bed after a busy day or needing a Friday night reprieve. It's more than a sore throat or needing to eat more than granola bars. Exhaustion is deeper, as it seeps into your life, pressing on your soul.

Phones rang, and four people were already waiting in my office one day. Papers were piled on my desk, and an unfinished email was waiting. Parents stood gabbing, the band was practicing, and construction workers repaired walls in the adjacent building. My bladder was full, my stomach was empty, and my jeans were the same pair I wore yesterday. I felt my mind collapsing, my spirit willing it to wait! It was the end of the school year and my twelfth year as secretary. I was tired. It was as if the seashore were before me, and I was on all fours, clawing at the sand to pull myself away from the hectic waves. I wanted to collapse in a heap on the shore with the sun glistening over me, kissing my spirit, yet I was too exhausted. What was wrong with me?

Then a woman walked in and softly said amid the noise, "Thank you, Heather." I looked up with "traffic stress" and asked, "What for?"

"For taking care of all of us all the time and doing it so well," she said. "You must be tired."

Tears flooded my eyes, and I buckled in my chair. I was a weary warrior, and it was OK.

There's nothing wrong with you. Breathe deeply, O precious woman of Christ. The Christian walk doesn't mean you never get tired. It means you've been out serving everyone and tackling everything from to-do lists to the laundry, using everything you've got. Women have warrior souls. We've been created with poise and power to persevere, plan, rise up, and roll. At times we tire, not from weakness but from living life on this earth. There's compassion in the tenderness of Jesus, inviting warriors to rest. And on that day, when the skies split and the majesty of angels rushes forth, God will shout, "Thank you for taking care of My people all the time and doing it so well. The Son is glistening over you and kissing your spirit!"

Heather VandenHoven

HOPE

*May the God of hope fill you with all joy and peace
as you trust in him, so that you may overflow
with hope by the power of the Holy Spirit.*
—Romans 15:13, NIV

The word *hope* brings a whole host of emotions. Those emotions can be anything from happiness to sadness to trust to waiting to being up all night praying—or something very simple. For example, I can say, "I hope the new recipe I am trying for dinner is good." That is a simple statement, but it is the expectation of an outcome, and we don't know what the outcome will be. Now on the tougher end of things, someone may say, "I hope I don't have this illness the doctor is testing me for" or, "I hope my loved one is going to recover completely from the accident they had." Again, it is the outcome we are waiting to hear. For someone in a war-torn country, or for those who don't know where their next meal is coming from, that word *hope* can truly mean "life" as in some of these earlier examples.

I feel that when we have hope in our lives, we have encouragement. Hope is God telling us to hang on. It is that light at the end of the tunnel. When we have hope, we feel we can continue moving forward, that we can breathe a sigh of relief—we can carry on. The admonition of Romans 12:12—"rejoicing in hope, patient in tribulation, continuing steadfastly in prayer" (NKJV)—has been an unwavering encouragement for me. Just this year, I have said so many times, "I hope and pray," because my wonderful husband has experienced a serious flare-up of his autoimmune disease. It's been tough at times. Whether you are a patient or a caregiver, a chronic illness is difficult and sometimes can leave a person mentally and physically parched. Through it all, though, both my amazing, brave husband and I still see our blessings. We have so much provided for us through great medical care and the loving support of family, friends, and our church. So when we are feeling particularly depleted, we remember "faith is the substance of things hoped for" (Hebrews 11:1, NKJV) and that God will give us the strength we need (Isaiah 40:31). We take one day at a time and know He is with us. He renews our faith each day and gives us hope while carrying us on wings like eagles.

Trust Jesus to be your hope too. He not only gives us hope, He is our hope. Put another way, no matter what our trials, He Offers People Eternity (HOPE).

Jean Dozier Davey

A Beautiful Thing

And let the beauty of the LORD our God be upon us,
And establish the work of our hands for us;
Yes, establish the work of our hands.
—Psalm 90:17, NKJV

I frequently walk on the Sabbath Trail, a one-mile trail adjacent to a historic church of my denomination which is located in Washington, New Hampshire. Visitors who hike on this trail will encounter thirty-one different sites at which they can rest and reflect. Each site features an engraved granite stone. Altogether, the messages on the stones serve to explain the history of the Sabbath from its origin at Creation to its observance in the new earth.

I enjoy resting on the bench at each site, surrounded by the peaceful beauty of the New England forest while I contemplate the message on each stone.

But the stones themselves have a story that speaks to my heart and reassures me that God has a masterful plan that includes me.

Over twenty years ago, the designer of the Sabbath Trail, Elder Merlin Knowles, drove past a granite quarry that was located in Enfield, New Hampshire. He noticed a number of discarded slabs of stone by the side of the road. These cast-off, asymmetrical rocks had one smooth side where they had been cut. The stones were of varying thicknesses and were no longer of any use for the needs of the quarry. The quarry owner was selling them for prices that ranged from five to twenty dollars—very low prices for New Hampshire granite.

These cast-off rocks became the stones on which the Sabbath messages were engraved. They are the focal points of the thirty-one sites and contribute to the exquisite beauty of the Sabbath Trail.

When I am feeling a bit left out, I remember the stones and how they were collected to make beautiful woodland masterpieces.

Dear sister, please know that as your Designer looks at you, He has a plan that beautifully includes you. He is well aware of your rough and crooked edges, but He still wants and needs you. You may feel cast off or abandoned, but He wants to include you as part of His masterpiece on this earth and beyond. Let Him establish His beauty in and through you today.

Marsha Hammond-Brummel

On the Banks of the Araguaia River

Praise the LORD, all you nations;
extol him, all you peoples.
For great is his love toward us,
and the faithfulness of the LORD endures forever.
—Psalm 117:1, 2, NIV

It was about 4:00 in the morning when a sharp pain awakened me. I could easily understand what was going on: our baby was coming! I called my husband and told him. He was quite surprised but soon called everybody to share the news. My sister was with me at that time and, with the wife of the nurse, helped me get ready.

We were living among the Karajá Indians, teaching at our church's mission school on Bananal Island on the Araguaia River, Brazil, Central Region. Our main problem was that the nearest hospital in São Félix do Araguaia was four hours by bass boat upriver—if the boat had a fifteen-horsepower motor. Our mission had only a twelve-horsepower boat, and with that less powerful motor, it would take the whole day to get to the hospital!

However, there was a nearby Karajá Indian who had a fifteen-horsepower bass boat, but when asked about going to São Félix, he answered that he would go there in two days. Nobody could convince him that this was an emergency and that we could not wait that long.

So people decided to use the twelve-horsepower motorboat to cross the river and call for the help of Brother Luis. He was a church member who lived on a farm on the other side of the river. His two children were studying at the school, too, and he had a fifteen-horsepower motorboat. A Christian Indian would go there to call him. As the man was crossing the river, the engine suddenly stopped. The boat often refused to function, and people would be obliged to row. My heart fainted. Brother Luis's boat was our only chance! Then suddenly, things started working again. Brother Luis came, and I was able to start my travel to the hospital at 8:00. We got there at noon. Our baby was born at night. Later, we were told that the Indian man had prayed when the boat motor stopped; it had started working again. God had answered his prayer. That was amazing!

Our mission station existed to teach the people about the true God. They had learned how to pray and applied that knowledge when helping us. Our mission had been fulfilled!

Het Jane Silva Carvalho

The Awesomeness of God

Before they call, I will answer;
and while they are yet speaking, I will hear.
—Isaiah 65:24, KJV

It is the small things that have me in awe of God. Don't get me wrong. I appreciate all God's blessings, the spoken prayers I expect God to hear and answer. However, it is the small, unspoken prayers that put me in awe of God. It's the things I have done that I don't even want to admit I have done, much less utter out loud in prayer.

It is these prayers that I whisper to myself when I don't want anyone to hear me, not even God.

I'm talking about those times when, for example, I have lost my keys for the twentieth time or when I have locked myself out of my van or when I am thirty minutes late for a business meeting. Of course, I ask for His help in situations such as these.

Yet it's the other times when I need God's help but I am too afraid to ask because my need seems so unimportant when God has more important prayers to answer.

One morning I received a phone call from my brother, who needed my help. He had left his wallet at the church the day before. I knew how important this was to him.

In my eagerness to help, I hung up the phone and headed toward the city. However, I had forgotten to get my brother's new address since he had relocated.

I tried calling him, but there was no answer.

I thought to myself, *If only he would look out his window and see me, that would be great.* As I drove around a block, suddenly my brother appeared! He looked around and began to walk down the stairs in the opposite direction of the van, not seeing me.

Nevertheless, I called out to him, and he turned around. What was so amazing is that he had no idea I was coming.

In a split second, God had heard my unspoken prayer.

God tells us in His Word that He will answer us even before we call. God knows our needs before we know them ourselves. Our God loves us. Not only is He aware of our needs and concerns but He is also willing to help us no matter how small our dilemma.

Avis Floyd Jackson

Slugs in the "Sonlight"

I am the world's Light. No one who follows me
stumbles around in the darkness.
—John 8:12, *The Message*

So what's all the fuss about slugs? Maybe it's the way they shrivel away and quickly die when exposed to sunlight. When the sun is shining, I can't find a slug, and my flowers blossom beautifully for all to behold.

While I am in my garden, I often wonder if I am tending to the spiritual "slugs" that try to invade my heart. Jesus shines His love on me so that I can grow and share His beauty with all. But too often, I let the darkness creep in, and the "slugs" of sin start eating away instead. Slugs can be the grudge I hold against the driver in front of me, who is still sitting at the green light because she hasn't finished texting. I detect the darkness in my heart and cover up what is left of my patience. Then Jesus, the Son, lights my mind with His words. "Carelessly call a brother 'idiot!' and you just might find yourself hauled into court. Thoughtlessly yell 'stupid!' at a sister and you are on the brink of hellfire. The simple moral fact is that words kill" (Matthew 5:21, 22, *The Message*).

Sometimes a slug creeps in, eats away at my faith, and leaves trails of anxiety and worry. Again, the Son's desire for me is to rest in His comfort, and then peace blossoms. "Don't fret or worry. Instead of worrying, pray. Let petitions and praises shape your worries into prayers, letting God know your concerns. Before you know it, a sense of God's wholeness, everything coming together for good, will come and settle you down. It's wonderful what happens when Christ displaces worry at the center of your life" (Philippians 4:6, 7, *The Message*).

The hardest slug to weed out is the bitterness I hide, deeply rooted from years of feeding its hurt, doubt, and mistrust. Yet that which is hard for me to release the Son uproots. In the place of bitterness, He plants fragrant forgiveness and His sweet, sweet Spirit. "For if you forgive other people when they sin against you, your heavenly Father will also forgive you. But if you do not forgive others their sins, your Father will not forgive your sins" (Matthew 6:14, 15, NIV).

Won't you let the Son's light destroy the slugs in your heart today?

As told by Ila Cockrum to Wendy Williams

Blessed Are the "Unlikelies"

But the LORD said unto me, Say not, I am a child:
for thou shalt go to all that I shall send thee, and whatsoever
I command thee thou shalt speak.
Be not afraid of their faces:
for I am with thee to deliver thee, saith the LORD.
—Jeremiah 1:7, 8, KJV

If I asked you, as you read this devotional, about the expectations folks had of you when you were in school, I would expect to hear something like "most likely to succeed," or, "She will make a very good teacher [or preacher, lawyer, doctor, nurse, scientist, or engineer]." Perhaps someone expected that you would be a "good wife" or "good mother." These affirmations might even have been written in your yearbook.

But what about those who did not hear such laudable and uplifting comments? Perhaps they overheard that "she will never amount to much in life." Maybe someone told them they were lazy or lacked discipline or capabilities. In many households, children are described as dumb, clumsy, foolish, selfish, and uncaring. Have you ever heard this expression: "Sticks and stones will break my bones, but words will never hurt me"? That is a fable—words matter greatly! Words can make or break a person. Words can lift us up as much and as quickly as they can bring us down. In fact, Scripture tells us that "a word fitly spoken is like apples of gold in pictures of silver" (Proverbs 25:11, KJV). Otherwise stated, "How delightful is a timely word!"

Gideon was not a warrior when God called him to lead His people into battle against the Midianites. Teenager Mary was called by God to be the mother of Jesus under unusual circumstances. Jeremiah was also very young when he was called to be a prophet in Judah. Moses was saved from the Nile River to become an Egyptian prince before becoming a murderer, a shepherd, and then the chosen leader of the children of Israel. Future king David was only a shepherd boy when God called him to slay Israel's nemesis, the Philistine giant, Goliath. Ellen G. White was a sickly teenager when God called her to exercise a prophetic gift. *Nothing is impossible with God.*

Dear sisters, I encourage you to trust God with your life. What He has done for others, He can certainly do for you. God loves to honor and bless the "improbables" and the "unlikelies." Our God is indeed awesome!

Avis Mae Rodney

My Family Tree and Yours

*And Adam lived an hundred and thirty years, and begat a son in his
own likeness, and after his image; and called his name Seth:
And the days of Adam after he had begotten Seth were eight
hundred years: and he begat sons and daughters:
And all the days that Adam lived were nine hundred and thirty
years: and he died.*
—Genesis 5:3–5, KJV

I love genealogy. I love reading and hearing about my family's history. I love finding old photographs of my grandparents, great-grandparents, and great-great-grandparents. I love seeing pictures of them in their day-to-day settings. I love figuring out who belongs to whom and how I'm related to each person. Years ago, I found a book, copyrighted 1809, in my grandparents' attic. The back page of the book had been used to list the owner's parents, siblings, and birthdays. These people were my ancestors who lived in the late eighteenth and early nineteenth centuries. One even had the same birthday as me! I also want my children, grandchildren, and other descendants to know who their ancestors were. I want them to come to the same realization that I have: that without any one of those individuals in their family tree, they wouldn't be here. If the owner of that book hadn't existed, I wouldn't exist. And without me, there wouldn't be at least four others—my son, my two daughters, and my granddaughter.

I also love reading genealogies in the Bible—you know, all the "begats." I enjoy reading about the day-to-day activities in the lives of Bible characters—the ones that God told writers to include in His Book. Years ago, when my son was being homeschooled, we sat together and worked out a timeline of whose son was who and how long each one had lived. I had a great time (I'm not sure if my son did). I'm fascinated with the idea that my family tree and yours, whoever you are, all meet back at the Flood and then again back at Adam and Eve. No matter who you are, no matter what nationality or ethnicity you are, I am related to you. And not just through Noah and Adam and Eve, but through the blood of Jesus. Without Him, none of us would have the hope of existing beyond this life.

I'm really looking forward to meeting all of my relatives in heaven—all of my ancestors and you. It will be great fun figuring out exactly how we're related. And who knows? We just might even have the same birthday!

Kathy Pepper

God's Taxi

And it shall come to pass, that before they call,
I will answer; and while they are yet speaking, I will hear.
—Isaiah 65:24, KJV

Knowing how my mother hated to be late anywhere—especially for her first time to fly back home to visit relatives in Virginia—I made a point of making sure I allowed more than enough time to load up and make the eighty-mile trip from Cushing, Oklahoma, to Will Rogers World Airport in Oklahoma City and hoped for time to spare. Things went well until I prepared to enter I-35 heading south. My car began to slow down and then came to a stop as I pulled onto the shoulder of the on-ramp. I sat there, stunned. My mother's eyes revealed panic. Before she could say anything, I quickly stated, "We need to pray." As I said "Amen" and lifted my eyes, I spotted another vehicle pulled onto the shoulder in front of us. A middle-aged woman carefully made her way to my side of our station wagon. Rolling down the window, I waited until she greeted us.

"Is everything OK?" She seemed genuinely concerned.

I shook my head. "I am afraid my car chose a rather inopportune time to quit on me. We're on the way to the airport for my mother to catch her flight."

The stranger's face lit up. "I'm headed to the airport, too, to pick up my daughter. Would you like a lift?" *Would I!* It didn't take long to transfer Mother's luggage to our rescuer's car. Within minutes we were on our way. As we rode along, our angel-in-human-form explained why she was at that spot at that moment. "Normally, I would have left for the airport much sooner than this, but today of all days, I had several students who needed my assistance with the class I teach at the university and couldn't get away." She smiled broadly before continuing. "At first, I was annoyed with the delay, but now I can see God's hand in it. I must confess I don't normally stop like this, but I felt impressed it was OK for me to do so."

Mother and I heartily agreed that our rescuer had indeed served a much-needed service as "God's taxi" and were thankful our benefactress had listened to God's promptings. My mother made it to the airport on time, and our new friend returned me to my vehicle, where my brother soon appeared to get my car running again. Once again, God made it clear that nothing takes Him by surprise. He had indeed answered our prayer before we prayed it.

Sharon Clark

July 24

Lifted

[He] sets me on my high places. . . .
Your right hand has held me up.
—Psalm 18:33, 35, NKJV

Our three visiting grandchildren, who live in a suburban California city, couldn't get enough of, well, *nature* here in the South—swimming in Bear Creek Lake, fishing, and just being out under the tall pine trees. One afternoon as we headed back to the car after a swim in the lake, four-year-old Kent turned to his dad (my son, Andrew), pointed to pine branches well above his head, and said, "Daddy, I want to touch some high places. Could you lift me up?"

Putting down an armload of beach towels, my tall son grasped little Kent just above his knees. "Hold your body straight and reach high," he instructed. Kent raised his short arms, stiffened his body, and looked up with expectation as his dad slowly lifted him higher and higher. Within seconds, at the end of his father's arms yet safe in the grasp of strong hands, the excited child strained for the closest pine branch above his head.

"Daddy, I'm touching the high places! I see more blue sky!" he cried with excitement. At that point, my memory "camera" recorded my grandson grasping a pine branch with both hands as his father's extended, steady arms held him high enough to achieve that little heart's desire.

Whenever I revisit this snapshot in my mind's photo album, I think of high places that I've been able to grasp, too, because *my* Father lifted me up, holding me securely. In high places among divine branches, I have surrendered the outcomes of a cancer diagnosis and family losses to focus on hope beyond. In high places, heavenly promises from God's Word replace fear, grief, and bitterness with fresh comfort, trust, and peace. In high places, we may even grasp dreams—despite thinking all has been lost—that we didn't know we had. With astonishment, I, too, have cried out, "Daddy—Father—I'm *touching* it! And I see bluer skies now!"

Words fail to describe what it's like to pray, *Father, lift me up*, then experience His strength replacing weakness, His fullness replenishing emptiness. All I can do is humble my grateful heart and pray His own truths back to Him: *I will love you, O Lord, my strength. You set me on high places, Your right hand sustained me, and Your gentleness encouraged me. You are the One who lifts me up* (Psalm 18:1, 33, 35, 48, author's paraphrase). Today, let Him lift you up.

Carolyn Rathbun Sutton

Tell, Tell, Tell—Part 1

But the wise took oil in their vessels with their lamps.
—Matthew 25:4, KJV

We were excited. Our son was graduating from the United States Coast Guard boot camp in Cape May, New Jersey. We received an official letter informing us of the date and time of graduation, along with other events taking place before graduation. The letter also informed us that proper identification would be needed for each of us to get onto the military base, but it didn't specify what documents would be acceptable.

After reading the letter, I called my sister to let her know that personal ID would be needed, and we discussed what documents to bring. Recently we had both gotten REAL ID–compliant driver's licenses (for increased security standards), so we felt confident our licenses would be sufficient. But not everyone in our family had had the REAL ID driver's license. Next, I called the Coast Guard's security office. The officer said a military ID was necessary to get on base, but he didn't know what a REAL ID driver's license was. Not sure what to do, I packed extra documentation for everyone, such as passports and birth certificates.

On Thursday, everyone was at my mom's house—my sister and her husband, my two sons, and, of course, my husband and I. The discussion around the table was how our youngest son would get to go to the graduation, as he had forgotten his driver's license in North Carolina! I mentioned bringing extra ID for him, so that problem was covered. Friday came. Our eldest son drove with us; our other son and my mom rode with my sister and brother-in-law.

As we neared the Throgs Neck Bridge in New York City, my sister phoned and informed us that Mom hadn't brought any identification with her. They would have to turn around to get it. I felt so bad and blamed myself for having forgotten to say anything to her earlier.

As I reflected on this event, it made me aware of something even more important. Jesus is coming again soon. Am I neglecting to tell others, directly and personally, that Jesus is the only way to enter heaven? Will I be the cause of their not being prepared? Jesus has a million and one ways to reach souls, but He also expects each of us to take part in reaching out. *Dear Lord, may I be like the wise virgins, filled with Your Holy Spirit and telling others of Your soon return.*

Rosemarie Clardy

Tell, Tell, Tell—Part 2

"Enter into the joy of your lord."
—Matthew 25:21, NKJV

Guilt! I felt consumed by it on the rest of the drive to Cape May for our son's graduation from the United States Coast Guard boot camp. If only I had told my mom to bring her ID, all of this delay could have been avoided. We had left at 6:10 A.M., figuring this would give us plenty of time to get to the military base for the 11:00 A.M. graduation. Now, with the other half of our family having to turn around to get Mom's ID, they would lose a half hour's travel time—or more. When we got close to the base, we gave my sister a call. She said they were about eight minutes behind us. I couldn't believe how they had been able to catch up with us so quickly. The long delay I was anticipating had not happened. And when they arrived eight minutes later, no word of complaint against me was made. I felt humbled and grateful for it all.

We drove to the gate of the base. The guard on duty smiled as he asked if we were there for the graduation. Yes, came our reply. He then asked for the last name of our graduate. As he looked it up on his sheet, he then asked for our identification documents. Everyone's driver's license was acceptable to get onto the base. Another blessing—no need for more ID.

We drove to the parking area, which was already filled, and parked on the street as directed. As we walked to the auditorium for the orientation part of the graduation, the recruits on duty who were stationed at each street corner gave us all a hearty "Good morning!" After the orientation, we were directed to go to the gymnasium. Before we entered the building, the whole company of eighty-one graduates in dress uniform marched by, chanting as loudly as you could imagine, with a straight face and form. It was impressive and beautiful to see and sent chills up and down my spine. We went into the gymnasium and took our seats on the bleachers and watched as Company Bravo-196 marched in. They stood at parade rest the whole time. After receiving their diplomas and marching back into place, they were dismissed. Everyone rushed from their seats, and graduates rushed to their loved ones. The love was flowing freely in that building as friends and family shared expressions of love and pride.

Thank You, Lord, for every blessing of that day. Thank You also for forgiveness, for family, and for the opportunity to tell others of Your love!

Rosemarie Clardy

The Hummingbird

Behold the fowls of the air: for they sow not,
neither do they reap, nor gather into barns; yet your heavenly
Father feedeth them. Are ye not much better than they?
—Matthew 6:26, KJV

I live in a very rural area in South Carolina, along with my husband, deer, rabbits, squirrels, raccoons, possums, bobcats, and all sorts of other critters. Early one morning, I was sitting on my front porch, still in my nightgown, having my morning devotion.

Somewhere between the stillness of the morning and the words I was reading, I began to sense the presence of the Holy Spirit. There was something about this devotion that caused my innermost soul to become energized. I've had devotionals that resonated within me and even made me tearful before.

But this one was different.

I finished my reading and moved to the top of the steps. As I stood there, I began to sing and lift my hands to the Lord. It was as though God had allowed me to step into a different dimension, and there I was—just the Lord and me. I could hear only the melodious songs of the birds and leaves rustling as small animals scurried along.

I began to pray. I prayed and cried. And then, I prayed and cried some more. That's when it happened. First, I heard the sound of what I thought to be a bumblebee. But when I opened my eyes, I saw a hummingbird. It was only inches from my face. Wow! I couldn't believe that a hummingbird was that close to me.

Often we experience trying times in our lives, times when it seems that our very souls are aching. Our husbands may stray, our children may get into trouble, and our finances may get out of control.

Yes, as Christians, we are not removed from the trials, temptations, and cares of this world. But we have God, who knows just how to feed our souls. He knows how to help us rise above our circumstances and He ministers to us. He constantly ministers, sometimes giving us an occasional moment to hear and see, yes, a hummingbird.

You may not see a hummingbird today, but I'm sure that God has something special in mind just for you as He whispers, "I'm near."

Cheryl P. Simmons

Meditation or Medication?

*I counsel thee to buy of me gold tried in the fire, that thou
mayest be rich; and white raiment, that thou mayest be clothed,
and that the shame of thy nakedness do not appear;
and anoint thine eyes with eyesalve, that thou mayest see.*
—Revelation 3:18, KJV

Grandma, I want my meditation," my granddaughter requested of me with urgency in her four-year-old voice.

"OK, dear," I replied. "Climb up in the bed with Grandma."

Neriah loves family worship and would learn snatches of Bible texts her older siblings were memorizing. One day, she beamed up at me. "Grandma, I know the text!" And she verbalized it: "Babylon is fallen, is fallen" (Revelation 14:8, KJV).

Well, meditation time it was! Cradling her in my arms, we sang together some songs: "Jesus Never Fails" and "Prayer Changes Things." A Bible story followed. Then we had prayer, and our meditation ended.

I started dozing off to sleep. Little Neriah climbed up and fetched her cough mixture, brought it to me, and said, "Grandma, I want my medication."

I smiled as the truth dawned on me. This lively little girl—that a cold was slowing down due to continued bouts of coughing—had previously asked me, not for meditation, but for her medication.

The Bible says that we are sick. "The whole head is sick, and the whole heart faint. From the sole of the foot even unto the head there is no soundness in it; but wounds, and bruises, and putrifying sores: they have not been closed, neither bound up, neither mollified with ointment" (Isaiah 1:5, 6, KJV). Jesus Himself said, "They that are whole have no need of the physician, but they that are sick: I came not to call the righteous, but sinners to repentance" (Mark 2:17, KJV).

What then do we need? We need to meditate upon God's Word, hiding His truths in our hearts that we will not sin against Him. Additionally, it would do us well to accept the medicated eyesalve, which God offers us so that we may see the wondrous things in His law.

For us, what will it be: Meditation, medication—or both?

Hyacinth V. Caleb

Surrounded

The LORD appeared to him from afar, saying,
"I have loved you with an everlasting love;
Therefore I have drawn you with lovingkindness."
—Jeremiah 31:3, NASB

I'm organized to a fault, and that's why I wasn't panicked about making my flight.

In the next hour and a half, before lurching forward down the tarmac, I'd load my car, drive, park, shuttle to the terminal, check baggage, walk through an expedited security line, and still have time for an email or two. It was routine. But as I walked down the steps of my apartment building and into the parking lot, my world collapsed. There was one empty space, and I knew that's where I'd left my car. A fist-sized lump forced its way into my throat—the parking pass. I'd forgotten to put it back on my mirror after cleaning my car the night before. My car had been towed! My world felt like it was crashing in on me. In the chaos and through tears, I called the one person who always knew how to fix things—my father.

I wasn't going to make it, and I would miss my meetings. The order had been replaced by chaos and the routine by fear. I was so angry with myself for what had happened. I was so fearful that I'd let people down that were waiting for me. And then before I knew it, the front of a truck I recognized turned a corner toward me. I recognized the steady hands on the wheel and the calm face of the man who has always been there—my rock, my world, my daddy.

Not a complaint came from his lips. Not a wagging finger or furrowed brow. No disappointment in his tone. Just, "Let's go." His calmness hid his determination to get me there. There was no panic within him that I could see. And with that look, and with that stare of what was ahead, I let him bear the burden of what I was feeling. I let him take the load and the doubt and the worry.

Did I make it? Of course.

And I was then quietly reminded of our God. If this mountain of a man could drop everything—every time his daughter needed him—with what I believe is immeasurable love, could you imagine how much more our heavenly Father loves us? To what lengths He would go to say, "I'm here. I've got you. Let's go."

Erica Jones

He Saved Me—Part 1

Yea, though I walk through the valley of the shadow of death,
I will fear no evil: for thou art with me;
thy rod and thy staff they comfort me.
—Psalm 23:4, KJV

On August 15, 2016, I was on a work trip to represent the Western Cape Education Department in a misconduct case. The day was sunny but very windy. I was driving a state car, which felt uncomfortable to me. I concluded that it was due to the windy weather. As I drove, I was listening to a song entitled "You Saved Me." I got caught up in the lyrics and increased the volume, unaware that my travel speed was also increasing. In a steep curve, just before I reached Riviersonderend, South Africa, I lost control of the car. I recall the car pulling toward the right in the direction of a cliff while I tried to steer it left. After swerving, my vehicle flew toward a big rock and rolled over several times, finally coming to a stop.

I was conscious throughout, thinking I would not survive. Yet I felt calm for some strange reason—almost as if I were in a bad dream with things happening I couldn't do anything about. When the car stopped, I was shocked to be alive. The back of the car was wide open, and I just walked out. Another miracle was that no cars were coming from either direction. Then I returned to fetch my bags and files.

While I was busy trying to retrieve my luggage from the car, a couple stopped nearby to inquire where the people were who had been in the car. I told them it was I, alone. They could not believe it. They asked me to sit down because the car's ignition was still on and the petrol was gushing out. They thought the car might explode at any time. A few cars stopped by us and an ambulance as well, and people managed to get my belongings out of the car. It was only when I was in the ambulance that my emotions started flowing as I realized what could have happened.

If someone asks me where God was when all this happened, I can confidently say, "He was there with me, and I felt His presence." He ensured no cars were coming from either direction because that would have resulted in a fatal accident. I cry whenever I think about this.

God prepared me from the moment I woke up that day. He was with me even when I walked in the shadow of death. He assured me again through that song, "You Saved Me," which was playing just before the accident. What an amazing God we serve!

Deborah Matshaya

He Saved Me—Part 2

*"All right, you may test him," the LORD said to Satan.
"Do whatever you want with everything he possesses,
but don't harm him physically."*
—Job 1:12, NLT

My brush with death during my automobile accident reminds me of the story of Job and how the devil had a meeting with God regarding Job. Satan challenged God that the only reason Job was faithful was because God had protected him. God gave the devil permission to test Job's faith. However, God placed a condition on the devil—he could not take Job's life.

In the end, Job passed the test, for he never wavered in his faith. He remained faithful despite every trial and loss the devil put him through.

I think back to my accident. I sustained no injuries except for chest pain due to the impact of the car and the safety belt. However, I struggled mentally for quite a while when having to drive on a hill or around a curve. But God was still faithful. The Western Cape Educational Department referred me to a wellness program for shock counseling. In the end, I realized that healing comes from trusting God and knowing that He will never leave me or forsake me. I am now driving again. Life goes on, and, in the end, God's name is honored.

All the trials we encounter will be in vain if, in the end, we don't honor the One who has placed a hedge around our lives. The One who said to the devil, "Yes, you may test the faith but not take the life." That is what my God did for me on August 15, 2016. He saved my life.

In Job 1:12, we read God's words to the devil concerning Job. " 'All right, you may test him,' the LORD said to Satan. 'Do whatever you want with everything he possesses, but don't harm him physically' " (NLT). Sometimes God can remove the hedge around you to test your faith, but He will still—and always—be around when the devil strikes. For me, the hedge was removed on August 15, 2016, and the devil struck. What he did not know was that God Himself was in the car with me. The devil will not stop trying to shake our faith, my dear sisters. Let us draw courage in the assurance that when the battle is over, our God will prevail in the end.

Be ye faithful until the end, dear sisters. Trust God, and know that He loves you in your situation and circumstances. It is my prayer, my sisters, that if the hedge is removed, your faith will not be shaken. Trust God, stand tall, and declare, "He saved me!"

Deborah Matshaya

My Delicious Monster Plant

To every thing there is a season . . .
A time to be born, and a time to die; a time to plant, and a time to
pluck up that which is planted.
—Ecclesiastes 3:1, 2, KJV

Today I found it much too hot to take my usual walk. So I decided to stay indoors, roll up the blind of my lounge window, and do some writing instead.

As I gaze out my window, I look upon my delicious monster plants. I have four of them growing in large containers. I like to watch for new shoots to appear from the last leaf that came out from the parent plant.

That little shoot grows longer and longer until it unfurls, slowly but surely, into a beautiful, large, green, almost circular leaf with holes and indentations that reveal a pretty pattern. This plant loves the warmth of the sun yet needs a bit of shelter. Otherwise, the edges turn brown. Many leaves are a bright and beautiful green, but, unfortunately, they don't stay that way.

Into the next stage, the color on the leaves begins to change. Only a slight bit of pale green remains on the rib of the leaf, then yellow and gold with brown edges. Then it's time to trim it off the main plant, but no! I wait a while longer to enjoy its beauty.

Now the time has come when the once beautiful leaf is brown and withered. Is there any beauty left in it now? Maybe, if only useful for the compost heap.

These transitions make me think of my life; I was born from my mother-parent. Birth is a miracle from God. Like a new leaf, I clung to my mother. She taught me about Jesus. I was a happy child. There were three siblings—I helped care for them. Mother always made me feel special. I was like the bright green leaf.

The time came for me to marry. Mom later died. I'm now in the golden-leaf stage. "A time to live, a time to die," as we might paraphrase the philosopher. I'll be like the brown leaf soon, withered by pains that come with old age. What influence have I left behind? Will people remember me as the green leaf, as the golden leaf, or as the brown leaf, only good to be cut down? Whatever my remaining time, may I use it as a positive influence for God.

God, help us brighten someone's life today and be the best for Your glory!

Priscilla E. Adonis

No Snow White Story . . .

*But each one must carefully scrutinize his own work
[examining his actions, attitudes, and behavior], and then he can
have the personal satisfaction and inner joy of doing something
commendable without comparing himself to another. For every
person will have to bear [with patience] his own burden [of faults
and shortcomings for which he alone is responsible].*
—Galatians 6:4, 5, AMP

Maybe some of you have never heard the fairy tale of Snow White. The evil Queen looks into her mirror and asks, "Who is the fairest of them all?" The mirror answers, "Snow White." The Queen then sets out to destroy the competition. Today, the mirror is social media.

Ladies, have we bought into the concept that we must compete with one another, rather than affirming one another? On social media, we show only the best: perfect occasions, outfits, meals—you know the deal. It's difficult for mere mortals to live up to such perfection.

I'm so glad to know that the Lord tells us that we are works in progress! Scripture reminds us, "And we all, with unveiled face, *continually* seeing as in a mirror the glory of the Lord, are *progressively* being transformed into His image from [one degree of] glory to [even more] glory, which comes from the Lord, [who is] the Spirit" (2 Corinthians 3:18, AMP, emphasis in original).

When I begin looking around, I can easily become discouraged: I'm not as talented or smart as someone else. Yet when I look up, I see my gracious, merciful Lord and His smile as He encourages me to be the *best me* I can be! He does not expect me to be anyone else but me. That makes me take a deep breath, stand a little taller, and start walking on *my* path. I don't have to best anyone else or replicate them. I have to develop all the talents and gifts given to me and smile because my Lord has called me to do something no one else can do. There is not another me. My God is so great—He needs me, and all of us, to show how great and good He is.

I can enjoy looking at social media and applaud others as they accomplish the tasks they feel called to do. I can cheer them on and not feel diminished. All I have to remember are the Lord's words to me: "Before I formed you in the womb I knew you [and approved of you as My chosen instrument], And before you were born I consecrated you [to Myself as My own]" (Jeremiah 1:5, AMP). "Who is the fairest of them all?" Actually, it's *fairest Lord Jesus*!

Wilma Kirk Lee

Weavers of the Fabric of Life

She spins her own cloth,
and she helps the poor
and the needy. . . .
She does her own sewing,
and everything she wears
is beautiful.
—Proverbs 31:19, 20, 22, CEV

"Abraham believed God, and God accepted Abraham's faith, and
that faith made him right with God." And Abraham was called
God's friend.
—James 2:23, NCV

My daughter, Kristin Marie, gave me the gift of a lesson with a master weaver. During the lesson, I learned to thread a lap loom and to weave fabric. For a seamstress, tailor, and lover of fabrics, this was the gift of a lifetime that filled a void. A void left thirty years ago by the untimely death of my fabric-loving mother-in-law, Lillian—and the wound that ripped my heart a few weeks ago by the all too early death of my sister, Marcia.

Lillian and I would roam fabric stores, caressing beautiful fabrics and imagining elegant garments draping and flowing. With Marcia, time did not matter when we entered a fabric store. She went immediately to the shelves overflowing with yarn. Simple rows of thread, undulating and overriding themselves, yet staying in place. Then there was fabric for crafting beautiful garments and elegantly dressing royalty, yet simple enough to shield the body of a pauper.

Death has a way of rending the fabric of our souls, tearing warp and woof, leaving holes, voids, and visual reminders of what once was. Something is missing. My loom is a reminder that fabric, like life, permits us to weave threads of beauty into something even more beautiful.

What beautiful threads will you encounter today? And what beautiful fabric will your threads weave?

Weave on, my friends. Weave on.

Thank You, Lord, for friendships. Thank You especially for calling me Your friend as I trust You to mend the rent fabric of my soul. Please help me be a friend to someone today.

Prudence LaBeach Pollard

A Small-Scale Scenario
of Self-Inflation

*Fear thou not. . . . I will strengthen thee; yea, I will help thee; yea,
I will uphold thee with the right hand of my righteousness.*
—Isaiah 41:10, KJV

G od is *so* good!
I've been going to New York from time to time since high school graduation. Since I had family there, someone was always available, and I never had to navigate the city alone. Fast-forward to a few years ago. I'm now a senior citizen with less energy; only my ninety-year-old aunt is in New York, and she is developing dementia. Her neighbor alerted us to some concerns that needed addressing as quickly as possible. At the time, it was not my desire to go to New York; the allurements of the city had faded. Someone had to go, but no one was able to go with me. What was I to do? I prayed and asked God to help me. My first step was to search the internet for directions from the airport to her apartment. Being a frugal person, I wanted to use public transportation. All the time, I was praying for strength, wisdom, and protection.

After a safe flight, I set out to find my way. After asking how to get a MetroCard (which I could use to pay for city bus and subway fares), I got on a bus and then on the subway—successfully. By this time, I was feeling quite exhilarated and proud of myself. Notice that I said *proud*. I had forgotten my prior feelings of anxiety and helplessness and was thinking, *Wow! I really am good at this!* I was beaming and feeling like a New Yorker.

However, before I arrived at my aunt's apartment, I made two navigational mistakes. Forgetting all my supplications to God for this trip, I had become absorbed in self-inflation. God used those mistakes to reel me back into reality. He was the one granting me this success.

Beware, sisters. Self-inflation can occur on any scale and at any age. Sometimes we forget that and think life is about our ability, skill, or knowledge. Don't let the enemy deceive you into thinking that your accomplishments are solely your own. The world sets us up to believe in and promote self. That is a tactic of the enemy. People may mock you for giving God the glory, but keep your eyes on Him and His goodness in your life. And be willing to speak of His goodness!

Sharon M. Thomas

Blowout on the Coquihalla

He shall call upon me, and I will answer him:
I will be with him in trouble; I will deliver him, and honour him.
—Psalm 91:15, KJV

Camp meeting was over for another year. I had my purchased blueberries, and we were on our way home—the air was smoky from forest fires around the province. Then we suddenly found ourselves crawling along the highway in slow traffic. An accident had occurred. A semitruck had lurched out of control, broken through the concrete barriers, and gone down the side of the mountain. Then our own emergency happened—our left rear tire had a blowout!

On this freeway, stops were not allowed; only a four-foot strip marked the shoulder and then concrete barriers. *What to do? What to do? O, Father!* An opening on the roadside suddenly appeared, just large enough for our car to glide into—our Father is never taken by surprise.

While Harmony unloaded the trunk of the car, I watched little John, her two-year-old live wire. I sat on the concrete barrier and fed him arrowroot biscuits and cherries, for he must not run to see what his mother was doing or he might be hit by a vehicle.

Harmony wrestled out the small spare tire and, shortly after, had exchanged it for the flat tire. The recommended speed for the small tire was about fifty miles per hour. We had many miles to go before reaching Kamloops and finding a Canadian Tire store.

"Yes, we can repair your tire on Tuesday," the clerk replied to Harmony's question. *Tuesday!* Today was Sunday. We had no time to wait. We must find another shop. But what shop would be open on a long holiday weekend? Harmony drove past several garages. The Lord impressed her to continue until she found the right one. Yes, one shop could repair the damaged tire and also replace it with a new one—within thirty minutes. It was nearly closing time. We had made it! This again was help from our Father. When the repair bill was presented after the work completed, Harmony was pleasantly surprised. The mechanics had rotated the tires, put on two new tires instead of one, and given a hefty discount on the tires.

Surely, God had worked overtime in order to answer our prayers. What an unfailing Parent! "Call unto me, and I will answer thee, and show thee great and mighty things, which thou knowest not" (Jeremiah 33:3, KJV).

Muriel Heppel

Fear, Ferret, and Funny

Peace, be still.
—Mark 4:39, KJV

Ah-h-h-h!" screamed Melissa, leaping onto the sectional sofa, popcorn flying up in the air. *"Ah-h-h-h-h-h-h!"* Turning, I saw a ferret, a domesticated form of the European polecat, streak across the carpet and disappear under the ottoman in the adjoining sunroom. Quickly closing the glass door, I pondered a course of action; this was difficult, though, since Melissa was still yelling, jumping, and sending popcorn flying. "Two weeks ago, a fat raccoon under the wheelbarrow. Last week a possum asleep on the clothes dryer in the garage. Today a . . . "

"Ferret," I said, intending to explain that the name means "little thief" and that the Romans used them for hunting. But the mayhem was deafening and too distracting. "Melissa, be still. You may go to your room and jump and scream and be part of the problem, or you can fetch the long-handled broom from the shed and be part of the solution. It's your choice."

Blessed quietness, momentarily. In a flash, she was back. Broom in hand, I stepped into the sunroom and, giving the ottoman a wide berth, opened the outside door. Back on the other side, I banged the broom purposefully on the floor before shoving the long handle under the ottoman. Voilà! The ferret streaked through the open door and disappeared into the woods.

"It's my fault," said Melissa contritely, pointing at the front door, still gaping ajar.

"It happens," I said. "What could you do another time to get a positive outcome?"

"Close and latch the door," she replied shakily. "I'll vacuum up the popcorn. Sorry I screamed. How could you be so calm? All I saw was a creature I didn't even recognize!"

"The calmer you are, the better your brain problem-solves," I said. I acknowledged being grateful there was only one ferret and not a whole "business," and then I knew how to proceed. "Thank you for fetching the broom. Keeping ferrets as pets in this state is illegal, so I bet this one used to be a pet and either ran away or its owners just set it free." In truth, I never intended to laugh. But remembering how funny Melissa had looked jumping, popcorn flying everywhere, screaming her head off, I started to chuckle. Before long, both of us were doubled over with mirth, tears of laughter running down our cheeks. Another memory to savor as the years go by.

Can you "be still"? You can have peace even in the midst of chaos.

Arlene R. Taylor

Ordinary People

*And whether one member suffer, all the members suffer with it; or
one member be honoured, all the members rejoice with it.*
—1 Corinthians 12:26, KJV

I love the culinary arts! It's a fascinating and dynamic world. The skill of food preparation is a useful one and can be a blessing or a curse, depending on how it's used and for what purpose. Here are two scriptural examples. One woman blessed the prophet Elijah with a meal and put herself in line for the boomerang effect of having her pantry continually full (see 1 Kings 17:8–16). Rebekah, Jacob's mother, was a good cook, but the dish she prepared included, sadly, ingredients such as deceit and strife that are still with us globally (see Genesis 27:1–45).

As I prepared a meal recently, I considered the process required for putting together a tasty dish: main ingredients, pots, pans, utensils, and cooking or baking heat instructions and duration. Of course, without the presentation, the planned effect may not be achieved. While adding a dash of this and that here and there, I found myself reflecting on the significance of each item to the finished product, and how blah the food would taste without salt: even a pinch of seasoning is vital to adding taste and flavor! In that instant, like a ton of bricks, I was reminded that each member of God's family serves an important purpose. This contemplation brought the words of the song "Ordinary People" that I love by Danniebelle Hall through my mind as I stirred. The lyrics share that God can use everyday people to accomplish His will if they will trust and obey Him. The little we have to offer Him can become much when placed in His hand.

Do you know what essence, what flavor or aroma you bring to the gospel commission within your sphere of influence? What is your gift, talent, or skill? Which "member" of the body of Christ are you? Without you, your input, your acts of worship, and your service to God, the body cannot be healthy and whole. Don't you ever forget that fact! And if you have any doubt whatsoever, deliberately omit an important ingredient from the next dish that you prepare, and let me know how it tastes.

Dear Jesus, please grant my heart's desire to be united with You and with Your remnant people (see Revelation 12:17).

Cloreth S. Greene

Climbing Mount La Soufrière

Let perseverance finish its work so that you may be mature and complete, not lacking anything.
—James 1:4, NIV

The quiet morning air was broken by the laughter and chatter of voices, young and old. Our family and friends were going to climb the four-thousand-foot volcanic mountain, Mount La Soufrière in St. Vincent. The first part of the journey was on level ground, lush with rain-fed vegetation. Tall, elegant bamboo trees stretched from some dark abyss below to absorb the bright sunlight. Wildflowers punctuated the vegetation and made it a pleasant hike. We easily climbed the first slope and cheered when the path leveled off before the next upward slope. As we climbed, the slopes became steeper. My brother, Branson, who worked for the Board of Tourism, had workers build log steps over the steep, slippery slopes to make the climb easier. But the steps were set so far apart that it took a stride to reach each one. One relative, Cheryl, struggled and fell behind, so three of us climbed slowly with her. The men made rough walking sticks to help us. In one place, the footpath on the level ground became very narrow. I shuddered as I glanced over the vegetation-covered slopes, which seemed to descend into the same dark abyss as the bamboos.

Two hours later, we saw the peak, but the last slope—about seventy-five feet wide—was covered with gravel. Young people, running down from the peak, loosened much of the gravel, yet with the help of the walking sticks, we made it to the top.

Before we got there, however, our guide admonished us to get down on our hands and knees and crawl to the summit because strong winds at the top could blow us over into the volcanic crater hundreds of feet below. He allowed us to peer over the precipice. There, glistening in the brilliant sunlight, was the crater lake, so calm and peaceful. It was hard to imagine that this could turn into a destructive force.

Climbing La Soufrière is like the Christian's journey. It's usually an upward climb. Sometimes the road is level and filled with many joys and blessings. Other times, we have to surmount challenges, trials, afflictions, and temptations. But with God's help, as with the walking stick, we'll reach the height that God wants us to achieve. Even then, at the top, we can slip or fall, but God, our Guide and Protector, will hold us safe till Jesus comes.

H. Anesta Thomas

August 9

The Blooming Faith of a Teenager

Be on your guard; stand firm in the faith; be courageous; be strong.
—1 Corinthians 16:13, NIV

In the early fall of 2017, as I settled into my sixth-grade year, the school's track coach asked me to be a member of one of the teams. Because of my agility and running skills, I was easily drafted into the team of runners. Due to the school's policy, there were many documents to read and sign in the process that would allow me to be engaged in practice sessions, travel, and, of course, the promise to continue getting good grades. My coach was impressed with my enthusiasm and progress. My mom told me that one of the forms stated that in early spring, I would have practices and meets on the weekend, which would include Sabbath. I felt disappointed already. I enjoyed track, especially since my dad tells me I will one day be a track-and-field star. On April 10, my coach said, "Alex-Anne, I am so sorry, but you can no longer participate in track and field because you will not be able to practice track on Friday and attend track meets on Saturdays." My heart sank. I was so disappointed—my spirit broke. That evening I came home, and my mom noticed that I was not energetic and lively. I told her the sad news.

My mom hugged me and reassured me that we would pray about the matter and leave it in God's hands. My mom continued to encourage and console me as she declared with conviction that if I was supposed to be on the track team, nothing could change that. She said, "Alex-Anne, you are a Bible-believing Christian, and you need to prove God for yourself with this issue." We prayed about the pressing matter and left it in God's hands.

Two weeks later, I went to school. As soon as I got situated in my classroom, I was summoned to the principal's office. This was such a dramatic situation—almost everyone was peeking at me. Some of my friends muttered concerns about my being summoned to the principal's office. As I headed toward the principal's office, I saw my coach; this was puzzling to me since I knew that I was off the track team. The principal directed me to the coach, who said, "Alex-Anne, you are my number one runner, and I am giving you another chance." He continued, "I will allow you to have your track meets during the week instead of on Fridays and Saturdays because I cannot afford to lose you." I texted my mom and told her the good news.

I want to continue to be faithful to God throughout my life.

Alex-Anne Riley

PreCheck

He died to sin once for all.
—Romans 6:10, NIV

As a music minister, I travel a lot. In my mind, I'm a seasoned traveler. Airport lines going through TSA (Transportation Safety Administration) or "security," as we call it, can be very long. They are categorized as General, Priority, and PreCheck lines. Priority means you have some status with your airline, which usually puts you in a shorter line to the security guard checking identification documents. Then you get put back with the general population to go through the scanning process. PreCheck is for people who have paid a fee, provided a background check, and taken the time to go to their local police station to give fingerprints. This elite group can sail through security without having to remove shoes, open laptops, or take off jackets! Sounds nice. Yet in times of heavy passenger traffic and excessively long lines, security guards will sometimes bump Priority passengers into the PreCheck line to balance things out. As you can imagine, this causes some ill will from some PreCheck passengers who paid the price to be in the fast lane—when others hadn't. It simply isn't fair!

I couldn't help but see a distinct similarity between this situation and the kingdom of God. Many of us lifelong Christians have been tempted to feel as though we are in the PreCheck line. After all, haven't we worked harder and longer at being good, faithful, and deserving than many others? The only problem is, God does not have a PreCheck lane. His salvation has no categories or boundaries. He cannot love us any more than He already does, no matter how hard we try, how hard we worship, how close to His principles we live. It's hard for some believers to swallow the fact that God loves the person who has served Him faithfully as much as He loves the person who has cursed and denied Him for years before being converted. In the end, there will be many that show up in heaven who, in some minds, couldn't possibly deserve to be there. (But truthfully, the ones who possess this latter frame of mind are the ones that won't deserve to be in heaven.) As you go about your day, I hope you will feel the love that God has for you. A love you could never earn, no matter how hard you try. We need a simple willingness to love God and others in that very same way that God loves you and me. Because when it comes to lines, I hope the one to heaven will be longer than any other line we have ever seen before.

Naomi Striemer

August 11

God's Printer

Give praise to the LORD, proclaim his name;
make known among the nations what he has done.
—Psalm 105:1, NIV

In 2012, I was the personal ministries director for my church in New York. Our pastor had had the blessed idea of giving away books during a soccer match between Brazil and Argentina. We bought four thousand books, bags, and water bottles. I decided to include a newspaper in our giveaways. After my file was ready to print, I realized that my printer would not be able to print eight thousand pages on time. I decided to buy a faster printer. A few days passed, but, to my dismay, the "Delivery delayed" message was still on the tracking records of my recent purchase.

Thinking about buying another printer in a store, I left to go to the dentist. On the way, my sister called me. She said, "The angel just delivered the printer!" I came home, and a twenty-hour, nonstop print journey started. With volunteers helping fold four thousand pages, we had everything ready on Sabbath to go to the stadium. Since that day, this same printer has been used to spread God's Word. I have printed thousands of kids' coloring sheets, music sheets, bulletins, and English lessons, among other ministry projects.

Six years after I bought the printer, its display gave this message: "Change the printer head." I checked the price of a printer head. It was the same price as a new printer! Then I knelt and "reminded" God that He is the owner of my printer. The message just disappeared.

In the middle of a special printing for the Orlando Brazilian Central Church Families Camping Meeting, smeared lines appeared in the middle of every printed page. I prayed, then restarted the printer but encountered the same problem. I repeated the same process again and again. I gave up and went to bed because it was late, and the meetings would start a few hours later. When I woke up, I hurried to the printer and turned it on. The first sheet came perfectly! I concluded God wanted me to recover my energies for the busy weekend. I know He was able to fix it at the very first prayer, but He preferred not. He knew I needed some rest.

I praise and worship this amazing God. He cares about our needs and works to fix things even while we are sleeping! How can I not let Him be the owner of all my belongings?

Kênia Kopitar

The Two Spies

And Joshua the son of Nun sent out of Shittim two men to spy secretly, saying, Go view the land, even Jericho. And they went, and came into an harlot's house, named Rahab, and lodged there.
—Joshua 2:1, KJV

After reading today's verse, my mind became riveted upon two phrases: "two men to spy secretly" and "go view the land." These phrases awakened questions, especially after I reread the verse with my personal context: "And Jesus the Son of God sent out of heaven two beings to spy secretly, saying, Go view the earth, even [the city where I live]. And they went, and came to a sinner's house, named [my name] and lodged there."

Joshua's mandate to the two spies was to leave their campground, enter Jericho, and secretly observe, investigate, substantiate, and gather information about the city's defense capabilities so he could prepare strategically for battle. Wow! What a task and an important assignment. As I thought about the responsibility of the spies, I thought, *Is it possible that I am going through the same secret scrutiny by spies as were the citizens of Jericho?* My answer is a conclusive yes. My guardian angel and the Holy Spirit, I believe, are my two secret spies. Both have the very important task of gathering evidence about my character, lifestyle, thoughts, and actions, which God, the Righteous Judge, has authorized them to do. This silent surveillance of the landscape of my life is how He keeps faithful records about me.

Although the people of Jericho were on high alert for enemy infiltration, they could not hinder the spies from doing their job. Despite the existing state of emergency and tightly guarded gates, the spies were detected only after they were lodged at the residence of Rahab the harlot.

I have come to realize that I cannot hinder the work of the "spies" in my life; they will fulfill their mission. I also realize that as Rahab was alert to the secret assignment of the spies, so must I be. I must be mindful of the presence of the Holy Spirit and my guardian angel each moment of each day. I should also endeavor to make my home (my life) an inviting, available, and habitable place where they will want to dwell. The Israelite spies were key participants in the scarlet-cord agreement of deliverance and salvation for Rahab and her family. I pray that the report of my "spies" will lead to my salvation and not to my destruction.

Maureen Thomas

Provoked to Jealousy

Have they stumbled that they should fall? God forbid:
but rather through their fall salvation is come unto the Gentiles,
for to provoke them to jealousy.
—Romans 11:11, KJV

For by one Spirit are we all baptized into one body,
whether we be Jews or Gentiles, whether we be bond or free;
and have been all made to drink into one Spirit.
—1 Corinthians 12:13, KJV

I have always loved the crape myrtle plant, so a few years ago, I purchased the deep pink variety to plant somewhere in my front yard. As I did not have much space, I did not want the tree to grow very tall, so I planted it in a large container. For about two years, I had medium-size blooms but comforted myself that the tree would produce larger blooms as it matured.

After two years, the tree died. This disappointed me deeply, but I was reluctant to toss out the trunk of the plant as it appeared to be so artistically formed. Then I had an idea: *I will use this trunk as a trellis for an annual runner* (a plant that "climbs" on some type of support and has a one-season life span). The first plant did well, producing lovely red flowers, but the flowers of the second plant looked sickly. I watered and fertilized the runner, but it continued to look even more sickly. I finally brought this to the attention of my neighbor, who is the unofficial plant doctor of the block.

Upon examination of the plant, she said to me, "Don't you understand what has happened? The crape myrtle became 'jealous' and did not want another plant running all over it, so it sent down roots and is alive again." As I write this (two years later), I am enjoying lovely blooms from the stump of the crape myrtle.

Paul, in Romans 11:11, explains that the salvation the Jews had so earnestly sought was also made available to the Gentiles, though Jews could still be saved. This turn of events made some Jews jealous. Since we, as Gentile believers, have been grafted into God's family tree, let us hold fast what has been given to us and "provoke" positive jealousy, encouraging one another to serve Christ and let "no man take thy crown" (Revelation 3:11, KJV).

Vashti Hinds-Vanier

From Darkness Into Light

"For I know the plans I have for you," declares the LORD,
"plans to prosper you and not to harm you,
plans to give you hope and a future."
—Jeremiah 29:11, NIV

Recently we witnessed (on television) the rescue operations for twelve young soccer players and their coach trapped inside a cave in Thailand. As the world rallied together to provide divers and rescue teams to get the victims out of the cave, people around the world were praying for the success of this rescue operation. The coach and the boys had been missing and trapped in the underground cave for more than two weeks and thought they didn't have a chance of getting out safely. They knew that some parts of the cave were underwater, and most of them didn't know how to swim. Furthermore, it was monsoon season in Thailand, and the rains could make flooding inside the cave more difficult for rescue.

When all twelve boys and their coach were ultimately rescued, we celebrated with Thailand and praised God for the rescue mission that had seemed impossible at first but had ultimately turned into a mission accomplished. This rescue story revealed humanity at its best—everybody helping one another. As I watched this event unfold on television, I thought about the sacrifices the rescue team was having to make to save those trapped in the cave. Although we grieve with the family of one diver who lost his life during the rescue operation, we know he did not die in vain. I believe that God has a plan for these young people who were rescued, and I thank Him for second chances.

Frequently we go through life not knowing what life challenges we are going to face—and sometimes end up in trouble before we know it. These young people didn't realize that a casual hike into the cave was going to get them trapped in the dark for more than two weeks. Thank God for His mercy and protective care that kept them safe throughout the whole ordeal. He sent angels in human form to help guide and lead these young people back to safety.

What a wonderful reminder of God's love and protection! Even though we may wander offtrack sometimes in our life journeys, God is always there to bring us out of the darkness into His marvelous light. He knows what is best for us and will always be there to rescue us from whatever cave of despair we find ourselves in.

Rhona Grace Magpayo

Angels in My Car Ride

For he orders his angels to protect you wherever you go.
—Psalm 91:11, TLB

It was April 4, and my mother was taking my sister and me to pick up our vouchers for WIC (Special Supplemental Nutrition Program for Women, Infants, and Children). I was pregnant, and Darla had just had a baby, so we had the benefit of the government assistance. On our way home, a pickup truck hit my mother's car. Mother was hospitalized and Darla suffered a broken nose, but we felt lucky that neither our children nor we had been severely hurt. Eight days later, my son Benton was delivered through cesarean section surgery.

Ten days after his birth, I planned to drive Benton back to the doctor for circumcision when my mother, who had been over to help me every day, commented that I didn't seem to be bouncing back as I had after my previous child's birth twenty-one months earlier. My sister, Darla, offered to take Benton and me to the doctor for his appointment.

Driving along our route, Darla suddenly asked, "Charlotte, what is the matter? Is my driving scaring you?" She stopped the car and came around to my side. Just then, I went into a grand mal seizure. The next thing I knew, our family doctor was standing beside me, saying, "Charlotte, do you know who I am?" I said I didn't. "Think about it awhile: I am sure it will come to you." I heard a baby cry and told Darla someone should be taking care of it.

"Charlotte," said Darla, "that is your baby." I thought, *What? I had a baby? Why didn't I know I had a baby?* Then I cried like the baby because the seizure had erased all memory of Benton's birth. When Dr. Tucker returned to the hospital room, I knew him.

More doctors and further tests suggested my seizure was a result of the earlier auto accident that my mom, sister, and I were in; I was also told my seizures would be a lifetime problem. One never knows when something will change in life, and you may find you are no longer the healthy person you were just a few weeks earlier.

As I look back on the incident, I realize that God sent my sister that fateful morning to drive, because if I had been driving, perhaps my son and I would have been killed on that trip to the clinic. Sometimes there are just small things that happen that make us realize God has His protective hand on us and His angels with us. Let's never forget His faithful care in our lives.

Charlotte (Swanson) Robinson

Does Jesus Care?

A thousand shall fall at thy side, and ten thousand at thy right hand; but it shall not come nigh thee.
—Psalm 91:7, KJV

As I awoke in the middle of the night, I thought of the lyrics of the song "We Shall Behold Him," by Dottie Rambo. The lyricist portrays nature's elements welcoming Christ, along with those who have been waiting for Him. I arose from my bed and peeked through my window to behold a beautiful scene I will never forget. I saw the clouds unfolding and a few stars appearing in the sky. My attention was immediately drawn to the half-moon I saw in the sky. At first, it appeared to be surrounded by dark clouds, but as I continued to observe, the moon became brighter and brighter; it looked as if it were being protected and surrounded by angels.

Pouring from my lips was the song "Does Jesus Care?" My answer was most confident: "O yes, He cares—I know He cares!"* Jesus cares because He sends the moon to remind me that He loves me. All my doubts at that moment were removed. I began to pray silently that the Lord would please help me trust in Him. I also asked Him to renew my faith. I told Him that I want my life to be a reflection of His life. He sent the moon to remind me He will keep His promise.

You see, for three days, I had been fearfully watching news reports of houses being flooded and rivers rising in another part of the country. Many people, including myself, were wondering if Florida was going to be covered with water too. Yet when I saw the moon and the beautiful rainbow, all my doubts disappeared. I enjoy awakening in the middle of the night to peek through my window and watch the stars and sometimes the moon when it does appear. They have become my friends because they remind me that God loves us and that He does care.

He reassures us through the psalmist David of His promise that though "a thousand shall fall at thy side, and ten thousand at thy right hand . . . it [destruction] shall not come nigh thee" (Psalm 91:7, KJV). If we trust in God and are obedient to Him, no flood can drown us.

The Lord will keep His promise. He will protect us.

Patricia Hines

---

* Frank E. Graeff, "Does Jesus Care?" 1901 in *The Seventh-day Adventist Hymnal*, no. 181.

Keep Your Eye on the Prize

"Seek first the kingdom of God and His righteousness,
and all these things shall be added to you."
—Matthew 6:33, NKJV

Our son was getting married on base at Fort Louis, Washington. Much to the delight of our six-year-old granddaughter, Makayla, he had invited her to be the flower girl. Adding to the adventure for her was a pretty dress and a flight from Michigan.

The base church was a large, older church with massive wooden doors leading from the foyer into the sanctuary. As a hospital chaplain, I was presiding at the wedding. The rehearsal began, and it was Makayla's turn to enter with her basket of flower petals. She hurried down the long aisle to reach the front. I tried to catch her eye to encourage her to slow her pace, but her eyes were on the floor.

At the hotel, I had one last chance to make suggestions. Makayla admitted to being nervous, afraid of messing up the wedding. After making pretend flowers from wadded-up tissues, we practiced. My instructions were simple: "When those huge wooden doors open, look at Nanna. Don't ever look down. With each step, drop one petal. Walk slowly. If you begin to walk too quickly, I will take my hands and move them slowly down from my face toward the ground. That's your signal to slow down. How does that sound?" Makayla was all for trying this out. We practiced a few times in the room, and all seemed well.

The next day brought the real test. Guests were in their places, and the groom was standing next to me up front. The organ music was playing. Those massive doors opened, and I could see Makayla. She looked so tiny! Her eyes were fixed on mine. She began walking, never losing eye contact with me. Her pace was slow and graceful as she daintily dropped her flower petals along the white runner. She reached the front with a smile on her face. Later that evening, I asked Makayla how she thought things went. She smiled. "Good. I did a really good job, and I'm proud of myself." So were we!

A couple of days later, as I entered my hospital, the lesson God had for me became clear. I need to keep my eyes on Him and notice where He is working and go there. Yes, I need to seek Him first with all my heart.

Carolyn J. H. Strzyzykowski

Before They Call

And it shall come to pass, that before they call, I will answer;
and while they are yet speaking, I will hear.
—Isaiah 65:24, KJV

Call unto me, and I will answer thee, and show thee great
and mighty things, which thou knowest not.
—Jeremiah 33:3, KJV

Scripture is replete with stories and narratives of God's miraculous provisions and protection for humanity, despite our spiritual shortsightedness. Because even when we do not necessarily call on God, He moves forward to meet our deepest needs. God is already in our future, shaping and fixing the intricacies of our lives to lead us to our divine destiny.

While it is important that we *ask*, *seek*, and *find*, we must never forget that even if we don't, God still pursues us and will, from time to time, show up in our lives in areas we had given up on, thinking that some battles were already lost. But it is not over until God says it is over. He invites us to call unto Him. He will give us a sneak peek or privileged glance into the perpetual harvest of blessings that He has provided for each of His children. His blessings provide for our every need: physical, spiritual, emotional, mental, and social.

Dear sisters, only an immortal God can solve the challenges of mortals. So today, know and believe that *before you call*, God will answer regarding your emotional and mental instability and give you His peace, which passes all understanding.

Before you call, He will bring physical healing and restoration to your broken body and spirit.

Yes, *before you call*, He will give you spiritual strength and fortitude that will guide you in every human storm.

Before you call, He will provide you with a social network that will meet all your social dilemmas.

Women of God, allow Him to show you great and mighty things, which you "knowest not" (Jeremiah 33:3, KJV). No matter the reason for your calling on Him, know and believe sincerely that He is listening. So call upon Him, audibly. Yes, *before you call*, He will answer.

Althea Y. Boxx

Standing in the Gap

Then I heard the voice of the Lord saying,
"Whom shall I send? And who will go for us?"
And I said, "Here am I. Send me!"
—Isaiah 6:8, NIV

I t was the strangest thing ever! Our school lost two teachers in a very short time and for the same class. When the first teacher left, it looked unfavorable for the school, but most of our parents were longtime stakeholders who were very familiar with the school. We carefully chose a replacement we believed—from experience—would do the job well and redeem us from our past failure. It was not to be. Within a month, the newest teacher was removed from the classroom. So two months into the school year, we had a room full of confused children and some very perturbed parents. Embarrassed and bewildered, I felt the Spirit of God directing me into that classroom. My administrative team worried that teaching would add a heavy load to my already-full plate of managerial work at this large school. A few teachers, however, believed that my presence would silence the anger and soothe the hurt (at the time, I had not taught full-time in almost nine years). Yet the requests from the teachers confirmed what the Holy Spirit had already impressed me to do. My team and I obeyed. Later as we met with the parents, we apologized and shared our plans to a group of anxious faces and rigid bodies. We ended with smiling faces, relaxed postures, and thankful handshakes. The parents were relieved, they were behind me, and they trusted me.

Throughout that experience, I thought of the many people in the Bible who obeyed when they were called. Abraham. Moses. Joshua. Deborah. Samuel. Esther. And many more imperfect ones like me. Then I think of the only perfect one—Jesus—who left heaven when my soul was in darkness and when all humanity was set to perish. He died on the cross so that we all may live with joy and the hope of a better home. Sometimes we, too, are called to stand in the gap. It may be to speak for the silenced or to work for the weak. It may be to stand between children and danger. And evil. Or to hold the helpless. When God calls, He empowers, and we need to go.

My sisters, today, if you see the evidence, feel the impression, hear the calling, go. Defend the powerless. Cherish the rejected. Heal the hurting hearts. Your calling is uniquely yours, and no one else can fill your spot. Go. By the power of the mighty Spirit of God—go.

Rose Joseph Thomas

The Miracle of the Pears

God is my strength . . . and he maketh my way perfect.
—2 Samuel 22:33, KJV

My daughter is an avid homemaker. She loves to bake bread, make granola, and try all kinds of new recipes. She also loves to can peaches, pears, and applesauce, and even though there may be some canned food leftover in the fruit room from the year before, she will add to the count when the fruit comes on each summer.

One Monday morning, she bought some pears, hoping they would be ready to can by the following Sunday or Monday. Pears never ripen at the same time, and some can take as long as a week to be ripe enough to use. So she put them in the basement where it was dark. Three days later, she thought she would check on them and see how they were coming along. Imagine her surprise when she found that every single pear was ripe and ready to be canned that very day! She called her sister and asked if she would be willing to come and help her, and she could have some of the canned pears as well. Our younger daughter was available, and by late morning, they were busy canning pears. Later that day, the pears were all in their jars, canned, and ready to be eaten this winter. The girls were delighted with all forty-two quarts and especially delighted to know that they would not have to can anymore until next year. When they told me about it, I was shocked to find all those pears had ripened at the same time. In all my fifty-something years of canning, I had never heard of such a thing.

Early the next morning, my oldest daughter's father-in-law, a retired pastor, passed away. He had been in the hospital, but his passing was still a shock. Her heart was broken. She had always felt very close to him and had even nicknamed him Uncle Charlie when he was a church youth director. The name had stuck, and thousands of young people came to know him as Uncle Charlie. Now he was gone, and she was very involved, along with her husband, in doing all that needs to be done when a family member dies.

God knew what she would be facing, and we all believe He performed a little miracle to ripen those pears all at once, so she could get that job finished before she needed to move on to something else.

What a wonderful God we serve!

Anna May Radke Waters

God's Bountiful Supply—Part 1

But my God shall supply all your need
according to his riches in glory by Christ Jesus.
—Philippians 4:19, KJV

I completed my bachelor of law degree (LLB) in Guyana, having paid my way through three years of study—to a great degree with money saved from three years of post-degree work following the completion of my first degree. I also received assistance from my family members and continued to work and study, despite that combination being discouraged by the university. Following the completion of my LLB, I qualified among the twenty-five eligible for automatic admission to the prestigious law school in Trinidad and Tobago for two years of post-degree studies. Knowing that such a course of study would cost more than 4.1 million Guyanese dollars for tuition alone, plus an additional 2 million Guyanese dollars for living and other expenses, I sent out letters to many organizations requesting sponsorship or scholarship assistance. I received no positive responses and, though disappointed, I prayed earnestly and continued to make preparations to depart for school, trusting that the God who brought me through the LLB would make a way.

One month before the September starting date, my mother traveled to Trinidad for a work conference. She took the opportunity to explore housing for me with assistance from one of my pastors with whom I had worked voluntarily in our church's youth department headquarters. He had migrated to Trinidad. Being dissatisfied with the accommodations available and seeing the high cost of housing, my pastor and his wife offered to accommodate me free of charge for my two years of study. Upon hearing the news, all I could say was, "Hallelujah! Thank You, Jesus!" Indeed, the Lord was working all things together for my good.

With this reassurance, I traveled to Trinidad one week before the starting date with what little funds I had for registration—but with no money for my first year's tuition. I registered in faith, placed it all in God's hands, and He worked in miraculous ways. At the law school, with what I can only describe as divine intervention and favor, I was able to commence classes, pay 75 percent of my tuition before the May examination period, and complete my first year of study with excellent grades. I am assured that my constant reliance on God through prayer, fasting, daily devotions, and service to Him, despite challenges, were driving forces in my experience.

Telisha A. Williams

God's Bountiful Supply—Part 2

*Be careful for nothing; but in everything by prayer and supplication
with thanksgiving let your requests be made known unto God.*
—Philippians 4:6, KJV

After my first year of study at the law school, even with contributions received from my local church conference, family members, church, church members, and outside sources, I had still paid only 75 percent of my first year's tuition. As an expression of gratitude, I wrote thank-you letters and cards to all those who had helped me, even those whom I didn't know personally. I enclosed a copy of my examination results as well.

While home, I was on internship attachment as part of my course requirement, so I was unable to seek employment. I was totally at the mercy and providence of God for my second year's tuition. Throughout this time, I was encouraged by the promises of Psalm 50:10–15 and Philippians 4:19 and would claim them in prayer daily and receive comfort and hope, especially in moments of discouragement. At one time, a pastor friend of mine, after I delivered news that my sponsorship request was denied, said to me, "Don't give up hope. Your supply will come from another source." I was then reminded of a line from one of my all-time favorite movies, "When God closes a door, somewhere He opens a window."* So I pressed on in faith.

My second year at this school was a trying one. By God's grace and providence, I started it with the necessary funds to pay off my first year's tuition. I assisted a friend with babysitting and received money for travel and some basic needs. Many times I either walked the twenty-minute journey to and from school with colleagues or used the school's free shuttle service. My computer screen was damaged, but God kept it working, and I kept praying and fasting.

During this time, a close friend and sister started to study at the law school. Sharing our common experience, we prayed together and encouraged each other. One Sabbath afternoon, under inspiration, we typed a joint sponsorship-request letter to one of the church's organizations, offering to repay over time and donate voluntary service. At the same time, the mother of one of my friends and colleague at my school also sought sponsorship on my behalf.

Both sources simultaneously supplied my full tuition! I shared my excess blessings with two others who then completed their full payments. Thank God for His bountiful supply!

Telisha A. Williams

---

* *Sound of Music*, directed by Robert Wise, (1965, Los Angeles: Robert Wise Productions and Argyle Enterprises).

A Church for Charlie

*"A new command I give you: Love one another. As I have loved you,
so you must love one another. By this everyone will know
that you are my disciples, if you love one another."*
—John 13:34, 35 NIV

When my granddaughter Charlie was three years old, I visited her and her parents in Texas. I lived in Maryland, so I was able to see my son and his family only twice a year. Despite seeing me so seldom, Charlie came running with arms outstretched, shouting, "Nana! Nana! Nana!" and enveloped my legs in a tight hug. How my heart melted that my little sweetheart was as happy to see me as I was to see her! Now a teenager, she is still happy to see me but less exuberant. Yet the memory of that sweet welcome always warms my heart.

I have another memory of a "welcome" that had the opposite effect on me. One Sabbath morning, I was a first-time visitor at a small church where I had an afternoon speaking appointment. The greeter's stand was about six feet from the door, and three people were there talking. They saw me but kept talking to one another, so I stood in front of the stand and requested a bulletin. One of the three dutifully handed me one without saying a word, then turned back to the others. I wondered if that's how they greeted all visitors.

My idea of church is a place that welcomes everyone warmly, whether member or visitor. A place where the members are as happy to see visitors and one another as Charlie was to see me. A place that is safe for all who enter, where they are not judged by what they're wearing, the color of their skin, or their past. They don't have to be as exuberant as three-year-old Charlie, but they need to be warm nevertheless.

I envision church as a true haven for sinners (which includes all of us), not a club for "saints." A place where people can be real about their problems and not be judged as unworthy of fellowship.

A place where teenager Charlie is welcome and, yes, loved, despite her crazy clothes, gaudy jewelry, and colorful hair. I suspect all of us want our children and grandchildren to be welcome in our church. Since everyone is someone's child, why not treat everyone as if they are ours?

Carla Baker

The Best School

A good man out of the good treasure of his heart
bringeth forth that which is good; and an evil man out of the evil
treasure of his heart bringeth forth that which is evil:
for of the abundance of the heart his mouth speaketh.
—Luke 6:45, KJV

The following conversation gave me food for thought about what true education is.

"Hi, Ruhana. Have you decided where to send your child to school?" Emily asked.

Elita interjected, "Aren't you planning to homeschool yours?"

Ruhana responded, "Well, what school did Satan attend?"

Not expecting this answer, Emily chuckled. "The *heavenly* home school."

"Well, here's another question then," continued Ruhana. "What school did Jesus attend?"

Elita jumped in. "His *earthly* home school in Nazareth, I suppose."

"Well," Ruhana pressed, "do you remember the reputation coming out of that city?"

"I sure do," responded Elita without hesitation. As Nathanael asked Philip, "Can there any good thing come out of Nazareth?" (John 1:46, KJV).

"So, think about this," resumed Emily. "Satan, in a sense, 'grew up' in heaven where he learned values and morals from the purest of the pure. Yet, eventually, he sinned and was able to deceive a third of his angelic classmates [see Revelation 12:4]. Conversely, Jesus—being raised and educated at home in a city with a bad reputation—also learned the same pure values and morals. Though Nazareth was polluted, Jesus, the Son of God, made repeated decisions to live by the truths He'd learned at home. He would be the one to save the world from eternal doom."

Recalling this conversation reminds me, as a parent, to direct my child toward the kingdom of God and His righteousness, believing that all other good and necessary things will be added (see Matthew 6:33). Just as twelve-year-old Jesus was doing His heavenly Father's business in the temple (see Luke 2:49) instead of being with his earthly parents, we parents also must trust that our God will lead our children into doing the business of the heavenly Father.

Are we schooling ourselves—and our children—in and by the Word of the Lord (see Isaiah 54:13)? I'm so glad that if our children accept the truths that are taught by God Himself, through His Word, we don't have to worry about their future (see Luke 6:45).

Suhana Chikatla

The Story of My Life

Who shall separate us from the love of Christ?
Shall trouble or hardship. . . ? For I am convinced that neither death
. . . nor anything else . . . will be able to separate us from
the love of God that is in Christ Jesus our Lord.
—Romans 8:35, 38, 39, NIV

My whole world crumbled and I felt shattered when my husband passed away. And I became angry with God. I experienced negative emotions, went into denial, and was frustrated.

The questions I asked God were, "Do You exist? If You do, are You in control? Do You care? Where were You when my husband died?" I had so much faith in God. How could this happen?

For three months, I severed my relations with God; I did not attend church, and I did not read the Bible or even pray. My situation in life at that time did not depict my picture of God's love. Yet despite my state of turmoil, God did not leave me alone. His still, small voice urged me to search Scripture. His voice said that I would find love, peace, joy, and hope there. To me, that showed God's amazing love. I searched His Word and found His love and care for me. After that, I felt His hand firmly grip mine. A sense of peace that surpassed all understanding flooded my soul (Philippians 4:7). Acquaintances expressed amazement and asked how I could look so peaceful under so much stress.

In the Bible, I read the stories of Jonah, Job, and David. God reprimanded these three men for being angry, talking too much, and complaining of their circumstances. What had these three created or brought into the world? The obvious answer was nothing! Everything came from God; they had contributed *nothing*. The Lord commands that all praise be given to Him. God knew them before they were conceived in their mothers' wombs. And He knew us before we were conceived. I began to realize how the circumstances in these stories applied to my situation as well. (Some Bible passages that might encourage you as they do me include Jonah 4:4–10; Job 22:12; Psalm 3; Psalm 30:11, 12; and Psalm 139).

God's grace pulled me from the grip of the evil one, turned my mourning into dancing, removed my sackcloth of sadness, and girded me with gladness. I was healed of my despair, glory be to God! I will sing praises to Him forever.

I thank God for all His blessings throughout my life.

Dorothy Mooka

Surrounded by Fire

"When you walk through the fire,
you will not be burned....
For I am the LORD your God."
—Isaiah 43:2, 3, NIV

It was very windy at 11:30 A.M. on December 7, 2017, and then the fire engines started coming and coming—too many to ignore. I stepped outside and saw my neighbor had his dog in his van. I asked Michael if the situation was serious. "I just came home from work to get my passport and dog. You need to get your important papers and photos and then leave too." I could not believe this was happening to me. I heard more fire engines. This was happening!

Although I never saw the fire, the sky was almost black with this orangish circle (the sun) trying without success to show itself. I tried to make a left turn onto the street in front of my condo, but it was full of cars. I turned into the center lane, and a kind woman let me into the long line trying to flee the fire. I had no idea where I was going. I called my sister in Michigan and asked her to pray. My friend, Linda, heard about the fire on the radio on her way to the Los Angeles airport. She was going to Germany. I accepted her invitation to stay at her home eight miles from my place, but I had to evacuate her home later that night. I drove to church and spent the night in a sleeping bag on a back pew. I'd forgotten to bring my phone charger, so I had to turn my phone off. I felt so alone. God was my only companion. Early the next morning, my pastor came, bringing breakfast. That afternoon I was able to return to Linda's house as the Lilac Fire didn't materialize there. I spent three days at her house without television or the internet.

When I returned home, I saw that I really had been surrounded by fire. I live across the street from a horse-training center where fifty-six horses perished. Trees in the old golf course behind our condos had been turned into a charred mess. The carpet on my kitchen patio had about thirty burn holes on it. My red wicker chairs had burn marks, and the red patio umbrella had lots of burn holes. But my condo was untouched by the fire. The firemen said while the fire was ravaging through Bonsall, it suddenly changed direction and left many of our homes unscathed. They didn't understand why this happened. But I did. I believe it was because so many people were praying. God protected me and my home.

Patricia Hook Rhyndress Bodi

Face Time

If My people who are called by My name will humble themselves,
and pray and seek My face, and turn from their wicked ways, then I
will hear from heaven, and will forgive their sin and heal their land.
—2 Chronicles 7:14, NKJV

The new telephone technologies are amazing. I remember when a person could converse with another over a telephone, called a landline, stationary to a specific location. Today we have mobile phones. Using them, we can talk from almost anywhere in the world to almost anyone else who has a phone anywhere in the world. Beyond this, these new mobile phones can provide remarkable services. Most models provide automatic location and global positioning services.

Recently, my phone even provided me a powerful personal sermon. I had just learned about and activated the service that calculates the user's screen time. This service registers the user's face engagement with the phone screen. In the busyness of meetings and responsibilities, I promptly forgot about this service. One morning as I was in deep thought working on a spiritual lesson, my phone, which is always close by, gave one of those familiar signals that indicate a message. Of course, I dropped everything to check my phone immediately without the slightest hesitation. It was my screen time report—the report of my face time with the phone screen.

The report that flashed up told me that my screen time with my phone was up by 2 percent, to five hours per day. Could that really be possible? That was incredible. Then the Holy Spirit asked, *What would the statistics be if the phone were registering and reporting your Word time or face time with God in His Word?* Ouch! Would it be up or down in percentage over the previous reporting period? God says: "If My people who are called by My name will humble themselves, and pray and seek My face, and turn from their wicked ways, then I will hear from heaven, and will forgive their sin and heal their land" (2 Chronicles 7:14, NKJV).

Could these wicked ways simply be my getting caught up in my own will and pursuits—even in my service for God—that prevent me from spending time with God? The Word says that we should turn to Him, which I take to mean more face time with God, more often in His Word. He promises that He will heal our land—perhaps that is our families, our churches, our neighborhoods, our life situations. Let us increase our face time with God.

Ella Louise Smith Simmons

Wait on the Lord

"Your heavenly Father already knows all your needs. . . .
and he will give you everything you need."
—Matthew 6:32, 33, NLT

When I was a teenager, I had two goals: be a teacher and marry a Christian husband. To fulfill my dreams, I attended college. I did become a teacher, but I graduated without finding my dream husband. After teaching a couple of years, I went back to a university and received my master's degree—still, no husband. I decided that perhaps God's will for me was to stay single, but I still prayed for a husband!

That summer, I met Richard. He was funny, smart, and cute, but he was not a Christian. We dated almost every night until I left for a teaching job in Maryland. I was very firm in my belief that I should marry a Christian, so I tried to forget Richard. Richard's father was an army colonel, and the family traveled a lot. Richard had attended thirteen different schools in twelve years. Since he'd never had a long-term relationship, he was sure when I left that he would never see me again. I was lonely and disappointed in Maryland. I was unhappy in the school where I was teaching. It was a prestigious school near Washington, DC. The children's parents all worked around the area. The students were restless and hard to manage. The school district was "advanced" in their thinking. Senior teachers knew how to work around the system, but the new teachers did not. After one semester, I'd had enough. I went back home and was rehired in the school where I had taught my first year. I loved the children and the school. One dream fulfilled.

When Richard found out I was back home, we started dating again. It wasn't long until I knew I was in love with him. What a dilemma! Every time I thought about breaking up, a little voice would say, *If you don't teach him about Me, who will?* That summer, we studied the Bible together, and he was baptized. We married that fall. Now both my dreams had been fulfilled.

Sometimes God answers our prayers in mysterious ways. While I was busy looking for a Christian husband, God had already chosen just the right one for me. I just had to help him find God first. Fifty years later, we are still happily married and working in the church serving God.

So if you are praying for something, don't be surprised if God answers your prayer in ways you never dreamed.

Dalores Broome Winget

Protection

He calms the storm,
So that its waves are still.
—Psalm 107:29, NKJV

Having lived in the Caribbean all my life, I have encountered major as well as minor hurricanes. However, September 2017 recorded two major storms, Irma and Maria, both Category 5 hurricanes, which occurred within two weeks of each other.

My husband and I made the necessary hurricane preparation before Hurricane Irma struck St. Thomas, Virgin Islands, on September 6. We prayed and trusted God to protect us and our property. However, as the winds howled and flying debris crashed into vehicles as well as onto the roofs of our complex of sixteen apartment buildings, I became concerned and a little anxious. Would the roofs remain on the buildings? Would the vehicles be destroyed?

As the storm progressed, I continued to pray, "Lord, please protect us. Keep our roofs intact and shelter our vehicles." There was so much going on outside that we were not aware of. Then suddenly, I heard a crash on our roof and saw a hole appear in the ceiling of the dining room. Then another larger hole was created in the living room area. Subsequently, the top and sides of the pump room blew off, and something struck and broke the kitchen window.

When the storm was over, assessment of the damage in our immediate neighborhood was made. No roofs had blown off, but many were damaged by flying debris. Many vehicles had sustained major damage. The devastation in the wider community was heartrending—homes, churches, schools, the hospital, other buildings, roads, vegetation, and utility lines and poles were severely affected. The recovery process has brought numerous challenges. It has been a time to exercise deep faith and trust in God. I gained a deeper appreciation for amenities after living without electricity, phone, cable, and internet service—it took many months for some of these services to be restored.

There are a number of life lessons that can be gleaned from a major hurricane. First, God is the Great Protector. Second, life is precious—things can be replaced, but not lives. Third, I need the support of others in difficult times. Finally, trust in God helps ease the burden of dealing with the aftermath of any major hurricane in life.

Janice Fleming-Williams

On the Outside Looking In

And he shall turn the heart of the fathers to the children,
and the heart of the children to their fathers,
lest I come and smite the earth with a curse.
—Malachi 4:6, KJV

Have you ever felt as though you didn't belong in your own family? I feel that way sometimes, mainly because most of my family members are not Christian, so there are many lifestyle differences. The one relationship that has troubled me most is the one with my now-deceased father. My mom and dad divorced when I was about three. He disappeared from my life completely when I was around five. At sixteen, I found my dad and stepmother, as well as another younger sister I hadn't known about, and lived with them for a few months. Then my dad was out of my life again until I was in my late twenties. My younger sister contacted me, and eventually, my dad and stepmother reestablished a relationship with me. Growing up without my dad was hard, not even knowing who he was or if he ever thought about me or missed me or wanted me. My experience later on told me that he really didn't care if I was in his life or not. He had raised my younger sister and was very close to her. They shared so many interests—mechanics, technology, motorcycles—things that I couldn't relate to with them. They had no interest in my God or my church. I tried to have as good a relationship as possible with my dad, but his drinking and smoking added to the strain.

When my dad was dying, I asked him if he had any regrets—hoping beyond hope that he would take this opportunity to apologize for abandoning me as a toddler. But he said no, he wouldn't change a thing. Then he said he had no desire for God, heaven, or an afterlife. So the short time we had had together might be all there would ever be. That was so painful! Truly my heart was toward my father, but his heart was not toward me, as I had deeply desired for it to be.

At times, it's hard to trust God as a loving, caring Father who will never leave or forsake you (Hebrews 13:5) when you've had an earthly father who *did* forsake you and didn't truly love you in the way a little girl needs a father's love. I have often needed to remind myself that my Father in heaven is trustworthy, kind, compassionate, and loving and that He will *always* be here for me. If you've had a difficult experience with your earthly father, I invite you to join me in taking God at His Word. Let Him love you, be your Father. He will never disappoint you!

Samantha Nelson

Hot Chocolate Stain

Purge me with hyssop, and I shall be clean;
Wash me, and I shall be whiter than snow.
—Psalm 51:7, NKJV

One clear, crisp Monday morning in Saskatchewan, Canada, I saw evidence of God's salvific love. After my devotional time, I sipped a cup of hot chocolate while looking out the window. Several frozen, jagged icicles were hanging from the roof in a crystalline display, sparkling in the sunlight. Now, I cannot visualize the stark beauty of those spiked icicles without thinking of the intense pain my precious Savior, Jesus Christ, endured on Calvary's cross. I can almost feel the jabbing thorns pressed into that sacred brow. I remember moving closer to my window for a better view of the icicle display. Then I accidentally splashed the dark chocolate drink on my snow-white sweater. *Oh no*, I mourned, *I've ruined it, and the laundry won't be able to fix it. I'll have to throw it away.* But my new friend, Michelle, had another idea.

"Let me work on it," she urged. "I have something at home that I think will get it out." Two days later, Michelle brought back the sweater in its pristine elegance. I was overwhelmed. Today's theme text came immediately to mind. "Wash me, and I shall be whiter than snow" (Psalm 51:7, NKJV).

Michelle saw me as a neighbor in need, as was the robbery victim in Christ's good Samaritan parable (Luke 10:30–37). In a blink of her hazel eyes, she saw my need and took care of it. Her generosity was incredible. It didn't matter that cleaning my stained top required diligent labor. Nor did it matter that she had more pressing things to do. With her compassionate spirit, she used her experience to create the "cure" I desperately needed. And I was truly grateful.

Musing later, I understood that my life can be like that stained sweater. But I know only Jesus Christ can fix it when I let Him. Only He is the soap, the hyssop—the spiritual cleanser—that I need. I treasure my moments spent with Him when He cleanses my soul and deepens my experience with Him. My wonderful friendship with Michelle is but an infinitesimal reflection of Jesus' deep and abiding friendship with me. It's a bond that I pray will never be loosened.

Dear Lord, please cleanse my sinful soul. Show me Your glory. I know You can do much more to rescue each one of us than I experienced that particular Monday. Please help me be a compassionate friend to those around me who need Your love and rescue. Amen.

Glenda-mae Greene

About the Good Old Days

And the one seated on the throne said: "Look!
I am making all things new!" Then he said to me,
"Write it down, because these words are reliable and true."
—Revelation 21:5, NET

As I took the soft, warm sheets and underwear out of the dryer this cold winter morning, I thought about our foremothers and the "good old days." Were those days really so good?

I thought about my mother when we lived in North Dakota during my middle school days. We did not have a dryer. In the winter, when the clothes came out of the last rinse, they went out on the clothesline to be freeze-dried. And the generations before that had to carry water into the house, heat it over an open fire, and wash and wring the clothes by hand. Or go down to the river to pound out the dirt. Forget the "good old days"!

Now don't get me wrong—everything isn't so great now either. Every day the TV, the radio, or the newspapers and news magazines bring us stories and pictures of wars, fires, natural disasters, famines caused by warring factions, murders, unfaithfulness to spouses and other family members, destitute widows and orphans, corruption in government, labor unrest, homelessness, and the struggle to survive. Added to this is my very long list of friends and acquaintances who are suffering from a variety of ailments, some fatal, and those who are grieving from losses. The list goes on and on.

Scripture has something to say about remembering and forgetting. God, through Isaiah, tells us to forget former things and not dwell on the past. Why? Because, "I am doing a new thing! Now it springs up; do you not perceive it?" (Isaiah 43:19, NIV).

Then God, again through Isaiah, tells us to remember past events. Again, Why? Because, "I am God, and there is no other; I am God, and there is none like me" (Isaiah 46:9, NIV).

That is something to remember—God has led in the past. Peter tells us we are nearsighted and blind if we forget that we "have been cleansed from [our] past sins" (2 Peter 1:9, NIV).

I think the best thing about forgetting the past is that, as today's text says, we can look to the future. Praise the Lord! We remember He has led us in the past, but a better future awaits!

Ardis Dick Stenbakken

He Was There

The LORD is with me; he is my helper.
—Psalm 118:7, NIV

After years of study, I was finally ready to present my master's thesis to a board of teachers. A month before, I had made a reservation of the projector that I would need to use during my presentation. Everything was ready—almost.

When I got to the university and went to pick up the projector, it was not available. The person responsible for the equipment told me that the vice-rector, his boss, had taken it to use on the following day. He could not refuse to give it to his boss. I was devastated. There was another projector in the teachers' departmental room, but it was so bad that it could not help in any way. Since I was to show how machine translation worked on the internet, the lack of a good projector would destroy my presentation.

After praying, I thought about going to the vice-rector to explain my urgent need, but there was no time to look for him. I had to choose between the worst projector—or nothing. To my consternation, when I got to the location of my public examination, nobody was there but the board of teachers and a secretary. My family had moved to the South, and I had had to stay behind to finish my master's program. Friends, colleagues, classmates—nobody had come to give me support. I was completely alone!

Suddenly, one of my English university students came in and began recruiting other students to attend the presentation. I had invited them, as well, and now they came. When I started my presentation, the girl commented, "This projector is awful!" I agreed and explained that I could not get a better one. Then she told us that there was a good one in the teachers' room. It had been used in their class that morning! One of the teachers had the room key. That projector was brought in, and it worked perfectly. I used it for my presentation. After answering all the teachers' questions, I was awarded my master's degree.

What was amazing is that months before, the projector I ended up using had been sent elsewhere to be repaired. It had arrived back on campus that very morning and had been used in only one previous class—so they could tell me it was available. God had found a way to tell me that He was there with me! I was not alone. He will be with us always.

Het Jane Silva Carvalho

"God Bless You!"

"The LORD bless you and keep you;
The LORD make His face shine upon you,
And be gracious to you;
The LORD lift up His countenance upon you,
And give you peace."
—Numbers 6:24–26, NKJV

God bless you! These three words, totaling eleven letters, are sometimes uttered without thought of the impact they might have on the recipient—yet how profound and powerful! Not long ago, I entered a department store where I don't usually shop. As I walked through the door, I saw a friend whom I hadn't seen for a long time leaving the cash register. We chatted briefly, and then we parted. I looked back and said, "God bless you!" She responded with the same words. A woman entering the store remarked, "It's nice to hear someone say that." My friend and this stranger struck up a conversation before going their separate ways. Only three words, but they created a moment for total strangers to connect in a positive spiritual way.

On another occasion, as I assisted my friend, Evelyne (who had an injured hand), get into my car, a man driving his truck stopped and waited for me to help her. "Is everything all right?" he asked, approaching us.

I assured him it was and said, "Thank you, sir. God bless you."

He smiled broadly as he responded, "Thank you. I could use that!"

Not long ago, I was scheduled to speak at an alumni homecoming gathering and was overcome with fear. Paulette, my friend, gave a beautiful introduction, and then closed with these words to me, "Let me tell you what you usually tell people: 'God bless you.'" Hearing that dissipated my anxiety, replacing it with a feeling of tranquility. The fear that my hand would shake having to hold the microphone disappeared as well—three little words, but what an impact they had on me throughout the message. I was thankful to be the recipient of that blessing. God blessed the message, the people, and me too. I am thankful that He hears and answers prayers.

Dear reader, as you travel this Christian journey, I leave with you these three powerful and profound words with a prayer that they will encourage and inspire your heart: *God bless you!*

Shirley C. Iheanacho

September 4

No Family Resemblance

It doth not yet appear what we shall be: but we know that,
when he shall appear, we shall be like him.
—1 John 3:2, KJV

I am one of seven children of Anne and T. J. Floyd. While growing up, I bore no resemblance to either of my parents. Nor to my sisters and brother. I was so very different; I was very skinny, my hair was short. This always bothered me, but my mother assured me that I was part of the Floyd clan. Cousins and family members would always make funny jokes about how I looked or who I didn't look like. While on vacation one summer at my uncle's house, my uncle asked my father if I was another one of his sons. There were little debates between my parents about whom in the family I looked like. My father would say, "She looks like your mother's side of the family." My mom would shake her head and say, "Nah, she looks like your side of the family, especially your brother John." I took great offense at this. First, because Uncle John was a man; second, he always looked scary to me. Of course, when I would misbehave, I would hear one parent tell the other, "She gets that from your side of the family." If I achieved honors for something, then I would overhear that that talent came from my mom's side of the family.

Forty-seven years and five children later, I can say with all honesty that I have both my parents' features. It seems that the older I get, the more I resemble my family. Robert, my husband, confirmed this one evening when he asked me to read him some mail that was lying on the dining room table. I reached for my reading glasses. Just as I put them on, Robert exclaimed, "Do you know who you look like with those glasses on?" Not bothering to wait for an answer, he said, "Your mother."

This got me to wondering: *How do I look from a spiritual standpoint? Whom do I resemble? As I grow in my walk with God, do I look like Him? Do I have a godlike character? Do I bear any resemblance to my heavenly Father? Will others be able to see the family resemblance?*

I began to pray that God would help me become more like Him so others can plainly see whose family I belong to.

Avis Floyd Jackson

Stitch by Stitch

And we all, who with unveiled faces contemplate the Lord's glory,
are being transformed into his image with ever-increasing glory,
which comes from the Lord, who is the Spirit.
—2 Corinthians 3:18, NIV

Knitting is one of my favorite things to do. Often when I am sitting, either at home or elsewhere, I work on my latest project.

When I start a new project, I first must decide what I am going to make. Once that decision is made, yarn is needed. It is fun to shop for just the right yarn to make the item. Depending on what I am knitting, a plain color or a multicolor yarn may be my choice. Then it is necessary to have the right size knitting needles.

Through the years, I have knitted, among other things, many baby items. For several years I knitted bootie and hat sets for a hospital auxiliary to give to newborn babies. Lately, I have chosen to knit fourteen-point, circular dishcloths. They are easy to make, colorful, and useful. Most of them I give away as gifts, but some I enjoy using myself.

Our Creator, I like to think, is the Master Knitter. He has selected each one of us as His project. We are the yarn that, strand by strand, He fashions to make a beautiful character as we yield to Him. Unlike the knitter who makes mistakes and must rip out stitches and knit them again, He never makes mistakes. More than once, however, He may take us over the same path of physical, mental, or emotional pain or loss before we learn the lessons He strives to teach us. Through it all, He promises never to leave us or forsake us.

Knitting needles are of no value without the knitter and the yarn. The Holy Spirit in union with the Master Knitter makes the project of preparing souls for God's kingdom successful. He works on our hearts and minds, encouraging us to be like our Savior. Spending time with Him and submitting to His will day by day creates a pattern that is beautiful to behold, a Christian that not only talks the talk but walks the walk—a saint that is true to Him no matter what.

I want to submit to God's plan for my life, don't you? Each one of us can be a masterpiece for the kingdom as we allow our Creator and the Holy Spirit to knit our lives together, stitch by stitch.

Marian M. Hart-Gay

Hiding From the Hurricane

You are my hiding place and my shield;
I hope in Your word.
—Psalm 119:114, NKJV

The morning of September 6, 2017, brought anxious and worry-filled moments to my husband and me. Many family members—including our daughters and their families—live in the state of Florida. Hurricane Irma, a terrible Category 5 hurricane, was headed directly toward them. We kept a close watch on the Weather Channel and monitored each family member by phone. They decided to take the necessary precautions, though it was too late to evacuate to another state.

During one phone call to our daughter, we heard the excited voice of three-year-old Kyrah, our youngest granddaughter. She wanted to talk to us; she had something very important to tell us. "Hi, GG, and hi, Granddad," she said in her usual sprightly tone. "We are not at our house. We had to leave and stay with our friends because we are hiding from the hurricane. We closed all the windows and doors and cannot go outside to play. It's really dark in here."

"Hiding from the hurricane?" We laughed. It was so funny to hear her saying that. How do you hide from the hurricane? In her childish mind, when you close the doors and windows, pull the shutters down, and barricade the house, you are hiding. Her parents had told her that she could not go out to play because the hurricane was coming, and they did not want her to get hurt.

The phrase "hiding from the hurricane" certainly contains some truths and lessons. We are often bombarded with challenges, difficulties, trials, and mishaps. Life is filled with physical and emotional storms and hurricanes. Where can we hide? *We have to hide in Christ.*

Today, you might need a hiding place, where you can pause and catch your breath, a place to rest your weary legs and aching heart, a place to soothe your furrowed brow, a place to shelter from the storms of life. Our compassionate Lord is waiting for you there.

May this be our prayer: "You are my hiding place; You shall preserve me from trouble; You shall surround me with songs of deliverance" (Psalm 32:7, NKJV).

Gloria Barnes-Gregory

Guardian-Protector

*Now I saw heaven opened, and behold, a white horse.
And He who sat on him was called Faithful and True,
and in righteousness He judges and makes war.*
—Revelation 19:11, NKJV

The abrupt ring of the pastor's cell phone across the table halted our discussion. Noticing his wife's name on the screen, I indicated he should answer. He stopped explaining he was busy when he heard her anxious voice. She plunged into an account of being accosted moments before by a mentally challenged man. During the incident, he grabbed her hair and wouldn't let go. Two men nearby rushed to restrain the attacker, but many seconds sped by while they tried to disentangle the situation without hurting the confused man. In the end, the person hurt was his wife, who lost clumps of hair to her assailant's clenched fingers.

While listening to her story, an adrenaline rush caused the pastor's heart to pound. Unable to sit still, he paced. "I wish I had been there!" he declared emphatically. "I would have punched him in the ribs. I would have forced him to let go. I wouldn't have let him hurt you." Later he asked, "Do you need me to come and take you home?"

His blood pressure was still elevated when he returned to his chair. Feeling both ashamed and astonished by his unexpected, violent outburst, he exclaimed, "I'm sorry! I'm a pastor. And that was an ungodly reaction." But at that moment, I saw him as a husband, not a pastor.

"I would have been disappointed if you had not reacted that way with your wife in danger," I replied. "I know men are created to reflect God's own image as gardener-provider and guardian-protector. They are wired to fight for the safety of their families."

Our divine Guardian-Protector is engaged in a battle for His family. Our text today presents Him astride His galloping white horse, making war. He attacks the enemy, who is intent on destroying God's family. Satan grasps our heels, causing us to stumble. He seizes our heads, leading us into sin. He tears out clumps of hair, making us feel unworthy to receive the crown of life. We cannot escape Satan's ironclad grip without help. But take heart! Do not falter! Our Guardian-Protector drives His sword of truth against the lying accuser. We are only moments away from the final thrust, and then the conquering King Jesus will break through the clouds to rescue His family. He is coming soon to take us home!

Rebecca Turner

September 8

God Cares for His Children

*I have been young, and now am old; yet have I not seen
the righteous forsaken, nor his seed begging bread.*
—Psalm 37:25, KJV

In November 1972, my husband decided to visit a Christian college (now a university) to investigate the possibility of relocating there to complete his education. When we arrived on the campus, we were greeted by President C. B. Rock and his knowledgeable administrative assistant, Ms. Darleen Williams (Simmonds). We were sold. So we returned to New Orleans, quit both of our good-paying jobs, and packed our belongings into a U-Haul truck, which my husband drove. I drove our Ford Maverick with our ten-month-old daughter.

By January, my husband was enrolled, and we both had part-time jobs. I earned $2.50 an hour, and my husband earned $2.00 an hour. His GI Bill paid for his tuition. But once the semester was completed, my job as a secretary for the education department was put on hold until the fall. This was devastating news. How could we survive the summer?

Our decision-making skills kicked into high gear. We received permission to pay our monthly rent of $150 for our two-bedroom apartment in weekly installments. Next, we brought our mattresses and daughter's crib to the first-floor level to sleep at night since we could not afford to use the air-conditioner. My husband suggested we apply for government assistance in the form of "commodities," nonperishable food items in generic wrappings. I recalled my family mantra, "Each one must pull himself or herself up by his or her own bootstraps." I felt apprehensive. My husband decided that his family was not going to starve.

We heard of the colporteur ministry and knew that selling Christian publications would be an answer to prayer. My husband opted to sell, and I did the bookkeeping. Before long, we were walking the streets of Huntsville, Alabama, spreading the good news of Christ. We visited homes in the evenings and sold a large volume of books. On Fridays, we drove to Birmingham with a supply of *Message* magazines, which were sold for twenty-five cents. Needless to say, we survived the summer—the Alabama heat, ridicule, and even doors slamming in our faces. However, I learned very valuable lessons that have stayed with me throughout the years. Today, if you are experiencing challenges that seem insurmountable, trust and have faith in God.

Yvonne H. Donatto

The Tea Bag

Ye are the salt of the earth: but if the salt have lost his savour,
wherewith shall it be salted? it is thenceforth good for nothing,
but to be cast out, and to be trodden under foot of men.
Ye are the light of the world. A city that is set on an hill cannot be hid.
Neither do men light a candle, and put it under a bushel,
but on a candlestick;
and it giveth light unto all that are in the house.
Let your light so shine before men, that they may see
your good works, and glorify your Father which is in heaven.
—Matthew 5:13–16, KJV

As I reflect on the many financial struggles that my husband and I faced while he pursued his master's and doctoral degrees in the United States, many things come to mind. I think of the times our kitchen cupboards would go empty, and I would have to make the little we had stretch to serve us for two or three meals. I think of the times when having money to purchase the bus and train passes seemed almost impossible and, more than that, I think of the times when having the funds to pay the rent on time—or even to pay it at all—repeatedly put our faith to the test.

Interestingly enough, what really resonated with me was when my husband and I would have to share a tea bag. We had gotten to a point where we decided to share a tea bag in order to make the box of tea bags last twice as long. I would dip the tea bag in my cup of hot water first, just long enough for it to flavor the water. Then I would pass it on to my husband so he could have the full flavor of the bag since I basically just drank hot water every morning anyway. The amazing thing is that even for the short time the tea bag was in my cup of hot water, its flavor permeated the water.

I thought to myself, *Wow! That's the way we are supposed to be as Christians in this world. Even if we connect with someone for a brief moment, our "flavor" of Christ should remain with them through our words and deeds of kindness and compassion. Others should have a wonderful impression of Christ in those moments, because Christ is the most important part of our lives.*

So let us remember, as we go about our daily routine, that we can be the tea bag that "flavors" the world with the best "taste" of Christ that we can share (Psalm 34:8).

Candy Monique Springer-Blackman

God's Protection and Care

Be strong and of a good courage, fear not, nor be afraid of them:
for the LORD thy God, he it is that doth go with thee;
he will not fail thee, nor forsake thee.
—Deuteronomy 31:6, KJV

It was my birthday. That morning everyone wished me a happy birthday. Then my husband left for work; my mother-in-law and I got busy cooking and taking care of my one-year-old twin girls. My three-year-old son, Praveen, waved bye-bye to his father as he left for work. While I was busy with my chores, Praveen toddled out the door and bolted it from outside. Around 11:00 A.M., I called Praveen but received no answer. Frantically I called for him and searched every room. Next, I tried to go outside but discovered he had bolted the door from the outside. Desperately I called for someone to unlock the door. Finally, our neighbor ran over and opened it. In a panic, I asked all the neighbors, but no one had seen my boy. Dashing into the house, I called my husband and told him our son was missing. Then I organized my parents, sister, and brother, and we spread out to search in different directions, calling for my son.

As we searched, we silently and fervently prayed. My husband rushed to the police station to report the missing child. Frantically we searched for hours. As evening approached, we were in tears, fearing the worst. All the family fell on our knees, seeking God's guidance and His protecting hand over my son. Suddenly we heard a knock. It was the owner of the ice cream shop my husband and son frequently visited. Beside him was Praveen on his bicycle. Overjoyed, we hugged our son and heard this frightening story from the shop owner.

Somehow my son had crossed two roads bustling with traffic and headed to his favorite ice cream shop. There he sat on the steps waiting for his dad. Noticing the boy, the shop owner kept an eye on him. He saw a lady walk up to the child and ask him if he wanted candy or ice cream. "No, my daddy will buy the ice cream, and I do not want candy," he told her. She kept insisting, and he kept refusing. Because the shop owner knew that people in the area were kidnapping little children, he told the lady the child was his and took him inside. After he closed the shop, he brought Praveen home to us. What a joyful reunion! We thanked God from the bottom of our hearts for protecting our child. He used the kind ice cream shop owner for His marvelous plan. What an incredible God we serve, a God who cares and protects.

Premila Pedapudi

Together in Love

"Yes, I have loved you with an everlasting love;
Therefore with lovingkindness I have drawn you."
—Jeremiah 31:3, NKJV

The United States of America had just observed another anniversary of September 11, 2001. Let us never forget that day and the thousands who lost their lives during the attacks. So many heartwarming stories have come from the survivors. This tragedy changed our world.

Tragic events can draw people together, and it definitely did in and around New York City. Even other countries gave their support and sympathy—some erected commemorative 9/11 memorials. I've talked with friends who were overseas during that time, and they shared how people in countries they were visiting offered words of encouragement.

Other tragedies people face include hurricanes, tornadoes, floods, fires, and tropical storms that keep impacting our world. Yet events such as these can also draw community members closer together. And if we aren't living in those impacted areas, we still can send our financial support to Christian and other relief agencies who are helping in those situations. The Bible is full of stories describing the effects of sin when people turned away from God's leading, though Jesus said that disasters would continue until His return.

Years ago, before the life-changing event of September 11, 2001, another life-changing event occurred. It wasn't a natural or man-made disaster; it was an act of God. God sent His Son to help people have hope and deal with sin-caused disasters. In fact, Jesus' very life is an example of how we can live a full, complete life despite the ravages of sin. He challenged people to think outside the box, especially beyond the teachings of their religious leaders. All this came to a head when the leaders had Jesus crucified on a cross like any common sinner. The controversy between good and evil was being played out in that great event, and good won. However, division among those who had not accepted Christ continued.

So we have to ask ourselves, Shouldn't the cross of Christ draw Christians together? No other event in earth's history has such meaning as Christ's dying for our sins. Let's meditate more on this event. In doing so, we will draw closer to Him. And when we draw closer to Jesus, we draw closer to one another through encouragement, support, and love.

Louise Driver

September 12

Mission Safari—Part 1

You, my brothers and sisters, were called to be free.
But do not use your freedom to indulge the flesh;
rather, serve one another humbly in love.
—Galatians 5:13, NIV

Kenya sounded exciting! I think what drew me to it was an opportunity to visit Africa, but I also knew that with adventure would come challenges. It challenged me to find fulfillment in doing something for others rather than become too self-serving. I had spent twenty-one years encouraging pastors and churches to get involved in mission work. I believed in it and promised myself that I would do the same someday. I knew in my heart that I should go to Africa.

When considering the trip, I wondered what my role might be. I was leaning toward the medical clinics. I am not a doctor or a nurse, yet I felt called, so I volunteered. Every morning our team climbed into open-air land cruisers and traveled over muddy, bumpy roads. When we arrived at a shady spot, we'd stop and set up our clinic. Almost before we set up, the Maasai were already walking our direction to see the doctor. Mothers came with children. Men, young and old, left their herds to receive care.

A quick tutorial on checking vital signs at the registration table provided the perfect place for me. Before I left for Africa, our grandson and daughter met me at the dollar store to pick out things for the kids in Kenya. So I had packed jumping frogs, pipe cleaners, coloring books, and more. Every day I filled my bag with little gifts. When a mother brought her sick baby with a runny nose or tears running down his or her face, I would reach into my bag and give her a package of pretty tissues. Women with weathered faces and calloused hands received hand lotion. Children so dirty and ragged from playing in the dirt received a washcloth and soap.

Yes, it was dirty and dusty. Flies covered the faces of the patients we served, but God gave me the grace and stamina to be of service to those who needed to feel His love. It felt good to know that God was using me!

One author wrote, "The common people are to take their place as workers. Sharing the sorrows of their fellow-men as the Saviour shared the sorrows of humanity, they will by faith see Him working with them."*

Bernadine Delafield

---

* Ellen G. White, *Gospel Workers* (Washington, DC: Review and Herald*, 1915), 38.

Mission Safari—Part 2

Do not neglect to do good and to share what you have,
for such sacrifices are pleasing to God.
—Hebrews 13:16, ESV

Recently a group of twenty adventuresome people from my church embarked on a long trip from Orlando, Florida, to Nairobi, Kenya. It took parts of three days to reach Mara West Camp, our "home" near the Maasai villages. We planned to offer medical services and a day camp for children (Vacation Bible School) and to paint a new seminary building.

Most of us, having never been to Africa, didn't know what to expect; but we soon discovered that this mission trip would be different than any we had taken before. The Maasai have many needs and are so primitive by modern standards! They have no running water, no electricity, no cars, although the younger men may have a scooter. You will see them walking everywhere. They may have an outhouse with a hole in the floor or nothing at all. They cook over an open fire, preferring to start the fire by friction, and live in mud houses with little outdoor light to illuminate the room. The men herd their cattle, and the women do everything else, which includes carrying heavy containers of water every morning from a nearby pond. Education is an escape and an opportunity for change, especially for young women who have been steeped in tradition.

I wondered at first if it were possible for us to do anything for a people that needed so much yet required so little. We discovered very quickly that our part would not be so much the offering of clothing and other material things as it would be showing them love and respect—sharing a friendly smile; providing children with a few short hours of joy and happiness; bringing comfort and peace to the suffering; and, through prayer, teaching them to trust in the healing powers of a heavenly Father.

One author described what mission looked like in the life of Christ: "From His earliest years He was possessed of one purpose; He lived to bless others. . . . His life revealed the grace of unselfish courtesy. . . . Jesus worked to relieve every case of suffering that He saw. . . . He passed by no human being as worthless, but sought to apply the saving remedy to every soul."[*]

His example should be our mission.

Bernadine Delafield

---

* Ellen G. White, *The Desire of Ages* (Mountain View, CA: Pacific Press®, 1940), 70, 69, 87, 91.

The Hidden Fear

For I the LORD thy God will hold thy right hand,
saying unto thee, Fear not; I will help thee.
—Isaiah 41:13, KJV

Our son, Joela, had just finished his senior secondary school examination and was preparing to enter the university when my husband and I decided to have a final discussion with him about his future career. "I would like to be a laboratory technician," he announced. I prayed silently for God to help us give the right counsel to our inexperienced son. When I asked why he was choosing a medical field, his response revealed a hidden fear. "I love medical professions, but I learned how difficult, time-consuming, and financially demanding it is to become a medical doctor, so I decided not to pursue it," replied Joela. "In addition, I speak French and not English, so how can I cope in medical school in Nigeria?" He sighed, disappointment on his face.

At that point, I realized the need to help our son overcome his fear and spur him into achieving the true desire of his heart: becoming a medical doctor. With great patience and empathy, I began to share my personal life experiences with him, how God had led me to overcome my fear and given me the grace to excel in my area of study. The promise of God in Isaiah 41:13 gave Joela hope that he could achieve his dream. As days went by, we continued to prayerfully counsel and encourage our son. I began to notice the brightness of hope radiating from his face. He was overcoming his fear, praise God! He finally made his decision to trust God with his fear and enroll in a Christian medical school in Nigeria.

Today, Joela is in his fifth year of medical school, a happy young man who speaks fluent English and is succeeding in his studies. Anytime he comes home on vacation, he always thanks us for realizing his fears and helping him overcome them. We thank God.

How many times do we succumb to our hidden fears that limit our achievement in life! How many young people are in need of godly adults with empathy and love to guide their trembling steps toward the path of life and success! I encourage you, dear reader, to watch for such young people and teenagers, whether in your own home, in the church, or in your neighborhood. Help them overcome their hidden fears so that they can make the right choices in their lives.

Helping others prayerfully deal with hidden fear is a ministry that each of us can do.

Omobonike Adeola Sessou

Monkey on My Back

Blessed be the LORD,
Because He has heard the voice of my supplications! . . .
My heart trusted in Him, and I am helped.
—Psalm 28:6, 7, NKJV

I had a terrifying experience the other morning. I was lying on my tummy, enjoying the slumber of deep sleep when I felt a heavy pressure on my head and shoulders, pushing me into the pillow. I remember trying to glance over my shoulder, and I saw a figure sitting on my back with a fiendish smile on his face. I cried out in my mind, *Jesus, help me!* Immediately the pressure lifted, and the figure disappeared. At that precise moment, I woke up fully, opened my eyes, and looked around my room to double-check that there was no one there. A verse flashed through my mind: "The angel of the LORD encamps all around those who fear Him, and delivers them" (Psalm 34:7, NKJV). I repeated the words and clung to that promise.

While I do not know why this happened, I have learned two things. First, God cares about me and always answers when I call. He has written numerous times in the Bible, "Do not fear" because He will help me, come to my aid, and fight battles on my behalf. Despite experiencing bad times, God walks beside me through every experience. My God is infinitely more powerful than Satan, so why should I fear? What an amazing God we serve. He never lets me down!

The second thing that crossed my mind is that just like that "creature" was sitting on my back, maybe I have a burden, or "monkey" on my back that I am not aware of—but God is showing me that I need to get rid of it. This could be anything—a secret burden, a guilty pleasure, or even an addictive vice that shadows my walk with God. It could be hatred or bitterness that I harbor against someone else, whereas God wants me to fix the situation, forgiving the person so I can walk with His peace in my heart.

Friend, I implore you to search your heart for whatever your "monkey" might be, and give the burden over to God, laying it completely at His feet. Only Jesus can truly help you let your burdens go. Only Jesus can give you peace, purpose, and a renewed spirit within. God is calling you today and is waiting for you with open arms. Don't miss this wonderful opportunity for a relationship with God so you can spend eternity with Him.

Jenny Rivera

How Would You Describe God's Goodness?

The LORD is trustworthy in all he promises
and faithful in all he does.
—Psalm 145:13, NIV

A few months back, a friend said to me that, deep within, she struggles with believing that God is good.* It hurt knowing someone didn't think that God was good, and I wanted to respond. In Job 38, God answers Job and his friends after hearing them ramble on with their reasons for Job's suffering. God overwhelms them with many questions impossible for humans to answer. He asks where they were when He created the earth and if they truly understand what He did (see verse 4). He inquires, "Do you know the laws of the heavens?" (verse 33, NIV).

It appears God is saying we will never comprehend what He knows. Therefore, it would be good to trust Him with the details of our lives. Adam and Eve believed that God was good until the devil threw in doubt: "Did God really say . . . ?" Their son, Abel, focused with faith on God's plan as revealed in his acceptable sacrifice of a lamb pointing to Jesus, the promised Lamb, who would take our place. Satan tried to deter and block Jesus' ministry while He was on the earth. But Jesus responded to each temptation with "It is written . . . " (see Matthew 4). On the cross, Jesus triumphed over Satan. But Satan—the one who boasted that he wanted to be like the Most High (Isaiah 14:14)—still wants to be. However, evil now holds no power over those who are in Christ, as God "has rescued us from the dominion of darkness" (Colossians 1:13, NIV).

Sometimes when I have wondered at God's goodness, He has given me little reminders throughout the day. So I guess I wasn't surprised that, not long after writing my friend about God's goodness, a journal appeared in the mail from another friend. The thought came to me: *I could go through each letter of the alphabet and write a word describing God's goodness.* Just a few were these: *C* is for *caring*, *M* is for *marvelous*, *N* is for *nurturing*. How true that "the LORD is trustworthy in all he promises" (Psalm 145:13, NIV)!

Faith, followed by action, helps with belief. It's a joy to share about God's goodness in my life. It strengthens my understanding that He is good.

Diane Pestes

---

* This entry first appeared as blog post, "Job 38-39; Psalm 145" *Bible Experience*, (blog), May 30, 2019, https://hoodviewbible.com/blog/2018/12/28/job24-pw8aw-3e5p4-6pg43-z8zgd.

Not Without Hope

"I will give them comfort and joy instead of sorrow."
—Jeremiah 31:13, NIV

When my husband's phone rang at 3:00 this morning, I knew what he had ahead of him. Since retiring from pastoral ministry, he had been working part-time for a funeral home. Besides assisting with funerals, he was occasionally called to help with the removal of deceased persons from a home or hospital. And that was the reason for the early morning phone call.

After he left, I was unable to sleep. I thought of the family watching their loved one leave their home for the last time. Even though Solomon says there is "a time to be born and a time to die" (Ecclesiastes 3:2, NIV), this is always a heart-wrenching experience.

Death after a long life is expected, but when it comes suddenly, unexpectedly at a young age, it is even more difficult.

I well remember the phone call alerting us that my husband's sister had been killed in a car accident, leaving behind a husband and two young children. Then there was the phone call informing us that my young cousin had been killed in a car accident on his way to teach in a church school.

Death is so cruel, but for believers in Jesus, there is hope. Paul says we are not to grieve like those who have no hope (see 1 Thessalonians 4:13). Because Jesus died and rose again, we have hope for eternal life with Him.

Many years ago, a call came to the church from a family needing a pastor to conduct a service for a young mother who had died. Because they did not have a church and pastor of their own, they had come to our church seeking help. As my husband helped with that service, he witnessed a very distraught family with no hope.

Then there was the service for a three-year-old boy who had been killed in a tragic accident. At the cemetery, his mother said to me, "If I pray really hard, don't you think Jesus will bring my boy back to life?" I can still see her kneeling beside that casket, praying for her little boy to come back to life. Her prayer was not answered that day, but someday that grave will open, and she will see her son again. It is just a matter of time. "Let us hold unswervingly to the hope we profess, for he who promised is faithful" (Hebrews 10:23, NIV).

Sharon Oster

Blessed Are They
Who Wash the Dishes

So let us not become tired of doing good; for if we do not give up,
the time will come when we will reap the harvest.
—Galatians 6:9, GNT

L ive to bless others" was the motto of our home. Our parents practiced it, verbalized it, and my dad preached about it from the pulpit. When we displayed the "me-first" attitude, we'd always be sent to the end of the line. We would often sneak over to Grandma's cottage to do helpful secret tasks and be there to bless her with a visit even when we'd rather be playing outside. Putting others first is not a natural response for a child. I thank the Lord for giving me dedicated Christian parents who taught me to be kind and benevolent. It will not be difficult for us to show kindness if we have the love of Jesus in our hearts. It makes the world a better place.

General Robert E. Lee, though familiar with war, was by nature a kind man, as evidenced by several stories about him. One day, traveling in a train full of officers and soldiers, General Lee noticed a poorly dressed, elderly woman board his car at a station. Not finding an empty seat, she walked down the aisle toward the area where General Lee was seated. Immediately he arose, bowed courteously, and offered the lady his seat. Noticing this act of kindness on the part of their general, a score of soldiers instantly arose, offering their seats to their commander. "No, gentlemen," he said, "if you could not rise for an infirm, elderly lady, you need not rise for me."* Rebuked, most disappeared into an adjoining car.

Jesus tells us to love the Lord with all our hearts and our neighbors as ourselves. That neighbor may live next door or be of another nationality or ethnicity. She (or he) might speak another language. Jesus wants us to show love and kindness to all. A kind deed will always leave at least two people happier. Jesus says, "Inasmuch as ye have done it unto one of the least of these my brethren, ye have done it unto me" (Matthew 25:40, KJV).

Living to bless others is the secret to finding true joy. Surprise someone each day with a random act of kindness. Live the golden rule (see Matthew 7:12). Keep a song in your heart; it will encourage others. A benevolent spirit is a gift from God—so pass it on with joy!

Marcella Lynch with Ruth James

---

* "A Language the Whole World Understands," My Bible School, accessed February 20, 2020, https://www
.pathlights.com/My-Bible-School-2010/story-27.htm.

The Gift of Worship

Worship the LORD with gladness;
come before him with joyful songs.
—Psalm 100:2, NIV

Since I was a child, my greatest times of comforting peace have been born in nature. And it was this security that I now needed as I lay in a Johannesburg hospital after emergency surgery. Alone on this continent, confronted with a life-and-death health emergency, I had been deeply frightened and I needed reassurance! Then God directed my gaze beyond my big window where the setting sun was splashing a reddish hue against the backdrop of the sky—an unexpected reminder that the evening and morning were the first day. A reminder that the Creator God was still in His heaven. This spoke to the depths of my wounded, broken, depressed spirit. Tears welled up. Though I suddenly felt small in this big picture, I also felt very important. Then, as clear as I could hear, came the answer to the question I had asked before leaving on this trip to South Africa: "Does God really love me?"

"I love you, Gail, and you will just have to trust Me on this one!" Trust? Trust—while halfway around the earth? Trust—while in a country where I don't know anyone? Just trust. The message was profound and clear. If I was to recover—body, mind, and spirit—then I would have to trust. I must let God be God in my life. I would have to give Him my years of suppressed guilt, pain, hurt, sorrow, and depression. I must surrender and be willing to follow and learn.

There in that hospital bed by the big picture window—both given to me for such a time as this—I decided that for the first time in a long time, He and I would be on the same page. Restoration and recovery; Creator and creature; Giver and receiver; Father and daughter; Divine and human—together on the exact same page. This would be my very first experience as a pure act of worship, void of human applause, affiliations, or rituals. Just me and just Him. I knew I would never be the same because of what had just occurred in that hospital room. How grateful I am for the gift of worship!

Thank You, Father God, the Ancient of Days, for an opportunity of being human in the presence of the Almighty. This keeps me humble in spirit, and living in awe-inspired praise. Thank You for the gift of worship.

Gail Masondo

Colored Perceptions

"Who can know the LORD's thoughts?
Who knows enough to teach him?"
But we understand these things, for we have the mind of Christ.
—1 Corinthians 2:16, NLT

For my thoughts are not your thoughts,
neither are your ways my ways, saith the LORD.
—Isaiah 55:8, KJV

My husband and I had been driving the highway as we ran different errands. In our speed, we passed an SUV parked on the highway with a sticker on the back. Out of curiosity, I asked what the green sticker meant. "What? A *green* sticker? Oh no, that sticker was *orange*!" my husband exclaimed. I was sure that I had seen a green sticker, and he was sure he saw an orange sticker. So, he quickly suggested that we return later to confirm the color of the sticker. We continued to Home Depot, where he did his bit for almost half an hour. When he returned to driving, I noticed that we were not heading home.

"Do we have another stop before home?" I asked, because I did not believe that he would actually go back to look at the sticker. Well, that is exactly what we were about to do. We drove for almost ten minutes before seeing the same parked vehicle on the opposite side of the road.

"I am almost sure I saw orange!" he exclaimed! "Am I color-blind?" He continued to rationalize why he thought he'd seen orange. And it all had to do with his past and background.

He explained that in New York, where he was born and grew up, vehicles on the side of the roadway would have orange stickers on them; so, even though the one we saw here in Georgia was green, in his mind, he had seen orange despite my stating it was green.

Life can do that to us many times. Our colored perceptions about other people sometimes prevent us from getting to know them in "their color" because we see them in the "colors" that we are familiar with or know from experience. Our perceptions not only affect our relationships with other people but sometimes even our relationship with God. This happens when we see Him through the lenses of others rather than through our personal relationship with Him. We know God through our parents, church teachers, elders, and TV personalities instead of knowing Him for ourselves. Yet He has given us full access so we can get to know Him for ourselves.

Nadine A. Joseph-Collins

A Lesson From
the Book of Numbers

God loves a cheerful giver.
—2 Corinthians 9:7, NIV

I'm reading through the Bible slowly—though some parts with more enjoyment than others. I loved Genesis and Exodus but felt tempted to skip most of Leviticus. I didn't, though, and continued reading until I reached Numbers 7. Partway into the chapter, I ran out of patience.

I always tell my students, "Don't say in twenty words what you can in ten." But this chapter totally violated that rule. It detailed the gifts that representatives from each of the twelve tribes of Israel brought for the dedication of the tabernacle, and by the time I reached the third listing of gifts, it was pretty clear to me that they were all going to be identical. And indeed, the only variation was who brought the gifts and from what tribe. Then, as if to inflict a final insult on my frustrated mind, the chapter concludes by summarizing the twelve sets of gifts. *Why didn't it just do that in the first place?* I wondered. *Why make the reader go through all that repetition?*

Exasperated, I took my questions to God. I was amazed when a clear answer that I would have never thought of on my own almost immediately unfolded in my mind: *It's not about the gifts but rather about the individual who brings them!* No matter what the corporate involvement, for God, it's as though each giver were the only one, and each gift from that one individual is lovingly received no matter what anyone else may bring.

I immediately thought of tithing. Each time I return my tithe, it is a unique experience, sometimes involving a struggle or test of faith, sometimes coming easily or even eagerly. Fortunately, despite knowing everything and seeing the end from the beginning, God walks with me through my individual experience the way I live it.

What if all that mattered to God was how much He collected per month? Or what if His concern was centered on the sum total that I'll give over the course of my lifetime? Fortunately, that is not God's focus. Rather, He regards me as though I were the only giver on earth and treats each time I give as if I had never done so before or will do so again. The lesson in Numbers 7 is that every single gift that comes from a willing heart is exceedingly precious to God, for He indeed cherishes the cheerful giver.

Rachel Williams-Smith

Forgive and Be Forgiven

And be ye kind one to another, tenderhearted, forgiving one another, even as God for Christ's sake hath forgiven you.
—Ephesians 4:32, KJV

One day, Tracy was walking home when she encountered a young man who appeared to need help in finding his lost money. Becoming engaged in the conversation, Tracy forgot she was on her way home. She followed the young man, and gradually realized that the conversation had become strange and that she didn't have the willpower to leave. Other people also joined the conversation and told Tracy they needed money, but she could barely understand, even as they told her they were counting on her to help them.

Tracy grew oblivious to her surroundings and agreed to the people's demands. Eventually, she found her way home but remained withdrawn. She couldn't talk about what had happened because she had been threatened. The next day she took the money she had saved up to buy things she needed; luckily, her parents had left no money at home within her reach. Tracy returned to where she'd been the night before and gave the strangers her money. Gradually, they left, one after the other, giving various reasons for their departures. Later Tracy realized what had happened. It seemed as if she had been put under some type of spell. Yet when she became aware of what had happened, she couldn't speak to anyone about it but wept uncontrollably.

One day years later, while at the market, Tracy spotted the young man who had lured her to the strangers who had taken advantage of her. She grabbed him by his shirt and raised an alarm, hoping he would be beaten as punishment. When she explained what had happened, some nearby young men decided to take the law into their own hands and burn the criminal alive. At that point, Tracy wondered if that was the punishment she truly wanted for the young man. Would it be better to forgive or to take revenge since the opportunity had presented itself? When she remembered that everyone's life is in God's hands, she pleaded with the young men to release the criminal. When they did, she walked away with forgiveness and peace in her heart.

Do you struggle to forgive others of their misdeeds? We are to forgive others as we have been forgiven. Colossians 3:13 admonishes us—if we quarrel with anyone—to forgive them as Christ forgives us. We are to let go of our anger and forgive. Let us let go and let God.

Oguchi Ajaegbu

Lessons From the Queen of Tonga

I will be a Father to you,
and you will be my sons and daughters,
says the Lord Almighty.
—2 Corinthians 6:18, NIV

In an instant, my brain deciphered what my eyes saw and delivered this conclusion: "You have not dressed appropriately for the occasion."* Had the ground under me parted, it would have saved me from embarrassment. Alas, the ground did not part, so a plan B formed in my mind: "I will run back to the hotel and change what I'm wearing." Before I could move, however, another woman appeared and wrapped my hips with a *tupenu*, which fully covered my shorts and legs. I was pronounced fit to participate in the march through town. The sense of relief was short-lived. First, as I walked, the fabric loosened, and I needed to keep adjusting the cloth, so it didn't unwrap completely. Second, when we arrived at the destination, the royal palace, I was among those asked to sit next to the queen of Tonga. Yes, you read that correctly. I was asked to sit next to Nanasipau'u, the queen of Tonga! A *real* queen—with all the pomp and protocol that go along with royalty. As I sat next to her and observed the event, I reflected.

An immediate lesson emerged: it is much better to be overdressed than underdressed. Deeper reflections occurred to me later. I have said and done things in my life that have made me appear less than who I am. Who am I? I am a daughter of His Excellency and Majesty, the Most High King. Jesus came so I can have abundant life (John 10:10). If I don't believe this, I act in foolish ways, and I treat others the same. They, too, are His children and deserve the best.

I have no doubt that the queen of Tonga was perfectly aware that I was not dressed in clothes that fit the occasion. But because she knew who she was and how she deserved to be treated, she extended the same grace and love to me, regardless of the clothes I wore. Similarly, God knows that by myself, I will never be dressed well enough to be fit to sit next to Him, so He, like the woman who gave me cloth, provided through Jesus my robe of righteousness.

May God's love for you as His daughter help you love yourself and others as royalty!

Danijela Schubert

---

* This entry first appeared as "Month of Travel," *Going Places: Adventist Women in the South Pacific*, May 2019, https://women.adventistchurch.com/wp-content/uploads/sites/19/2019/05/going-places-1905.pdf.

Sing Us a Happy Zion Song!

Alongside Babylon's rivers
we sat on the banks; we cried and cried,
remembering the good old days in Zion. . . .
That's where our captors demanded songs. . . .
"Sing us a happy Zion song!"
Oh, how could we ever sing GOD's song
in this wasteland?
—Psalm 137:1–4, *The Message*

I understand God's people were being taunted to sing a happy Zion song and why they resisted. However, I would like to suggest that when we are being harassed, persecuted, disappointed, or just sad, singing one of God's songs may be the best remedy! We often ask, *Lord, how long must we wait till we see Your blessed face?* Though the wait seems long, the end result will be worthwhile. I am reminded of Naaman, the leper, who had to dip into the muddy Jordan seven times so he could come up shouting, "Oh, Lord, I see a change!" (see 2 Kings 5:14). When you get the promotion or raise you did not expect, do you sing like Moses? "I'm blessed in the city, I'm blessed in the field, I'm blessed when I come and when I go!" (see Deuteronomy 28:3–6). While we wait, sing His praise.

So, what are the blessings of singing a "happy Zion song"? First, "[The Lord] will quiet you by his love; he will exult over you with loud singing" (Zephaniah 3:17, ESV).

And finally, it is a rehearsal for heaven:

> I looked again. I heard a company of Angels around the Throne, the Animals, and the Elders—ten thousand times ten thousand their number, thousand after thousand after thousand in full song:
>
> The slain Lamb is worthy!
> Take the power, the wealth, the wisdom, the strength!
> Take the honor, the glory, the blessing! (Revelation 5:11, 12, *The Message*).

Are you singing happy Zion songs?

Sylvia A. Franklin

If You Believe

And all things, whatsoever ye shall ask in prayer,
believing, ye shall receive.
—Matthew 21:22, KJV

My husband had just been transferred to another state in the western part of my country, Nigeria, where he worked as a youth director for our church. To accompany him, I had to resign from where I was working in the local church elementary school. After arriving at the place of our new assignment, I couldn't find another job immediately. This left us financially challenged, living only on my husband's salary with two children, my sister-in-law, my mother-in-law, and several friends and relatives who visited often.

On a Friday, after cleaning the house all day in preparation for the Sabbath, I was already tired but still needed some groceries for the Sabbath meal. I had just a little money on me. I decided to walk down to the market instead of going with a taxi since the market wasn't too far from the house. That way, I could save money on transportation. The markets in Nigeria are usually open-air markets, and the particular section I went to was very busy. After making my way around the market, I exhausted all the money I had brought with me. Yet I was too tired to walk back home carrying the things I had bought. "Dear Lord," I whispered, "please send me someone to provide me with money for my transportation, so I don't have to walk."

While walking on, totally worn out, I looked behind me, thinking I had heard someone calling my name. But I couldn't see anyone doing so. Just a few minutes after, I heard a voice that said, "Shepherdess" in my language (Yoruba). I looked back and saw an elderly woman from my husband's hometown who attended the same church I did. She greeted me and said, "Take this money for the taxi!" It was like a dream that God answered my prayer for the taxi fare. I needed only one-fourth of the money she gave me for the taxi fare and went back home with the remainder. "God never will forsake in need the soul that trusts in Him indeed."*

He is the faithful keeper of His promise. If you believe His promises, He will never fail you.

Kehinde Adenike Abolarin

---

* George Neumark, "If You But Trust in God to Guide You," 1641, in *The Seventh-day Adventist Hymnal*, no. 510.

In Our Afflictions,
He Hears Us—Part 1

In the day of my trouble I will call upon thee: for thou wilt answer me.
—Psalm 86:7, KJV

One very strict mother became a burden to her daughter. The girl was restricted from socializing; as a result, the young woman snuck out to meet her friends. On several occasions, she was caught and physically and emotionally abused by her family members. Eventually, she got pregnant and was chased from home by her mother. "The only way I'll let you come back," said her mother, "is if you give away your baby after childbirth." However, the young woman began to love the baby growing inside her womb. *Give it away?*

Though the young woman lived quietly with her auntie, her mother arranged for another family to foster the baby after birth. The young woman sadly accepted this plan. At the same time, she poured out her heart to God. Having a child was all she had to look forward to. God heard the desire of her heart. As soon as the baby was born, the foster parents arrived at the hospital, saying they would not take the baby girl. They had wanted a boy. The new mother's heart leaped for joy. She was able to keep her own baby!

The next few years brought both physical and emotional pain. The little girl often cried when she heard her grandma barking abuse at her young mother. She felt her mother's pain and humiliation at the hands of her family—and sometimes her community.

I am that little daughter. I did not realize that my mother was all alone, except for her dependence on God. She and I were both sustained by her prayers of faith. "Even the babe in its mother's arms may dwell as under the shadow of the Almighty through the faith of the praying mother."* The truth of this statement, which my mother believed, helped carry her through depression and years of mistreatment. Only God understood her heartache. He kept the little one—me—under "the shadow of the Almighty" because of the faith of my praying mother.

Perhaps you, like my mother or Hannah in the Bible (the mother of Samuel), have been mocked and mistreated. As these women did, turn to God. He never overlooks the prayers of brokenhearted mothers. Pray in faith as you cling to His promises, especially while struggling through hardship. He has promised that He will always be near to hear and to strengthen us.

Lucy Taolo Julius

---

* Ellen G. White, *The Desire of Ages* (Mountain View, CA: Pacific Press®, 1940), 512.

In Our Afflictions, He Hears Us—Part 2

I love the LORD, because he hath heard my voice and my
supplications. Because he hath inclined his ear unto me,
therefore will I call upon him as long as I live.
—Psalm 116:1, 2, KJV

From an early age, I learned—from the example of my mother—that God hears the cries of our hearts and the prayers we offer up with faith in His promises. Therefore, I want to encourage you mothers around the world who face hardships in life. God the Father will strengthen us when we call on Him for help. He will listen to our prayers and help us with our needs. We may be struggling with so many different hardships, but God gives us unfailing encouragement through His Word. Are you alone today? "Be strong and courageous. Do not be afraid or terrified because of them, for the LORD your God goes with you; he will never leave you nor forsake you" (Deuteronomy 31:6, NIV).

Are you depressed? Cast all burdens on him "because he cares for you" (1 Peter 5:7, NIV). Do you have addictions? Let Jesus set you free (John 8:36). What about the need to unload your stress and find rest? "Come to me, all you who are weary and burdened, and I will give you rest" (Matthew 11:28, NIV).

Has someone betrayed you or cheated on you? "It is better to take refuge in the LORD than to trust in humans" (Psalm 118:8, NIV).

Are you struggling with temptation? "Pursue righteousness, faith, love and peace, along with those who call on the Lord out of a pure heart" (2 Timothy 2:22, NIV).

Have you been considering suicide? "The cords of death entangled me. . . . Then I called on the name of the LORD. . . . Our God is full of compassion" (Psalm 116:3–5, NIV).

Are you grieving? The heavenly Father Himself "comforts us in all our troubles" (2 Corinthians 1:4, NIV). He will also give us relief from guilt (see 1 John 1:8, 9; Isaiah 1:18).

Mothers, you are not alone. God is close to you with your struggles in life. Please be encouraged by the stories of His faithfulness and through His promises, which He makes to you.

Lucy Taolo Julius

Oatmeal Soap

Train up a child in the way he should go.
—Proverbs 22:6, KJV

While visiting with a relative of mine, I was introduced to a kind of soap for washing hands that seemed never to decrease in size or effectiveness, although it was constantly being used.

One morning, the energetic seven-year-old, ready for music lessons, headed directly toward the piano. "No, no," came the warning from his mother. "Come, wash your hands!"

"My hands are clean, Mum; my hands are *clean!*"

"You just had a pastry. Wash your hands before touching the piano keys."

"OK, Mum, OK," was the reluctant response as the youngster was led to the bathroom. Once in front of the vanity, he was able to see the color of the soap being handed him. Tearfully, he explained, "But my hands are clean. That thing in your hands looks just like oatmeal, and you know that I do not like oatmeal. That is oatmeal soap, and I will not wash my hands with oatmeal soap," he continued with a mournful groan.

"You know you can't touch the piano keys with pastry fingers."

"OK, OK," he replied, almost in tears. "But I hate oatmeal soap!" When the child finally washed his hands, we could hear him say, "Now my hands are clean, very clean!"

"Very clean," said his mother.

And I must agree—very clean! Apparently, the oatmeal we eat works inside our body as perfectly as the oatmeal soap worked on the outside of our hands. We understand that it performs a cleansing function.

What the child's mother demanded of him may have seemed unnecessary or even unreasonable to a seven-year-old's way of reasoning. But after the little boy complied, he finally agreed that obeying his mother produced satisfactory results.

Sometimes, when our Father in heaven asks us to trust Him when He asks us to do some specific thing or change our ways so that we will be clean, we hesitate and make excuses. But as we yield to His loving will, we find peace and experience real cleansing.

Quilvie G. Mills

My Court Case

Make haste to help me, O Lord my salvation.
—Psalm 38:22, KJV

Sabbath was rapidly approaching, and I had completed my cleaning and meal preparation. After supper, my grandchildren joined me for worship. Then we retired for bed.

I arose early to be ready to go to Sabbath School. I enjoyed the Bible study and then the worship service. Afterward, I stayed for choir rehearsal and finally started my return trip home. There was a chill in the air, but the sun shone brightly. *This is a high day in Zion*, I thought.

As always, when driving, I frequently observe my surroundings by glancing at my mirrors. Though I didn't hear a siren, I noticed the blue flashing lights of a police car behind me. I did not have a clue as to why I was being followed and then pulled over to the side of the road. Having never before experienced an encounter with patrol officers on the road, I went to the police car. "Why did you stop me?" I asked.

"Please wait behind my car," he requested. Soon he returned and said, "You were speeding."

I looked at him and responded, "But why did you stop *me*? The car ahead of me was the one that was speeding. I wasn't speeding."

I soon realized that I was fighting a losing battle, although I was truly innocent of the accusation made against me. Despite my anger, I accepted the ticket and no longer tried to convince the officer that I was not speeding. Immediately I made up my mind to take the matter to court. In all honesty, I was not speeding—which is why the accusation hurt so badly. In fact, it cut to the core! I decided to exercise my faith and put my trust in God.

I could not sleep that night and soon began to solicit the prayers of my family members, pastor, friends, and fellow church members. After all, the Bible promises, "Call upon me in the day of trouble: I will deliver thee, and thou shalt glorify me" (Psalm 50:15, KJV). Finally, the day of my court hearing arrived. Trusting in the Lord, I spoke very few words in court. The result? My case was thrown out, and my record remains clean.

God answered our prayers. To God be the glory! Try God today. He still answers prayers.

Gloria McPherson

My God Is Awesome!

"Fear not, for I am with you. . . .
I will strengthen you,
Yes, I will help you,
I will uphold you with My righteous right hand."
—Isaiah 41:10, NKJV

I was born into a family of nine children—six boys and three girls. Four of my brothers are older than I, but I am the oldest among the girls. Because I am older than my two sisters, washing and ironing the clothes, cleaning the house, and cooking became my lot.

My mother also requested that I drop out of school and go to work to supplement the family income. So at an early age, I learned to make cocktail bags that were exported to Hong Kong, Guam, and the United States. God blessed me in the ability to earn even more than a local elementary school teacher. This made my mother very happy and thankful. Since my three oldest brothers were all married and had their own homes, and my fourth brother was almost finished with his civil engineering course, he admonished me to go back to school. At first, I was not enthusiastic because I thought I was too old to go back to school. Besides, my former classmates in the elementary school were all in college now. I would feel embarrassed. However, my brother said that I wouldn't grow younger, even if I didn't go to school. That stuck in my mind; therefore, I decided to go back to school.

To ease my embarrassment, I went to night school. However, I chose not to attend school on Friday nights, as that is when my day of worship began. One evening, one of my teachers asked me why I was always absent on Fridays. I told him the reason. He became unhappy with me and announced that he would give his chapter tests only on Fridays.

I still didn't attend his class on Fridays, but I always asked him each Monday if he would be willing to give me the missed test from the previous Friday. At the end of the year, God was honored, I believe, by helping me obtain the highest grade point average in all the classes. When I graduated from high school with three hundred other students, the faculty made me salutatorian, due to my absences, rather than valedictorian.

Thank God that when we honor Him, His response is to bless us.

Ofelia A. Pangan

Peaches—Part 1

A new heart also will I give you, and a new spirit will I put within you:
and I will take away the stony heart out of your flesh,
and I will give you an heart of flesh.
—Ezekiel 36:26, KJV

I had wanted a kitten for a long time, but my grandmother, who lived in my home with me, didn't want a cat in the house. Sometime later, when my birthday came around, one of my coworkers walked into my office with a small tote bag in her hand. "I have a gift for you!" she announced. In the bag was the most wonderful birthday present I could ever have imagined, a tiny yellow and orange kitten! I couldn't say no. I promptly named the kitten Peaches and took her home.

The first night Peaches and I shared the same pillow. She placed her tiny paw into my hand as I drifted off to sleep. For the next few weeks, everything went fine. Then, one day when I picked Peaches up, she suddenly did a backflip right out of my arms and ran away from me! After that, she never again wanted to sit in my lap and wouldn't permit me to hold her. I was mystified because up until that particular day, she had been very loving.

One day my grandmother called me from her bedroom and said, "Terry, come and get Peaches out of my closet. When she goes in there, I pull her out by her tail, but now I can't reach her." Just a few days later, I witnessed another episode where Peaches was being treated unkindly. At that moment, I knew what had caused Peaches to jump out of my arms. She had been frightened by rough handling and wasn't going to risk letting anyone ever do that to her again. For the next few years of Peaches's life, she would jump up on the back of my sofa, just to be near me, but that's the closest she ever got.

One day as I had my Bible study, I read Ezekiel 36:26, where God told Ezekiel to tell the Israelites that He was going to take out of them their hearts of stone and give them hearts of flesh. Suddenly, it struck me! I thought, *I'm going to ask God if He will take away Peaches's stony little heart toward me and give her a soft heart so that she could love and trust me again and allow me to love her back.*

Friend, God wants us to come to Him with every perplexity in our lives. No concern of ours is insignificant or unimportant to Him.

Terry Wilson Robinson

Peaches—Part 2

*"And I will give you a new heart, and I will put a new spirit in you.
I will take out your stony, stubborn heart
and give you a tender, responsive heart."*
—Ezekiel 36:26, NLT

My birthday-gift kitten, Peaches, had become distrustful of me because someone else had treated her unkindly. So I began praying. Every day for more than five years, I prayed that God would replace the "hard" heart in my pet and give her a "soft" heart toward me in its place.

Then one day, things changed.

I was sitting close beside my bed in a large, comfortable chair while having my morning devotions. Peaches jumped onto my bed, then curled up and went to sleep. In just a short while, she sat up and then stood up. But she didn't jump off the bed. She just stood there for a few seconds looking right into my face. Then, very slowly and carefully, she took two steps toward me. I thought, *Perhaps she just wants to come from the bed over to the large arm of my chair because she likes to be close to me—but not too close.* My cat then placed her two front paws on the arm of my chair but kept her back paws on the bed.

I continued my reading.

When I felt something on my leg, I looked again at Peaches and caught my breath! She was sitting on the arm of the chair, but one of her front paws was now on my leg. We continued to look into each other's eyes as she put her other front paw on my leg, followed by her back paws. Then she calmly turned around once and plopped in my lap—for the first time in five years!

I was stunned, yet could not keep from crying out, "Oh, thank You, Jesus! Thank You!"

The rest of the story is even more precious to me. I told the children's story at church one Sabbath and shared my experience with Peaches. Immediately after the worship service, one of the members came to me and said, "Several years ago, my daughter was hurt by someone in the church, and she never went back. I have been praying for her for years. I don't think I knew exactly how to pray for her until I heard your story about Peaches this morning. Now I know how to pray. I'm going to pray the same prayer for my daughter as you did for Peaches."

May God give each of us soft and forgiving hearts toward one another.

Terry Wilson Robinson

Waiting

Wait on the LORD, and keep his way.
—Psalm 37:34, KJV

Wait. *But I don't like to wait.* If I have to be given a ride at a specific time and it's not on time, I get frustrated and start to pace. I don't like to wait in lines, and I don't like to keep anyone waiting, either, so I am always early.

I wonder, *Am I too impatient?* Isn't this a way to develop patience? David encourages us to "Wait on the LORD: be of good courage, and he shall strengthen thine heart" (Psalm 27:14, KJV). Then I realize how patient the Lord is with me. He is always waiting to receive my praise, thanks, and requests. He is patiently waiting for all who give their lives to Him before He comes. We should not wait to give our hearts to Him.

Life today is lived in the fast lane—everyone is in a hurry, and no one wants to wait. I have learned to wait on the Lord, realizing that my timing is different from His timing. When I pray, I wait. I know the Lord will answer. Sometimes waiting can save us from trouble. If Abraham and Sarah had waited on the Lord, they would have avoided much pain in their family. King Saul did not wait for the prophet Samuel. In his haste, he sinned and eventually lost his kingship. The disciples were encouraged to tarry in the city until they received power from on high. They obediently waited and received the Holy Spirit.

Let us endeavor to wait on the Lord since that is God's desire for us, as David emphasized in Psalm 27:14. "Wait on the LORD. . . . wait, I say, on the LORD" (KJV).

There's a hymn entitled "Wait, and Murmur Not!"* It encourages us to wait patiently in times of sorrow or unanswered prayer. We are in a waiting period right now and in a time of preparation. Let us be ready to meet Jesus when He comes.

And let us remember to wait faithfully. When we pray, we need to wait for the Lord to answer our prayers. We cannot do anything to speed up His answers. On the other hand, waiting does help us develop patience. Paul wrote, "If we hope for that we see not, then do we with patience wait for it" (Romans 8:25, KJV). Let's continue, with patience, to wait for the glorious return of the loving Savior. Let us not grow weary, for He is near.

Ena Thorpe

---

* W. H. Bellamy, "Wait, and Murmur Not!" (Biglow & Main Co., 1890), public domain.

The Big Rock

A brother offended is harder to be won than a strong city.
—Proverbs 18:19, KJV

When my children were little, my youngest boy, Garry, usually played with his sister, Kathy. At other times his two older brothers would play with him, but he didn't like their constant teasing.

One day Garry came to me and told me he didn't like his brothers. He said he was going to run away. We have forty-five acres, and he knew all the hiding places. I told him I loved him and didn't want him to go. He said he loved me too. Then he decided he would meet me out at the big rock at the back of our property. He didn't want to run away from his mom; he wanted to run away from his brothers!

"A brother offended is harder to be won than a strong city," says our text. If you want to acquire a city, you go out and conquer it. Even a strong city can be won by brute force, and you may be strong enough to win, even strong enough to quell the rebellion that follows.

When you want to establish a lifelong bond with your brother, however, you cannot force his loyalty, and you cannot make him love you. You must first rule yourself by practicing self-discipline and self-denial. That is hard! But worth it. Your brother can be won over by learning to trust your deep love and true acceptance.

Our text also means that a grudge provides fuel for strong resistance and can outlast most sieges. It can take a long time for your love to seep through the stone walls protecting your brother's heart. That is laborious but worth it! Your brother can be won over by watching the consistent change in your behavior, attitude, and nature.

As they grew up, my children learned to love one another. The boys brought three new "daughters" into my family, and now I have sixteen grandchildren and six great-grandchildren! More than ever, the next generation of brothers and sisters and cousins must learn to be bound by cords of love, to build their homes solidly on the Rock of Ages. Only this foundation is strong enough to withstand the brutal force of an assaulting enemy.

I never forgot about Garry wanting to meet me at the big rock on the hill. I pray that all my family will meet me at the Rock of Ages on the hill of Mount Calvary.

Anne Elaine Nelson with Rebecca Turner

God Is Always With Me

For he shall give his angels charge over thee,
to keep thee in all thy ways.
—Psalm 91:11, KJV

It was the third week of the new year, and we were bombarded with twelve inches of snow. As a rule, I try to be cautious when caught up in inclement weather, especially ice and snow. In any event, life goes on, and my chores had to be completed.

One day, during this storm, I went outside to dispose of a bag of garbage. I was under the impression that I was stepping in a puddle of water when suddenly I found myself lying on a sheet of ice. The garbage went up in the air and landed everywhere. I made several attempts to get up but to no avail. I kept slipping and sliding. There wasn't a soul in sight.

I prayed, *Lord, what must I do? I can't get up!*

The Lord impressed this answer on me: *Slide downward until you touch dry land, and you will be able to get up.* I followed His instructions and was able to pick myself up without a problem. What a relief!

As I tried to pull myself together, I heard a voice asking, "Miss, can I take you where you need to go? Please let me take you where you need to go. It's very cold out here." I admit that I was shaken and wondered if I should accept the offer of this young man. I quickly prayed about it and was convinced that I would be safe.

The young man and I witnessed to each other by sharing how good the Lord has been to us in our lives. We soon reached the house, and I thanked him profusely. I continued to praise and thank God for His constant love, mercy, and grace toward me.

Safe at home, I realized I had not even been injured as a result of my fall. Several of my fellow church members came over to see for themselves that I was not hurt. After all, I'm only eighty-seven years young!

In their amazement and my gratitude, we joined together in giving God thanksgiving and praise for His blessings. That day I experienced the truth of Psalm 91:15: "He shall call upon me, and I will answer him: I will be with him in trouble; I will deliver him, and honour him" (KJV). God kept every word of that promise. Will you join me in giving God thanks today for your blessings as well? He is extremely good, and His mercy endures forever.

Harriet Langley

The Dislodged Sink

So, if you think you are standing firm, be careful that you don't fall!
—1 Corinthians 10:12, NIV

On Good Friday 2019, one of our new care partners came over. Michelle was helping Mom, sitting in her wheelchair, transfer to the restroom. In that cramped area, Michelle—who is quite tiny—became entangled with the sink. Suddenly it fell from the wall to which three rusty nails had attached it about twenty-five years earlier. Horrified, the three of us surveyed the catastrophe on the floor. Then we remembered: Nobody in the maintenance department would be available until Tuesday after Easter Monday (a paid holiday in Canada).

Silently, we all prayed for help. Nothing happened immediately. But much later that evening—before sunset—Marcos, a Christian plumber on staff, appeared with a wry smile and his electric drill. The sink was reattached securely in what seemed like five seconds. We thanked him and God, who sent him. He simply said, "I know how difficult life would be without access to water."

He was right on several levels—both physically and spiritually.

Physically, our bodies need to be washed thoroughly by that pure, cleansing liquid to avoid contamination and disease. Second, we need to drink water to survive. When we are dehydrated, we feel thirsty long after we need that thirst-quenching drink. Spiritually, it is essential to drink of the Water of Life to maintain a close relationship with God. We must delve into His Word to grow in faith because we can do absolutely nothing on our own.

Using water as a metaphor, Jesus explained this truth in His interaction with the Samaritan woman at Jacob's well. Ellen G. White's pen records this conversation and makes the following observation: "The cisterns will be emptied, the pools become dry; but our Redeemer is an inexhaustible fountain. We may drink, and drink again, and ever find a fresh supply."*

Master Repairer, please use Your tools to make our daily moments of praise, adoration, and prayer lead us to be seekers of the only requisite for eternal life—connection to You. I pray that my influence will inspire my new friends to a closer relationship with You.

Let's drink and drink again from the Fount of Life.

Glenda-mae Greene

---

* Ellen G. White, *The Desire of Ages* (Mountain View, CA: Pacific Press®, 1940), 187.

The Truth

"Sanctify them by the truth; your word is truth."
—John 17:17, NIV

One day I was browsing the internet and saw a notice from a mother looking for a family that would be willing to adopt her thirteen-month-old girl. *Wow*, I thought, *she's desperate!* I told my husband, but he didn't seem interested. I was too curious to forget it and called the phone number for more information.

The divorced woman, Christy, already had two little ones. She attended school at night, had a full-time job, and was worn out. Christy invited me to her house to talk. The similarities between this woman's situation and the birth mother of our now adult (adopted) daughter were uncanny.

When I arrived at her home, Mama Christy was drying the girl's hair after a bath. Little Lolana had dark eyes and short platinum hair. She was so cute and shy as she stood next to her mother. The three of us took a short walk down the street to talk. Lolana walked warily on the other side of her mom, avoiding me. With plans to move to another state, Christy needed closure as soon as she finished school. When she suggested I take Lolana home for a week to see how she would fit in, I was not only shocked but also excited. Then I wondered what my husband would say.

I took the little one home, dropped the "na" from her name, and adopted Lola, our little girl *dog*.

Did this true story deceive you? I led you to believe the little girl was human, but for me, she was a dog all along. In the Garden of Eden, Satan didn't tell Eve the whole truth, but it was close enough for her to accept it. The apostle Paul said, "But I am afraid that just as Eve was deceived by the serpent's cunning, your minds may somehow be led astray from your sincere and pure devotion to Christ" (2 Corinthians 11:3, NIV).

Deceptions abound, especially in the spiritual world. Jesus warned us to "watch out that no one deceives you." (Matthew 24:4, NIV) The only way to prevent deception is to know Jesus and study His Word, the Bible. As Christian women, we don't want to be naive and accept beliefs that don't reflect the teachings of Scripture.

Donna J. Voth

The White Coat

Being confident of this very thing, that He who has begun a good work in you will complete it until the day of Jesus Christ.
—Philippians 1:6, NKJV

Nervous and anxious just a couple of days before my medical board exam, I ran out of time to order (online) a white lab coat, which I was required to wear. So I Google-mapped some locations of stores where I could shop. I didn't have the time to be running around, so I tried calling ahead. The first place said, "No coats." The second place was so close that I just started driving before calling. Thankfully the answer was affirmative! "Yes, we do have white lab coats." Happily, I hurried to the store—or should I say warehouse? It was huge, with rows and rows of medical apparel.

A lady asked, "How can I help?" I told her I was looking for a white lab coat. She said, "Let me call the manager." *Manager?* A very pleasant man came forward to hear my request. I was beginning to pick up that this business didn't sell to individuals.

"A white lab coat?" he said. "We don't sell like that—only to medical supply stores." I thanked him and was turning to leave when he asked, "Do you work for a doctor?"

I almost answered, "I *am* a doctor," but instead explained, "I have an exam, and I need a white lab coat." He asked me what size I wore, then he left and came back with a white coat. It was perfect. "How much is it?" I asked, hoping for a good price since the exam, the two-hour road trip, and an overnight hotel stay was already costing me. But I was a desperate buyer!

The manager shook my hand and said, "All the best on your exam."

He began to walk away, so I quickly asked, "Uh, where do I pay for this?"

He responded, "I said, 'All the best on your exam!' "

As I carried my white lab coat out the door, I felt as if my smile was glowing like the sun. God is so amazing! Not only did I have a white lab coat but one at no cost. But the real priceless gift here was God's message of reassurance: He was with me and would see me through. *Thank You, Jesus!*

I am looking forward to wearing another white garment soon. Until then, though, this white lab coat will remind me that He is faithful to complete the work He has begun in me.

Glenetia Carr O'Connor

A Warm Blanket

Two people are better off than one, for they can help each other succeed. If one person falls, the other can reach out and help. But someone who falls alone is in real trouble.
—Ecclesiastes 4:9, 10, NLT

My friend was in real trouble. Struck out of the blue by crushing, debilitating depression, she was helpless to save herself. She had, of all things, just begun to explore a relationship with Jesus. She'd just commenced Bible studies and started attending church services. The enemy of souls must have been most displeased indeed.

He hit her hard!

I spent hours praying for and with her, talking to and encouraging her. We talked about the cosmic battle we're engaged in—the great controversy between Christ and Satan, who challenged the goodness of God's character, law, and sovereign reign in the universe. Satan continues to rebel against God and harass those who follow Him. This provided some context for her current struggle.

I shared pertinent Scripture promises with my friend. Every single day I texted her at least one Bible verse, which I prayed would be helpful to her.

Then one day, when my discouraged friend began to feel a little better, she said to me, "You're like a warm blanket in a cold place."

Those words took my breath away. That the Lord would use me as relief is awesome.

And the fact that He's provided *me* many warm blankets and much relief over time, as well, is something for which I'll be eternally grateful. He uses us to touch one another, reach out to one another, and help one another. We're all in this together.

Heaven itself is Warm Blanket Central, but it allows us to participate in this life-giving process. Every one of us has fallen and will fall again. And there are many down all around us. You don't have to look far at all.

I resolve to be a warm blanket to all those the Lord places in front of me who need one. Will you do the same?

Carolyn K. Karlstrom

Rest Assured

And he said, My presence shall go with thee, and I will give thee rest.
—Exodus 33:14, KJV

The LORD your God hath given you rest.
—Joshua 1:13, KJV

When you hear the word *rest*, what comes to mind? For me, *rest* has many different meanings. After teaching twenty-plus energetic kindergarten students, I truly enjoy rest from a hard day's work. God knew what He was doing when He created the Sabbath for our rest, worship, and fellowship with Him. This weekly one-day "vacation" is something I relish and would not exchange for anything. I must be honest. I wish the Sabbath could last longer each week, for as soon as it is over, I am back in a rush.

There will come a time when I will rest in the sleep of death if Jesus does not come before then. Yet how about resting while we are still living? Do we take the time to "rest assured" that the Father is in complete control and that He is capable and able to take care of all our needs? Is there anything too hard for the Lord?

When we are truly resting in God, we can go to sleep and go through our daily activities free of anxieties. It is easier said than done, of course, but when we take God at His word, He will come through for us. God cannot lie. He says what He does and does what He says.

The Bible tells us to "be anxious for nothing, but in everything by prayer and supplication, with thanksgiving, let your requests be made known to God" (Philippians 4:6, NKJV). God carries the weight of the world on His shoulders, and He will carry us through.

So what is holding us back from claiming the promises of God?

By His strength, I am renewing my commitment to accept the invitation: "Come unto me, all ye that labour and are heavy laden, and I will give you rest" (Matthew 11:28, KJV).

Won't you join with me in this renewal?

Joan M. Leslie

An Unforgettable Experience

For the Lord Himself will descend from heaven with a shout, with the
voice of an archangel, and with the trumpet of God. And the dead in
Christ will rise first. . . . And thus we shall always be with the Lord.
—1 Thessalonians 4:16, 17, NKJV

My mom was diagnosed with breast cancer in January 2009. She did quite well for several years, but in 2017 I watched her grow weaker. Since we did not live in the same place, I had to travel to visit her. In recent years I had visited her twice annually. It was so painful to see her decline in health. I remember, many years ago, that my mom spent my fortieth birthday with me. Now in the summer of 2017, while visiting her, I celebrated my birthday again. On the morning of my birthday, my mom asked my sister (who was her caregiver) to hand her a special handbag. My mom took money from the bag and gave me the same amount of dollars that matched my age. Instantly I was overwhelmed with emotions of gratitude and sadness. Never again would I have the opportunity to receive another gift from my dear mother. I hugged and thanked her and then left her room as my emotions overcame me. I did not want her to see me crying. As I stepped outside, I cried, pouring out my heart to God.

That year I was able to visit Mother in April, June, July, and again at Thanksgiving time in November. We spent a lot of time talking to her and singing for her. Inspirational songs were also played for solace. The November visit to see Mother was the most difficult one. By this time, she was saying very little and couldn't do much for herself. After being with her for nine days that November, I had to return home. On Sabbath, December 16, 2017, my mom passed quietly to her rest in Jesus. (In 2008, she'd been preceded in death by her dear husband, my dad.)

As much as I didn't want to lose my mother, I comforted myself with the knowledge that Mom was no longer suffering. As she expressed her readiness to go to sleep in her Savior, I prayed that God's will would be done. She had lived a full life and touched many. At eighty-four, she could say, as had the apostle Paul, "I have fought the good fight, I have finished the race, I have kept the faith" (2 Timothy 4:7, NKJV).

How I look forward to the day when she and I will be reunited. Thank God for this blessed hope! Thank God, as well, for fond memories of our loved ones until then.

Janice Fleming-Williams

Unseen? Unheard? Never.

Praise be to the LORD,
for he has heard my cry for mercy.
—Psalm 28:6, NIV

One day early in my first semester as a full-time professor, I awoke with a sick feeling in my stomach. I loved my new job, but it overwhelmed me. Not only was I prepping six new classes and running the writing center, but I was also worried that I might lose the position. You see, I lacked a doctorate and had accepted a job with the proviso that the institution would reopen the search toward the end of the year. I was doing my best, but I never felt I was doing enough. Not at work, and certainly not at home as a mother to my two preschoolers.

Who can I tell? My heart cried for a while on that dark morning. I lay there feeling sorry for myself—and sorry that I couldn't express my insecurities to my coworkers because, soon, they would be responsible for either firing or rehiring me. In the predawn hours, I prayed, *God, please encourage my heart today.* Later that day, God answered. After my last class, within just minutes of one another, a student and then a colleague stopped me to tell me, privately and sincerely, that my presence and teaching that semester had already made a difference to them.

Gratitude welled within me. God had opened the eyes of not one but *two* gentle souls at my workplace—and allowed them to really "see" me that day— even though I had never voiced my insecurity or my need for affirmation. I didn't end up being rehired for the next year, but that news eventually came as a relief. I had started my PhD program during the spring semester, but grad school, added to the job and motherhood, was too much at once. I realized there had been no time that year to tend to relationships with friends and prayer partners. It's no wonder I had felt unseen and unheard.

As I write, I am headed back to graduate school full-time, with plans to return to full-time instructing afterward. The next few years will be busy, but more flexible, with more opportunities to express my heart to Christian sisters or even fellow teaching assistants at my secular university. I believe God saw this need for fellowship just as He saw my need for affirmation that dark day—just as He saw my need "to taste" my calling so I'd re-enroll in grad school after seven years away. God always sees, just as He always hears. Cry out to Him.

Lindsey Gendke

Appreciating Mothers

Charm is deceptive, and beauty is fleeting;
but a woman who fears the LORD is to be praised.
—Proverbs 31:30, NIV

In the United States each May, we celebrate Mother's Day. I was blessed being raised by two mothers: Mama, my biological mother, and Granny, my grandmother.

Mama became a widow early in life, and singlehandedly nurtured and provided for three daughters and a son. Being the mother of one son, I can scarcely imagine what life was like for her, especially when we "malfunctioned"! Being a skilled seamstress, she always had us smartly dressed, sometimes using the same fabric for dresses and shirts to economize. She became a culinary magician, stretching and varying the food we had to give us tasty, nutritious meals. We were educated and taught love and respect for God and our elders. Mama was a good and loving mother. However, with time, providing for us became a challenge, and she had to do what many Jamaicans did to better provide for her children: She left the warmth of our beautiful tropical island for the much colder continent. There she went back to school and worked. The mothering baton was temporarily passed to Granny.

Granny did not have to provide for us materially since Mama did; she just loved us. She went to extremes to "make sure that nothing happened" to us. She was calm because she started her day with prayer, covering each family member, friend, stranger, and the island of Jamaica.

I often wonder how I measure up to my two mothers. I believe I have blended traits from both and have adapted various actions and responses appropriate for raising my son. I did not have a manual with his name on it, so I depended heavily on prayers. After thirty-three years, I continue to lift him daily in prayer. Someone once said, "It takes a village to raise a child." How true! Many times, I sought advice and compared notes in the "village." I am confident that with God's help, I have done the best that I could. Mothers in the household of faith, let us don our spiritual armor and unite in continuous prayer for our children, our own as well as others in our "village." Let us defeat the efforts of Satan in his spiritual warfare to snatch them from the Lord.

Cecelia Grant

Staying Connected

Keep thy heart with all diligence; for out of it are the issues of life.
—Proverbs 4:23, KJV

My awareness of my surroundings was on high alert, and my senses were almost overwhelmed. It was a glorious sight to behold—the majestic trees, the variety of unique plants, the kaleidoscope of colors offered by the flowers. A breathtaking fragrance filled the air; visiting birds made a musical racket; running water gently bubbled in the nearby stream. I felt the damp, fresh grass beneath my feet. I could almost taste the beauty of it all as my mind was engulfed, and I closed my eyes in wondrous rapture. This was real. God was present! I had discovered this secluded spot one day while traveling through the countryside. Since then, it had become my secret hiding place where I retreated for those special, private days shared with God alone.

Even in my thoughts, this site always brings calm and joy to my soul. It elevates my thoughts and sends my imagination soaring: if—despite sin and its corrupting force—such a masterpiece of nature still exists, then what does heaven look, smell, sound, feel, and taste like? If the presence of God can be so palpable when one is surrounded by His creation on this earth, then what will it be like to be in His presence, face-to-face?

We all need a private space or place with nothing to distract us from refreshing, rejuvenating, reconnecting, and rebuilding our relationship with God, our only Source of strength. Where our souls are watered as we pour our hearts out to Him and He breathes into us the reassurance of His love and watchful care. The location need not be exotic. Whether it's at home, at church, at the home of a relative or friend, in a park or garden—it doesn't matter. What does matter is that we identify such a place where we can reflect on His sacrifice, provisions, protection, leading, and purpose for our lives. If you haven't already identified one, find a secret hiding place that can be your place of quiet rest. It's always an uplifting, life-changing experience to recharge our spiritual batteries by intentionally drawing close to God's heart. And there is no better place to do this than in nature!

Lord, teach me to hunger and to thirst after Your presence. Cleanse me and then fill me with Your sweet Holy Spirit.

Cloreth S. Greene

Past, Present, Future

"The LORD himself goes before you and will be with you; he will never leave you nor forsake you. Do not be afraid; do not be discouraged."
—Deuteronomy 31:8, NIV

Joshua was about to take on the biggest responsibility of his life—leading the children of Israel—and Moses was giving him words of encouragement. I know these words have been so meaningful to me when facing new challenges or opportunities, but this morning in my Bible study, it struck me clearly that each day the Lord Himself leads the way for us. He does not assign a surrogate or a substitute. The Lord Himself goes before us into each new day.

Each new day is a clean slate. We don't know what the day will bring, but God knows, and He is going into that day ahead of us, leading the way, blazing the trail, and even taking the hits for us.

Not only does He go before us but He also promises to be with us. What could be better than that? To have the God of the universe with us no matter what we encounter is such a precious promise. But that isn't all: "For the LORD will go before you, the God of Israel will be your rear guard" (Isaiah 52:12, NIV).

Think about it. He is also our rear guard. He has us surrounded by His love, care, and salvation! The whole idea of God going before us, going with us, and going as our rear guard implies that He has our future covered, that He takes care of our present, and that He deals with our past.

We don't have to worry about what happened in the past. We can let it go and let it rest in God's capable hands.

No matter what happens today in our present, He's got that covered too. Not to worry!

And, as far as the future goes, He has great plans for us, to give us hope and a future (see Jeremiah 29:11), so no need to worry about that either.

What an awesome God we serve! May you sense His presence today. May you feel His arms around you, holding you up. Rejoice in Him always. He is our risen Lord. He lives, and He is continually present with us in all aspects of our lives—past, present, and future!

Myrna L. Hanna

First Responders

"Love your neighbor as yourself."
—Mark 12:31, NIV

My husband's cousin, John, was one of several thousand first responders at the World Trade Center during the 9/11 disaster in New York City in 2001. The responders were of different skills and professions, but they were united in the goal of finding people and saving their lives. They were intent on treating their neighbors as themselves. Most were volunteers. John, however, was employed by the National Disaster Medical System, a huge federal organization whose purpose is to help people. John was a hero—the governor of the state of Missouri, where he lived, presented him with a plaque of appreciation.

Did you encounter a first responder today? I do—daily—and most first responders will never get an award for their deeds or even get thanked. They don't even know they did anything out of the ordinary. There's the gentleman who held the door open for me at the store yesterday. On the same day, an unknown driver let me change lanes with my car in a very awkward place. They certainly met my needs at the minute; they were first responders for me. We can be first responders by simply making a phone call.

While John was at Ground Zero, he was the chief medical officer, working eighteen hours a day for three weeks. There were 1.8 million tons of wreckage, and the rescue mission lasted nine months. Nearly three thousand people died, and six thousand were injured in the attacks.

First responders put their lives in danger every day. Police officers are shot, EMT workers and firefighters die as they are trying to save "their neighbor." They may not know these people or like them, but they love them anyway. Their passion and calling is to help people.

Jesus Christ, our Savior, responded to the needs of fallen humanity. He was the great First Responder. He may not always like what we are doing, but He loves us anyway. He died on the cross for people who hated Him. Cousin John now has asthma and pulmonary issues from breathing the dust and smoke at the 9/11 site. He is eager for Jesus to come and heal him.

Will you try to be a first responder for someone in need today, thus loving your neighbor as yourself? Encourage a child or write that long-neglected letter. "Love your neighbor . . . "

Barbara Huff

Dirty Money

Come now, and let us reason together, saith the LORD:
though your sins be as scarlet, they shall be as white as snow;
though they be red like crimson, they shall be as wool.
—Isaiah 1:18, KJV

My father has a tradition of saving coins. When we were younger, he'd save them in an antique fire extinguisher. Then when we'd take summer trips with him, he'd count the change and use it for our vacation "fund." Over the years, he began filling five-gallon plastic jugs. With all the technology we have today, including coin-counting machines in many stores, you'd think it would be an easy process for him to "cash in" his savings. Well, my dad doesn't think those machines are accurate and prefers to count the coins himself.

This year he enlisted my sister and me to help count coins since his jug was almost full. The weather prohibited us from traveling to his home on the first designated counting date. So Dad decided to start the process by sorting all the quarters, dimes, and nickels. Father's Day was picked as our next designated counting day. We would be able to spend the day with our dad and help him count all his coins.

I am the treasurer of my church. I must admit that sometimes when I hear all the coins hitting the offering plates, I cringe a little. Not only is counting coins time consuming but it's also a dirty job! Some coins come with dried chewing gum attached to them. Others are so dirty you can't tell what denomination they are.

So, after spending hours counting coins on Father's Day, my hands were disgustingly dirty. I would wash them periodically just to get rid of that feeling of disgust. Even though dirty, each quarter was still worth twenty-five cents. Each dime was still worth ten cents. Each nickel was still worth five cents. And when they were all added together, my dad had saved a nice chunk of change. The coins being dirty didn't decrease their value at all.

Driving home after that day with my father, I reflected on this: We, too, are disgustingly dirty with our sinful selves. We may look at one another and wonder what value we hold, due to our sinfulness. Yet—praise the Lord—we are all God's children. Like those dirty coins, our filthiness doesn't decrease our value in God's eyes. One day soon, He will gather us all home to count us among the redeemed. Hallelujah!

Angèle Peterson

Persistence

What then shall we say to these things?
If God is for us, who can be against us?
—Romans 8:31, NKJV

We don't even know the name of a widow that Jesus referenced in a parable. This woman was in trouble, and the judge who could help her did not fear God or care about the problems of others. "Now there was a widow in that city; and she came to him, saying, 'Get justice for me from my adversary' " (Luke 18:3, NKJV). However, Jesus said, the widow was so persistent that the judge rushed to try her case and obtain justice for her.

Then there was the Canaanite woman. She was a desperate mother seeking Jesus' help for her demon-possessed daughter. At first, He seemed not to hear her. His apparent attitude of not caring made her persist even more in her search for a miracle. Her persistence overcame the hostilities, fears, and suspicions that had beclouded her mind. When the ethnic barriers were overcome, the woman declared before all present that she believed in the power of Christ to heal her daughter. Jesus revived her faith and set her troubled heart free.

God is no respecter of persons. Although the desperate mother and the possessed daughter were of a foreign race, Jesus healed anyway. In the end, Jesus used this incident as an example of persevering faith and honored it, declaring: " 'O woman, great is your faith! Let it be to you as you desire.' And her daughter was healed from that very hour" (Matthew 15:28, NKJV). Persistence is something we must learn to cultivate. Many women give up the fight for faith by anticipating defeat even before the battle. They fear they are not strong enough to win. But it is in the face of struggle that faith is strengthened. In hope and prayer is where God reveals His plans for us. If He goes ahead of us, we will never be defeated by an enemy.

Dear friends, in the face of this divine reality, let us raise our heads and—like the Canaanite woman, the widow, and many others—persist toward our goals. We need justice for our causes, freedom from our fears; we must believe that we have not been forgotten and that we are loved. God is for us in our internal and external struggles. He is for our families, our work, our friends, and especially our faith. We do not have to be discouraged by the "giants" ahead of us because there is a great God to fight our battles—with Him, we are more than conquerors!

Sueli da Silva Pereira

Skunk!

The LORD is my rock and my fortress and my deliverer;
My God, my strength, in whom I will trust;
My shield and the horn of my salvation, my stronghold.
—Psalm 18:2, NKJV

A few months ago, I was driving down the road in Arizona when a pungent, foul odor hit my nose. I instantly knew what it was. A skunk! Skunks are small mammals (about the size of a large cat or small dog) native to North America and South America. While their coloring can vary, typically they are black with a long white stripe down their back to the tip of their bushy tail. Skunks have the ability to spray a putrid-smelling liquid (which contains sulfur chemicals) as a means of defending themselves. Once you smell a skunk, you don't forget it.

As I continued driving down the road, the stench got worse and worse. As I expected, I soon drove past the carcass of the little skunk. Skunks spray people, dogs, and anything else they consider their enemies—including cars and trucks. The poor skunks have no concept that their bad odor is not going to prevent a vehicle from running them over.

I kept driving, feeling sad for the poor little skunk, and then I started thinking about the spiritual parallels. Skunks try to defend themselves against cars by using their nasty smell. But inevitably some get run over and killed anyway. Likewise, we alone cannot defend ourselves against the wiles of our enemy, the devil. Only a saving relationship with Jesus Christ will keep us safe! We can claim this promise: "Through God we will do valiantly, for it is He who shall tread down our enemies" (Psalm 60:12, NKJV).

On our own, we cannot protect ourselves—just as a little skunk cannot protect itself against a vehicle. But our mighty God is the King of the universe, and He and His angels stand ready to protect us. Let's not be like the skunks who futilely try to defend themselves. Instead, let's claim the promise, "And the Lord will deliver me from every evil work and preserve me for His heavenly kingdom. To Him be glory forever and ever. Amen!" (2 Timothy 4:18, NKJV).

Amanda Nicole Gaspard Collins

A Wonderful Surprise

Now the God of hope fill you with all joy and peace in believing,
that ye may abound in hope, through the power of the Holy Ghost.
—Romans 15:13, KJV

In August 2018, I accompanied my husband to Kigali, Rwanda, where he was a guest speaker during a camp meeting at a large church there. After our first evening program, some ladies approached me, asking if I could provide some presentations uniquely for the women. (At the time, I was the coordinator for our denomination's Shepherdess program* in West-Central Africa.) When I agreed, they arranged through their district pastor to schedule some evening programs for the women. For three evenings, we ladies enjoyed seminars together as we explored the topic "How to Stay Young and Beautiful Without Damaging Our Bodies."

One evening after the program, a lady came to me and said, "I know you very well. Do you remember that several years ago, in 1994, you came to our dormitory, prayed with us, and read Bible texts to encourage us?"

Yes, I remembered. My husband and I had stopped at our Christian university in Rwanda, after month-long evangelistic meetings in Kisangani in the Democratic Republic of the Congo. At the end of that week, the girls at the university pleaded with us to come and pray in every dormitory room. We did so from 7:00 P.M. until 2:00 the next morning! In the last room, after we prayed, two young ladies presented us with two Bibles and church hymnals in their native language, Kiswahili. It was hard to say goodbye. I left Rwanda with that scene in my mind. Some weeks later, war broke out. When I learned that many had perished on that very campus, I thought of those two young ladies, remembering their faces and feeling the sadness of separation.

Twenty-four years had passed. Now here, in Kigali, this woman said to me, "I am one of the young ladies you prayed for in the last room of the dorm. God saved us, and we are serving Him as pastors' wives here in Kigali." What a joy!

I believe it will also be a wonderful experience to meet our loved ones in the heavens when Jesus comes, as He promised in the Bible. There we will stay and live with Him forever and ever. Amen!

Angèle Rachel Nlo Nlo

---

* A program that provides support and encouragement for pastors' wives.

Staying in Airplane Mode

Love not the world, neither the things that are in the world.
If any man love the world, the love of the Father is not in him.
For all that is in the world . . . is not of the Father, but is of the world.
And the world passeth away, and the lust thereof:
but he that doeth the will of God abideth for ever.
—1 John 2:15–17, KJV

My phone was in airplane mode, and I missed a very important interview!" cried Roylette.

"Did you pray about it and ask God for His will?" asked Royce.

"Of course," exclaimed Roylette.

"Well, then, God's will is not in that job, and He wants you to wait patiently."

Airplane mode offers a quick way to disable many functions on our electronic devices that connect us to wireless communication services. When in airplane mode, however, we have to wait patiently until the right time before receiving our communications again. It seems to me that several patriarchs and other noteworthy individuals in the Bible also had to remain in airplane mode. They had to remain spiritually "disconnected" from the things of the world but still trust that God would make good on His promises to them.

Noah persevered in building the ark though the world mocked him—and rescued his family in the process. Abraham left his homeland with only a promise from God that his descendants would become a great nation. Joseph resisted temptation, serving a "silent" God until the time was right for God to use Joseph's faithfulness to save Egypt and Israel. Moses, though surrounded by the riches of Pharaoh's palace, searched for God's leading in his life. And then there were Joshua, David, Elijah, Daniel, Esther, and Job. All had to "disconnect" from the world, keep their hearts faithful while in airplane mode, and await God's timing.

This world is not our home (John 17:16); our citizenship is in heaven (Philippians 3:20); and we are to set our minds on the final victory and destination (Colossians 3:2). If we love this world, the love of our Father is not in us (1 John 2:15).

We, as Christians, need to practice being in airplane mode, disconnecting ourselves from anything in this world that would distract us from our relationship with, and service for, Christ.

Suhana Chikatla

Loyal and Faithful

God's love is meteoric,
his loyalty astronomic,
His purpose titanic,
his verdicts oceanic.
Yet in his largeness
nothing gets lost.
—Psalm 36:5, 6, *The Message*

It is hard times for Naomi, so she leaves her home and moves to Moab with her husband and two sons. In time, her sons marry Moabite women. This is not how Naomi has pictured her sons' futures. While there, she experiences tremendous loss. All three men in her life die. Tragedy. Hopelessness. What can be her future now? In her sadness and despair, her heart turns toward her Bethlehem home. So she decides to leave Moab. She plans to return alone without her daughters-in-law, which would mean even more loss. But one, Ruth, is loyal. Understanding her mother-in-law's heartache, Ruth vows not to leave Naomi, nor the God Naomi has taught her about. Approaching her former home in Israel, Naomi is broken in her spirit. She doesn't even want to be called by her name anymore and asks others to call her Mara, which means *bitter*.

Naomi is so swallowed by her sorrow that she can't recognize that God has blessed her with a faithful daughter-in-law. Ruth tries to make life easier for Naomi in every way she can. She offers to go to work so they can have food. Then Naomi remembers she has a close relative, Boaz, who is wealthy and owns the barley fields in which Ruth finds herself gleaning grain. Isn't God wonderful to put us in the right places at the right times?

Enter Boaz. He is impressed with Ruth's dedication to Naomi and how hard she works in the fields. (And her being young and attractive isn't a deterrent either!) Naomi, who now has turned matchmaker, suggests a plan to Ruth. The young woman boldly follows Naomi's plan to let Boaz know of her interest, and he responds favorably.

As the Bible story goes, Naomi sees her daughter-in-law's devotion rewarded with a husband and family. Ruth is even mentioned in Jesus' genealogy! The loyalty and faithfulness of both women were rewarded. God has a plan for each one of us. Let us listen for His voice today.

Louise Driver

Drifting

The tongue has the power of life and death,
and those who love it will eat its fruit.
—Proverbs 18:21, NIV

I really liked this guy! He approached me, introduced himself, and welcomed me to his church—it was my first time attending. After our introductions and small talk, he promised me a gift that the church gives their visitors. But he didn't come back; he got distracted.

Miraculously, a second opportunity presented itself for us to connect. He came to the house where I'd been invited to have lunch. We ended up having a conversation that caused him to miss the meeting he was scheduled to attend. The conversation was enchanting; there was a real connection. We exchanged phone numbers and decided to keep in touch. He also promised to ensure that I would receive the visitor gift from his church—pens. He kept his word.

Because I still had six more days of visiting family, he later asked if I wanted to spend some time with him. I was happy to. He picked me up and took me to the beach. We walked, talked, and got to know enough about each other to realize that we had a real interest in staying connected. So we did—for a while.

We talked every day for a solid week. It was thrilling! The more we talked, the more I wanted to talk to him. The more we talked, the more I learned about him and he about me. I mean, it was amazing! I felt as if all my prayers about a lasting relationship were working.

But then, his calls became fewer, and his text messages got shorter. I sensed a shift. I noticed right away that something was different about him too. Yet I wanted to give him a chance to demonstrate if he was serious or not.

Days later, I gently voiced my awareness of a change. He proposed that I not worry. He said he had just been busy and that we would talk again soon. But our conversations were never the same; the distance grew. So, how similar does this sound to your relationship with God?

Healthy relationships take effort, vulnerability, and frequent communication. God is most eager to be in a relationship with us, but are we too busy to notice when we are drifting? Life lies in the power of our tongues to communicate with our Creator. He has more time for us than anyone else. Let's not allow neglect on our part to bring death to our relationship with Him.

Rachel Privette Jennings

An Unforgettable Journey

Wherefore . . . let us lay aside every weight,
and the sin which doth so easily beset us, and let us run
with patience the race that is set before us.
—Hebrews 12:1, KJV

As the education director of an area that includes eight schools on five different islands, attending the 2019 graduations took me on a seventeen-day journey. My greatest challenge was not all the standing during my public presentations. My greatest challenge was not filling in for a keynote speaker who couldn't keep the appointment. Neither was my greatest challenge the annoying airport security lines and delayed flights. Actually, my greatest challenge was the large amount of luggage I had to take from place to place because of my extensive itinerary.

At the beginning of my journey, my husband expressed his concern as to how I would be able to manage so much luggage. I assured him that I was on God's mission, and He would make a way. And He did. On several occasions, He sent good Samaritans to assist me with my hand luggage and, at other times, tipped the scales in my favor so that my checked luggage fell within the allotted weight. As I reflected on my arduous journey this year, it reminds me that we are all on a journey to heaven. What luggage are we taking with us? Are we lugging around the works of the flesh such as "adultery, fornication . . . witchcraft, hatred . . . wrath, strife, seditions, heresies, envying's, murders, [and] drunkenness" (Galatians 5:19–21, KJV)?

The apostle Paul provides us with some sound advice for our Christian journey when he says, "Lay aside every weight, and the sin which doth so easily beset us, and let us run with patience the race that is set before us" (Hebrews 12:1, KJV). Author Ellen G. White also counseled, "The path to eternal life is steep and rugged. Take no additional weights to [slow] your progress."* As we run the race, our luggage should consist of the fruit of the Spirit, which is love, joy, peace, long-suffering, kindness, goodness, faithfulness, which may be considered lightweight luggage (see Galatians 5:22, 23).

I look forward to participating in that grand graduation in heaven, where I will be a graduate. Jesus will spare no pains to make this the graduation of graduations! The angelic hosts and the redeemed of all ages will be there as cheerleaders. I long for heaven. Don't you?

Gerene I. Joseph

---

* Ellen G. White, *The Adventist Home* (Nashville: Southern Publishing, 1952), 67.

Brave Choice

Your love, LORD, reaches to the heavens,
your faithfulness to the skies.
—Psalm 36:5, NIV

My husband, John, and I had been married for almost forty years and were proud parents of two grown sons. We welcomed our daughters-in-law into our hearts and were then blessed with two grandsons, Andrew and Micah. I vividly remember the day I heard, "Your tests are positive for breast cancer." John was my rock. He and I prayed together more than we ever had, surrendering to God's will as Jesus did. Our Lord received the strength to go to dark Calvary; I received strength to go on a less strenuous journey—through surgery, chemo, and radiation.

Then my faith wavered slightly one morning. As my precious John was getting ready to take me to treatment, he succumbed to a massive heart attack—how I missed his loving arms around me. *You can do this, baby,* I seemed to hear him say.

Time passed. I was now a healthy six-year survivor, enjoying being cancer-free. Then my doctor informed me that my tests were positive again. *No, Lord!* my heart cried. *My prayer warrior, my rock is gone. How can I make the brave choice this time? How can I bear to start over in this battle for my life?*

I sat on the couch, surrounded by my grandchildren and their friends, enjoying their favorite game of hide-and-seek. Oh, how they giggled when someone was found! *O, Lord,* I prayed, *please find me, Your loving daughter, and rescue me from death's door. I want more time. I want more days of laughter with these loved ones. I want to watch them grow up.*

So, I trusted Jesus to go with me and give me the strength to begin again. Surgery, weakness, uncertainty, bald head, chemo—on and on it went, but He never left me. Again, I am a survivor, way beyond the typical five-year expectancy. I praise my forever Friend, Jesus, for each new day. My grandchildren are still my world. I have always encouraged them to do their best in life: Andrew was valedictorian in his senior high school year and has now completed his second year of college. Micah recently graduated from high school and has enrolled in a nearby college. I praise God for the extra time He has given me with them. My prayer now is that I may use it wisely, spreading the good news of a loving Savior.

Jane Wiggins Moore

God's Different Plan for Us

"For I know the plans that I have for you," declares the LORD, "plans for welfare and not for calamity to give you a future and a hope."
—Jeremiah 29:11, NASB

We had planned a vacation to Tennessee to spend time with our son, Jamie, and his family during the latter part of September. Stan and Jamie would be enjoying a father-son fishing and camping trip. Meanwhile, Ana Paula, our daughter-in-law, Izzy, our granddaughter, and I had plans to do girly things. For some reason or another, our plans did not seem to be coming together smoothly. At the last minute, I canceled the kennel reservations for our pets. Still disappointed about our plans, I was toying with the idea of making the trip by myself. Stan was not in favor of my idea, for it would involve a two-day drive from Texas to Tennessee. I finally gave up the idea of driving by myself and consoled myself with the fact that I would be making three weekend trips to Albuquerque, New Mexico, during October.

On the last Friday of September, while sitting under the hairdryer at my weekly hair appointment, I received a frantic call from our daughter, Joquita. She was unable to reach Stan and needed to convey the message that our friend, Dennis, was being moved to hospice care. Dennis had refused any further medical treatment because he realized his condition was terminal, and he didn't want to suffer anymore. When I arrived home from my hair appointment, I found Stan packing and making arrangements to cover his responsibilities at church the next day. I volunteered to teach his Sabbath School class since he couldn't find a replacement for that duty. Stan then left for Fort Worth, Texas, to pick up Joquita and head for Austin. They would stay there with Dennis until he was laid to rest. After Stan's return to Amarillo, the pieces of the puzzle of God's plan came together. I realized that if our vacation to Tennessee had taken place, Stan and Jamie would have been in a remote area that would not have had cell phone service available. I also realized that had I driven to Tennessee by myself, I would not have been able to care for our three furry friends while Stan was gone.

As I pondered how God's plan had overruled in this experience, the words of a couple of praise songs came to mind: "What a Mighty God We Serve" and "My God Is an Awesome God." Not only is our God amazing and awesome, but He is also worthy of honor and praise.

Anna Ivie Swingle

An Angel's Touch—Part 1

The angel of the LORD encampeth round about them
that fear him, and delivereth them.
—Psalm 34:7, KJV

May 8 dawned bright and sunny over lovely Grants Pass in southern Oregon. The songs of the meadowlarks filtered through the breakfast nook windows as we rejoiced in our morning worship experience. What a beautiful day to be alive! My husband and I had promised to take a recently widowed friend to her favorite restaurant for her birthday. Then we would spend the afternoon helping her pack up her late husband's clothing to donate to community needs.

As we relaxed comfortably in our Jeep, I noticed my husband looked very tired. We had been staying up late preparing invitations for our fiftieth wedding anniversary celebration. "Dear, would you like me to drive today?" I asked cheerfully. He agreed, and we swapped places.

We had barely started down the road when I noticed he was already asleep. I also noticed that we were running a few minutes late, so I accelerated to sixty-five miles an hour on that last steep mountain pass. And that's *all* I remember. Folks in the car behind us later shared that they saw our vehicle suddenly go airborne, flying completely over a road sign before crashing down on the left front wheel. They witnessed our car, glass spraying into the air, roll over three times before coming to an abrupt stop on its roof a few feet from a one-hundred-foot precipice.

"Are you all right?" my husband asked in a subdued tone. He told me later that my response was to cry out three times, "Honey, I'm so sorry!" That Jeep Grand Cherokee had been his favorite car. With shock setting in, we hung upside down in our seatbelts, feeling the pressure of being squeezed to death or cut in half. My left foot had gone through a window, yet a sweet face suddenly pushed through the broken glass, asking, "May I help you?"

"Don't move her!" shouted a voice from the gathering crowd. "The ambulance is on its way!" A hand came through the jagged edges of the glass, turned off the car's engine (we had a full tank of gas), and took the keys from the ignition. Gentle "angel hands" on our shoulders let us know that we would survive. Long ago, Jesus' compassionate hands touched people with comfort and healing. The prophet Daniel testified, "One having the likeness of a man touched me and strengthened me" (Daniel 10:18, NKJV). Let Jesus touch and strengthen you today too.

Patty L. Hyland

An Angel's Touch—Part 2

Then the one who looked like a man touched me again,
and I felt my strength returning.
—Daniel 10:18, NLT

Before I was lifted out of the car, I felt little footsteps going across my back and saw Sparkles, our bichon frise pet dog, frantically dash out my window. The sweet lady who had spoken to me a moment earlier returned and assured me that she would care for Sparkles and bring her to the hospital. *Another angel touch?*

The next thing I knew, strong hands lifted me through the jagged glass, gently placing me on the ground. *An angel?* (No one in the crowd seemed to know him.) Blood trickled down my face and into my hair. My head ached from repeatedly hitting the steering wheel as our car had rolled. Someone else thoughtfully held an umbrella over my head.

My husband, Verne, also extricated from the car now, wandered about in a daze, losing blood from an injured hand. He spotted my purse resting under a bush and his glasses nearby. *God's touch in the details!* The emergency room doctor was sure that I had internal injuries after hearing the report from the responding highway patrol officers. He examined me three times before having me wheeled away for X-rays. The officers said they'd never seen anyone walk away from our type of accident and had certainly never seen an animal survive. Yet our beloved Sparkles didn't have even a scratch on her little furry body—*another evidence of God's care.* And little did we know that many kind residents of the Illinois Valley were bringing garbage bags to pick up *for us* as many of our things as they could find, along with more than two hundred anniversary reception invitations that had been tossed and scattered everywhere!

That Sabbath, my dear husband, a retired pastor, and I preached the sermon. It turned into a praise service as the congregation viewed our black eyes and bruised faces. The crushed Jeep was the least of our worries as we praised God for angels shielding us from the jaws of death.

The photo of our crushed vehicle appeared on the front page of the city newspaper. We now have that picture on our refrigerator as a constant reminder of God's love and care through His angels. Let it also remind you that when *you* are in the most desperate of circumstances, Jesus will touch you with assurance and strength, which you will notice—even in the details.

Patty L. Hyland

Won't He Do It?

Don't worry about anything; instead, pray about everything.
Tell God what you need, and thank him for all he has done.
—Philippians 4:6, NLT

After a good night's sleep, I should have felt rejuvenated and ready for the day, but instead, I awakened feeling extremely anxious, my heart racing. Several months ago, my thyroid had drifted out of normal range, so my prescription had been changed. However, there was comfort in knowing that the waiting game to have it rechecked was almost over.

I got out of bed, put on my robe, and quietly slipped out of the bedroom. My hypochondriacal nature wanted to Google thyroid symptoms, but I refrained. As I paced from room to room, too anxious to sit down, all kinds of questions started going through my mind. Should I take my blood pressure? What if my heart rate is way too high? Should I awaken my husband? Should I go to the emergency room? I got the blood pressure machine out but was too anxious to use it. Suddenly, I just stopped, sat down, and prayed, "Lord, calm my nerves." I closed my eyes and breathed deeply. Then I felt a strong urge to read my women's devotional book's reading for that day (July 21 from *In His Presence*). *OK, Lord, if I'm going to be all right,* I prayed, *let there be no doubt that this reading is meant for me . . . today.*

The title was "Just Be Still." The theme text was Mark 4:39, 40, "Then He arose and rebuked the wind, and said to the sea, 'Peace, be still!' And the wind ceased and there was a great calm. But He said to them, 'Why are you so fearful? How is it that you have no faith?' " (NKJV).

As I continued reading, I saw my favorite text, "Be anxious for nothing, but in everything by prayer and supplication, with thanksgiving, let your requests be made known to God; and the peace of God, which surpasses all understanding, will guard your hearts and minds through Christ Jesus" (Philippians 4:6, 7, NKJV). The Lord had answered my prayer and sent exactly what I needed. I thought, *Thank you, author Akosua Ntriakwah, for your devotional thought this morning!* It ended with, "Let Him calm every storm in your heart and mind and life. Ask God to strengthen your faith in Him. If you need an extra dose of His peace in your current season of life, He will lavishly pour it over you. All you need to do is ask."* He'll do it every time!

Shirley Sain Fordham

---

* Akosua Ntriakwah, "Just Be Still," in *In His Presence*, ed. Carolyn Rathbun Sutton (Nampa, ID: Pacific Press®, 2018), 210.

Slow Down

"Are you tired? Worn out? Burned out on religion? Come to me. Get away with me and you'll recover your life. I'll show you how to take a real rest. Walk with me and work with me—watch how I do it. Learn the unforced rhythms of grace. I won't lay anything heavy or ill-fitting on you. Keep company with me and you'll learn to live freely and lightly."
—Matthew 11:28–30, *The Message*

A m I the only one who wants to trade in my smartphone for a regular rotary-dial landline?* It seems that the invention of this one-stop device has changed social norms and quickened the pace of society. We no longer wait to get home to check our *answering machine.* Yes, I said, "Answering machine." We are now expected to pick up calls as we go, and if by awful chance we miss a call, we are held to the standard of returning the call the moment we retrieve the message. Texting has become the new communication norm, and responding in more than a few minutes is construed as rude and dismissive.

We are now expected to multitask at every moment. Our cell phones rest on our nightstand, so we check them right before going to bed and first thing in the morning. This little device gives us the news and weather, keeps us connected to family and friends, sends us work emails, and gives us endless access to the World Wide Web.

I miss the slower pace of the eighties and nineties. Now I sound old. We have become a society whose minds are so constantly engrossed with "something" that we miss the present. Did you notice the leaves budding this spring, or did you just happen to realize one day that the trees are no longer naked?

Simply put, we are too busy. One of the lessons I've had to learn during my recent hospital recovery is to slow down. What I didn't realize was that this lesson was priceless. There is power in being present. Being present in each moment and focusing on the matter at hand, even if it was just focusing on eating that grape tomato on my plate.

Before my hospitalization, I was moving so fast that I missed the beauty that can be found in each moment. God provides such joy for us each day, but we've got to slow down long enough to appreciate it.

Tricia (Wynn) Payne

---

* This entry first appeared as "Slow Down," Tricia Wynn Payne (blog), May 14, 2018, https://triciawynnpayne.com/tag/patience/.

The Palace Welcome

"Let not your heart be troubled; you believe in God,
believe also in Me. In My Father's house are many mansions. . . .
I go to prepare a place for you. . . . I will come again and receive you
to Myself; that where I am, there you may be also."
—John 14:1–3, NKJV

The long-awaited day had arrived. Six hundred Christian women from islands all over the South Pacific (including Fiji, Tonga, Western Samoa, American Samoa, the Solomon Islands, Vanuatu, Kiribati, Tuvalu, and Niue) converged at a designated center in the city of Nuku'alofa, Tonga. From there, they would begin a march to the palace to meet the queen of Tonga. It was a most colorful gathering as the women stood in groups according to their local island groups. Led by the Tongan police band, the march began. An invitation to visit the queen at her mansion is a rare opportunity in Tonga and usually accorded only to nobles, chiefs, and other high-ranking individuals. Every woman on the march looked forward to entering the palace compound through the front gate and seeing Her Majesty, the queen of Tonga, face-to-face.

As the women marched through Nuku'alofa, crowds of excited people lined the sides of the street to wave and cheer. School children waved flags and sang songs of welcome to the women of the Pacific. The happy throng reminded me of the Bible story in which children waved palms and cheered Jesus when He rode into Jerusalem on a donkey.

As the marching women approached the royal palace, they were ushered into the huge compound by nobles who monitored palace activities. The queen stood at the entrance to the palace, beaming a huge smile and welcoming the women. Each country's representatives took their places in designated spots, and all were seated. Speeches and formalities, along with a devotional and prayer, followed. Women presented gifts to the queen, and she stood to receive them and thank the women. It was a solemn occasion, yet a happy one. The women were pleased to have that firsthand encounter at the palace and cherished the visit.

We also cherish the hope of visiting another palace—a home that God is preparing for us. At this palace, which also belongs to us, God will welcome and receive us in person. He is the builder of this palace that far surpasses worldly mansions. We will enjoy its beauty and comforts for eternity. Let us accept His invitation and prepare to meet Him in this glorious home.

Fulori Sususewa Bola

Mary or Martha

But one thing is needful: and Mary hath chosen that good part,
which shall not be taken away from her.
—Luke 10:42, KJV

My son had graduated from eighth grade. For a couple of years, we had been trying to move to Michigan, where he could attend a Christian high school. And then our house sold—the "green light" sign for which I'd prayed. We closed on Wednesday for the sale of our home and planned to close on our new home in Michigan on Friday. It was a whirlwind, but it went quite smoothly. Soon we began having several young people (sometimes up to thirty) to our house from the nearby college after church on Sabbath.

One week I noticed that the girls and some of the guys who would offer to help me while others preferred to sit, visit, and relax. Of course, I didn't mind the extra help with so many at our house on Sabbath. We had a wonderful time getting to know the students, and many of them would also ask to bring their friends. We usually ate cafeteria-style as we had a large middle island from where they obtained their food before sitting down. I would tell my husband, Brad, that this fellowship was a little taste of what heaven will be like.

Entertaining was a lot of work. Sometimes my boys would complain when I elicited their help. But after everyone had left, our family would say what a great time we had.

As I think about the story of Mary and Martha, I am concerned that I may have been more of a Martha than a Mary. I am a people pleaser, and whenever I am invited to someone's house, I always try to help. Would I have missed out on sitting and talking with Jesus had He been visiting? Would I be the one complaining that it wasn't fair that so much of the work and preparation fell on my shoulders? Would I have viewed Mary as being lazy?

I am often coming and going, busy with all my multitasking. But the Bible reminds us to "be still, and know that I am God" (Psalm 46:10, KJV). How often do we judge people by what we see them doing or not doing—and miss the point? Jesus knew He had a short time on this earth, and Mary knew that her time with Jesus was so precious that she hung on His every word. She had "chosen that good part." She didn't just happen to be there visiting with Jesus—she had chosen to be there!

Gyl Moon Bateman

The Anointing

"Before they call, I will answer;
And while they are still speaking, I will hear."
—Isaiah 65:24, NKJV

The shrill ring of the phone awakened Pastor Richard. He looked at the clock. It was midnight. *This can't be good,* he thought. "Pastor, can you come to the hospital right away?" asked Madlyn. "Mike is very, very sick, and we want you to anoint him."

"Of course," responded the pastor, "I'll be there right away." When he arrived at the hospital, he found a very sick seven-month-old baby with sores all over his body, and part of his tongue eroded. He also found two parents who were in shock.

"He's been diagnosed with acute leukemia," Madlyn wept. "The doctors said all his blood cells are immature. He will not live through the night. Our only hope is that you will anoint him, and God will perform a miracle." Pastor Richard knew that God can perform miracles. He placed his hand on little Mike's head and prayed for a miracle. Tears streamed down the faces of Mike's parents. While the pastor prayed, he felt an electric shock run down his arm. After the prayer, much to his surprise, he said, "Your baby is healed!" He had never told anyone before that they were healed after an anointing. There was a look of shock on the parents' faces as well as his own. Could this be true? It was a long night, but in the morning, the doctors came in and took blood samples. They were shocked by the results. Baby Mike's blood samples revealed the blood cells to be mature. Several weeks later, his tongue was restored. It took a little more than a year for the sores to be completely healed. Clearly, God had performed a miracle! The baby remained in the hospital for one month. Though he still has scars from his ordeal and is deaf in one ear, Mike is now forty-five and a successful attorney. He has mentored two young fatherless boys. Madlyn says, "He is very kind and so thoughtful to his grandparents and us."

Pastor Richard was my brother, who always delighted in telling this story. Sadly, he passed away several years after his prayer over Mike. But I think he will rejoice when he meets Mike in heaven. Our God is so good. He knows what is best for each of us, whether He chooses to heal someone or let them go to sleep until Christ returns. Someday those who are faithful will meet Him and never be sick or face death again!

Dalores Broome Winget

Walking With Jesus

*Whoever says he abides in him ought to walk
in the same way in which he walked.*
—1 John 2:6, ESV

We become like those we are around. For instance, as I grew up, I began to walk like my mother, picking up many other physical characteristics from her. However, from a spiritual point of view, there is Another in whose steps we are to walk. A walk with Christ is necessary for anyone who works for Him. God has not called us to find fulfillment in the quantity of our work for Him but in the quality of our walk with Him. Let's look at five aspects of walking with Jesus.

1. *Walking with Jesus in faith:* The woman with the flow of blood exercised faith in Jesus' healing power (Matthew 9:18–22). Walking in faith means living in confidence, obedience, and righteousness.

2. *Walking with Jesus in newness of life:* Mary Magdalene was among the brave followers of Christ who walked in newness of life (Luke 8:2). After Jesus healed her, Mary displayed a great desire to be with Him. As a result, she had the privilege of being the first to see the risen Christ (John 20:10–18). When we have the desire to be with Jesus, it will lead us to Him.

3. *Walking with Jesus in good works:* Dorcas was "full of good works and charitable deeds" (Acts 9:36, NKJV). Jesus said, "Let your light so shine before men, that they may see your good works and glorify your Father in heaven" (Matthew 5:16, NKJV).

4. *Walking with Jesus in truth:* Deborah, the only female judge of Israel, was courageous (Judges 4). She was a prophetess and a judge, and she led Israel into battle to help liberate Israel.

5. *Walking with Jesus in the Spirit:* The woman at the well in Samaria met Jesus at noonday. She began her walk with Him when He told her, among other things, that "God is Spirit, and those who worship Him must worship in spirit and truth" (John 4:24, NKJV). Jesus says that those receiving the Spirit can know that "He dwells with you and will be in you" (John 14:17, NKJV). The Holy Spirit gives us the power to bear the greatest burdens and adversity. He is also a guide, knowing the ways of Christ when on this earth. He fills us with joy and peace.

Walking with Jesus should be our utmost goal while living on this earth. No matter our circumstances, means, or situations, we, like these women in the Bible, can walk with Jesus.

Premila Pedapudi

The Warning

*"Call to Me, and I will answer you, and show you great
and mighty things, which you do not know."*
—Jeremiah 33:3, NKJV

October 10, 2018, is a day I will always remember. It was a day that everyone in the path of Hurricane Michael had been expecting. As the hurricane got closer to the United States, I began to listen more intently to the weather report. Eventually, we got a warning that we were in its path. I became frantic as I rushed to shop for the necessary provisions for me and my dog, Precious. With my shopping done and gas in the car, and stressed out from the pressure of long lines, I drove home. After settling down, I listened eagerly to the radio. The landfall was expected around noon the next day. In the wee hours of October 10, I got a text: "Marilyn Wallace, go to a shelter." I ignored it and went back to sleep. Around 4:00 A.M., I got another warning, which stated that all shelters would be closed at 6:00 A.M., so I decided to heed the warning. I got dressed and drove to my church. Earlier, I had received permission from my pastor to stay there with my dog since the designated shelters allowed only service pets.

I arrived at the church with just enough time to unload my things. I got inside and watched as trees snapped. Some fell on the church, and water pooled everywhere. I prayed, asking God to keep my dog and me safe. Finally, the hurricane subsided. I wanted to go home but didn't want to drive through so much water. I prayed for a miracle, and God sent a gentle breeze to sweep away the water. It took a long time to reach my house. When I arrived, I was shocked to see that half of the roof of my house was gone, ceilings were down, and insulation was everywhere. However, the Lord kept me calm and sent people to help me.

After the hurricane passed and the situation settled down a little, I asked my neighbor about the warning texts. He said that he hadn't received any warnings. I believe it was God who sent me those warnings to save my life.

A greater hurricane is coming on this earth. Warning signs are everywhere. Will we give heed to them? If I hadn't obeyed the warnings, I could have been killed because the ceiling, insulation, and roof fell on my bed, covering it completely. I thank God for the two warnings that helped preserve Precious and me. I pray that I will always be obedient to His voice.

Marilyn P. Wallace

Divine Instruction

I will instruct thee and teach thee in the way which thou shalt go:
I will guide thee with mine eye.
—Psalm 32:8, KJV

God has fulfilled this promise in my life experience! We sometimes get to a point in our lives when we do not know how to handle disturbing situations. We try to figure out solutions but in vain. At such times, we need to remember a faithful Father of love, God—our best Friend, who is able to instruct us and teach us the best way to get through difficult situations.

Ebenezer, my youngest son, was always falling sick, being in and out of the hospital with diagnoses ranging from infections and malaria to colds. I became troubled as I had to leave him many times to meet the travel demands of my job. In desperation, I prayed, "Instruct me on the solution to my son's poor health, or I will quit my job." As I continued in claiming this promise, my son fell sick again. I took him to the community health-care center instead of the pediatric clinic. It was a public hospital with less care and attention for patients. Health workers seemed busy with different cases. There was no air-conditioning, no toys and playground for the children, no snacks to pacify a crying toddler, and no television on which to watch cartoons. The center was totally different from the pediatric clinic my son was used to.

"Mummy, let us go back home. This is horrible. I don't like this clinic. I am fine now!" my son yelled. I calmed him down, and we finally had a medical consultation with the doctor. On our way back home, my son whispered, "Mummy, what can I do so that I will never come here again?"

"Son, you simply need to be well and not fall sick again," I replied. Since that day, I noticed a totally different situation with my son. He prays every day for good health, obeys simple health rules like washing his hands before eating, washing his fruit before eating, drinking enough water, and taking his afternoon naps. His sicknesses are gone. My seven-year-old Ebenezer enjoys good health, and we are all happy now. Going to a public, less-than-optimum health center instead of the child-friendly pediatric clinic worked wonders on my son psychologically and helped him make conscious efforts to overcome sickness.

How wonderful that God will teach us simple ways to deal with our challenges! Try Him!

Omobonike Adeola Sessou

The Torn Shopping List

My God shall supply all your need according to His riches.
—Philippians 4:19, NKJV

The pot of beans simmered in the slow cooker as the children and I knelt in the dining room. "Father, You know our situation. You know how little food we have left. I know You will provide . . ."

My prayer was interrupted by a knock at the front door. Rising from my knees, I was pleasantly surprised to find a very dear friend and fellow church member on my porch, holding a bulging brown paper bag. "Could the boys help me carry these bags in?" The boys scampered out to the car and hauled in several more bags. Shaking her head, Nelda watched me unload each item. "It was the strangest experience. I was in the store and felt this urge to pick out all these things. I wasn't even sure why. I'm elderly and live alone. When I got into my car, I said, 'Well, Lord, what am I supposed to do with all these groceries?' Then, sure enough, God said, 'Take it to the Todds'. They need some help right about now.' So here I am."

Shortly after Nelda left, a second visitor knocked on the door. Throwing the door open, I greeted another dear friend and fellow church member, "Linda! It's so good to see you. Nelda was just here. Too bad, you missed her." Linda, too, had her arms full of bags. Again we helped unload a vehicle. "When we had our little prayer group here yesterday," she said, "I noticed the way your table was all set as if you were expecting company." She continued a big grin on her face. "I remembered a story I had read in the Uncle Arthur's Bedtime Stories series about the family that was out of food. They set the table as an act of faith that God would provide. [And, yes, we, too, had set the table in faith.] So I went shopping. I have a can of gasoline too. Something told me you could use it." I nodded again. Then I realized something remarkable.

"Did you tell Nelda you were shopping for us?"

Linda shook her head.

"There's not a single duplicate item on our shelves. It's as if God wrote out a shopping list and tore it in half, giving each of you your part." How amazing is our Great Provider! Not only did He take care of our family but the food lasted until my husband's finances were straightened out with the military—and God did it with flair. To this day, I still shake my head in awe over the time God filled our cupboard and refrigerator using a "torn shopping list."

Sharon Clark

Half Hour Late

Through the LORD's mercies we are not consumed,
Because His compassions fail not.
They are new every morning;
Great is Your faithfulness.
—Lamentations 3:22, 23, NKJV

My elder son attends one of our island's institutions, which allows the students to attend the campus most convenient to them. Because he lives on the south side of the island, his primary campus is in the south. In order to complete his associate degree on time, though, he attends the north campus once a week. That means leaving home very early in the morning to take public transportation so he can get to class on time.

However, on one of those mornings, he seemed to be unconcerned about time. Being the typical mom, I became a bit annoyed and began to lecture him on the importance of time management—this, though, did not disturb my son. When he was ready to leave, he called out, "Bye, Mummy" and sauntered out the door. He usually called us when he got on the bus and then upon his arrival in class. As the morning progressed, though, we got breaking news that there had been a major accident on the very highway my son traveled. A delivery van heading south had crossed the median and collided with a bus traveling north. I began to worry as I had not yet heard from my son. Numerous attempts to contact him proved futile. How I prayed for his safety as the time and place of the accident coincided with the bus route he usually took!

Eventually, my cell rang. It was not a number I knew. I began to tremble, fearing the worst. Thankfully, it was my son. His cell phone had been giving him trouble that morning, so he had been unable to contact me by phone. Because he had not been in a hurry that morning, he missed his usual bus and took a bus half an hour later. His usual bus had been involved in the accident resulting in the death of individuals seated identically to where he sat on the later bus.

At times, we tell ourselves that God is taking far too long to work out our circumstances. We feel like He has taken a back seat and forgotten all about us. Yet we must always remember that God's timing is not our timing. As the Bible writer put it, "He has made everything beautiful in its time" (Ecclesiastes 3:11, NKJV)—in *His* time. He is our on-time God.

Jill Springer-Cato

Beauty Through the Ashes—Part 1

"When you walk through the fire,
you will not be burned. . . .
For I am the LORD your God,
the Holy One of Israel, your Savior."
—Isaiah 43:2, 3, NIV

One month ago today, as I began my morning worship time, I noticed that the sunrise was extraordinarily beautiful. I went outside to take a picture. Then I saw that what sounded like rain showers on our two opened deck umbrellas was actually falling *ashes!* I called Ben, my husband, to look outside. "Those clouds are black with smoke, soot, and haze!" he quickly informed me. Back inside, I phoned my cousin, Carrie.

"Feather River Hospital is being evacuated right now!" she informed me. "We are hooking up our RV and loading our trucks. We're evacuating as soon as we can." Ben came in to tell me he had located on Google a fire burning thirty-five miles away from where we lived.

"Mary, you need to get all the clothes into the RV and anything else you want to take." Having just returned from a discipleship seminar in New York, I still had a partially unpacked suitcase into which I threw two pairs of jeans, a couple of tops, a sweater set, a skirt, and a camisole. *That will be enough to last a week or so,* I told myself. *Then we'll be back home again.*

We'd previously had to evacuate four times since moving to Paradise, California. This would be the fifth—but we had always returned. So I didn't worry about what-if. I simply grabbed my computer, my Bible, Dad's Bible, my iPad, phone, and CPAP machine with all the battery connections. At the last minute, I said to Ben, "Better get your passport in case we need identification documents." As Ben backed our RV down Crestmoor Drive, I was strangely convicted to take a picture of the RV and the house. (Later, we learned that the first thing insurance investigators request is a recent picture of one's property.) I followed Ben in the truck with our dachshund, Buster. Soon I could barely see the backlights of our RV. As telephone poles burst into flame and crumbled just feet away from my vehicle, the heat inside the truck became intense—even with air-conditioning. Buster trembled.

In a sinful world, disaster can burst upon us without a moment's notice. Are we walking so closely with Jesus each day that our faith will look beyond our circumstances? I pray we are.

Mary H. Maxson

Beauty Through the Ashes—Part 2

"I will lead the blind by ways they have not known,
along unfamiliar paths I will guide them;
I will turn the darkness into light before them
and make the rough places smooth.
These are the things I will do;
I will not forsake them."
—Isaiah 42:16, NIV

I fled the Paradise Fire (November 2018), following in our truck as Ben, my husband, drove the RV ahead of me. The Skyway was congested. We found ourselves suddenly driving through an inferno of towering fire columns, wreaking disaster in every direction. Roadside transformers burst into flame and then exploded. Trees, homes, underbrush—all appeared to be engulfed in the crackling fingers of fire. At one point, I touched the side window with the back of my hand and quickly jerked it away. I checked to see if my hand was burned because it was so hot. When we left home, I had texted our children to let them know we were evacuating. Now I tried to stay in touch by phone as I could. Each of them prayed with me for God's protection.

Yet I still had to concentrate. I could see abandoned cars whose tires had burst into flame. People were evacuating their burning vehicles with no place to go. One man was in such a frenzied state that he stood, just kicking one of his burning tires. A few yards down the road was another vehicle in the median engulfed in flames and in the very process of exploding.

As we began emerging from the worst fire zone, I glanced back at Paradise and saw only a boiling, monstrous black cloud of smoke looming over the city that was now being consumed by fire. As I looked in my rearview mirror, I suddenly had a strong conviction that our home would also be destroyed. We later learned that the same fire through which we were driving was the same fire that reduced our home to ashes just one hour later. Yet God had not abandoned us.

Maybe a personal disaster in your life has led you down "unfamiliar paths" too. Yet God has promised that He will be by your side, guiding you. He has promised to turn the thick clouds of "darkness into light"—just when you need it most. He will make the "rough places smooth" and show you comfort, even beauty, just when you need it most. He will never, ever forsake you!

Mary H. Maxson

Beauty Through
the Ashes—Part 3

*"Be strong and courageous. Do not be afraid or terrified ... for the
LORD your God goes with you; he will never leave you nor forsake you."*
—Deuteronomy 31:6, NIV

After Ben and I, in our ash-covered vehicles, found our way through the worst of the fires, we continued driving toward Modesto, where our son, Benjie, and his family live. It's usually a three-hour trip, but because of the Paradise Fire, it took another five hours.

Where is God in the midst of such devastating loss of home, property, and human life? Well, each day here in Modesto, God showed us the beauty of His presence and compassion through people. Each day people who heard our story gave us a discount, a free meal, a free manicure, among other kindnesses. They wanted to assist in some way and help out a fire victim.

In a discount clothing store one day, an associate asked if she could help me find anything. I shared my story; she hugged me and began to cry. When I inquired about possible discounts, the manager informed me their store didn't offer them. Evidently, the associate overheard, for a few minutes later, she sought me out and handed me a wad of bills—sixty dollars.

One Sabbath, Ben spoke at a church in Turlock, California. A gentleman named Gary visited with me about our loss. When we left the church, he slipped me (as we shook hands) a hundred-dollar bill. Shocked, I thanked him for his generosity. He said he hadn't planned on coming to church that day but had decided, at the last minute, that he would. "Now I know why God brought me to church," he affirmed. "To help out you and your husband."

I pray that God will continue to remind me that He is alive and well and overseeing my losses, my emotions, and my life. I continue to learn that God is faithful—and I hang on to His promises. The first morning after sleeping in the RV outside our son's home in Modesto, God reminded me of His promise in Isaiah 43:2, 3. There may be fires all around me, but they will not consume me. The next day, God gave me another promise. Not only will He be my Guide on "unfamiliar paths" (Isaiah 42:16, NIV) but He has also covenanted never to forsake me in the midst of loss and trial (see today's text). Finally, He assures me—and you—that in Him, we can be strong and courageous because He is a compassionate and real presence at our side. And, quite often, through people, the beauty of His love for us will show up through the ashes in our lives.

Mary H. Maxson

Creation Testifies

You were shown these things so that you might know
that the LORD is God; besides him there is no other.
—Deuteronomy 4:35, NIV

There is a tree in my front yard that, over the years, has shown evidence of dying. Its sprouting leaves appear ready to die at the onset. Each ensuing spring, I would hear my husband, with exasperation in his voice, declare, "I am going to cut down that tree! We can replace it with a new one." This was his vow—until the spring of 2019.

That was the spring that my dear ninety-two-year-old mother died. With a heavy heart, I saw Mother engaged in her personal death struggle. I saw her one vespers evening joyously welcoming the Sabbath day, heard her singing her love to God with gusto. I witnessed her acceptance in Him, her tribute to Him. I was holding on to Mom, who had made peace with God. She was now ready to rest from the burdens of this world and await Christ's second coming when death would no longer be victorious.

As the spring of 2019 approached, the dying tree in my front yard appeared to be doing something different. That spring it produced beautiful white blossoms with hints of pink shades that later heralded brilliant green leaves full of health and life. The tree was giving evidence of the newness of life. My heart soared when I observed the change in this tree, for I almost heard God's loving words remind me that Mom was now asleep in Him, peacefully awaiting His promised return. I was reminded that someday soon, she and all those who have died in Christ will be raised in newness of life—for all eternity.

I recalled God's thrilling promise through John of what we will witness in heaven: "Then the angel showed me the river of the water of life, as clear as crystal, flowing from the throne of God and of the Lamb. . . . On each side of the river stood the tree of life, bearing twelve crops of fruit, yielding its fruit every month. And the leaves of the tree are for the healing of the nations" (Revelation 22:1, 2, NIV). Until that day, I join with David in declaring, "But as for me, it is good to be near God. I have made the Sovereign LORD my refuge; I will tell of all your deeds" (Psalm 73:28, NIV).

Cynthia Best-Goring

In the Moment

"If you remain in me and I in you, you will bear much fruit;
apart from me you can do nothing."
—John 15:5, NIV

My top sin is self-sufficiency. I'm goal-oriented and purpose-driven, so I'm going and doing for God a lot, but am I doing it *with* God? Many times, as a hospital chaplain, I've had a meaningful interaction with a patient, provided emotional and spiritual support, and had prayer with them, only to realize afterward that I hadn't been in two-way communication with God throughout the visit. The patient was blessed and encouraged, but how much more healing had God wanted to accomplish if I had been actively in tune with Him at the moment?

Growing up, I often had to rely on myself, but in growing up to be more like Jesus, this trait is a huge liability. Many verses come to mind. "I can of mine own self do nothing" (John 5:30, KJV). "The words I say to you I do not speak on my own authority. Rather, it is the Father, living in me, who is doing his work" (John 14:10, NIV).

Of all people, you would think that Jesus could have relied on Himself. He was God in the flesh! Yet His life shows complete, total, moment-by-moment dependence on God. He was so aware of the frailty of His humanity, the potency of Satan's cunning, and the dynamite power of God. Over the years, I have learned this and forgotten it just as quickly; relearned and forgotten it again and again.

Recently on a break during some meetings, I started up a conversation with a woman I'd not met before. Thankfully I was also dialoguing with God in my heart. As I listened closely to her and God, a thought formed in my mind: *Shift back to the broken relationship she lightly mentioned earlier.* God helped me to weave it back into the conversation seamlessly, and this person I'd just met opened up about the pain of that experience. She needed to share it and receive further healing from God. It would not have happened if I hadn't been in two-way communication with God, depending not just on the keen listening skills and compassion God has developed in me but also on His guidance at the moment.

Let's not rely on our God-endowed gifts and talents, but instead tune in each moment to God's voice, so He can lavishly do His deeper work of healing in the world.

Heide Ford

Our Eyes Grow Dim

Because of this our hearts are faint,
because of these things our eyes grow dim.
—Lamentations 5:17, NIV

In the past few years, I realized that my eyesight was slowly worsening. Not only was it more difficult to read the small print but also everything started to appear less colorful and bright. I often felt I was missing key parts of what I was viewing. Glasses enlarged the print so I could see up close or read, but my distance vision was terrible. *This is just another part of getting old*, I decided sorrowfully. *Why didn't someone tell me before now?*

As a senior citizen, I'd started hearing more and more talk about cataracts and surgery to improve one's eyesight. I even knew a few people who had had the surgery, including my husband. The testimonies that he and others shared of wonderfully improved eyesight sometimes bordered on the ridiculous. How could such a surgery restore eyesight to the point that people were eager to stop strangers to exclaim how much better their sight was? As my sight worsened, driving through glaring lights became very difficult and almost deadly at times. I decided to see my ophthalmologist, only to discover that my eyes needed correction-cataract surgery. Weeks later, my left eye was done, then my right. Wow! My world became clear, bright, and colorful again, practically in an instant. How could I have gone so long, unaware of how terrible my vision really was? I began sharing my story with people I knew—and didn't know!

Isn't dim vision what we get when we concentrate on the world's pleasures, forsaking a crucial focus on Jesus? Inevitably our eyes grow dim to spiritual things as bold enticements dance before them. Our connection to Christ fades, and we adjust to a new normal. The spectacular view of the life God promised becomes less clear, and we think, *Oh, that's life; it happens.* But when the Holy Spirit prompts us to recognize how bad our vision has gotten, we willingly undergo our Master Physician's corrective surgery. Again we will see all He has done when we're faithful. We will eagerly tell everyone we encounter—even strangers—why our sight on heavenly things is great and encourage them to repair their dim eyes, so they will see how good God is too. *Help us, Lord, to seek You in all things so we can see the brighter, bolder, better world You are preparing for us rather than the dim world we live in and stumble through.*

Iris L. Kitching

A Triad of Miracles

Is any thing too hard for the LORD?
—Genesis 18:14, KJV

Waiting in the reception area of a medical office is not my favorite place to spend time. One day I was waiting because my primary care physician was concerned about two areas on my face and thought I should see a dermatologist.

My name was called, and I went into the examination room. The physician assistant who saw me took samples of what looked suspicious, bandaged me, sent me home with instructions for wound care, and told me I needed to wait for the diagnosis.

The results confirmed I had skin cancer. It was suggested that I go to the main office in Bend, Oregon, about 135 miles from my home, for the surgery. The earliest available appointment was more than a month away. On Sunday, I was talking with my longtime friend, Pam. She mentioned she had to take her husband to Bend for a medical appointment on Tuesday.

"You're going to Bend next Tuesday?" I almost shouted. "Pam, if the Lord—who does amazing things—decides to part the sea of filled schedules to create a path that leads to an appointment, may I go to Bend with you?"

"Of course," she answered with a grin. The next morning I called the Bend office. I explained the situation and told the receptionist that I believed in miracles and that I needed one for the next day. After checking, she told me she did find one patient opening, and she gave it to me. I thanked the Lord profusely for His miracle.

But that created another problem. I had a dental appointment on Thursday of the same week. I knew that if I could change the appointment, then I wouldn't have to wait until the surgery healed for the next appointment. I prayed and phoned the dental office, explaining the situation. The receptionist said she'd let me know if they had a cancellation for that day. Two hours later, I had a second miracle. The dental office called: they had just had a cancellation.

A third miracle came after the surgery when I learned that the tests showed that all cancer had been successfully removed.

God does things like this quite often. Some may call my experience a coincidence, but Christians know they're just His miracles in disguise.

Marcia Mollenkopf

God's Unexpected Revelation

Behold, I am the LORD, the God of all flesh:
is there any thing too hard for me?
—Jeremiah 32:27, KJV

Have you ever had a strong impression to do an act of kindness for someone? This is what happened to me a few weeks ago:

My twenty-eight-year-old Toyota Camry had been parked in the garage for a few days. I kept smelling gasoline intermittently but could not ascertain the source. My husband and I checked both of our cars but found no leaks, even though I had a suspicion that the strong odor was coming from my car.

Two days later I saw a friend at church. For some time, I had been concerned about him. He had been battling a persistent cough. This was of concern to me since he rarely ever came down with a cold. If and when he did, it was usually gone within a few days. Now here he was—still coughing and appearing pale and tired.

On the following Monday morning, I felt a strong urge to do something for this brother. I thought about a home remedy treatment in my medicine cabinet, which had worked for me in the past. It was as if someone suddenly spoke and instructed me to take some of my remedy to him.

Without delay, I called and told the brother that I was on my way with some cough remedy for him. I drove my car to his house, and he met me outside in the parking area.

"I am smelling gasoline!" he exclaimed as he came up to my car. "Why don't you turn off the engine," he suggested. "Then I'll be able to check for leaks."

Even though he did not locate a source of leakage, he still seemed convinced that gasoline was escaping from somewhere and that my car needed to be examined by a mechanic. My friend stressed the hazards of driving a vehicle from which gas is escaping. "You can certainly drive one of my cars," he offered. "At the very least, drive your car home and park it until it can be checked." My habit has always been to pray and ask the Lord to be my silent Partner in operating the vehicle. So I prayed and asked Him to get me home safely—and He did. My heavenly Father is awesome. He speaks, listens, hears, and answers prayers.

What situation in your life do you need to take to Him in prayer today?

Kollis Salmon-Fairweather

Room Enough
to Receive Blessings

I will . . . open [to] you the windows of heaven, and pour you out a
blessing, that there shall not be room enough to receive it.
—Malachi 3:10, KJV

I was not prepared for this medical situation, even though I knew I had an ailment that could worsen. My concentration was on completing postgraduate studies; all my finances and energy were directed toward this project. How was I going to manage to meet these medical expenses (which would include two surgeries), pay my regular bills, and provide for my basic needs? I needed a change in my financial situation. Attempts at change, however, proved futile to improving things. There was only one way left to try, and that was to consolidate my loans. Yet which financial institution would want to buy my exorbitant loans to relieve me of financial pressure? I prayed for God's intervention.

One day, a close friend suggested I try a particular financial institution. I was reluctant at first but then decided to act on her suggestion. I qualified during the introductory process, but the approval process was still to come. Weeks passed while my loan was being reviewed—and with a request for more documents. I became frustrated but was encouraged by my loan officer not to worry and just provide all the required documentation. Another document was requested, which would probably raise questions about my unstable financial situation. I grew frightened and doubted that the loan would be approved.

I promised to inform my loan officer a few days later of my decision to withdraw the loan application. But God's grace abounds, and the mighty hand of my loving Savior began to reveal itself. The telephone rang. It was my loan officer. "Ms. Cain," he said, "I have great news for you: your loan has been approved on condition that you provide us with the last required document."

Experiencing God's mercy and grace during this financial crisis was overwhelming. I could barely comprehend and contain this blessing. I am reminded of the song that tells us any "river" we have to cross or any "mountain" we need to tunnel through is not too big of a challenge for God. In fact, doing the impossible for His children is something He delights to do. Trust our merciful Father, my sisters. He will do the impossible for you!

Elizabeth Ida Cain

Secret of the Sun

Let your light so shine before men, that they may see your good
works, and glorify your Father which is in heaven.
—Matthew 5:16, KJV

When I opened my eyes this morning, the light coming through the shades was unusually bright. I went to the window and saw beautiful sunlight in a cloudless azure sky. Reveling in the light and warmth flowing through the glass, I lowered my gaze and noticed frost on every blade of grass, every branch of the shrubs—a field of glittering diamonds. Noting the snow on the nearby Blue Mountains at a lower elevation than yesterday, I shivered. *Br-r-r-r.* Winter is coming!

After ten minutes of first-thing-in-the-morning prep for the day, I wandered back to the window. Shocked, I went to look at the thermometer. The air temperature was still below freezing. Back at the window, I marveled that grass and shrubs showed moisture, but no frost.

Gazing on the scene, I noted one area where frost still clung—that one frosty area was in the shadow of a tree. Despite the freezing air temperature, the warmth of the sun had melted the frost everywhere else.

A memory popped into my mind. Two days before, I'd attended a memorial service. During the sharing time, one woman said, "When Janell walked in, she lit up the whole room like a ray of sunshine." Throughout the group of mourners, heads nodded in agreement—including mine. This friend had captured Janell's essence. Other people who spoke echoed the same.

As I looked at the frosted and frost-free areas in my yard, I pondered. Janell had faced disappointments, grief, and very difficult and discouraging situations. But with God's help, she had risen above her own pain. Perhaps because Janell knew pain, she understood how devastating it can feel. She accepted God's love and healing and shone it into the hearts of others. She cared.

Soaking in the sunshine at the window, I prayed, "God, shine Your Son into my heart. Help me warm the hearts I meet today—the grocery store clerk, post office worker, my husband, and other family members. Help me be a ray of sunlight that melts stress, negativity, hard feelings. Care through me!"

Helen Heavirland

The Big Picture

I waited patiently for the LORD. . . .
He lifted me out of the pit of destruction. . . .
He stood me on a rock
and made my feet steady.
—Psalm 40:1, 2, NCV

In 2019, I had my sixth knee surgery and first back surgery as a result of problems caused during physical therapy after my knee surgery. I was home for five months on medical leave.

If you know anything about me, you know that being inactive is not one of my strengths. I love the work God has called me to do. I am passionate about women's ministries. I love to encourage my sisters through God's Word, empower them through training, listen to their challenges, and much more. But now, for five months, I was unable to travel, unable to go to work, and even though I tried to do some work on my laptop, pain medication had my mind too fuzzy to concentrate and focus. So what was I to do?

I had been home for a few months each time I had had other knee replacements. But five months was more than I could bear. After month three, I began to get frustrated and felt my life had no purpose. I could not stand, walk, or sit for more than a few minutes at a time. That's when God and I began to have long conversations—I did a lot of talking. "Why, Lord, would you allow this back injury and surgery when my knee recovery was going so well?" God knew my heart. He knew I only wanted to serve Him and my sisters around the world. "So why, Lord?"

One day, as I lay in bed, I could see in my mind a long straight line that was my life. It began at my birth, but I could not see where it ended. Along that line were marked out the major trials in my life. Then I saw my current trial. The time for these trials, though seeming long at the time, were but short periods in my life's timeline. Suddenly I realized that seeing my trials one at a time while going through them made them seem enormous and lengthy.

Sometimes we look too long at our trials. We need to step back and focus on the big picture and see what God has done in our lives because of each trial. Are we the same after a trial as we were before it? Each trial can strengthen us and draw us closer to God if we allow it to.

I pray we allow God to work His perfect will in our lives each day.

Heather-Dawn Small

What's the Point?

The Spirit itself beareth witness with our spirit,
that we are the children of God.
—Romans 8:16, KJV

I've attended many presentations or sermons where the presenter was all over the place. I've sighed and wondered, *What's the point?* Or, *Will he ever get to the point?* Don't misunderstand me, I like the funny stories, the intellectual quotes, the backflips on stage, and the eloquent vocabulary, but really: What's the point? My attention span is not what it used to be.

Have you found yourself faithfully attending church, yet deep inside, you are wondering, *What's the point?* Your spiritual condition is what led you to ask. Maybe you do not see in your life what you had hoped church membership, obedience, and attendance would produce—peace, joy, power, and victory over sin. But when you look into the mirror of your heart, there is only emptiness, a weakening desire to go through the expected motions, and mounting resentment and rebellion. Whether we admit it or not, a lot of us are in this condition, for multiple reasons. So, what's the point? *We've missed the Point.*

When my children were babies, people wanted to hold them. Things went fine for a while, but then the baby began looking around, getting fidgety and making sounds that soon led to unhappy cries. I sensed what was happening: my baby wanted me. When I reached out to take my baby, the kind people told me, "I've got this. I know how to handle babies." Well-meaning ignorance or stubborn pride made them unwilling to return my baby. Finally, when my mother-bear instinct hit my Enough button, I took my baby. That adorable infant belted out a cry of joy and gave me a smile worth five million words.

The Point. God is our parent, we are His children, and we need Him. It's nice that churches, and even people, want to cuddle us, entertain us, control us, and try to meet our every need, but they must never forget that they are to work *with* our Parent, not *as* our parent. All the fidgeting cries of discontent and complaining and tears of despair are most likely a sign that we want and need our Parent, desperately. In reality, our deepest need can be satisfied only through Jesus Christ, our Lord. If we want to see a 360-degree change in our spiritual walk, we must get back and stick to the Point (see Philippians 4:19; 1 Corinthians 1:30).

Sharon Pergerson

Jesus, Our Advocate

My little children, these things write I unto you,
that ye sin not. And if any man sin, we have an advocate
with the Father, Jesus Christ the righteous.
—1 John 2:1, KJV

One day, I was driving back from the market with my daughter when I saw the Federal Road Safety Corps (FRSC) on the highway stopping vehicles to check on the validity of vehicle and driver's licenses. In Nigeria, the FRSC is a body set up by our government to regulate road use and reduce accidents on our roads while overseeing that drivers are operating their vehicles with a valid driver's license. Silently, I began to pray. *Dear God, please don't let the FRSC stop me because we both know I don't have a driver's license.*

However, I found myself in a line of vehicles waiting to go through the checkpoint. When it was my turn, one of the officials told me to pull off of the road.

At that point, I knew I was in trouble. Another officer approached. "May I please see your vehicle license?" I gave the paperwork to him. After looking through it all, he asked, "Now, may I please see your driver's license?"

"I think I forgot it at home," I responded, knowing it was a lie. I did not even have a driver's license. The reality of what I had just done struck my conscience. The officer read the last name on his paperwork and asked who that person was. "He is my husband and a pastor."

He asked, "Which state is he from?"

I told him.

Then he said, "Your husband was my pastor and youth director. Ma, you can go."

I felt deeply ashamed of myself because I had lied in front of my daughter. "I lied so quickly," I exclaimed as she looked at me with surprise.

In the middle of the night, I woke up and could not sleep. The Holy Spirit was convicting me of the sin I had so quickly committed (John 16:8). I felt deep remorse for having told a lie. Throughout the night, I prayed, asking God to forgive me—but also taking comfort in that truth that Jesus is our Advocate before the Father if we sin. He also said that if we confess our sin, He is faithful to forgive our sin (see 1 John 1:9; 2:1). No matter how grievous the sins we commit, we should go to our Advocate, Jesus Christ, and confess them to Him. He will faithfully forgive us and give us the power to repent and forsake our sins!

Kehinde Adenike Abolarin

In the Womb of Singleness

Before I formed thee in the belly I knew thee;
and before thou camest forth out of the womb I sanctified thee,
and I ordained thee a prophet unto the nations.
—Jeremiah 1:5, KJV

God formed you and knew you first—even before you were in the womb. To be in a relationship with someone, we need to spend time with them. To be in a relationship with God—or renew your relationship with Him—sometimes God needs to isolate you again and get you in a position to know Him. For a relationship to be birthed, God wants first to spend alone time with you. God's not going to birth you into something without making sure that He knows you're ready to be born into it. Do not rush or make hasty decisions prematurely—let God do His work in you. Learn to enjoy this growth process in the womb. Be like a child with Him. Learn from Him and seek His ways.

It takes nine months for a baby to develop in the womb before it can be born. Eventually, the time comes for that baby to be born. Likewise, the time will come for you to be fully the person God is crafting you to be.

If God is saying to you, "Be single in this season in your life," then stay in the "womb" and stop kicking and fighting what God is doing in your life. Stop wrestling, be patient and silent, and ask God for guidance. Your time to be birthed into a relationship will happen if it's in God's will. While you were in your mother's womb, you were never alone. During those prenatal months, when you didn't know what was going on, the person who was carrying you did.

In this seasonal womb of singleness or isolation, God is giving you what you need. He is able to understand and see things you don't see. He is still molding and creating you; He wants to feed you His Word and His love. He also wants to remove the unclean parts of your character. In His time, He wants you to experience a shared union and time of affection and care with the person He has for you—just like a baby spends time with its mother and father getting affection and feeling loved. While you're in this seasonal womb, allow God to be first in your life. Allow Him to give you the affection and love He has for your needs. In due time, you will be ready to be "birthed" into the union of His will.

Maranatha Byrd

Groping in Darkness

The people who walk in [spiritual] darkness
Will see a great Light;
Those who live in the dark land,
The Light will shine on them.
—Isaiah 9:2, AMP

"I am the Light of the world. He who follows Me
will not walk in the darkness, but will have the Light of life."
—John 8:12, AMP

Have you ever tried to find something in the dark? Have you ever tried walking into a dark room where someone is sleeping, and you did not want to disturb them?

Well, if you are like me, you have fumbled around in the dark, looking for shoes, keys, or books. In the darkness, your frustration grew because you could not find what you were looking for. You felt around aimlessly, thinking that whatever you were searching for should be "right here" or "right over there"— but to no avail. You were being so careful not to awaken the person sleeping in that room, yet perhaps you finally decided, *I need some light!* Once the light illuminated the space, you instantly found what it was you were searching for— and guess what? It was right there all along. I know I am not the only one who has had this experience.

That's what it is like when we try to grope around in the darkness of this life without Christ. We fumble around for this or that but never find what we need until we realize that even a candle would shed light in the midst of this darkness. We need to invite Christ into our dark place. The Bible tells us that He has brought us out of darkness into His marvelous light (see 1 Peter 2:9). Once we have the light of Christ in us, others will find their way too. We must allow His light, through us, to illuminate the dark places in the lives of those we meet, those who are hopeless, helpless, depressed, and addicted to the wrong things or people.

Our responsibility is not to see how we can keep from waking that sleeping person. Rather, our light should shine so brightly that they can no longer sleep! May they walk into God's marvelous light because you decided not to hide yours.

Our challenge is to light the world wherever we are.

Sabrina Crichlow

Angels Are About

The eyes of the LORD are in every place,
Keeping watch on the evil and the good.
—Proverbs 15:3, NKJV

My husband, Adjei, and I landed in Lisbon, Portugal. After settling down to wait for our connecting flight to Accra, Ghana, I realized that my cell phone was dead. I had wanted to let family members know where we were, so we needed to recharge the cell. Adjei tried to help, but he soon discovered that our charger was not compatible with the type of electrical sockets available in the airport. While we had square pins, the airport had round ones.

As we were discussing this problem, a young man appeared from nowhere and handed us an adapter with round pins and square holes. Just what we needed. Wow!

He said, "I had the same problem another time when I got here, so I carry different adapters with me all the time now." We thanked him for his kindness in allowing us to charge our cell phones with his adapters.

But that was not the end of the story.

From his bag, he gave us two more connecting pieces that were compatible with different sockets. We were thinking of using his chargers and giving them back to him when it was time for him to get on his flight.

"You can keep whatever I have given you," he said, surprising us. "I have enough for myself." Then he was gone as quickly as he had appeared. We never set our eyes on him again, even though we waited ten hours for our connecting flight.

Readers, where did that young man come from? How did he know that we needed help with our cell phones? Where did he go after helping us? The Lisbon airport is very big, with numerous travelers from around the world. But this man was there at the right time to give us exactly what we needed—and even more. *Oh, Abba! How does God do it?*

"The eyes of the LORD are in every place" (Proverbs 15:3, NKJV). Truly, we have an omnipresent and omnipotent Father. He is able to surprise us with blessings when they are most needed. He knows the end from the beginning. Just trust Him. Period. Remember how He promised to be with us always (see Matthew 28:20)? Well, just take His word as it is. I do.

Mabel Kwei

Whiter Than Snow

*Purge me with hyssop, and I shall be clean: wash me,
and I shall be whiter than snow.*
—Psalm 51:7, KJV

On the Wednesday before Thanksgiving (which I will call Thanksgiving Eve), while I was having my morning worship, I heard my husband get up to put a load of laundry into the washing machine. Then he returned to bed. I continued my worship until I heard him calling me. He sounded like one of our sons when they were in trouble! "We have a big problem!" *What could it be? No fire. No burglary. What in the world could it be?* I followed him into the laundry area, and there he began sloshing around in ankle-deep water. The washing machine had gotten stuck in the filling mode. After the machine filled, it did not go into the wash cycle, so the water had been running out of the machine for about an hour. What a mess!

Looking at that water, I could think of only one thing to say: "If God allowed this problem, He has it solved already." As I helped "gather up" the water, I thought, *We are going to have to replace the flooring in the laundry area and the kitchen—not to mention the carpet in the other rooms.* This probable need became more evident later as the carpet began to dry, and a certain stench filled the air.

Of course, on Thanksgiving Day, our family came as planned. Somehow, we got through the day. Yet from that Thursday through the following Sunday, we had to deal with wet carpet and then the smell. By Monday, the floor had dried significantly, and the odor was less noticeable. By Tuesday morning, the floors were completely dry, and the stench was completely gone. I could hardly believe it! Then I saw the spiritual lesson in all of this.

Like the water flowing out of the washing machine for an hour, sin—for years—has flooded our lives, and we are saturated with it to the uttermost. When we accept Christ as our personal Savior, however, God says, "That's enough." With "hyssop"—the blood of Jesus—He begins to cleanse us. As we begin our walk with Him, the stench of sin may still be evident until the day when we realize that it is finally gone. Thank You, Jesus!

"If we confess our sins, he is faithful and just to forgive us our sins, and to cleanse us from all unrighteousness" (1 John 1:9, KJV).

Mattie E. Johnson

What Makes Me Happy Working for the Lord?

Now to Him who is able to do exceedingly abundantly above all that we ask or think, according to the power that works in us, to Him be glory in the church by Christ Jesus to all generations, forever and ever. Amen.
—Ephesians 3:20, 21, NKJV

The question was asked: "What makes me happy working for the Lord?" After pondering the words for a few minutes, I realized it comes from being thankful and blessed. I must admit that there are things I feel more comfortable doing than others. However, comfort is not what God has in mind for me. He's always pushing me in directions I wouldn't have chosen for myself. He's always challenging me, and I'm never sure what's next on His agenda.

It is my choice to be happy in whatever situation He places me. Since I'm His ambassador, I try to represent Him well. I shouldn't let circumstances control my feelings or actions. There's a world out there that needs to know what a loving, caring, and compassionate Savior He is. I can't rightly represent Him by going around with a sad, sulky face, because no one will believe that He's a wonderful God. When I look back at the many blessings I've received, my soul is flooded with happiness and joy, and I want to share that with others. Someone once said that happiness doesn't come when problems disappear but rather when we see them as opportunities, especially to exercise our patience as we learn. I agree.

There are three questions I've asked myself through the course of my life: *Who am I? Why am I here? What is my purpose?* The answer? I am a child of God whom He thought about with such love that He made me unique, to fulfill His purpose. My purpose is to live a meaningful life and share Christ with others.

The more I give of myself in whatever way God wants me to, I am blessed. Whether it's a smile, a card, a visit, a phone call, a text message, food, friendship, or a prayer—as long as I give willingly from a cheerful heart, I'm blessed. As someone once said, we have only one life. And we should do our utmost in the time we have to make a positive difference in the lives of others.

My prayer is that God will give me the strength to live this life to the best of my ability, to honor Him, and to be a blessing to others.

Maple Smith

Coincidence?

*"It shall come to pass
That before they call, I will answer;
And while they are still speaking, I will hear."*
—Isaiah 65:24, NKJV

Have you ever had one of those experiences that convince you that "someone" had laid everything in place for you? My son and his family live on the island of Oahu, Hawaii. In late May, I received a call to come over and spend time with two of my three Hawaiian grandchildren as the other one was going with her mom to a volleyball tournament in Florida. My son had travel obligations to Japan. I flew to Oahu and brought my two grandchildren home with me. On arrival home, I carefully put their passports away. At the end of June, the rest of the family visited in British Columbia. We touched base at my home a couple of days before they were to leave for Hawaii. Then they went to my daughter's home (an eighty-minute drive) with plans to fly home from there to Oahu early Tuesday morning.

On Monday, due to an insect bite, I had low energy, minimal appetite, and had to depend on others at times for transportation. Unable to sleep until approximately 2:00 A.M., I was surprised to awaken at 5:00 A.M. feeling quite well. At 6:00 A.M., after breakfast, I was preparing food for my waiting dogs when the phone rang. It was my daughter calling. "Mom, do you have the kids' passports?" After spending a few frantic moments on the phone, I hurriedly fed the dogs, dressed, convinced my daughter I was OK to drive, grabbed the passports, and said I'd meet someone halfway. As I drove through town, I encountered only one red light—almost unheard of here in our city! Just before 7:00 A.M., I pulled into our gas station rendezvous point. After a quick hug and my handing over the passports, my son-in-law was on his way. The family's flight was due to depart just after 8:00 A.M.

As I drove back home along the lake through the cities of Westbank and Kelowna, I could think only about what an amazing God we have. I kept thanking Him for His care. Who else could have laid everything in place so the grandchildren could receive their passports just in time to board their family's flight home?

Beverly D. Hazzard

At the Red Sea

And Moses said unto the people, Fear ye not,
stand still, and see the salvation of the LORD, which he
will shew to you to day: for the Egyptians whom ye have seen
to day, ye shall see them again no more for ever.
—Exodus 14:13, KJV

A colleague, John,* read the foreclosure notice and then put it aside. He was about to lose the family home. This dilemma occurred during the Great Recession when so many things were going awry. His wife had been ill for some time and could no longer work. The part-time evening job John had been promised to supplement his full-time position fell through. It had been this family's daily prayer that things would somehow improve. Now mounting bills, failing health, and possible homelessness threatened the couple's future. John and his wife were facing their Red Sea.

Pharaoh had finally relented and allowed the Hebrews to depart Egypt. He had seen his people and their land suffer through ten plagues—water to blood, frogs, lice, flies, livestock disease, boils, hail, locusts, and darkness. Then the last plague: the death of the firstborn sons. Now with the Hebrews gone and on their journey beyond Egypt's borders, Pharaoh rethought his decision and gathered an army to bring back God's people. Moses and this great multitude spotted Pharaoh's horses on the horizon. They had nowhere to turn. Pharaoh was behind them and the waters of the Red Sea were before them. Moses informed the multitude not to fear for the army behind them would be seen no more. Our Father parted the Red Sea!

Perhaps you are facing your own figurative Red Sea—the enemy is at your back and in front of you as a reminder that there is nowhere to go. We have all been there. Life with all its challenges of sickness, unreliable employment, marital disharmony, errant children, insurmountable debt, and broken dreams may haunt our every footstep, causing us to believe that only destruction lies ahead. But friends, we serve a God who is able to part the Red Sea and take us through on dry land.

Have you shared your problems with Him today? He is waiting to perform that miracle. Fear not. Hold on to your faith. Remember, God is able!

Yvonne Curry Smallwood

---

* Not his real name.

Flies and Fungi

Do not let your heart envy sinners,
But be zealous for the fear of the LORD all the day;
For surely there is a hereafter,
And your hope will not be cut off.
—Proverbs 23:17, 18, NKJV

In nature, we learn very important life lessons. Through my balcony gardening pots, God has taught me about His love, patience, and the futility of appearances time and again.

One day while tending one of my plants, I noticed that it always had beautiful flowers and rich green leaves, even when I forgot to water it. This got me thinking about how sometimes we think that maybe other people, based on appearances, have perfect lives and that maybe we have ended up with the short end of the stick. We make the mistake of pitying ourselves and thinking God doesn't have the same considerations for us as He may have for His other children. This, my sister, is a big mistake.

As I felt that life wasn't fair, a thought occurred to me: *Turn over the leaves.* First, I continued looking at flowers but finally turned over some of the plant's leaves. To my surprise, I discovered that the undersides of the leaves were covered with fungus and whitefly. My jaw just dropped in amazement and, honestly, in embarrassment.

Then and there, God wanted me to understand, through nature, that not all we see around us is as perfect as it appears. Every family and every person has their fungus and whitefly—some area in life that is being or has been touched by sin. Of course, these areas God wants to clean and sometimes prune, if necessary, to promote spiritual growth. I ended up chopping that flowering plant to the bare minimum. It grew back pest-free and more beautiful than ever. God wants to do the same with us.

God wants to transform our hearts, help us grow into beautiful fruit-bearing plants that can give testimony about His love and governance in our lives. He wants us to shine and glorify His name in every area of our lives, not just in the areas people can see.

May God continue to give us the lessons we need to learn and help us grow in spiritual health until we are transformed into His image.

Yvita Antonette Villalona Bacchus

God's Plans

*For I know the thoughts that I think toward you, says the LORD,
thoughts of peace and not of evil, to give you a future and a hope. Then
you will call upon Me and go and pray to Me, and I will listen to you.*
—Jeremiah 29:11, 12, NKJV

As it was dangerous for a woman to be alone in the dark, my father accompanied me every morning to the taxi stop since I had to leave home at 5:30 to be on time to the private school where I worked as a secretary. I had to ride two taxis from home to work each day, and some workdays stretched to eleven hours, though my salary was low. I often hoped my effort and dedication would receive verbal or material recognition from my superiors. But I hoped in vain.

Tired of the situation one day (as I sat laboring over a difficult task on the computer), I cried out to God. "Father, I am tired of this situation. Such hard work for so little pay that does not reward my efforts. Please allow me to work for You, even if it's for free. I do not have to be paid because what the Lord has done for me is priceless. I would be happy to work for You for free. In the name of Jesus, amen."

In fewer than three months, I learned that our church headquarters in my region needed two secretaries. Forgetting what I had prayed, I did not consider these openings as an answer to prayer. Yet I asked my brother to take my résumé information to the office needing the secretaries. Maybe I could work for God. After a few days, I was called in for a competency test, followed by an evaluation process. Then I was informed that one of the positions was mine, though my salary would be half of what I'd been receiving at the college. Yet I was still happy. Now my "boss" would be God, and I would have just one taxi ride a day and I would not have to leave home until 7:00 in the morning.

To my surprise, the salary turned out to be twice as much as I had received at the previous job. God told me, "Daughter, I heard your prayer and will pay you double." It was a joyful moment because I did not expect God would give me so much. Just as today's text states, God has the best plans for us. Let us only trust Him. He will deliver everything into our hands, according to His will. Today, reaffirm this promise in your life and ask Him to fulfill it. Truly, the hand of the Lord will always be open to all who seek rest in Him.

Tereza Makanzo

Thinking Right

"Even before they finish praying to me, I will answer their prayers."
—Isaiah 65:24, GNT

In my insurance business, sometimes people tell me interesting stories. Here is one that I thought would be an inspiration.

After I helped her take care of her business needs one day, Rhonda* told me this personal experience. For years, Rhonda had felt financial pressures and let her credit rating slip because she was afraid that if she paid one bill, there wouldn't be enough money for other things. It became a habit to think of herself as "poor" and not able to have things in her life that others have. As Rhonda struggled through life day after day, she found herself murmuring and complaining. Her siblings had all bought houses and told her she should too, but Rhonda thought that would be impossible. She was living with a poverty mindset.

One day, Rhonda was reading in her Bible about the children of Israel and suddenly saw that she was just like them in their complaining. Something had to change! She was tired of living with her negative, poverty-oriented mindset, so she prayed.

God opened her eyes. She suddenly remembered that years before, her father had set up a trust fund for her and one for her son. When Rhonda asked a friend, a real estate agent, if this trust fund could be converted to use as the down payment on a house, she was told, "This is done all the time!"

So the house hunting began. Finally, Rhonda's family found a lovely townhouse they could afford. To their delight, there was money left over for insurance and even for some new furniture. After going to settlement and getting moved to her new home, Rhonda recalled the promise of Isaiah 65:24 and realized that God had answered her desperate prayer long before she had even thought to ask.

Have you found what it is that you should ask God for? He may have already answered your prayer and is just waiting for you to ask!

With God, nothing is impossible, and He does want to give His children good things. Ask Him today to show you what it is that He has prepared for you.

Peggy Curtice Harris

---

* Not her real name.

Testing God

"Bring all the tithes into the storehouse,
That there may be food in My house,
And try Me now in this,"
Says the LORD of hosts,
"If I will not open for you the windows of heaven . . .
That there will not be room enough to receive it."
—Malachi 3:10, NKJV

There wasn't enough food in the house. For the second month, we were running short on key items. Because we shopped monthly, it meant that we would have to borrow from somewhere else to top off our supply. The budget was tight. "Borrowing" would make us short in another area. We were discouraged. "Why does this keep on happening?" my husband wondered. "We tithe. We're not robbing God. So why don't we have enough food to eat?" We hadn't always been faithful. We had both gone through periods where we had not tithed. Strangely enough, it seemed that when we *weren't* tithing, we had enough. So why was it that when we were faithful, we ran out of food?

I reached for my Bible and read Malachi 3:8–10. If we were going to claim the promise, we would have to make sure that we were meeting any stipulated conditions. The words "And try Me now in this" leaped off the page. "That's it!" I said to my husband. "It's a conditional promise—there are two things we're supposed to do, but we've only been doing one. We're to bring the tithes into God's house *and* try Him. To try God is to test Him to prove that He is faithful." We prayed and reminded God that we were being faithful and asked Him to be faithful to us. This happened in November. My husband worked in a supermarket as the warehouse supervisor but had recently been transferred to the shop floor. Usually, at the end of the year, warehouse personnel would receive gifts from various suppliers. Since he was no longer in the warehouse, we knew there would be no gifts that year. But that was *before* we tested God.

In December, the gift baskets started rolling in. When my husband brought home the first basket, I was surprised. That year he received more gift baskets than he had ever received. We had a surplus of food, which we shared with our family. God had proved Himself to be faithful.

Aminata Coote

Handicaps and Husbands

*Moses said to the LORD . . . "I have never been eloquent,
neither in the past nor since you have spoken to your servant.
I am slow of speech and tongue."
The LORD said to him, "Who gave human beings their mouths?
Who makes them deaf or mute? . . . Is it not I, the LORD? Now go;
I will help you speak and will teach you what to say."
—Exodus 4:10–12, NIV*

I am handicapped in a certain area, and my husband is awesome in that area. If I think about it much, I can beat myself up over my weakness. But recently, I realized that I didn't have to lament my handicap; I could rejoice over my husband. "God is so wise," a friend said. "He was so wise to put you two together." Amen. And while I'm looking, staring, obsessing over what I'm not good at, I totally forget all the other things I'm good at—I also forget whose daughter I am. I forget that God's strength is made perfect in my weakness.

Lately, I found myself meditating on Exodus 4. This is where God calls Moses to speak to Pharaoh and lead the Israelites out of Egypt. Moses protests: "Lord, I'm a bad speaker. Lord, I can't—send someone else." Well, God's not pleased with this complaining. Yet despite Moses' whining, God does *not* choose someone else. *Instead,* He sends a helper—Moses' brother, Aaron—to speak for Moses. I've been wondering why God didn't just choose Aaron in the first place. Why not choose someone eloquent for a job that demands eloquence?

Here are three reasons I can think of: First, God chooses weak vessels so His glory can shine. Second, God wants us to work with others to accomplish His plans. Our work in this life is not about our own strength; as we rely on others, we can learn more fully to rely on God. Third, God sees the bigger picture that we do not. It seems to me that some of Moses' traits, such as the stubbornness he displayed at the scene of his calling, made him an ideal candidate for leading the whiny Israelites in the desert for forty years.

At the end of the day, if I can't thank God for my handicap, I can thank Him for His provision of Aaron—or, in this case, my husband, Buc. I can thank God for His wisdom in putting us together and for His larger view that sees what I don't see in this situation.

What handicaps are you facing? How can you thank God for providing what you lack?

Lindsey Gendke

December 3

In Over My Head

Some were fools; they rebelled
and suffered for their sins.
They couldn't stand the thought of food,
and they were knocking on death's door.
"LORD, help!" they cried in their trouble,
and he saved them from their distress.
He sent out his word and healed them,
snatching them from the door of death.
—Psalm 107:17–20, NLT

Do you feel in over your head? Maybe you are. I remember being on a family vacation in Jamaica, at my dad's favorite place, Doctor's Cave Beach. This particular day, my dad's sister joined us. Her laugh could lift the atmosphere, drive away storm clouds, and cause everyone around to join in her jubilee. Dad and Auntie were getting ready to jump into the beautiful blue Caribbean. She was laughing and ready to experience the deep blue. Before jumping in, Dad cautioned me, "Now, Tricia, don't do what I'm about to do." Then off he ran, speeding into a running long jump and diving into the Caribbean. I was always enamored with my Dad's swimming ability. I could not swim, but he made it look so easy. So I decided that I would disregard my Dad's command and try what I saw him do. Let's just say I soon found myself in over my head.

I was drowning. I saw my short nine years flash before me. Why was I in over my head? I had disregarded my dad's instruction. Now I found myself flailing for my life. As I struggled to find the surface for what felt like an eternity, the deep blue Caribbean seemed to be winning. Then suddenly, I felt warm arms pull me up. It was my aunt! She saved my life.

Have you ever felt as if you were in over your head? Could it be you are in over your head right now? In an unpleasant position—health challenges, financial ruin, a bad relationship, an unfortunate circumstance—because you decided to disregard wise counsel or even God's instruction? The good news is God is not happy to see us suffer even when it's our fault. He loves us. Like my aunt, He is willing and able to save us.

Tricia (Wynn) Payne

What's That Smell?

For He shall give his angels charge over you,
To keep you in all your ways.
—Psalm 91:11, NKJV

When God created us, He thought of everything that we would need; therefore, He gave us five senses: touch, sight, hearing, taste, and smell. I was recently reminded of their importance in our daily lives. I had just finished cooking a delicious dinner of Trinidad and Tobago East Indian rice, dal, spinach bhaji, and fried fish. I washed the dishes, cleaned the stove, mopped the kitchen, and retired to the porch for some relaxation.

Upon reentering the house, I inhaled a strange smell. I believed it was probably coming from some stuff my neighbor had put out (seeing that the windows in that direction were open). So I got dressed and went off to Wednesday evening prayer service. On my return, I noticed that the smell had increased and was the strongest in the kitchen. I thought, *This must be a rotten vegetable.* So I searched the area for the source of the odor but found nothing.

That night I had problems sleeping. Although our bedrooms are upstairs, the doors had to be closed to keep out the smell. When I awoke the next morning, the smell was so awful that I began having problems breathing. I had to go outside for some fresh air. On my way out, my husband mentioned that gas can have a similar odor to the one we were smelling.

Shortly after, while my husband was preparing breakfast, he called out to me from the kitchen: "I've found the source of that smell! Gas has been escaping from the stove because one of the knobs was not turned off properly." Apparently, I had accidentally turned the knob back on while cleaning the stove after cooking. I immediately began saying, "Thank You, Jesus!" We could have all died. Besides that, just one little friction or spark could have ignited a fire in the house. I'm grateful for the sense of smell!

All day long, our guardian angels are at work protecting us. We are unaware of the numerous times they have just snatched us up from dangerous situations in which we might have lost our lives. Every new day that God gives us is another opportunity to live for Him. Time is running out; we have no time to waste. Tell someone of God's goodness today. Let's create a fire in the souls of men and women so that our Master can come quickly in a blaze of glory.

Jill Springer-Cato

Life's Plans

"For I know the plans I have for you,"
says the LORD, "plans to prosper you and not to harm you,
plans to give you hope and a future."
—Jeremiah 29:11, NIV

My parents were divorced when I was very young, so I don't remember living with my father. He was attentive to my sister and me by sending us birthday and Christmas gifts, and child support for my mother. We saw him from time to time, and I even spent a two-week vacation with him, his new wife, and their daughter when I was about ten years old. He attended my wedding, even though I didn't ask him to take part in it. He met my children when they were very young, but gradually the communication became less frequent—perhaps just a note on a Christmas card. Well, after I retired, I acquired the email address for my stepsister, who was just a toddler the only time I had seen her.

I wrote to her, giving her a short rundown of my life; I held my breath as I clicked the Send button on my computer.

Her response unnerved me at first. She told me which college she had attended and what scientific courses and jobs her two daughters had taken and were now pursuing. She told me of her interesting career and her husband's death with lung cancer. Then she spoke of her retirement.

Wow, I thought, *her life was so different from mine. Maybe if my parents had stayed married, my life would have been much different.* "Wait a minute," I said out loud. "My life has been great." I was still living with my husband of sixty-three years. We had two successful, professional children who gave us three wonderful, ambitious grandchildren. We had served as a pastoral couple in several places. We were privileged to have been missionaries and had started new churches. We had actually lived in, of all places, Moscow, Russia. And most important of all, we had Jesus in our hearts! Yes, Jesus was and is more important than degrees, jobs, houses, and lands. He had specific plans for us, and it was satisfying to take His hand and trust Him as He led us, not as we might have planned, but according to His master plan.

Loving Jesus is the most important thing for all of us. Our purpose in life is to live for Him and to tell others of our wonderful Lord, whom we know and love.

Barbara Huff

A Godly Example

Strength and dignity are her clothing,
and she laughs at the time to come.
She opens her mouth with wisdom,
and the teaching of kindness is on her tongue.
—Proverbs 31:25, 26, ESV

A godly mother will model strength, dignity, and wisdom for her children. She will also teach them how to be kind to others. A week or two before Mother's Day 2019, I decided to sell five bunches of artificial carnations for eighteen dollars to buy a cake for my mother. I used my WhatsApp and took a photo of them to send to church members, the majority being mothers. Though I received several responses, no one was interested in buying my carnations. One response I received said, "I don't need the flowers, but if you need help with finances, I may be able to help. I don't usually have or plant flowers at home."

I responded, "I just wanted to show you my flowers for purchase so I could have money for a cake for my mother. Thank you for your concern." Finding no one who wanted to purchase my flowers, I made some floral bouquets from them and sent them to people I knew, along with Mother's Day greetings. I kept a few flowers for display on my glass shelf at home.

Two days before Mother's Day, I went to a Christian gift shop. There I met Doris, a sales assistant. She insisted on giving me money with no strings attached. "There's no need," I gently declined. "I have a budget for my family's special occasions. In fact, I've given away most of my flowers as gifts, and I enjoyed doing that." After all, I had been taught while growing up the truth and joy of Christ's words: "It is more blessed to give than to receive" (Acts 20:35, ESV).

On Mother's Day, friends and family joined in singing "Happy Mother's Day" (to the tune of "Happy Birthday to You") to my mom. My youngest sibling and his family were there, along with our mother's domestic helper. My sister-in-law took pictures and posted them on Facebook. I shared with my mother all the well-wishes that resulted from that social media post. It did my heart good to see that the qualities Mother had instilled in us, along with the kindness she had modeled and taught to others, were coming back to her in abundance on that day.

What are we teaching others by the attitudes and choices we model in our daily lives?

Yan Siew Ghiang

A Light in the Darkness

For my life is spent with grief,
And my years with sighing;
My strength fails.
—Psalm 31:10, NKJV

We moved around California a lot—from the north to the south. About the time we moved to Glendale in Southern California, Pearl Harbor was bombed, and the United States found itself directly involved in World War II. So our government imposed blackout restrictions on West Coast communities to make things more difficult for the enemy, should they want to attack our mainland. Therefore, we had to turn off all the lights when the siren sounded. If a light accidentally got left on in the house, someone would invariably knock on the door and tell us to turn it off! My mother would take us into the closet, and there she would tell us stories or sing with us. It was really scary for us, but we got used to it. Mom would tell us stories about when she was a child. My sister and I would be so happy—and distracted—listening to her that we'd almost be surprised when the all-clear signal was sounded. One night, the blackout time lasted for several hours. When the all-clear signal was sounded, we were so happy and relieved to be able to turn our lights back on and go outside.

Our mom also taught us to pray to God each day. We learned that we had to rely on God for our safety in these trying times. Practicing our growing faith brought us even closer to Jesus and taught us to hold on to the promises of His Word. He was the Light in our darkness, and we learned how to draw closer to Him each day. As we grew in faith, we also grew in the knowledge of how very much He loves us! Of course, we were glad when we finally got through this part of our growing-up history. Although we had loved hearing all of Mother's stories in that closet, we were relieved after the war to have our lives back to normal again.

The Bible tells us that in this life, we will have experiences that bring us grief and uncertainty. But our strength does not have to fail. As Mother taught in that closet so long ago, God is our safest Refuge in the dark. He is our Light. "The Lord is the strength of my life; of whom shall I be afraid?" (Psalm 27:1, NKJV).

Anne Elaine Nelson

Pain—Part 1

Be kind to each other, tenderhearted, forgiving one another,
just as God through Christ has forgiven you.
—Ephesians 4:32, NLT

A few years ago, I attended a women's ministries prayer day.* To be transparent, I used to hate these types of events. Because of my work and travel schedule, I thought other women saw me as an inadequate mother and wife. I rarely had time for tea parties or retreats. Yet one of my friends talked me into attending an event after I moved to Houston. After parking the car, I checked into the hotel and entered the meeting room a few minutes after my friend had.

The hotel ballroom was decorated with symbols of the cross and a woman praying. Then I saw my friend sitting near the front at a table with someone I knew from church, someone with whom I had had an issue in the past. Somewhat shocked, I said to myself, *Oh boy! This is going to be interesting.* I quickly decided there was no way I would walk to the front in front of all those people. I was already late, and I knew this woman from my church did not care for me. Previously, I had been cordial to her, but I had avoided her ever since we'd argued a few years earlier. So I decided to sit in the back.

Yet my friend indicated that she wanted me to sit with her. I realized that I had never told her about the confrontation with this other woman. After my friend sent a few text messages, I moved to the front table with her.

I'm a Christian lady from the South. My mother always taught me to speak when seeing someone, so I sat down at the table and spoke to the woman. Actually, there was no way to avoid her, as she was the only other one sitting at our table. We exchanged the proverbial, "How are you doing?" Then silence reigned.

Have you ever found yourself in a situation that called for grace, but your hurt feelings from the past pulled you in another direction? That's the best time to claim God's promise to help you be tenderhearted. Why not say a prayer today for someone who has hurt you? Ask God for His heart of tenderness toward others.

Paula Sanders Blackwell

---

* This entry first appeared as a blog post as "Unlikely friends," *Devotable* (blog), accessed April 15, 2020, https://devotableapp.com/daily-devotion-luke-418-unlikely-friends/.

Pain—Part 2

"The Spirit of the LORD is upon me,
for he has anointed me to bring Good News to the poor.
He has sent me to proclaim that captives will be released,
that the blind will see,
that the oppressed will be set free."
—Luke 4:18, NLT

After a long, awkward silence, the woman I'd unexpectedly encountered at this women's retreat courteously inquired about a mutual friend, then we grew silent once again.* Later we heard a sermon about Hannah's struggle to get pregnant and how God blessed her with a son. During dinner, we discussed the sermon. The lady whom I wanted to avoid spoke from her heart—about her struggles raising children and her painful divorce. I asked her how long she was married. She said, "Thirty years." There it was! Our common ground, our painful divorces.

I shared that I had been married for eighteen years. As we mutually shared, I listened to her pain. I realized that no matter what differences we may have with others, there is something that connects us all—pain. I told her God heals and restores. She said it had taken a long time to recover, before her remarriage to "the love of my life," and then losing him after only a few years. The pain in her eyes deeply moved me. I realized that God had used my friend to set in motion something I probably would have avoided: closure. Over the next few days, I reflected on the events of that day. The sermon about Hannah and my new kind of experience with a former "adversary" had lifted me to another level. As women, we don't always support one another. We find fault with one another. What keeps us from supporting one another?

I also realized the issue this lady had had with me in the past wasn't really about me. She was more upset with someone else; I had gotten lumped in by association. I thought I had forgiven her when she had apologized a few years ago, but, clearly, I had not let it go because I'd been avoiding her. But after that conversation that day, I was done avoiding her. I made the decision not to hold on to the past anymore. I learned the lesson.

Paula Sanders Blackwell

---

* This entry first appeared as a blog post as "Unlikely friends," *Devotable* (blog), accessed April 15, 2020, https://devotableapp.com/daily-devotion-luke-418-unlikely-friends/.

He Never Lets Go

"The LORD himself goes before you and will be with you; he will never leave you nor forsake you. Do not be afraid; do not be discouraged."
—Deuteronomy 31:8, NIV

"The Spirit of truth. The world cannot accept him, because it neither sees him nor knows him. But you know him, for he lives with you and will be in you. I will not leave you as orphans; I will come to you."
—John 14:17, 18, NIV

There are glorious days in my relationship with God! My morning devotions are rich, and His praises are constantly on my lips. Everything in my life is humming along. I am on the mountaintop. And then there are those other days—days when I don't want to pray, and my morning devotional time is nonexistent. The humming along has stopped. Nothing is going right: the job promotion didn't come through; I have regained those ten pounds; I am in the valley. During these times, I struggle to connect with God.

However, it is also during these times that I am most aware of how much He loves me.

The Holy Spirit is relentless: He gives a gentle prod, a firmer nudge, and sometimes a push, especially when my heart is stubborn, resentful, and willful. God is aware of every pitfall. He sees where the wrong desires of my heart may lead and doesn't let up until I am reminded that He—not I—is in control.

" 'For I know the plans I have for you,' declares the LORD, 'plans to prosper you and not to harm you, plans to give you hope and a future' " (Jeremiah 29:11, NIV).

And silently, my heart cries, "Hold on to me, God! Don't let me go. Get me through this valley." And He comes through and leads me back to the mountaintop.

I am reminded that "the LORD himself goes before you and will be with you; he will never leave you nor forsake you. Do not be afraid; do not be discouraged" (Deuteronomy 31:8, NIV).

God has been a very real presence in my life. He guides my path. When I stray, He—like a relentless shepherd—seeks me and reminds me that He has been there with me all along.

He never lets go!

Terry Roselmond-Moore

Without Warning

*Now the Spirit of the LORD had left Saul, and the LORD sent a
tormenting spirit that filled him with depression and fear.*
—1 Samuel 16:14, NLT

*But an evil spirit from the LORD came on Saul as he was sitting in
his house with his spear in his hand. While David was playing the
lyre, Saul tried to pin him to the wall with his spear,
but David eluded him as Saul drove the spear into the wall.
That night David made good his escape.*
—1 Samuel 19:9, 10, NIV

It began the night before. Or did it?

You see, I had been divorced for eight years and was finally ready to try a relationship again. So I downloaded a dating app suggested by one of my friends and began chatting away. On this particular app, the woman initiates conversation so that the men, who might be attracted, can chat back. So I started by asking this one guy a question. He wanted me to answer the question first, and then he would answer.

Well, seeing we were connected only through text messaging, which doesn't give much nonverbal information about the other, I gently restated my question. He answered and let me know that he was a Christian and grew up in a Christian home. Knowing that not all homes have the same practices in exercising their Christianity, I then posed a follow-up question: "What was your experience like in your home?" Immediately, I got a response for which I was not prepared. "Sorry to say, you seem controlling and are micromanaging this conversation. Even a non-Christian would be able to tell a Christian home." My emotions flared up. It felt as if a spear had been thrown in my direction without warning. He didn't know me, and he was making judgments instead of asking questions. He called me names that did not fit my character. He carried the name Christian yet became defensive to my question instead of taking the opportunity to share his faith. I quickly blocked him and escaped that potential disaster.

How can we recognize whether the Spirit of the Lord has left us? How can we recognize an opportunity to share a spiritual tool that may help someone else in his or her walk with God? You never know who may need what you have or who may be hurt by the fact that you didn't ensure the Spirit of the Lord was still with you.

Rachel Privette Jennings

The Helicopter

*"Come to me, all you who are weary and burdened,
and I will give you rest."*
—Matthew 11:28, NIV

Early one spring morning, long before dawn, I awoke to a loud, roaring noise close by that didn't go away. It sounded as if it was circling above our street. While waiting for the noise to stop, I wondered why my husband didn't wake up.

Living on Howell Mountain above the Napa Valley is a unique experience. Vineyards surround us, and we are the envy of visiting friends and family who view our area as a beautiful, peaceful retreat from city life.

So what's with this noise I hear?

The only sound I could think of in the middle of the night would be that of a helicopter flying a patient to the local hospital. *Helicopter! That's it. The helicopter pilot must be in trouble and looking for a place to land, or maybe he can't find the hospital. Perhaps he is lost.*

The longer the droning helicopter circled, the more worried I became. *What might I do to help? Maybe I could find a phone number and call the small college airport nearby, but would anyone be there to answer the phone? Or, maybe I should call 911 and at least report this situation to the police! Should I wake up Al? No, he needs his sleep.*

After a couple of hours of "problem solving," I decided that by now, the helicopter must be running out of fuel. *What if it crashes in a vineyard or on a house?* My anxiety level was rising like a space shuttle. Out of pure exhaustion and the frustration of not knowing what to do, I fell into a deep sleep.

In the morning, I awoke to a comforting silence. My first thought was, *What happened to the helicopter?*

My husband was in the kitchen eating breakfast, so I sauntered in and asked, "Did you hear the helicopter circling us for hours last night?"

"You mean the motors of the big fans in the vineyards? Yes, I heard them."

Do you worry unnecessarily? Remember to "cast all your anxiety on him because he cares for you" (1 Peter 5:7, NIV).

Donna J. Voth

An On-Time God

Great is his faithfulness;
his mercies begin afresh each morning.
—Lamentations 3:23, NLT

I don't know about you, but there are some days when I need just a little reminder that God sees me and cares for me. Yesterday He gave me just such a glimpse of His attention to the details of my journey through this world.

Over time I have been building steps up my hillside with various scavenged materials. To date, I have succeeded in building sixty-three steps. I have been using them for part of my workout, doing nineteen to twenty laps a day, up and down the hill.

But earlier this year, I broke some bones in my foot and tore some tissue in my ankle. So I haven't been able to do my laps in almost two months. It's been slow healing. Yesterday I got to thinking I would try the steps, just to see how the healing is coming along. I'm eager to get back into my little exercise regime. A sedentary life is not something I can tolerate for very long.

So I got out there and began my exercise. I was about halfway up the steps (where they "swing over" to parallel the fence line) when I began hearing the sounds of a bird in distress. Other birds were singing in sympathy with the unfortunate one. A few steps farther, I saw a young thrush caught in the fence. His legs were hopelessly entangled around one of the horizontal wires. I carefully unwound his legs from the fence and carried him to a clear spot in the woods where I could put him down. There he could rest before trying to fly again.

What a reminder of God's love! Not even a sparrow falls to the ground without God seeing it. If I had decided to chill for the rest of the day, instead of rallying myself to get out and try, the poor thrush would have died there in the fence. That's where I would have found him at a later time.

Isn't that so like God! He shows up, right on the money, when we need Him. He never disappoints.

Why do we worry and fret about things that we have committed to Him?

He will teach us of His faithfulness if we give Him full control of our lives each and every day.

Sylvia Sioux Stark

Friendship of a Child

"Let the little children come to Me, and do not forbid them;
for of such is the kingdom of heaven."
—Matthew 19:14, NKJV

During my twelve-day visit to Siale's home at Vaini in Nuku'alofa, we got to know each other. He was about a year old when I arrived in April 2019. His working parents schedule their day around Siale's need. Big sister Jolene, a nursing sister, takes a turn at making sure Siale is comfortable, clean, and well-fed. Siale has three older brothers who attend the nearby school and spend time after school each day playing with him. Siale has a loving family that keeps him happy and secure.

During my first week, Siale was fearful of me and my attempts to befriend him. He would watch when I played with his older brothers. At the end of my first week, the barrier between us began to open. He would hold on to my chair during mealtime, waiting for my attention. Soon my effort to make friends with him worked. He would crawl up to my room to check on me early in the morning. The fear disappeared. By the second week, Siale and I were friends. We built with blocks, read, and ate together. I taught him how to stand and walk. By the end of that second week, Siale was able to stand alone and take several steps before falling. He enjoyed the walking sessions outside and little games of hide-and-seek in the house. While I was visiting, many other adults came to the home. It felt gratifying when Siale would choose to come to me rather than anyone else. I cherished and loved his faithfulness to our new friendship.

This growing friendship experience with Siale reminds me of how Jesus engaged with children. However, He did not need to take one week to develop trust with children. They were attracted to Him by His love, care, and concern for them. Jesus had time for them and never turned them away. It was no surprise that one day, a child shared his lunch with Him and five thousand others on a hillside.

The Lord reminds us today that in order to become citizens of God's kingdom, we must become like little children. May our prayer be that God will give us the innocent heart of a child to love, forgive, live, and trust Jesus as little children do.

Fulori Sususewa Bola

"The Soul Felt Its Worth"

*"But God showed his great love for us by sending Christ
to die for us while we were still sinners."*
—Romans 5:8, NLT

There is nothing more glorious at Christmas than hearing "O Holy Night" sung by a choir or someone whose heart for Jesus and beautiful voice come together. Just reading the lyrics can give you chills in remembrance of Christmases past. We feel the intensity of the song as it rises to the chorus: "Fall on your knees!" We sing our hearts out as we finish with "O night divine!" And yet there is a line in this song that I never consciously picked up on before: "Long lay the world in sin and error pining till He appeared and the soul felt its worth."*

As I meditated on these words, I realized that this sentence in this song contains vital truth. Our individual worth is directly tied to Jesus. Have you ever felt unworthy or unloved? I certainly have, and it took me many years of being a Christian to understand and genuinely accept the truth of my worth. Maybe you have entertained the lie from Satan that no one cared if you lived or died. The world may have taught you that your worth came from how well you performed. Through experience, you concluded that your talent, intelligence, or good looks were the only reason you mattered to others.

The number one thing on Satan's to-do list every day is to deceive you into thinking that God is against you. He wants you to believe that in order for God to accept you, you must shape up and measure up to earn His love. But God placed in us all a desire to feel valued and loved, and there is only one Person that put so much value upon you that He gave His life for you.

On the night Jesus was born, He showed through His birth, and later, His life, death, and resurrection how worthy He is and how valuable we are to Him.

So this Christmas season, as we hear and sing this powerful Christmas carol, *fall on your knees*, and remember that Christmas is about Jesus, yes. But also remember the reason He came—because of His great love for us.

Lee Lee Dart

---

* John Sullivan Dwight, trans., "O Holy Night," public domain.

Keeping Christ in Christmas

*Let your light so shine before men, that they may see your
good works, and glorify your Father which is in heaven.*
—Matthew 5:16, KJV

Every year when I finish decorating for Christmas, I'm always enraptured by the light and beauty around me. Yet I can't help but remember that Christmas wasn't always like this. When I was young, strict religion took Christ out of Christmas and reduced the season to one thing only: winter—and winter constituted a harsh reality.

When I turned six, believing the world was about to come to an end, my parents decided to separate us from society, ultimately landing us on a rural tract of land in Tennessee. Isolated on the top of a steep hill, we lived without running water, electricity, or telephones. Our old wooden house had no heating apart from woodstove fires that always died out at night. By early morning, the house would be only about ten degrees warmer than the temperature outside.

One night, which will always remain frozen in my memory, the temperature dropped to –10°F outside and 0°F inside. I woke up in the morning to discover that my heels were frozen solid, white, and hard like golf balls, despite sixteen blankets and four pairs of thick socks.

Looking back, I marvel because though we were Christians, we did not believe in even acknowledging Christmas. At a time when the world is most likely to think of Jesus, we refused to mention His birth. We focused on pagan origins and associations, forgetting that Christ did not leave heaven to come to heaven, but rather to a very pagan world. And He came to bring light and overcome the darkness, just as my gently winking Christmas tree always reminds me.

I see such a contrast between Christmas then and Christmas now. Then, the season was isolated, lonely, and cold; now, it is beautiful, cozy, and warm. Then, in our effort to be right in every facet of our beliefs, we excluded Christ. Now I embrace Him and rejoice in His love.

Despite possible concerns about pagan origins, I want to encourage you to embrace every opportunity to bring light and hope to this world, talk about Jesus, and build warm and wonderful memories in your home. Don't let it be that your children have little to think back on when it comes to Christmas—or religion—except frozen, harsh, or lonely memories. Instead, let their memories be of the warmth, beauty, and light of Christ's love!

Rachel Williams-Smith

If Mary Magdalene Had Twins

Jesus said to her, "Woman, why are you weeping?"
—John 20:15, NKJV

The tears I'd suppressed for weeks now stained my pillowcase; tired in ways that sleep would never ease, I craved rest. Mothering twins had never been on the to-do list. Being a single mother had topped my *never*-in-this-lifetime list! But alas, through strange turns, single-mother-of-*twins* was my new reality. I'd heard that parenting isn't easy, but no words can describe how truly, incredibly difficult it is. For months I'd been praying for help—for any change that would make this season brighter or its burdens lighter. God's only answer? A calm, deafening silence. Falling into a restless sleep, I prayed again, a single, silent sentence: *Lord, if You don't move soon, I will shrivel up and die.*

The next day, I met my own twin for lunch. Her quiet discomfort hung between us. Sensing her struggle for words, I waited, wearily. Eyes downcast, she lined chips across her sandwich wrapper. Inhaling loudly, she blurted, "Did you tell God that if He doesn't move soon, you'll die?" The pain of God's prolonged silence sharpened into the realization that my silent prayer had been heard and shared from the sacred halls of heaven. Bitterly, I asked, "What else did *He* say?" Shielding her eyes behind a broken chip, she whispered, "He said, 'Remind her I am Lord of the Resurrection too.' " God's silence is painful, but so is the echo of His voice in the dreary walls of His waiting rooms. Through each season of single-parenting two incredible girls, the story of Mary Magdalene at the tomb has sustained me. In her story, I've learned that God works best in the darkest nights. While Mary navigated narrow streets on that dark, lonely night, God defeated death and left an empty tomb. As I navigate the darkest nights of this season, He empties the tomb of buried dreams. Mary cried. Her tears did not make Him—nor the angels guarding the empty tomb—wish she'd visited at a better time. When grief and confusion overwhelm my heart, it's OK to cry. Jesus called Mary's name. Though she had not recognized His face, her name from His lips was unmistakable. When disappointment, fear, and loneliness obscure His face, He calls my name.

In the darkest nights of every season, God empties tombs. He sees our tears, and He knows each name. Listen to Him call. Witness Him, Lord of the Resurrection still.

Melissa Martinez

The Christmas Ornament

The end of a thing is better than its beginning.
—Ecclesiastes 7:8, NKJV

It doesn't matter that it's ugly. It goes on the Christmas tree every year and has for more than sixty-five years, a testament to one of my childhood attempts at creativity. Styrofoam was a newfangled miracle for craft-makers in the fifties. Spectacular orbs with sequins, gold braid, and iridescent beads were displayed by triumphant homemakers who became artisans with a few craft materials and some straight pins. My family was no less inspired. Mama bought me a five-inch diameter ball, pure in its white nakedness, and a whole packet of gold sequins to do with as I willed. The mere thought of such a creative license had almost made me giddy.

I planned to make a perfect, symmetrical application of those gold sequins, covering the entirety of the ball so that it would sparkle under the lights on the tree. It wasn't long until my thumb became sore from pushing the short pins into the ball. And getting the sequins lined up wasn't nearly as easy as I had imagined. Then to my dismay, after a few shaky revolutions around the ball, I realized there were not going to be nearly enough sequins to cover the whole thing. So I began to space the sequins further and further apart, and as a result, the lines circling the ball became even more erratic. So much for symmetry.

To my mother's credit, she did not make fun of my efforts, and the ornament assumed its place on the tree, as it has in all the years since. My parents have long passed, so one might wonder why I have kept it into my golden years. Why would I stir up the recollection of my failed artistic effort every year at holiday time?

Well, it does remind me that even though my well-intentioned plans don't always work out the way I first envision, I can learn to live with the results. The ornament does still sparkle—a little. Beyond that, it helps me remember that happiness is not directly tied to things always being perfect. And in a sense, isn't *life* like that? Most of us discover, at one time or another, that things don't work out exactly as we had planned or expected. But we become *who we are* as a result of the sum of our life experiences. The Master Potter takes all those experiences into account as He molds us into His likeness, the good, the bad—and even the ugly.

Linda Nottingham

God's Goodness

I know the thoughts that I think toward you, says the LORD,
thoughts of peace and not of evil, to give you a future and a hope.
—Jeremiah 29:11, NKJV

God has a work for everyone, and He is honored when we use the gifts He gives us to bless others. I was born into a poor family, and no money was available to attend a Christian school, but I always wanted to work for the Lord. When I moved to the mainland, the Lord provided a way for me to attend a Christian school where I was able to work on campus to pay my tuition and expenses. After graduation, I returned to the island, where I worked at my area's church headquarters for two years. Later, I served as a missionary in a foreign country; however, circumstances out of my control brought me to the United States.

Although my life was difficult and filled with twists, turns, detours, and mistakes, the Lord kept a watchful eye over me and honored my desire to work for Him. My daughters and I had a major challenge because we were in a foreign country on a student visa that was about to expire. With the help of God, Christian friends, and my daughters—who felt that no job was beneath them—we survived. We never went hungry, and we always had a place to stay.

One thing that concerned me, though, was our visa situation. My family, who lived on the island, encouraged me to return home with the girls, but I didn't want to do that, although I didn't know what plan the Lord had for me. The awesome God that we serve brought a Christian man from another state to Huntsville, Alabama, to fulfill His plan. He was a loving man, but he had a difficult time trying to capture my attention (I was not interested in his romantic overtures). However, the Lord was not finished with me. The gentleman made everything possible for himself, my girls, and me. As a result, we were able to stay in the country legally.

The Lord blessed my family, and the girls completed their education and obtained jobs in their fields of study. I became an employee at the college where it had all started. I give praise and honor to God for His great love and mercy.

Dear reader, no matter what you may be going through, I encourage you to stay connected with God because His words are true: "I know the thoughts that I think toward you, says the LORD, thoughts of peace and not of evil" (Jeremiah 29:11, NKJV).

Flore Aubry-Hamilton

Nighttime Vigil

Casting all your care on him; for he careth for you.
—1 Peter 5:7, KJV

It had been a long and sleepless night—one of many as I watched three of my four grown children gradually forsake the church of their childhood. On my knees beside our bed where my husband lay sleeping, I wept and prayed for each of them, finding no solace or comfort. I knew my health and ability to function were giving out as a result of these nighttime vigils, but I seemed helpless to stop them.

About 3:00 A.M., I felt as though a hand had been placed on my shoulder, and it seemed I heard a gentle voice speaking: *You know, you are not to do this anymore. You cannot save your children by sacrificing your life. I am the only One who can save your children.*

Where had I heard those words before? I crept silently downstairs to find my Bible concordance and look up the word *save*. Finally, reaching the book of Isaiah, I read the words, "I will contend with him that contendeth with thee, and I will save thy children" (Isaiah 49:25, KJV). What a wonderful promise! Surely I had read that passage before, but somehow it had never registered. I dropped to my knees once more and accepted Christ's invitation to cast "all [my] care upon him" (1 Peter 5:7, KJV).

It seemed a heavy load had been lifted from my shoulders. A feeling of peace, such as I had not experienced in years, swept over me. The verse repeated over and over in my mind as I made my way back to bed just as the morning light began peeping through our eastern window. My dear, not-yet-retired husband had recently expressed his concern that when he came home at night, he never knew whether he would find me dead or alive. I realized what a burden I had placed on him. I told him about my night's experience and asked for his forgiveness. His relief was as palpable as mine!

During the years that followed and through my husband's last illness, our hearts continued to ache for our children. We knew we could not save them. All we could do was love them and lift them up in prayer. Now widowed, I daily claim Jesus' promise that He gave me in the wee hours of that long-ago morning: "I will contend with him that contendeth with thee, and I will save thy children" (Isaiah 49:25, KJV).

Donna Ritchie Casebolt

Bullying at the Feeder

"They shall not hurt nor destroy in all My holy mountain."
—Isaiah 11:9, NKJV

When April comes to North Carolina, it brings with it those bejeweled and fascinating ruby-throated hummingbirds. Their frenzied activity and acrobatics have always been a source of wonder and delight. In fact, when the time came last fall for their migration, I so much regretted seeing them leave that I composed a little song:

> Oh, the hummingbirds have gone away,
> They'll be coming back another day;
> And I really, really hate to see them go.
> I will miss the little things, I will,
> With their busy little wings, but still
> They just had to leave before the cold winds blow.

Now summer was passing. One day I realized that the activity at the birdfeeder had slowed almost to a standstill. Only one ruby-throat was in sight, perched on the red ant guard above the feeder, looking this way and that in case a rival should approach. Sadly, Mr. Bully Bird had taken over! Eventually, I decided to bring the feeder inside and let Mr. Bully find a new territory.

As for the hummingbirds, my song changed to a lament:

> Now I have no hummingbirds at all,
> Though it isn't even nearly fall.
> Mr. Bully Bird has driven them away.
> Though it's true, they are no longer here,
> Maybe they'll come back another year;
> And I hope the bully bird will let them stay.

Bullying is not restricted to the animal world. Statistics of bullying-caused suicide among children are shocking. We adults need to be sensitive to the emotions of children and youth within our spheres of influence. Love can go a long way toward winning their confidence. Yet only when Jesus returns will perfect peace and harmony be restored. How wonderful that will be!

Lila Farrell Morgan

God Surprises!

"For My thoughts are not your thoughts,
Nor are your ways My ways," says the LORD.
"For as the heavens are higher than the earth,
So are My ways higher than your ways,
And My thoughts than your thoughts."
—Isaiah 55:8, 9, NKJV

The year was 2014. My home was filled with gloom. I had been out of a job for six years and had moved from one state to another trying to sort out an immigration situation but to no avail. My children requested that I join them so we could all struggle together under one roof. We were all experiencing different levels of privation due to our immigration problems. There was always an ever-present sense of fear and uncertainty as we wondered, *What next?*

One Friday morning, I picked up the mail with indifference, believing that it was mainly junk mail anyway. As I sorted it, I reminisced about happy days when I was part of the hospital team. I was filled with nostalgia as I reflected on past moments of collegial collaborations with fellow graduate students and, subsequently, with other hospital chaplains. I had an active commissioned minister license, which enabled me to work and support my family, but sadly, it expired correspondingly with my work authorization. Moreover, I wondered why I was still wallowing in joblessness, with feelings of helplessness and hopelessness, after acquiring an expensive training in original medicine. I was, however, impressed that God led me into this area, first to heal me from bursitis and, later, to use me as an instrument to help others.

With these thoughts in mind, I noticed an unusual envelope in the mail addressed to me. I settled down to open it. Twice, I had experienced a denial of work authorization; therefore, with trembling hands, I opened the strange envelope last. To my greatest astonishment, it was my green card (the authorization to live and work in the United States permanently). Tears of joy welled up in my eyes. I ran to share my surprise with one of my daughters. We rejoiced and thanked God for showing me hope—that He was not done with me. He brought me up from the depths of despair. His ways and thoughts are beyond our understanding!

Ekele P. Ukegbu-Nwankwo

Fog

Cast all your anxiety on him because he cares for you.
—1 Peter 5:7, NIV

It was early morning. My bags were ready for one more trip. As I always do, I looked through the window before loading the car for the drive to the airport. To my surprise, a densely foggy day awaited me. I don't like foggy travel days. On those days, my mind immediately sets the pace toward worry and fear. I am anxious about safety during fog anyway, but if I am inside a plane, I battle with feelings of insecurity because I don't have a clear view of what is ahead. OK, I admit it: I battle because I'm not in complete control.

Are you also battling a day of fog? Have you unnecessarily created your foggy day in your own mind? Have you let circumstances overwhelm you with doubt and fear? Have you allowed the fog to seep inside and guide your emotions? Have you forgotten the things for which you are grateful? I had. I just wanted a bright sunny day!

I was sabotaging my journey without knowing it because my mind created thick, dark clouds of fear and ingratitude. My heart was not happy that day, so God reminded me of how important the *journey* is. It's not always about getting to the destination. The fog, the slow travel, and the detours are all part of God's purpose for our lives. My plane was delayed for hours, my plans were changed, and my patience was tested. Yet surprises like this teach us what to do on a foggy day—cast our anxiety on God. You gave your day to Him, so let Him deal with it.

I love the image of created by the word *casting*. It involves an action—to throw something. And we know in what direction, don't we? Toward God! Let Him carry the burden of fear and anxiety—He is in complete control. Women such as Hagar, Jochebed, Ruth, Naomi, Hannah, Esther, and Mary all cast their anxiety at the feet of the Lord during the fog-filled days of their lives. They expected Him to take control. Some begged for it.

Whatever circumstances you find yourself in today—whether you have just celebrated an uplifting mountaintop experience or, on the other hand, have just scrambled blindly through the darkest night of your life—know that God is the same on the sunny, clear day as He is in the wet, foggy night. "Cast all your anxiety on him" (1 Peter 5:7, NIV). Why? Because He cares about you. He wants to carry your burden, and He knows the way. Believe it, my friend, and enjoy the journey!

Raquel Queiroz da Costa Arrais

What a Gift!

No eye has seen, no ear has heard,
and no mind has imagined
what God has prepared
for those who love him.
—1 Corinthians 2:9, NLT

One Christmas Eve some years ago, I sat under the tall, lighted tree at my parents' house. The whole family had gathered for our tradition of opening presents—one at a time, from youngest to oldest.

The youngest was Julie, my niece. As she opened a My Twinn doll, she looked at it adoringly and then hugged it. We took a few pictures, and she contentedly cradled the doll as we moved to the next family member.

Her brother, Sam, opened a box of LEGOs. "Oh, little LEGOs!" he shouted. "Thank you!" Running to an open area on the carpet, he dumped the box out and began to assemble the set and play with it.

After we'd gone around the circle a few times, I began to notice a pattern in reactions. Julie lined up her gifts and admired them. Sam paused to play with each one. Doug, my brother-in-law, put all his gifts to immediate use; soon, he was wearing two pairs of socks, a new belt, a hat, and a new flannel shirt, while reading a humor book he'd received.

But my German grandma—the oldest—was the most fun. She had just turned ninety-four, and after opening each gift, she'd exclaim, "Ach, I've never seen anything like it!" or, "*Ach du liebe Zeit* [Dear me]! I've never seen anything so nice in all my life!"

We found that a little hard to believe, considering that she'd lived so long and traveled extensively. But it sure made us gift-givers feel good.

That was my grandma's last Christmas on earth. But I can't wait to hear her say those words again—and this time I'll know they will be absolutely true: "*Ach du liebe Zeit* [Dear me]! I've never seen anything like heaven! I've never seen anything so nice in all my life!"

I'm so grateful that Jesus came the first time—and I'm even more grateful that He's coming back—for Grandma and the rest of us.

Lori Peckham

God Knows Where I Live

In the sixth month the angel Gabriel was sent from God to a city of Galilee named Nazareth, to a virgin betrothed to a man whose name was Joseph, of the house of David. And the virgin's name was Mary.
—Luke 1:26, 27, ESV

At six years of age—when my school friends talked about Christmas and the legend of Santa Claus who delivers gifts to good boys and girls, flies in a sleigh drawn by reindeer, lands on the rooftop, slides down the chimney, and leaves gifts under the Christmas tree—I was skeptical.

How did Santa know where I lived? We just had moved. Or perhaps he wouldn't leave gifts because we didn't have a chimney. But then, why should a chimney be the deciding factor for receiving a gift, I reasoned, when many of the little boys and girls of the world live in homes and huts without chimneys? And most don't have a Christmas tree to receive those gifts.

My parents assured me that my gifts came from our family. More than that, God knew where I lived, and the Christ child was the greatest gift I receive on Christmas morning—and every morning—because Jesus was born to die for my sins.

From heaven, God sent Gabriel to the right country, region, city, street, house, and woman. He even knew her name was Mary and that she was engaged to marry Joseph.

No matter where Mary was, Gabriel knew where to find her. She was not at home when Jesus was born, but Gabriel told the shepherds how to find the Baby in a manger. When wise men came looking for the Baby, they were guided to where Mary and Joseph were living.

God knows where we are at anytime, anywhere. We are not hidden, forsaken, or lost. Jonah learned this in the belly of the great fish, Peter found out in prison, and David learned while on the run. God always knows where to find us—because He follows us!

> Surely [the Lord's] goodness and mercy shall follow me
>   all the days of my life;
> and I shall dwell in the house of the LORD
>   forever (Psalm 23:6, ESV).

Jesus is called Immanuel, "God with us." He follows because He wants to dwell with us forever. The assurance that God gave His only Son to save us is our greatest Christmas gift.

Rebecca Turner

What Do I Behold?

*But we all, with unveiled face, beholding as in a mirror the glory
of the Lord, are being transformed into the same image
from glory to glory, just as by the Spirit of the Lord.*
—2 Corinthians 3:18, NKJV

A few days ago, a homeowner told me, "If I had known all of this kitchen remodeling would take so much time resulting in ruined counters a year later, I would have never done this. You know, the remodeling projects on *television* look so easy. I'm never doing this again! Next time we're going to pay for someone to do the work." This comment about being influenced by television made me reflect on children. How often parents don't realize the danger that lurks behind cartoons and movies that children are exposed to. Impressions imprint on their little minds and memory files, inviting trust and belief in what they see and hear.

I also reflected on the fact that the majority of television programs are meant not only to entertain but also to capture, if not enslave, one's attention, time, and memory. It makes us adults want to be—or look like—someone else. It can make us want a bigger home, new furniture, or more decorations for our home, among other things.

On a very personal level, whenever I have allowed any of these thoughts to jump into my mind, it has not been a coincidence but more of a purposeful choice to watch and contemplate. When I have chosen to spend my time caught up in decorating and remodeling programs, I suddenly have new desires in my heart for different things. I start to put my time and focus on the things of this world that do not have lasting value for my spiritual growth. These thoughts sometimes rob me of my happiness, especially when they come between Jesus and me. I lose focus on my true journey because I am now beholding and contemplating other things that start making me believe that this or that will make me happier. Have you ever experienced your time and money being consumed by that which is unnecessary in your life?

God has begun a good work of transformation in us, and He wants to continue it until we are transformed into His image. Therefore, let us continue to behold and contemplate Him as in a mirror by spending more time with Him through the reading of His Word, prayer, and praise through hymns and songs of worship. I invite you to focus anew on beholding Jesus.

Lily Morales-Narváez

Missing the Blessing to Our Cravings

For He satisfies the longing soul,
And fills the hungry soul with goodness.
—Psalm 107:9, NKJV

Have you ever craved something very specific? You could almost taste it, and you wanted to taste it! I don't know where the craving came from, but one week, I couldn't get peanut butter blossom cookies off my mind. Small round peanut butter cookies with a Hershey's Kiss placed in the middle, fresh from the oven—I battled the craving all week.

Finally, at a bakery filled with every imaginable kind of cookie, except the one I craved, I saw peanut butter cookies partly dipped in chocolate. They'd have to do. "What were you looking for?" asked a lady at the counter. When I told her, she said, "Wait, they might be baking some in the back." Returning, she reported, "Yes, they have been baking them this morning. The first tray just came out of the oven, and they're putting the chocolate Kisses on them now."

"No, thank you," I replied. "These will do." As much as I wanted peanut butter blossom cookies, I didn't want anyone to go to any extra trouble just for me. I left without the fresh-baked cookies I'd been craving and with only a "good-enough" cookie instead.

Eating my good-enough cookie, it suddenly struck me that I could have had what I was craving, but I said no to the generous offer to pack up warm cookies. Crazy!

But how often do we say, "No, thank you" when others offer to do something for us or give us something? Even something we'd like or have even been wishing for. How many times have we missed out on a blessing because we didn't want to "bother" someone? Didn't want anyone to go to any extra trouble for us? (Yet often those of us who say, "No, thank you" the most are the first to offer and truly want to do something for others!) And how many times does God attempt to bless us with something our heart desires, and we miss out because we haven't learned to accept gifts graciously or feel that we are worth the effort?

I want to challenge you (and myself): Let others bless you. Accept their offers of kindness. Simply say, "Thank you!" Enjoy. Ask God to open your eyes and heart to see the ways He's attempting to bless you and say yes to Him. Don't miss out on the gifts of kindness, encouragement, and joy He's already preparing just for you!

Tamyra "Tami" Horst

The Perfect Fit

Peace I leave with you, my peace I give unto you:
not as the world giveth, give I unto you.
Let not your heart be troubled, neither let it be afraid.
—John 14:27, KJV

I left my sixth job interview, where I was told to expect a call the following day. I was still waiting to hear back from a second-stage interview with another company that was dragging the interview process. My frustration was coupled with anxiety and fear of failure, and I tried to find peace reciting John 14:27. On the way to my friend's home, I stopped at a department store.

I needed a long-sleeve black shirt, which was the required uniform for a part-time job. I had been searching for size six in several stores, including in London and Leeds. A week earlier, I messaged my supervisor asking if I could wear something else as I had not found a black shirt, and she offered to bring me a shirt. To my utter dismay, I opened the package to find a large men's-size shirt. I had no choice. I tucked it in, rolled up the sleeves, and wore it with feigned confidence. But there was no way I was going to wear that shirt again!

Yet, a week later, I still could not find a size six. I told my friend's sister about my dilemma. She quickly said, "I'm the queen of black shirts. I have so many! I can give you one."

"Yeah?" I asked unbelievingly. "It has to be a shirt, you know, with buttons on the front."

"Yes, I know," she nodded her head in understanding.

"And it must have long sleeves," I emphasized, pointing to my wrist.

"Yes! I have that," she responded.

When I picked up the shirt she gave me, I heard God's whisper, "Don't I always provide for you? I will find you the perfect fit." The Perfect Fit was a tagline for an employee recruitment campaign I managed three years ago. God had just reassured me that He would replace my part-time job with a job that is just right for me. This gave my frustrated, anxious, and fearful soul much-needed peace.

To my surprise, while I thought I needed size six, the perfect fit turned out to be size eight! God is able to do exceedingly, abundantly more than we can ask or imagine (Ephesians 3:20).

We don't know what the future holds, but we can know His promises are sure.

Kimasha P. Williams

Give Her Your Eyes, Lord!

"I will give you a new heart and put a new spirit in you; I will remove from you your heart of stone and give you a heart of flesh."
—Ezekiel 36:26, NIV

My sister, Damaris, suffered from glaucoma. She consulted with many doctors but to no avail. Her sight continued to deteriorate until she could not read any text. She had to depend on her ten-year-old son to read the Bible to her. For several years, family and friends prayed for Damaris without any positive results.

Recently a friend of mine shared Ezekiel 36:26 with me, and it occurred to me that if God could do a heart transplant, then He could do an eye replacement. The thought of an "eye replacement" excited us. I called my sister and asked her to join us in asking for an eye replacement. We prayed for ten days asking that Jesus replace my sister's eyes with His all-seeing eyes.

The first Sabbath of October 2014 was a day of prayer and fasting for the sick in my home church in Edmonton, Alberta. I focused on my sister, and I kept repeating the prayer for an eye replacement. While we prayed in Canada, it was nighttime in Uganda, and as Damaris slept, she had a dream. She saw her church pastor wearing big eyeglasses with six lenses. She requested that she try on the glasses, and the pastor granted her request. To her surprise, she could see everything clearly. She returned the glasses and said she should get a similar set for herself. At that point, she woke up with very itchy eyes.

As Damaris started to scratch her eyes, she remembered the dream. She turned to the bedside stand and picked up an English Bible study guide, which had lain there unopened for over a year. To her surprise and utter amazement, she could read the words on the page! She tossed it down and picked up a guide in her vernacular. She could read those words too. Damaris jumped out of bed and picked up a Bible—the words stood out clearly on the pages. She opened two more Bibles and read. Praise God! At that moment, the thought struck her: *God has restored my vision!* He had replaced her blind eyes with His eyes. My sister could see! She called me at 10:30 P.M., crying, "Jesus has given me His eyes! My vision has been restored!" I felt so humbled. We both started to cry, overwhelmed by God's kindness toward His children.

Edith Kiggundu

The Shepherd's Psalm

The LORD is my shepherd; I shall not want.
—Psalm 23:1, KJV

The Lord is my Shepherd. He formed me within my mother's womb and took me in his arms as I was born. He chose me—to love me, protect me, and give me the opportunity of experiencing a relationship of fellowship, trust, and victory in Him. No other has a greater interest in my present and eternal well-being than Christ. That's why I trust and depend solely on Him and His grace. I shall not want. He will supply all my needs according to His riches in glory.

He diligently searches for soft, green pastures where I find nourishment and refreshment for my soul. He leads me into situations that will cause me to reflect. He bids me rest from all worries, leading me where His Spirit can renew me.

He leads me beside still waters, that I may quench my thirst for His wisdom and the knowledge of His love. If worries, sadness, or troubles arise, He will comfort my soul and encourage me along the way.

My Shepherd knows my comings and goings. He knows my thoughts and is aware of my frailty. That's why He's always by my side. He promised to guide me in the path of righteousness, honoring His name. I know His character is love, and He proves that in the way He treats me day by day.

Even when I walk the valley of trials, temptation, and sorrows—even if I face death—I need not fear, for You are by my side. When others forsake me, You remain. You don't condemn me when I falter. Instead, You invite me to turn my eyes upon You. Your commandments act as a staff, protecting me from evil, and Your rod returns me to the path of life.

My enemies stand in awe, as they notice Your faithful provision for me. You honor me before them by treating me as a child of the King. With the Holy Spirit, You anointed me as a sign that I belong to You. For this and countless blessings, my cup overflows with gratefulness!

Your mercy and grace shall follow me unendingly until I arrive in Your everlasting home, where I shall live eternally before Your holy presence.

Let the Lord be your Shepherd today.

Rhodi Alers de López

A New Year Dawns

" 'He will wipe every tear from their eyes. There will
be no more death' or mourning or crying or pain,
for the old order of things has passed away."
—Revelation 21:4, NIV

It was midnight on December 31, and the "world" said it was 2019. However, as a Bible-believing Christian, I had entered 2019 hours earlier—at sunset, while in church for a vespers program. I must confess that I have a weakness for fireworks, so I did join the midnight celebrators by viewing our annual "Jamaican Fireworks at the Waterfront" on television. Vespers was more inspiring, though, consisting of uplifting musical renditions and a powerful charge from our pastor, interspersed with testimonies. Almost every testimony started with, "This year has been the worst year of my life." Loved ones or jobs lost. A motor vehicle accident. Illnesses. Family problems. Yet all expressed faith in God and hope for the future. Sadly, we lost two of our children for whom the church had offered intercessory prayers for healing, but God allowed them to go to their rest. One day, if we are faithful, we will know why.

As I reflected on the daily world news throughout 2018, it appeared that the world was skiing downhill. Irrational mass murders were frequent. Children in schools could no longer focus only on reading, writing, and mathematics; they were also being taught how to escape attacks by shooters and avoid predators. Tales of abuse were increasingly being aired on news media. Cyberbullying and human trafficking continued to take place internationally. Finally, politics in many countries could only be described by one word: *bizarre*. The bad news is that, as students of the Bible, we expect things will get worse before they get better.

Yet there is good news that far surpasses the bad! John 14:1–3 comforts and assures us with the promise that Jesus will return to rescue His children and make all things right. So, at the dawn of this New Year, we can look forward to the time when Jesus, seated on His throne, declares, "I am making everything new" (Revelation 21:5, NIV). "Those who are victorious will inherit all this, and I will be their God and they will be my children" (Revelation 21:7, NIV).

John, in Revelation 22:20, states, "He who testifies to these things says, 'Yes, I am coming soon' " (NIV). I join John in exclaiming, "Amen. Come, Lord Jesus" (Revelation 22:20, NIV)!

Cecelia Grant

2021 Author Biographies

Kehinde Adenike Abolarin, a shepherdess (pastor's wife), lives in Ogun State, Nigeria. She is a chaplain, working at Babcock University as both a campus and a hospital chaplain. She loves caring for people and impacting lives for the kingdom of God. **Sept. 25, Nov. 20**

Priscilla E. Adonis writes from Cape Town, South Africa. She likes writing, card making, and working in the flower garden. She has two daughters and two grandsons that live in the United States. As a widow, she thanks God daily for keeping her safe and for His blessings on her. **June 6, Aug. 1**

Harryette Aitken loves to travel and has coordinated group tours to the Middle East and Europe. She and her pastor husband, John, live in Southern California, United States, where she assists her husband in ministry. She's served her church in many capacities, her last position being a development director for a North American Division ministry. Her greatest joy in life is being grandmother to two precious boys, John III and James. **May 14**

Oguchi Ajaegbu, PhD, is a lecturer in the Department of Mass Communication at Babcock University. She lives with her husband and their son in Ogun State, Nigeria. **Sept. 22**

Brenda Alexis, MA (in counseling psychology), lives in Silver Spring, Maryland, United States. She enjoys the relaxing hobby of photography. Capturing photographs of people tells a story. Her most memorable photo shows her grandfather in his brown leather chair reading the paper. She was privileged to have it become part of an art exhibit at the Library of Congress. She has received degrees from Loma Linda University and Washington Adventist University. **June 17**

Ginny Allen, a retired school nurse, lives with her pastor-husband (of more than fifty years), David, in Vancouver, Washington, United States. She is best known for her interest in prayer. She founded Joy! Ministries, which encourages others to bring joy to the heavenly Father's heart while they listen for God's love song (*God's Love Song* is also the title of her recent book). She is a frequent speaker who is committed to living God's will for her life—"nothing more, nothing less, nothing else!" **Jan. 23**

Sue Anderson is retired from the United States Department of Agriculture, Forest Service. She lives in the Pacific Northwest of the United States and has been married to Chuck for more than fifty years. They have two married daughters, a granddaughter, two grandsons, and two great-grandsons. She enjoys writing and spending time with family and friends. **Feb. 24**

Lydia D. Andrews is a certified nurse-midwife, mother of three adult children, and grandmother of four delightful boys. She and her husband reside in Huntsville, Alabama, United States, where she works as a labor and delivery clinical instructor. Her hobbies include reading, cooking, travel, music, and spending time with family. She is involved in the prayer and women's ministries of her church. **Mar. 23**

Raquel Queiroz da Costa Arrais is a minister's wife who developed her ministry as an educator for twenty years. Currently, she works as associate director of the General Conference Women's Ministries Department in Maryland, United States. She has two adult sons, two daughters-in-law, and four adored grandchildren. Her greatest pleasures are being with people, singing, playing the piano, and traveling. **Jan. 15, Apr. 5, Dec. 23**

Jean Arthur is an attorney living in Silver Spring, Maryland, United States. When not at work, she is either in her very large fruit and vegetable garden; at home baking, reading, or knitting; traveling around the world; or running, bicycling, or boxing. **June 26**

Flore Aubry-Hamilton loves the Lord, and she wants her light to shine for Him. She and her husband, George, live in Huntsville, Alabama, United States. They enjoy working with disabilities ministries. **Dec. 19**

Yvita Antonette Villalona Bacchus is a graphic designer and violinist living in the Dominican Republic. She works in the music and communication departments of her local church. She is grateful for the opportunity to bless and be blessed. **Nov. 28**

Noella (Jumpp) Baird, born in Jamaica, is a registered nurse living in Edmonton, Alberta, Canada, with her husband, Alan, and two young daughters. She loves reading, singing for the Lord, adult coloring, cooking, meeting new people, and entertaining with her gift of hospitality. **Apr. 23**

Carla Baker lives in Maryland, United States, and is the director of Women's Ministries for the North American Division of Seventh-day Adventists. She enjoys walking, cooking, reading, and spending time with her three grandchildren. **Aug. 23**

Jennifer M. Baldwin writes from Australia, where she works in risk management at Sydney Adventist Hospital. She enjoys family time, church involvement, Scrabble, crossword puzzles, and researching her family history. She has been contributing to this devotional book series for twenty-three years. **June 20**

Gloria Barnes-Gregory is inspired by nature and her precious granddaughters. She seeks to motivate others to make positive life choices. Currently, she and her husband, Milton, serve at the Victory Church in New York, United States. **June 9, Sept. 6**

Dottie Barnett is retired and lives in a beautiful country setting in southeast Tennessee, United States. For more than fifty years, she has been involved in children and adult Sabbath School leadership. She has written a devotional blog for the past several years called *Whispers of His Wisdom*. She loves working with plants and flowers, mowing her large lawn, photography, and camping with her family. **Jan. 7, May 22**

Gyl Moon Bateman lives in Niles, Michigan, United States. She has three grown sons and was widowed in February 2018. She enjoys writing, music, cats, cooking, and traveling. She went on her first cruise in May 2019 to the Caribbean. **Feb. 10, Nov. 1**

Dana M. Bassett Bean is an educator from Bermuda who loves God, food, the color orange, photography, writing, children, and granola. She works for the Lord as church clerk, Sabbath School teacher in cradle roll, and Adventurer leader. **Jan. 3, Apr. 1**

Elizabeth Bearden is an English education and history major at Union College in

Lincoln, Nebraska, United States. Her mom, Pauline, has been telling her the raccoon-in-the-jam-jar story her whole life, which led to Elizabeth's love of small, fuzzy animals. She loves curling up in a warm quilt with a good book on rainy days. **June 23**

Dawna Beausoleil, a retired teacher, and her husband, John, lived in a retirement community in London, Ontario, Canada, before recently passing away. She always praised God for the wonderful care with which He had blessed them. **June 30**

Cynthia Best-Goring lives in Glenn Dale, Maryland, United States, where she is the principal of a pre-K to sixth-grade elementary school. Her passion lies in helping children learn, teachers teach, and all become acquainted with our heavenly Father. She is a wife and mother of two adult children. Her hobbies include writing, playing the piano, and reading. **June 27, Nov. 11**

Paula Sanders Blackwell is an educator and writer who resides in Houston, Texas, United States. She is the author of the devotional book entitled *Lessons from My Hard Head*. She also has a ninety-day prayer journal. **Dec. 8, Dec. 9**

Patricia Hook Rhyndress Bodi is a happy senior living in Bonsall, California, United States. She enjoys mild ocean breezes every evening. Asking God for guidance, she is trying to live a life committed to His purposes for her. **Apr. 9, Aug. 26**

Fulori Sususewa Bola, a retired schoolteacher, is serving as a volunteer with Hope Channel Fiji. She enjoys working with women, being involved in prayer ministry, and working with young people to share God's love through media and television. **Oct. 31, Dec. 14**

Tamar Boswell is a marriage and family therapist intern in the state of California, United States. **Apr. 17, July 8**

R. Bowen, a Canadian woman teaching English and living for Christ in Northeast Asia, enjoys traveling, meeting new people, and watching God work to draw others closer to Him. She is supported by her family living in Toronto, Canada, and her international family of prayer across the world. **Feb. 22**

Althea Y. Boxx, MPH, is a registered nurse with backgrounds in critical care and emergency nursing. She has authored a motivational devotional entitled *Fuel for The Journey*. She enjoys writing, photography, and traveling. She lives in Jamaica. **Apr. 28, Aug. 18**

Sonia Brock from Palmer, Alaska, United States, lives with her faithful dog, Banjo, in a small cabin she built on a little more than nine acres. She has been privileged for almost thirty years to drive a school bus in the rugged but beautiful forty-ninth state. She finds service to her church a joy and privilege, whether it's mowing the churchyard in the summertime or caring for the little ones in Sabbath School class and during church service. **Jan. 17, May 7**

Vivian Brown is a retired educator residing with her husband of nearly sixty years and her children in Huntsville, Alabama, United States. She enjoys photography, reading, her six grandchildren, family, technology, and traveling. She teaches computer classes at the local senior center in Huntsville. Her lifetime goal is to witness of the love of Christ to everyone, reminding them that Jesus is coming soon. **Jan. 20**

Joy Marie Butler, originally from New Zealand, has lived with her husband, Bob, in the Pacific Islands, Australia, Zimbabwe, and Kenya. She has worked as a women's ministries director, secretary, teacher, chaplain, fund raiser, speaker, and writer. Living in Australia, she is a mother of three grown children and has a passion to help the hurting women of the world. **Apr. 30**

Maranatha Byrd is a student majoring in theology at Oakwood University in Alabama, United States. She enjoys sharing the gospel of Jesus Christ. She also loves to sing and write music and poetry. She enjoys spending time with loved ones. She loves kids and wants to be a role model to the youth and those her age. Her desire is to continue to strive to spread God's love to others. **Nov. 21**

Elizabeth Ida Cain is an administrator at a leading farming company in Jamaica where she resides. She is a professional florist who enjoys teaching the art and finds spiritual blessings in writing devotionals for these women's devotional books. She is looking forward to completing her master's degree in education. **Jan. 30, Nov. 16**

Hyacinth V. Caleb was raised in the West Indies and presently resides in Saint Croix, United States Virgin Islands. University educated in Trinidad and Jamaica, this retired educator loves reading, writing, and working outdoors in her garden. **Apr. 26, July 28**

Florence E. Callender is an integrative educational and wellness consultant and an author and speaker. Her passion is to inform and inspire women to develop a strong relationship with God, build strong minds and bodies, and live by biblical principles. Florence lives in New York, United States, with her young adult daughter. **Apr. 12**

Jenel A. N. Campbell-McPherson is the wife of Pastor Mark McPherson and the mother of a three-year-old son. She has a passion for young people with a special emphasis on nurturing young women. Jenel lives in Trinidad and Tobago. **Apr. 16**

Laura A. Canning lives in Berkshire, England. God has gifted her with the talent of writing. She enjoys country life, photography, gardening, and her pets. **Mar. 16**

Het Jane Silva Carvalho graduated in literature from the Federal University of Rio de Janeiro and has a master's degree in human sciences from the Federal University of Amazonas, Brazil. She worked as a teacher at various levels, including university, as well as in the literature evangelism area. She likes music, traveling, and reading. She volunteers in her church in the areas of music, treasury, missionary work, and children. Her favorite activity is distributing literature. **July 18, Sept. 2**

Donna Ritchie Casebolt is a volunteer writer and editor at Gospel Outreach in College Place, Washington, United States. Widowed in 2011, she is the mother of four adult children, grandmother of two, and great-grandmother of one. She and her new husband, Don, a retired family practice physician, are active in promoting the plant-based diet prescribed by God for mankind at Creation. **Dec. 20**

Camilla E. Cassell writes from Manchester, Pennsylvania, United States. A retired United States Postal Service employee, she attends Berea Temple Seventh-day Adventist Church. She especially treasures her grandson, Amari. Camilla has great compassion for families and feels they should spend time with one another in love and unity, enjoying God's gift of life. **May 5**

Pamela Catalán is thirty-two years old and from Argentina. She was married four years and seven months ago to José Aragonés, who is from Ecuador. They have been living in Kyrgyzstan as missionaries. She is a geography teacher and executive assistant but currently teaches Spanish. She loves to teach, meet new people, and visit new places. More than anything, she enjoys time with friends and being out in nature. **Mar. 19**

Suhana Chikatla, born in India, has two master's degrees and one doctorate degree. She volunteers in children's, youth, and social leadership positions at her Hanceville, Alabama, church in the United States. She is an executive council member for the Gulf States Conference Women's Ministries Department. She and her husband, Royce Sutton, have a beautiful young daughter, Rehana. **Aug. 24, Oct. 21**

Rosemarie Clardy volunteers at church and at the Asheville Humane Society in North Carolina, United States. She enjoys the company of her retired husband, as well as their menagerie of pets. **July 25, July 26**

Sharon Clark was born in Virginia, raised in Texas, and served as an educator for more than twenty-five years. She enjoys eating produce fresh from the garden that Joe, her husband, grows at their home in Arkansas, United States. This published author also enjoys reading, writing, hiking, and traveling. Active as a speaker, she loves to encourage others to trust God, be grateful for His many blessings, and support Adventist education. **July 23, Nov. 6**

Amanda Nicole Gaspard Collins earned a master's degree in public health and is an environmental health specialist at San Bernardino County Department of Public Health in California. She is a Sabbath School teacher, pianist, and song service coordinator at Advent HOPE in Loma Linda, California, United States. Her hobbies include traveling, reading, collecting coins, and snorkeling. **Oct. 19**

Aminata Coote is currently serving as women's ministries coordinator in her local church in Montego Bay, Jamaica, where she lives. She is the wife of one man and has one son. Both keep her on her toes. She dreams of becoming a writer and created a website, www.Hebrews12Endurance.com, which focuses on the type of endurance featured in Hebrews 12:1. **Dec. 1**

Joanne Cortes currently serves as a defined contribution specialist for the Retirement Office of the North American Division of Seventh-day Adventists. Together with her husband, Jose Cortes Jr., who leads evangelism and church planting, as an associate ministerial director of the North American Division, they are the proud parents of Jose III and Joel. She is an author, a worship leader, and an influencer who loves empowering people to be all God calls them to be. **Apr. 4**

Patricia Cove, married for more than sixty years and blessed with many offspring, is a busy member of her church and community in Ontario, Canada. Her fourth book was published in 2018. She enjoys freelance writing, outdoor pursuits (such as sailing), multiple hobbies, baking, and learning to use a one-pot electrical appliance. Who says old dogs cannot learn new tricks? **Apr. 20, July 5**

Sabrina Crichlow resides in Clifton, New Jersey, United States, with her husband and two children and attends the First Seventh-day Adventist Church of Montclair. Her goal is to serve God and see everyone through the eyes of Christ. She self-published a thirty-day devotional book, is a certified health coach, certified life mentor, motivational speaker, and founder of iNAY (it's Not About You) homeless ministry. **Nov. 22**

Shana Cyr-Philbert is a family practice physician with a special interest in diabetes. She lives in Saint Lucia with her husband and young son, Nate. She loves music and has sung in choirs from childhood and is still actively involved in the music ministry of her church. She is passionate about using music and medicine to change lives. **Feb. 8**

Lee Lee Dart is a pastor at the Adventure Seventh-day Adventist Church in Windsor, Colorado, United States. This wife and mother of two is passionate about being a conduit of God's love to others. **Mar. 14, Dec. 15**

Jean Dozier Davey and her husband, Steven, live in the beautiful mountains of North Carolina, United States. A retired computer programmer, she enjoys family, cooking, walking in Pisgah National Forest, reading, sewing, photography, and encouraging others. **July 16**

Bernadine Delafield writes from Florida, United States, where she is involved with women's ministries at her church, is an active member of the Sweetwater Oaks Garden Club, and values time spent with family. She loves to travel the world, so she takes every opportunity to do so. **Sept. 12, Sept. 13**

Yvonne H. Donatto resides in Huntsville, Alabama, United States. She enjoys camping, photography, and traveling. She has lived on three continents and has been active in the King's Daughters organization for more than thirty years. She and Anthony have two adult children, Yolande and Anthony II, and three granddaughters: Ayana, Maya, and Brianna. She is a member of the Oakwood University Church. **Sept. 8**

Kay Dorchuk lives in northern Arizona, United States. She enjoys camping, gardening, teaching Sabbath School, and telling stories. She lives with her husband, Ron, and Sally, their bullmastiff. **June 8**

Dagmar Dorn is women's ministries director for the Inter-European Division and lives in Switzerland. She is a nurse-midwife who has worked in different countries. She enjoys traveling and meeting people and is impressed over and over again by God's love. **Feb. 28**

Louise Driver is a retired pastor's wife, whose husband still preaches nearly every Sabbath in the state of Idaho, United States. Her sister, three sons, and their families live nearby. She enjoys gardening, reading, and traveling. **Sept. 11, Oct. 22**

Aiyana Duran is pursuing a major in English and a minor in psychology at Southwestern Adventist University. She lives in Arlington, Texas, United States, where she enjoys reading, writing, and drawing in her free time. **May 10**

Shevonne Dyer-Phillips is a loyal wife and the young mother of two children. She is devoted to serving God and actively leads women's and family ministries at College Station Seventh-day Adventist Church in Texas, United States. Through writing she rehearses her testimonies of answered prayers, amazing blessings, and learning life's toughest lessons. She hopes that by beholding God's glory in her life, she will be changed and affect a change in others. **Mar. 5**

Ruby H. Enniss-Alleyne writes from Guyana and is still passionately in love with youth activities, family life, her three adult children, daughter-in-law, son-in-law, and two adorable grandchildren, Alaric D'Metri and Rhyea Aria. She anxiously looks forward to the return of Jesus. **May 15**

Mona Fellers is women's ministries leader in her church. She is the multicounty ambulance inspector in Colorado, United States. She lives in the mountains with her husband, two dogs, and two cats. She has two grown daughters and two grandsons. Her biggest joy is to share Jesus with friends and family. **Apr. 24**

Maureen Ferdinand is from the spice island of Grenada. She is the women's ministries director of the Ambassador Seventh-day Adventist Church. She resides in Fort Lauderdale, Florida, United States. She was married to the late Ezra Ferdinand. She has four adopted daughters, five grandchildren, and one great-grandchild. **May 28**

Carol Joy Fider, a retired educator, writes from Mandeville, Jamaica. She serves her church as a local elder, education director, and Sabbath School teacher. The yearning of her heart is to go with Jesus when He gathers the saints of all the ages. She and her husband, Ezra, have two adult daughters. **Mar. 6**

Janice Fleming-Williams is a schoolteacher and certified family life educator. She is family ministries leader at her church and works for its associated school. She and her husband live on Saint Thomas in the United States Virgin Islands and have two adult sons. Her favorite pastime is reading. **Aug. 29, Oct. 11**

Heide Ford, a commissioned minister, has served as a hospital chaplain, pastoral counselor, Women's Resource Center director, associate editor of *Women of Spirit* magazine, and registered nurse. She loves exploring history with her husband, Zell, spending time in nature, and developing friendships with local refugees in Chattanooga, Tennessee, United States. **Nov. 12**

Shirley Sain Fordham is a retired educator, wife, mother of three married children, and grandmother of eight. She enjoys family and friends, technology, crocheting, and scrapbooking. She also loves befriending transfer members at her home church in Atlanta, Georgia, United States. She has learned to occupy well—living, loving, laughing, and learning until Jesus comes again. **Mar. 12, Oct. 29**

Andrea K. Francis is a teacher at the Clement Howell High School in Providenciales, Turks and Caicos. She is actively involved in church life and works in children's and young adult ministries and Adventurer and Pathfinder clubs of her church. She has a passion for young people and seeks to nurture them and build characters for eternity. **Mar. 15**

Sylvia A. Franklin resides in San Bernardino, California, United States, and works as an administrative analyst at California State University, San Bernardino. She is a Sabbath School superintendent at her church and has been happily married to Joe for ten years. She also volunteers as the administrative assistant to the Pacific Union Women's Ministries director. **May 13, Sept. 24**

Edith C. Fraser is a retired college professor, counselor, wife, mother, and grandmother. She currently lives in Alabama, United States. She was an educator for more than thirty years and speaks nationally and internationally about issues regarding women, families, and spiritual growth. She has been married for more than fifty years. **Apr. 21**

Forsythia Catane Galgao served as a missionary in Ethiopia for eighteen years and in Madagascar for seven years—a quarter of a century in Africa! At present, she is the English as a Second Language program coordinator at Asia-Pacific International University (formerly Mission College) in Thailand. **May 4**

Claudette Garbutt-Harding has just retired after forty-three years as a K–college Seventh-day Adventist educator. She has shared forty of those years in pastoral ministry with her husband, Keith. They reside in Orlando, Florida, United States. **May 20, May 21**

Lindsey Gendke is a writer, wife, teacher, and mom whose passion is sharing God's redemptive work in messy lives. The author/coauthor of three books, she is currently pursuing her PhD in English, with an emphasis in composition pedagogy. She lives with her family in Texas, United States. Connect with her at www.LindseyGendke.com. **Oct. 12, Dec. 2**

Marybeth Gessele is retired and lives in Gaston, Oregon, United States, with her husband, Glen. For many years she did in-home caregiving, the last eighteen years with hospice. She enjoys country living, including her garden and orchard. Making and donating baby quilts to two different organizations is a rewarding outreach for her. **Feb. 6**

Kareal Getfield, a practical nurse and phlebotomist and mother of three young children, lives on the beautiful island of Jamaica. She hopes one day to start a foundation for children who have lost their fathers to crime. **May 1**

Carol Wiggins Gigante lives in Coalfield, Tennessee, United States, with her husband, Joe, and their lovable pets: Buddy, Charlie, and Skipper. Carol loves reading, writing, photography, and the work she does in the Coalfield Seventh-day Adventist Church. She and Joe have two grown sons, Shannon and James. *Even so come, Lord Jesus.* **Mar. 8**

Beverly P. Gordon is a health-care provider, lay preacher, and psychology professor. She lives in Pennsylvania, United States, with her husband, David. She is the mother of two adult sons. She is a committed Christian with a passion for fostering strong relationships. She ministers through sermons, seminars, and support group facilitation. **Mar. 26**

Kaysian C. Gordon is a mother, author, speaker, and Bible teacher living in New York, United States. She has published a devotional, *Walking by Faith, and Not by Sight: Learning to Be Still in the Midst of Life's Chaos.* She also guest blogs for Devotable, a devotional app and website, along with the Recraft Devotional Group, a group dedicated to recrafting lives. She teaches her church's youth class and speaks to various women's groups. **Feb. 9, June 10**

Alexis A. Goring is a passionate writer with a degree in print journalism and a master's of fine arts in creative writing. She is an author of contemporary romance with books published by WestBow Press and Forget Me Not Romances. She's a total foodie who lives in Maryland, United States, and enjoys photography as a hobby. **Feb. 14, May 30**

Cecelia Grant is a Seventh-day Adventist medical doctor retired from government service and living in Kingston, Jamaica. Her hobbies are traveling, gardening, and listening to good music. She has a passion for young people, to whom she is always giving advice. **Oct. 13, Dec. 31**

Mary Jane Graves is a mother, grandmother, great-grandmother, sister, and friend. She enjoys family, reading, writing, gardening, and table games. She lives in North Carolina, United States, and recently celebrated her ninetieth birthday. **June 28**

Carmalita Green lives in Montgomery, Alabama, United States, where she works as a nutritionist for the state office of Women, Infants, and Children (WIC) for supplemental nutrition. She is also active in women's ministry at Bethany Seventh-day Adventist Church. **Feb. 19**

Briana Greene is a first-year medical student at Loma Linda University in Southern California, United States. She splits her time between studying, working on her nonprofit, From Hearts 2 Hands, which focuses on improving the lives of children in Tanzania, and exploring the waves of California. **July 1**

Cloreth S. Greene is an education and communications consultant from Jamaica who currently resides in Canada. She appreciates the outdoors, enjoys music and cooking, and is passionate about prayer, youth, and children's ministries. **Aug. 7, Oct. 14**

Glenda-mae Greene writes from her wheelchair at the Sunnyside Adventist Care Centre in Saskatchewan, Canada. Crafting devotionals is her way of sharing the faith she lives by. **Aug. 31, Oct. 6**

Zandra LaMar Griffin-Willingham is a retired captain from the New York City Department of Correction. She resides in Alabama with her husband, Stanley, two cats, and one dog. Zandra attends the New Bethel Seventh-day Adventist Church in Columbus, Georgia, United States. Her current ministry positions are Sabbath School teacher, church chorister, prison ministry participant, and senior citizen exercise instructor. **June 29**

Darlene Joy Grunke, a retired teacher, currently serves on four scholarship committees plus the boards of NAMI (National Alliance on Mental Illness) and Daughters of Norway. She writes from the Pacific Northwest, United States, and avidly supports the global church outreach initiative, enditnow: Adventists Say No to Violence. Find the rest of her story at montereybayacademy.org/history/LealGrunke. **Mar. 25**

Caroline Guchu is from Overland Park, Kansas, United States, and was a senior communication major at Union College who graduated in May 2019. In her spare time, she enjoys reading, cooking, and spending time with family and friends. **July 9**

Marsha Hammond-Brummel is a teacher living in Claremont, New Hampshire, United States, who wrote about her experience during a snow day from school. From May through October, she can often be found at the historic Washington, New Hampshire, Seventh-day Adventist Church and Sabbath Trail where she helps her husband, Ken, welcome guests to the site. **May 17, July 17**

Myrna L. Hanna is assistant vice president for administrative affairs and alumni and donor relations at Loma Linda University Health in California, United States. Her favorite things include traveling, spending time with family, and encouraging others to make the most of the talents God has given them. **Apr. 3, Oct. 15**

Peggy Curtice Harris, born and raised in the states of California and Washington, has lived in Maryland, United States, since 1996. She is widowed, retired, a great-grandma, and a writer of fourteen books. Peggy is still active in Destination Sabbath School, prayer ministry, abuse prevention, and creative hospitality in the Beltsville Seventh-day Adventist Church. **Nov. 30**

Marian M. Hart-Gay lives in Florida, United States, with her husband, David. She is a mother, grandmother, and great-grandmother. Knitting and volunteer mission trips are two activities she enjoys. **Apr. 11, Sept. 5**

Beverly D. Hazzard is retired from health-care administration. She lives in Kelowna, British Columbia, Canada. Mother of two adult children and grandma to five, she enjoys time with family, her dogs and cats, travel, sailing, and mission trips. She is a church elder and the school board chair at Okanagan Christian School. **Nov. 26**

Helen Heavirland is an author, speaker, and encourager who lives in Oregon, United States. She has written numerous articles and four books, including *My God Is Bigger*. For more information or inspiration, go to www.HelenHeavirland.com. **Nov. 17**

Muriel Heppel has been a teacher and principal for more than thirty years in Canada, the United States, and the Philippines. She enjoys nature and has a telephone ministry encouraging others. **June 25, Aug. 5**

Kathy-Ann C. Hernandez, PhD, is a professor in the College of Business and Leadership at Eastern University. She is the author of several journal articles and book chapters and blogs at www.ValueWhatMatters.com. She lives just outside Philadelphia, Pennsylvania, United States, close to a natural park where she enjoys spending time outdoors with her husband and two daughters. **Mar. 4, July 11**

Denise Dick Herr was an English professor at Burman University, Alberta, Canada. She enjoys the blessings of reading, travel, and family. **Feb. 1**

Vashti Hinds-Vanier, born in Guyana, South America, recently celebrated her fiftieth anniversary of entering the nursing profession. She has widely traveled throughout Europe, Africa, and the Caribbean. Her hobbies include cake decorating and gardening. She enjoys spending time with her grandson, Jaden, and resides in Brooklyn, New York, United States. **Mar. 9, Aug. 13**

Patricia Hines was born in Jamaica in the West Indies. She worked as a teacher then migrated to the United States and lived in Orlando, Florida. Just recently she has moved to Sebring, where she enjoys writing, music, and gardening. She loves the Lord and is anxiously awaiting His return. **Apr. 27, Aug. 16**

Roxy Hoehn is retired in Topeka, Kansas, United States, after many happy years doing women's ministries in the Kansas-Nebraska Conference. She's involved with Sabbath School and social occasions in her local church and has happy times with eleven grandchildren. **May 25**

Tamyra "Tami" Horst writes from Paradise, Pennsylvania, United States, where she lives with her husband of more than thirty years, Tim. An author, speaker, and communications director for the Pennsylvania Conference of Seventh-day Adventists, she loves being a mom to her two young adult sons, being a friend to an amazing group of women, enjoying quiet with a great book and a cup of chai, and sharing adventures with those she loves. **Dec. 27**

Jacqueline Hope HoShing-Clarke has served in education as a principal, an assistant principal, and a teacher since 1979. She currently serves Northern Caribbean University in Jamaica as the chair of the Teacher Education Department. She is married and has two adult children. She enjoys writing and gardening, but most of all, spending time with her grandson. **Apr. 14**

Claudine Houston, a former research financial analyst and online university instructor, resides in Atlanta, Georgia, United States. She teaches an adult Sabbath School class at her church. Currently, she facilitates a book club on social media. **Jan. 19**

Lynn Howell is a learning support teacher who lives on the Sunshine Coast, Queensland, Australia. Her hobbies include painting, computing, photography, and reading. She enjoys traveling with her husband, Reg, in their van and spending time with their two married daughters and their husbands. **June 19**

Kristen Hudson enjoys spending time with her daughter and relatives. She believes God blessed her with her daughter, Autumn, because He gave her the courage to love with an open heart. Kristen resides in Huntsville, Alabama, United States. **June 14**

Barbara Huff is the wife of a retired pastor and church administrator. They have one remaining child and three grandchildren. She is a freelance writer who enjoys finding spiritual lessons from nature. She and her husband live in southwest Florida, United States, where nature is abundant. **Oct. 16, Dec. 5**

Patty L. Hyland is a retired teacher, her final position as an instructor at Rogue Community College in Grants Pass, Oregon, United States. She and her pastor husband, Verne, served as missionaries for fourteen years in Sri Lanka and on the island of Palau in Micronesia. At present, she is a chaplain at Asante Three Rivers Community Hospital in Grants Pass, Oregon. **Oct. 27, Oct. 28**

Shirley C. Iheanacho resides in Huntsville, Alabama, United States, with Morris, her husband of more than forty-seven years. She enjoys visiting the sick and shut-in, encouraging people, traveling, spending time with her children and grandchildren, and writing. Her newly published book, *God's Incredible Plans for Me: A Memoir of an Amazing Journey*, is available at www.amazon.com. **Jan. 1, Sept. 3**

Ericka J. Iverson and her husband, Jeff, are parents to two children, Brody and Bonnie, and they live in the sticks of northern Minnesota, United States. She loves being a homeschooling mom and getting to see all the little aha moments in teaching her children! They greatly enjoy traveling, camping, and visiting waterfalls as well as Lake Superior and Lake Michigan. **Jan. 22**

Avis Floyd Jackson lives in Pleasantville, New Jersey, United States, and is a mother of five. She does business out of her home and is a party planner. She is active in her local church. **July 19, Sept. 4**

Rachel Privette Jennings attended Pine Forge Academy and graduated from Kettering College of Medical Arts as a registered diagnostic medical and cardiac sonographer. She is a member of Central Seventh-day Adventist Church in Columbus, Ohio, United States. She is passionate about theatrical arts. She has acted, directed, and written plays and devotional messages. **Oct. 23, Dec. 11**

Greta Michelle Joachim-Fox-Dyett is a potter, writer, blogger, and educator from Trinidad and Tobago. She is married to her love, Arnold, and is also the proud mama of an adult daughter. **Jan. 8, Apr. 29**

Elaine J. Johnson has been a contributor to several of these devotional books and delights in sharing her experiences with you. She loves her country living, reading, writing, and card ministry. She and her best friend, Peter, just celebrated fifty-one years of marriage and have four children. She writes from Alabama, United States. **Feb. 4**

Mary C. D. Johnson is a free-spirited high school Spanish teacher in California, United States. When she is on her vacation breaks, she travels the world doing mission work. Her favorite things to do on mission trips are children's ministry, preaching, and translating. When she is at her home church, she teaches the Spanish adult Sabbath School lesson and serves as a deaconess. **Feb. 25**

Mattie E. Johnson is a wife, mother, and recently retired educator from the Dayton public school system in Dayton, Ohio, United States. She spent her last twelve years as a first-grade teacher at the Dayton Boys Preparatory Academy. Currently she is an elder, the director of the disabilities department, and a Sabbath School teacher in the Junior/Earliteen class at the Ethan Temple Seventh-day Adventist Church in the Allegheny West Conference. **Nov. 24**

Erica Jones is assistant director of Women's Ministries at the North American Division of Seventh-day Adventists in Columbia, Maryland, United States. She loves working with young adult women. **July 29**

Gerene I. Joseph is married to Elder Sylvester Joseph. They have two children, Sylene and Sylvester Jr. At the time of this writing, she had served the North Caribbean Conference for twelve years, first as director of Women's Ministries and Children's Ministries and the now as director of education and coordinator of prayer ministries. In the Virgin Islands where she lives, she enjoys writing poems and playing the piano. **Oct. 24**

Nadine A. Joseph-Collins, PhD, is a women's leadership expert and spiritual wellness coach who has dedicated herself to full-time ministry. She currently resides in Atlanta, Georgia, United States, and travels globally empowering the prayer lives of others. She appeared on 3ABN's Dare to Dream Network's *Urban Report* episode entitled "How To Pray." She recently launched the very first online prayer training program: Creating a WOW Life Through the Power of Prayer. **June 16, Sept. 20**

Lucy Taolo Julius is the mother of one daughter. She and her husband currently minister with Sonship in the western Solomon Islands, taking free medical care (aboard the *Medisonship* mobile clinic) to isolated areas. She's worked as a registered nurse in the Atoifi Adventist Hospital. This reader and lover of inspirational music feels blessed to be able to minister to the bedridden, listen to the needs of little children, and even attend mothers who give birth in canoes. **Sept. 26, Sept. 27**

Carolyn K. Karlstrom is a Bible worker in the state of Washington, United States. She is a speaker and writer whose articles have appeared in various publications. She is married to Rick and loves reading, writing, friends, family, and their sweet kitty, Dusty. **Jan. 5, Oct. 9**

Grace A. Keene was born December 31, 1935. For twenty years she lived in New Rochelle, New York, before moving to Florida, United States. There she raised her family (and some other people too), whom she still points to the lovely Lord Jesus and His joy and comfort. Recently widowed, she resides in a Tennessee retirement center and remains intensely interested in doing what Jesus asks all of us to do: "Go and tell." **Feb. 17, June 22**

Sonia Kennedy-Brown lives in Ontario, Canada. She recently completed her autobiography, *Silent Tears: Growing Up Albino*. She is active in her church but uses every opportunity to speak on behalf of those who are different and socially ostracized for this reason. For more information, email her at Soniab47@msn.com. **Jan. 14, Apr. 15**

Edith Kiggundu, PhD, is a visiting assistant professor in the faculty of education at Memorial University of Newfoundland, Canada. She is a Ugandan but now lives in Canada with her husband, Fred, and their three children. She serves as a Sabbath School superintendent, adult Bible lesson teacher, and prayer ministry leader. A prayer warrior, she enjoys singing and studying the Word of God. **Dec. 29**

Iris L. Kitching enjoys creative endeavors, spoken word poetry performances, and writing for children. She has worked at the General Conference of Seventh-day Adventists in Maryland, United States, for more than twenty years, first in Women's Ministries and then in Presidential. She and her husband, Will, appreciate the joys of spending time with family and friends. **Mar. 7, Nov. 13**

Kênia Kopitar is Brazilian but now lives in Florida, United States. She enjoys gardening, writing, reading, teaching music and piano, and taking care of animals. Her greatest desire is to meet God and her loved ones at the second coming of Jesus. **Mar. 13, Aug. 11**

Betty Kossick continues as a freelance writer of varied genres—as a journalist, author, and poet for both religious and secular publications. She says, "I'm a blessed woman to serve my Lord and friend, Jesus." She developed and edits *Front Porch Visits*, the newsletter for Florida Living Retirement Community. She lives in Florida, United States, and much of her work appears on Google. She can be contacted at bkwrites4u@hotmail.com. **Feb. 13, June 2**

Patricia Mulraney Kovalski, a longtime contributor to these devotional books, lived in Collegedale, Tennessee, United States, at the time of this writing. She had many hobbies and often traveled to several states to visit family before she passed away in 2019. **Feb. 21**

Mabel Kwei, a retired university and college lecturer, did missionary work in Africa for many years with her pastor husband and their three children. Now living in New Jersey, United States, she reads a lot and loves to paint, write, and spend time with little children. **Apr. 18, Nov. 23**

Harriet Langley resides in Maryland, United States. She is an active church member and loves witnessing and winning souls to Christ. **Oct. 5**

Wilma Kirk Lee, licensed clinical social worker, currently directs the Center for Family

Wholeness in Houston, Texas, United States. She serves with her pastor husband (of five decades), W. S. Lee, as codirector of Family Ministries in the Southwest Region Conference of Seventh-day Adventists. Both her bachelor's and master's degrees are in social work. Wilma has authored two books: *The Reason Is . . .* and *Launching Eagles*. **Jan. 18, Aug. 2**

Loida Gulaja Lehmann spent ten years selling religious books in the Philippines before going to Germany and getting married. She and her husband are active church members and are both involved in radio, prison, and laymen's ministries. Her hobbies are traveling, nature walks, writing, and photography. **May 26**

Joan M. Leslie is a native of Kingston, Jamaica. She is a teacher by profession and currently teaches in New York, United States. She takes great pleasure in reading, writing, traveling, and crocheting. **Mar. 17, Oct. 10**

Sharon Long retired in 2015 from a thirty-four-year social work career. She is an associate certified coach and is excited to serve God in Edmonton, Alberta, Canada, and abroad. **Jan. 10, June 24**

Rhodi Alers de López writes from Massachusetts, United States. Her ministry, ExpresSion Publishing Ministries, aims to inspire others to a closer relationship with Jesus. She's an author, singer, songwriter, and speaker who also leads a prayer ministry. Her bilingual website is: expressionpublishingministries.com. **Dec. 30**

Erika Loudermill-Webb lives in Tucson, Arizona, United States. She is a mother of two beautiful young ladies. Her bachelor's degree is in television production, and she has an associate degree in biomedical technology. She enjoys writing and volunteering her time in the media department at the Tucson Sharon Seventh-day Adventist Church. **Feb. 27, June 11**

Lynn Mfuru Lukwaro was born and raised in Tanzania. She and her husband, Gureni, live in Sharjah, United Arab Emirates, with their two beautiful daughters. They serve the Lord in their church. She enjoys traveling, stories, nature walks, teaching, and reading. **Mar. 10, June 3**

Marcella Lynch is a home economics teacher, the author of *Cooking by the Book*, a 3ABN cooking show host, a vegetarian/plant-based cooking instructor, and has been a member of the General Conference of Seventh-day Adventists Nutrition Council for twenty-five years. Now retired with her husband in southern Oregon, United States, she enjoys grandchildren nearby, teaches NEWSTART classes, and supports community health and wellness projects. She coauthored this year's devotional with Ruth James, her sister. **Sept. 18**

Rhona Grace Magpayo enjoys going on mission trips with her husband, Jun. A photo enthusiast, she loves traveling the world and capturing sunsets with her camera. She always returns home to Maryland, United States. **Mar. 20, Aug. 14**

Tereza Makanzo writes from the Southern Africa–Indian Ocean Division. **Nov. 29**

Zandile Mankumba is married with four children. She is a certified teacher. Her hobbies are reading, gardening, and dressmaking. Zandile writes from South Africa. **Feb. 20**

Melissa Martinez lives on the beautiful island of Grand Cayman but needs frequent trips to see mountains, the one wonder of creation that Cayman is not blessed with. However, she has been blessed with not only an amazing twin sister but also twin daughters. **Dec. 17**

Gail Masondo is a wife, mother of two adult children (Shellie and Jonathan), women's and children's advocate, songwriter, chaplain, life in recovery coach, and an international speaker. She has authored *Now This Feels Like Home*. A New York native, she now resides in Johannesburg, South Africa, with her musician husband, Victor Sibusio Masondo. **Sept. 19**

Deborah Matshaya writes from South Africa, where she is a teacher. She enjoys gospel music and has contributed many times to this devotional book series. **July 30, July 31**

Mary H. Maxson, the "King's daughter," is a third- and fourth-grade volunteer Bible teacher at Central Valley Christian Academy, women's Bible fellowship leader, and prayer ministries coordinator at Modesto Central Seventh-day Adventist Church. She lives in Modesto, California, United States. Mary served as director of Women's Ministries for the North American Division from 1999 to 2005. **Nov. 8, Nov. 9, Nov. 10**

Theresa M. McDonald hails from Jamaica and now serves as lecturer and chair of the Department of Curriculum and Teaching in the School of Education at Rusangu University, Zambia. She holds a doctor of health sciences degree from Nova Southeastern University. As she awaits the return of her best Friend, Jesus, she finds joy and satisfaction in meeting the needs of the less fortunate. **July 2**

Gloria McPherson lived in Trinidad and Tobago prior to coming to the United States. She is a retiree and currently resides in Georgia, United States. She is an active church member and enjoys working with children, singing, and spending quality time with her family. **Sept. 29**

Judelia Medard-Santiesteban is from an island in the Caribbean called Saint Lucia. She is a high school teacher and is involved in women's ministries and youth ministries. She is learning to lean on Jesus. **Feb. 23, May 12**

Annette Walwyn Michael writes from Saint Croix in the United States Virgin Islands. In her retirement, she enjoys spending time with her husband, a retired pastor, her adult children and grandchildren, and her Central Seventh-day Adventist Church family. **Jan. 16, Apr. 2**

Cynthia Mighty, a Jamaican, resides in Apopka, Florida, United States with her husband, a pastor and chaplain. Together they have three grown children and five grandchildren. She is an experienced music teacher and organist and one of the musicians at the Solid Rock Seventh-day Adventist Church, where she is a member. She enjoys listening to music, teaching piano students, and traveling. **Feb. 26**

Quilvie G. Mills is a retired community college professor. She and her husband are members of a Seventh-day Adventist church in Port Saint Lucie, Florida, United States, where she serves as a musician and Bible class teacher. She enjoys traveling, music, gardening, word games, reading, and teaching piano. **Sept. 28**

D. Reneé Mobley, PhD, is trained in clinical pastoral education and has owned a

Christian counseling practice for more than ten years in Alabama, United States. A member of the National Christian Counselors Association, she trains and facilitates numerous workshops, seminars, and conferences. She is the mother of two adult women, mother-in-law to the greatest son-in-law in the world, and grandmother to three grand-dogs. **May 9**

Marcia Mollenkopf, a retired teacher, lives in Klamath Falls, Oregon, United States. She enjoys church involvement and has served in both adult and children's divisions. She loves to share God's Word. **Nov. 14**

Dorothy Mooka, PhD, is a mother of four children. She was a nurse and lectured at different nursing schools in Botswana. She earned her PhD in home-based care. She is active in her church and in community outreach projects, being one of the leaders who feed a group of people at three sites every Wednesday and Thursday. She is retired from nursing and is now an active businesswoman. **Aug. 25**

Jane Wiggins Moore lives in Coalfield, Tennessee, United States, where she is community services leader for her church and active in their food ministry program, Hope for the Hungry. A retired registered nurse, she has two grown sons and delights in her granddaughter, Micah, and grandson, Andrew. She still mourns her beloved husband, John, who went to sleep in Jesus in 2001. **Oct. 25**

Lily Morales-Narváez lives in Texas, United States, and presently works for the Texas Adventist Book Center. She has a bachelor's degree in psychology and has written articles for these women's devotionals and the *Adventist Review*. Active in her church, she is involved with personal ministry, "Build Your Ark," and preaching. Lily likes to sing, write, read, and decorate. She especially loves her husband and family. **Dec. 26**

Lila Farrell Morgan especially enjoys country living, family, friends, reading, writing, baking, table games, and exercising regularly in a SilverSneakers® class. She writes from North Carolina, United States. She is a widow, mother, grandmother, and great-grandmother. She enjoys keeping in touch with family and friends. **Dec. 21**

Valerie Hamel Morikone works for the Mountain View Conference office in West Virginia, United States, and leads out in the Communication and Women's Ministries departments. She loves to read, cook and bake, and do internet research. **Mar. 2**

Bonnie Moyers lives with her husband in Staunton, Virginia, United States. This freelance writer is a mother of two, a grandmother of three, and a musician for several area churches. **May 31**

Esther Synthia Murali works as honorary director for Women's Ministries in South Karnataka Section, Mysore, India. She is a physiotherapist by profession, but her passion is ministering with her pastor husband. She has a son, Ted, and enjoys playing guitar, painting, gardening, and photography. **Jan. 2, May 29**

Jaclyn Myers is a college student at Southwestern Adventist University in Texas, United States, where she is majoring in English. She enjoys reading and preaching. **Mar. 1**

Jannett Maurine Myrie is currently employed at AdventHealth Orlando hospital in United States. She serves as women's ministries director and Sabbath School superintendent in her church. A proud mother of one son, her hobbies include reading, cooking, going on cruises, and serving as a medical missionary overseas. **Apr. 19**

Cecilia Nanni earned a degree in psychology, a master's degree in mediation and conflict resolution, and a master's degree in education, management mode. She has received an international diploma in volunteer management from UNESCO. Currently, she works as volunteer coordinator in Central Asia. **Feb. 11, May 27**

Regina Jele-Ncube was born in Zimbabwe but now resides in the United Kingdom. She has served in women's ministries at her local church. She considers it a blessing from God to be able to reach out to others through her writings. She is not driven by reason but by purpose as she reaches out to others through the words she pens. **Feb. 2**

Judy-Ann Neal is an international speaker, author of *Time With God*, and as a retired chaplain. She enjoys the winter sun of Florida, United States. She is a mother and grandmother who keeps busy quilting, writing, and learning. Judy's greatest joy is walking alongside others as they learn to recognize and listen to God's voice through His Word. **Feb. 15**

Anne Elaine Nelson, a retired elementary teacher, lives in Rockford, Michigan, United States. She is assistant Sabbath School superintendent at the Belgreen Seventh-day Adventist Church in Greenville, Michigan. She has four children, sixteen grandchildren, and six great-grandchildren. **Oct. 4, Dec. 7**

Samantha Nelson is a pastor's wife who loves serving alongside her husband, Steve. She is also the CEO of The Hope of Survivors, a nonprofit organization dedicated to assisting victims of clergy sexual abuse and providing educational seminars to clergy of all faiths. She and Steve live in Wyoming, United States, and love traveling, hiking in the mountains, and enjoying the beauty of God's creation. **Jan. 12, Aug. 30**

Judith Nembhard, PhD, a retired English professor and administrator, is the author of two books of Christian fiction and a memoir. She blogs at her website, www.JudithNembhardBooks.com. She lives in Chattanooga, Tennessee, United States. **May 3**

Angèle Rachel Nlo Nlo and her husband served more than twenty years at the Seventh-day Adventist Church headquarters in Abidjan, Ivory Coast. While there, she held the position of West-Central Africa Division Shepherdess Coordinator. She has degrees in family law and public law. She is back in her home country, Cameroon, where she founded an evening school for difficult young people. Her hobbies are reading, traveling, conducting evangelistic campaigns, meeting new friends, and cooking. **Oct. 20**

Linda Nottingham lives in Florida, United States, and teaches an adult Bible study class at her church. She is semiretired but serves as a mentor to women business owners. She was also a 2012 honoree of the Florida Commission on the Status of Women. **Dec. 18**

Margaret Obiocha has been married to her husband, Fyneboy, for fifty years. They are now retired in Connecticut, United States. She has served her local church as Sabbath School teacher, deaconess, and treasurer. She and her husband are involved in church projects to help poor village churches in eastern Nigeria. She enjoys supervising her grandchildren with their schoolwork. **June 13**

Ngozi Obiocha-Taffe lives in Ellington, Connecticut, United States, with her husband, Marlon, and their two daughters, Sidney and Ashley. She loves gardening, traveling, and spending time with her parents, Fyne and Margaret. She is passionate about human rights, education policy, and spreading God's love. **Jan. 24, June 5**

Glenetia Carr O'Connor was born and raised in Jamaica to Pastor Glenville and Patricia Carr of the East Jamaica Conference. She studied medical technology at Northern Caribbean University, Jamaica, and later medicine at the University of Montemorelos in Mexico. She worked for a couple of years as a physician before she got married and migrated to New York, United States. She has a five-year-old boy and a three-year-old girl. **Oct. 8**

Elizabeth Versteegh Odiyar of Kelowna, British Columbia, Canada, has served God through church, Pathfinder Club, and mission trips. She has managed the family chimney sweep business since 1985. She is married to Hector. They have twin sons and a daughter—all married, all serving God—and three delightful grandchildren. **Mar. 24**

Pauline Gesare Okemwa is married to a pastor with three grown children. She is a counselor by profession and earned a master of philosophy degree in public health specializing in health promotion. Pauline is currently pursuing a PhD in public health. She loves singing and listening to Christian music. She loves God, who has blessed her with different talents and enjoys sharing her experiences to help young women. She is Kenyan from the western region (Kisii). **Mar. 18, July 10**

Monique Lombart De Oliveira is retired and lives in the United Kingdom. She is busy adapting *The Desire of Ages* into stories for children. She makes laminated religious bookmarks to insert into the book *Steps to Christ* to give away. **May 6**

Sharon Oster is a retired teacher assistant living in Evans, Colorado, United States, with her retired pastor husband. She enjoys automobile day trips in the nearby Rocky Mountains. She and her husband have three children and eight grandchildren. **May 11, Sept. 17**

Naomi N. Otore lives with her husband, a retired pastor (James C. Otore), in the Nyamira Conference in Kenya. They have four adult children (Cleopas, Nicodemus, Deborah, and Neema) and five grandchildren. Her greatest joy as a wife and mother is that all their children are faithful followers of the Lord Jesus Christ. Naomi's interests include reading spiritual books and working in the family garden, where she grows vegetables and other produce. **Jan. 9, May 18**

Hannele Ottschofski lives in Germany, where she has been active in many facets of women's ministries. She has published the story of her family in the book *Das Hemd meines Vaters (My Father's Shirt)*. **Jan. 11**

Ofelia A. Pangan and her husband just came back from Hawaii, where they ministered to the members of the Molokai and Lanai churches for a year and a half. They recently returned to California, United States, to be near their children and minister again to their grandchildren. **Mar. 28, Sept. 30**

Revel Papaioannou and her husband, who live in Greece, were privileged recently to celebrate their sixtieth wedding anniversary, with twenty of their twenty-four family members present. She also had the joy of seeing the publication of her little book of Bible-based poetry entitled *Glimpses of God's Grace*. Praise God! **Mar. 21**

Tricia (Wynn) Payne serves in the Lake Region Conference as the lead pastor of the Conant Gardens Seventh-day Adventist Church. She resides in the Greater Detroit area, United States, with her loving husband, Shawn. **Oct. 30, Dec. 3**

Lori Peckham teaches English and communication at Union College in Lincoln, Nebraska, United States. She lives on a small lake with her husband, Kim, and teenage son, Reef. Her father, who is now eighty-nine years old, lives in Michigan and still sends his love. **Dec. 24**

Premila Pedapudi is the administrative assistant for the Department of Women's Ministries at the General Conference of Seventh-day Adventists and lives in Maryland, United States. **Sept. 10, Nov. 3**

Kathy Pepper is a pastor's wife living in Pennsylvania, United States. She and her husband, Stewart, have a son, two daughters, a daughter-in-law, a son-in-law, and a granddaughter. They were blessed with their first grandson, William Bradley, in January 2020, who joined his older sister Makayla. She enjoys babysitting her grandchildren, graphic design, and working with her husband in ministry. **July 22**

Sueli da Silva Pereira lives in Brazil in Patos de Minas and works in the local city hall. She is married and has three children: Arthur, Eric, and Samuel. She likes to read, write, and study music. **Feb. 5, Oct. 18**

Sharon Pergerson is an educator with a love for pointing people back to Christ and the matchless beauty of His character. Her hobbies include teaching, writing, sewing, and curriculum and program development. She has two precious college-age children. She is in the process of relocating from Michigan to Texas, United States. **Nov. 19**

Diane Pestes, author of *Prayer That Moves Mountains*, published by Pacific Press®, is an international speaker. She is known for her commitment to Christ and ability to memorize Scripture. She resides in Oregon, United States. She can be contacted at www.DianePestes.com. **Sept. 16**

Angèle Peterson lives in Ohio, United States, where she uses her talents of organization and efficiency to serve her church as clerk and treasurer. She enjoys yearly family trips and looks forward to heaven, where we'll never part again. **July 4, Oct. 17**

Roxi Peterson grew up in Lincoln, Nebraska, and is completing her bachelor of arts degree in communication with an emphasis in public relations at Union College in Lincoln, Nebraska, United States. She spends her time having fun with friends and family. She's grown up in the Seventh-day Adventist Church and has worked at a Seventh-day Adventist camp for seven summers. **July 13**

Karen M. Phillips, writing from Omaha, Nebraska, United States, is happily married to her husband, John, and has four children and three grandchildren. Along with a full-time job as a human resources manager, she partners with John in their worldwide ministry, HeReturns. She is also a Bible teacher and the vice president of communications for ASI

Mid-America. Her passion is proclaiming the Lord's end-time message and being an instrument in saving souls. **Mar. 22, June 18**

Prudence LaBeach Pollard, PhD, MPH, RD, SPHR, is vice president for research and faculty development, professor of management, and principal investigator for Career Pathways Initiative at Oakwood University in Huntsville, Alabama, United States. She has authored the book *Raise a Leader, God's Way* (available at www.AdventistBookCenter.com or as an e-book at www.amazon.com). **Aug. 3**

Alex-Anne Riley was twelve years old and in the sixth grade at a charter school in the United States when writing her devotional. She loves singing, dancing, and playing the piano. She is a baptized member of her church and involved in Pathfinder activities as well. She believes that Jesus is her Friend and wants to see Him when He returns. **Aug. 9**

Marli Elizete Ritter-Hein was born in the city of São Paulo, Brazil, married an Argentinean doctor more than forty years ago, and worked with him as a missionary in Nepal and now Paraguay. The mother of two young adult sons, she is a teacher by profession who loves music that points to heaven. She also enjoys nature, flower arrangements, visiting family, interior decorating, and coordinating her church's music ministry. **Mar. 27, July 3**

Jenny Rivera lives and writes from Brisbane, Australia, where she is a registered nurse. She is an active member at the South Brisbane church, where she plays flute in the church orchestra, sings in the youth choir, and serves as a deaconess. She is also a proud auntie of six nieces and nephews. Every day she is just overwhelmed at how God blesses her life. She loves spending quality time with her family and friends, traveling, reading, and looking after her cockatiel, Luigi. **Jan. 21, Sept. 15**

Denise Roberts is prayer ministries coordinator for her church in Leicester, England. She works as a clinical team leader in public health nursing, has two adult children, plays piano, writes poetry, and loves hiking. **Mar. 29, July 12**

Taniesha K. Robertson-Brown has been a devotional contributor since 2013. She enjoys writing, listening to hymns, and serving in church. She writes from Pennsylvania, United States, where she is cheered on by her children, Courtney and Preston. **Jan. 25, June 4**

Charlotte (Swanson) Robinson has spent most of her life working and helping her husband raise three children. She has been published in *Our Little Friend, Primary Treasure, Guide*, and *Insight*. After living seventeen years with her parents near Ozark Adventist Academy, she moved to nearby Decatur, Arkansas, United States, when she married. She now lives on her late mother's property, where she lived as a child. **Aug. 15**

Pauline E. Robinson, Esq., is an administrative law judge living in Florida, United States. She is a widow with five children. After twenty-years of marriage, she became a widow on January 27, 2018. Pauline is from Jamaica and has fourteen brothers and sisters. Her family finds comfort in God's promise that He will never leave them or forsake them and that His plan for their future is that they prosper. **Feb. 7**

Terry Wilson Robinson lives in Hendersonville, North Carolina, United States, with her husband, Harry, who is an ordained minister. She enjoys working side by side with him in teaching Revelation Seminars. **Oct. 1, Oct. 2**

Andrea Rocha is from Brazil but has been living in New York City, New York, United States, for more than seventeen years. She is a registered pediatric nurse at Lenox Hill Hospital in Manhattan, taking care of kids who have had surgery. She has a seventeen-year-old son named Joseph and has been married to Carlos for eighteen years. She is the director of the Women's Ministries department at the Luso Brazilian Church. **Apr. 13**

Avis Mae Rodney writes from Guelph, Ontario, Canada. She is a retired justice of the peace who continues to work on a per diem basis. She is a mother and grandmother who enjoys gardening, writing, and her role as women's ministries leader for the Guelph Seventh-day Adventist Church. **Feb. 3, July 21**

Terry Roselmond-Moore is a native of Barbados, a tiny Caribbean island, but has lived most of her life in the United States, her wonderful adoptive country. She is a nurse executive with Kettering Health Network in the metro Dayton, Ohio, area; a proud mother of her daughter, Taryn Lynch; and the Pathfinder and Adventurer Club leader of the New Life Aviators' Pathfinder Club in Dayton, Ohio. Heaven is her destination. **Dec. 10**

Teresa A. Sales was a retired journalist, editor, and language arts/creative writing teacher, who lived with her husband of sixty-six years, Pastor Don J. Sales, in Pueblo, Colorado, United States. Before passing away, she was published in several magazines and story compilations. She and Pastor Don also self-published three daily devotionals. **Jan. 26**

Kollis Salmon-Fairweather, an ordained elder, is retired from the profession of nursing. In retirement, she remains busy working for the advancement of God's work in Florida, United States. Her hobbies include giving Bible studies, visitation, cooking, and reading. **Nov. 15**

Deborah Sanders lives in Alberta, Canada, with her husband, Ron, and her son, Sonny. In 1990, God blessed her with a writing and prayer outreach ministry, Dimensions of Love. In 2013, she compiled a book of sacred memories entitled *Saints-in-Training*, a book she hopes Sonny can use to continue his witness for Jesus. She wrote this year's devotionals with her mother, Lila Bailey Romp, who lives in Oregon, United States. **Mar. 30, Mar. 31**

Danijela Schubert lives in Sydney, Australia, where she works in the South Pacific Division caring for Women's Ministries and women in pastoral ministry. Originally from Croatia, she lived, studied, and worked in France, the Philippines, Pakistan, Papua New Guinea, and Australia. She is happily married to Branimir. Together they have two grown sons. **Sept. 23**

Shirley P. Scott resides in Huntsville, Alabama, United States, with Lionel, her husband of fifty-four years. They have three children, two granddaughters, and a son-in-law. She enjoys traveling, reading, and family and friends. She currently serves as Women's Ministries director for the Southern Union Conference and is the coordinator of Prayer Ministries for the South Central Conference. **June 15**

Omobonike Adeola Sessou is the Women's Ministries and Children's Ministries director at the West-Central Africa Division of Seventh-day Adventists in Abidjan, Ivory Coast. She is married to Pastor Sessou, and they are blessed with three children. Her hobbies include teaching, counseling, making new friends, and visiting with people. **Sept. 14, Nov. 5**

Cheryl P. Simmons, MDiv, MEd, BCC, is a staff chaplain with Healing Hearts Grief and Bereavement in Clinton, South Carolina, United States. She lives by the motto, "Things could always be worse, but never with God." **Feb. 16, July 27**

Ella Louise Smith Simmons is a vice president at the General Conference of Seventh-day Adventists world headquarters in Silver Spring, Maryland, United States. She is the first woman to hold this position. A veteran educator, she has served as provost, academic vice president, and professor in church and public sector universities. She is married to Nord, and they have two children, three grandchildren, and one great-grandson. **Aug. 27**

Heather-Dawn Small is director for Women's Ministries at the General Conference of Seventh-day Adventists, in Maryland, United States. She has been Children's Ministries and Women's Ministries director for the Caribbean Union Conference, located in Trinidad and Tobago. She is the wife of Pastor Joseph Small and the mother of Dalonne and Jerard. She loves air travel, reading, and scrapbooking. **Mar. 11, June 1, Nov. 18**

Yvonne Curry Smallwood, writing from Maryland, United States, enjoys spending time with God, family, and friends along with reading, writing, and crocheting. When she is not writing, you can find her in a craft store purchasing yarn for the many crocheted items she creates and donates to local charities. Her articles and stories have appeared in several publications. **Nov. 27**

Maple Smith writes from Huntsville, Alabama, United States, and is a nurse by profession; she was born in Guyana. She enjoys spending time with Jesus and with family and friends, traveling, gardening, animals, and nature. In church, she has held many leadership positions. She has been married for more than twenty-nine years and is the mother of two adult children. **Nov. 25**

Sharon Denise Smith lives in Orlando, Florida, United States. She enjoys working with the Adventurer children's group and singing in the church choir. She also enjoys reading, traveling, and bicycling on the nature trails where she lives. **Feb. 18**

Debra Snyder was raised in Massachusetts, United States, but moved to Nebraska in 2012. She works as a medical biller/coder in her town. Her greatest accomplishments are being a wife and mother. She enjoys writing and sharing the story of how God brought her husband and her together and how she came to Nebraska by God's providence. Debra and her husband are both active in their church and continue to look for God's leading in their lives. **Apr. 6, May 24**

Candy Monique Springer-Blackman is from the twin-island Republic of Trinidad and Tobago. She attended Caribbean Union College (now the University of the Southern Caribbean) and graduated in 1999. There she met her husband of fifteen years, who is from the island of Barbados where they currently reside. They attend the King Street Seventh-day Adventist Church in Bridgetown, Barbados. She is an administrative assistant, but her passion is doing décor for church, events, or just at home. **Sept. 9**

Jill Springer-Cato lives in the lovely twin-island country of Trinidad and Tobago and is mother of two boys in their late teens. She is a music minister who loves working with women and youth ministry. **Nov. 7, Dec. 4**

Sylvia Sioux Stark is an artist who lives in Tennessee, United States. Her artwork is displayed in several North American states and in South America. She enjoys being in the outdoors, hiking, camping, backpacking, and enjoying the work of the Master Artist. She has been published in *Guide*. **Dec. 13**

Eva M. Starner is an assistant professor in the psychology department at Oakwood University in Huntsville, Alabama, United States. She is a graduate of both Oakwood University and Loma Linda University. She currently has three adult daughters, two sons-in-law, and three wonderful grandchildren. She believes that God has called her to her current position, and she knows that when God opens doors, they stay open! **Apr. 7**

Ardis Dick Stenbakken has edited these devotional books from her home in Colorado, United States. She has done this since she retired as director of Women's Ministries at the General Conference of Seventh-day Adventists. She and her husband, Dick, love their two children and their spouses and four grandchildren. She is still hoping to find time to once again pursue some hobbies. **Jan. 6, Apr. 8, Sept. 1**

Rita Kay Stevens is a church administrator's wife whose family recently moved to Olympia, Washington, United States. She has been working as a medical technologist in a hospital. Until their recent move from New Mexico, she was a liaison for Women's Ministries and sponsor for the ministers' wives in the Texico Conference of Seventh-day Adventists. She is the mother of two grown sons and is thankful for a daughter-in-law, grandson, and granddaughter. **Apr. 22, July 14**

Barbara Stovall, DBA, MBA, lives in Huntsville, Alabama, United States. She is a docent for the Anna Knight Center for Women's Leadership and archivist for Oakwood University. Her travels to a myriad of places at home and abroad, afforded a deep appreciation for different cultures and people from diverse backgrounds. She loves to read, take long walks on the beach, travel, and is a firm believer and follower of Jesus Christ. **Apr. 10**

Naomi Striemer lives in Franklin, Tennessee, United States, with her husband, Jordan, and dog, Bella. She is a best-selling author, a chart-topping Christian singer and songwriter, and a sought-after speaker who tours around the world singing and speaking. In her spare time, she enjoys baking, board games, and the outdoors. **Jan. 27, Aug. 10**

Carolyn J. H. Strzyzykowski and her husband, Stan, live in St. Joseph, Michigan, United States. They have six children, twenty-two grandchildren, and two great-grandsons. After being a special education and adult education teacher for eighteen years, Carolyn became a chaplain for the next twenty-eight years, working in hospitals, hospice, and long-term care. She's a church elder and volunteers at the pregnancy care center. **May 19, Aug. 17**

Carolyn Rathbun Sutton edited this year's Women's Ministries devotional book from her home in Alabama, United States. In addition to spending time with her across-the-country children and grandchildren when she can, she enjoys teaching the Kindergarten class at her local church. She and her husband, Jim, are also ambassadors for Adventist World Radio. **May 16, July 24**

Anna Ivie Swingle—born in California, raised in New Mexico, and educated in Texas and Nebraska, United States—is a retired government administrative specialist. This published author of devotional articles is a mother of two and grandmother of one. She loves Jesus Christ, volunteering at a hospital, visiting with family and friends, traveling, and being involved in music and church activities. She has been a church clerk, pianist, and organist for more than twenty-five years. **Oct. 26**

Evelyn Porteza Tabingo is a retired cardiac nurse living in Oceanside, California, United States. She and her husband, Henry, are from the Philippines and have served as missionaries to East Africa. She enjoys reading, writing, gardening, music, traveling, and spending time with family and her grandchildren. **Feb. 12**

Arlene R. Taylor recently retired from health care after decades of working with Adventist health facilities. Still living in the Napa Valley of Northern California, United States, she devotes her time and energy to brain function research, writing, and speaking. **Jan. 29, Aug. 6**

H. Anesta Thomas is a retired English teacher who resides in Florida, United States. She is the mother of two daughters and the grandmother of a precious granddaughter. She served as Sabbath School superintendent for many years, has worked with women's ministries, and is currently the visitation ministry leader. She enjoys writing, traveling, cooking, friends, and collecting teapots. **Aug. 8**

Maureen Thomas lives in Waynesboro, Tennessee, United States. She is a retired teacher who enjoys gardening, the outdoors, decorating, and writing poetry. Reading the Bible and finding interesting nuggets from God's Word are also great delights to her. **May 23, Aug. 12**

Rose Joseph Thomas is a school administrator at Forest Lake Education Center in Longwood, Florida, United States. She and her husband, Walden, have two precious children, Samuel Joseph and Crystal Rose. **Jan. 28, Aug. 19**

Sharon M. Thomas is a retired public school teacher. She still enjoys working part-time in Louisiana, United States. Her other interests include quilting, reading, walking, biking, and piano. She is always grateful for the omnipotent, omniscient, and omnipresent God of love whom we serve. **Aug. 4**

Stella Thomas works at the General Conference headquarters in Maryland, United States, as an administrative assistant. She enjoys being with her grandson and twin granddaughters and has a passion to share God's love with the world. **May 2**

Bula Rose Haughton Thompson is a member of the Goshen Seventh-day Adventist Church in the West Jamaica Conference of Seventh-day Adventists. She has been married to Norman for twenty-one years. **May 8**

Ena Thorpe is a retired nurse who attends the Hamilton Mountain Seventh-day Adventist Church in Hamilton, Ontario, Canada. She has three married children and five adorable grandchildren. Ena loves to travel, play Scrabble, and solve sudoku puzzles. **Oct. 3**

Rebecca Turner belongs to several small groups and studies the Bible deeply. Her mission in life is encouraging her friends and family, particularly two tiny grandsons, to fall in love with Jesus. She is editorial assistant at the General Conference of Seventh-day Adventists Women's Ministries department and lives with her husband, Charles, in Maryland, United States. **Sept. 7, Dec. 25**

Ekele P. Ukegbu-Nwankwo is a Nigerian-born, board-certified chaplain with a doctor of ministry degree in health-care chaplaincy from Andrews University in Michigan, United States, and a doctor of naturopathy from the International Institute of Original Medicine in Virginia. Her life challenges and walk with God have increased her passion for coaching and empowering others to holistic and sustainable life transformation through the power of the Holy Spirit. She lives in Columbus, Ohio, United States, and is the mother of four young adult professionals. **Dec. 22**

Ellen Porteza Valenciano writes from Mugonero Adventist Hospital in Rwanda, where she works as a physician. She and her husband, Harville, have been missionaries to Zambia, South Sudan, and Kenya. She is actively involved in the health and music ministry. She enjoys playing the piano and organ, traveling, and collecting coins and stamps. **July 6, July 7**

Heather VandenHoven is a freelance writer from Northern California, United States, has been married twenty-five years to her best friend, and is mama to a beautiful daughter. She's on a journey, as is everyone, and seeks to serve Christ through writing about life. Her devotionals can also be seen in the *Adventist Review* from time to time. She is currently in the process of writing a devotional book. **July 15**

Donna J. Voth, a retired teacher and health educator, lives in Angwin, California, United States, with her husband, Al, and Lola, a Maltipoo dog. She enjoys volunteering, writing, watercolor painting, and traveling. They have one adult daughter. **Oct. 7, Dec. 12**

Cora A. Walker resides in Atlanta, Georgia, United States. She is a retired nurse, editor, and freelance writer. She enjoys reading, writing, sewing, swimming, classical music, traveling, and spending quality time with her family. **Jan. 4, June 7**

Marilyn P. Wallace and her dog, Precious, reside in Panama City, Florida, United States, where she and her husband (now deceased) established the first South Central Conference regional church, the Maranatha Seventh-day Adventist Church. She is a retired educator, church elder, treasurer, and South Central Conference Women's Ministries State Director for the Gulf Coast area. She loves to help people, travel, exercise, crochet, and work in her yard. She is the mother of two adult children: a son and a daughter (deceased). **Nov. 4**

Anna May Radke Waters is a retired administrative assistant at Columbia Adventist Academy in the state of Washington, United States. She and her husband of sixty-six years enjoy living near their three daughters, four grandsons, and four great-grandchildren. They just wish the other members of the family were nearby also. **Apr. 25, Aug. 20**

Lyn Welk-Sandy lives in Adelaide, South Australia. She has worked as a grief counselor, spent many years as a pipe organist, and loves church music, choir work, and playing the hand chimes. She enjoys nature, photography, and caravanning around outback Australia with her husband, Keith, and serving where needed. She is mother of four, grandmother of nine, and great-grandmother of five. **Jan. 31, June 21**

Kimasha P. Williams is currently working as a communication professional in Teddington, United Kingdom. She enjoys sharing her testimonies with family and friends and is discovering a passion for vegetarian cooking. **Dec. 28**

Telisha A. Williams lives on the East Bank Demerara in Guyana. She has a passion for children and youth development and has worked with youth for eighteen years. She loves reading, cooking, and spending time in nature. She currently functions in several roles in her local church and conference, including youth elder and women's ministries leader. **Aug. 21, Aug. 22**

Wendy Williams lives in Ohio, United States. Her favorite pastimes are writing, photography, traveling, hiking with her husband, and eating the world's supply of chocolate. **Mar. 3, July 20**

Rachel Williams-Smith is a wife, mother, writer, and speaker. She has a bachelor's degree in language arts, a master's degree in professional writing, and doctorate in communication. She chairs the Department of Communication at Southern Adventist University in Collegedale, Tennessee, United States. Her December 16 devotional is adapted from her autobiography, *Born Yesterday*, which was published by the Pacific Press® but to which she owns the copyright. **Sept. 21, Dec. 16**

Dalores Broome Winget is a retired thirty-year elementary teacher living in Warwick, Pennsylvania, United States, with her husband, Richard. This much-published author has two children and two grandchildren. She enjoys being with family, reading, and traveling. **Aug. 28, Nov. 2**

Cyndi Woods is a mom of two and wife to a wonderful God-fearing man for twenty years. She is a blogger and writer in Michigan, United States, and has written articles for The Disability Network for more than a year. Her heart is in ministry and leading others to know Jesus. She is also blind. Visit her on her blog at www.CyndiWoods.com **Jan. 13, June 12**

Yan Siew Ghiang is a Singaporean Seventh-day Adventist Christian who works as the in-home caregiver for her mother. The hawker center, an open-air complex where food is cooked and sold from vendor stalls, is her "evangelism network." She loves to read and write and do indoor exercises. **Dec. 6**